MW00845529

THE PSYCHOLOGY OF SCIENCE TEXT COMPREHENSION

THE PSYCHOLOGY OF SCIENCE TEXT COMPREHENSION

∂ ∂

Edited by

José Otero
Universidad de Alcalá

José A. León
Universidad Autónoma de Madrid

Arthur C. Graesser
University of Memphis

2002

LAWRENCE ERLBAUM ASSOCIATES, PUBLISHERS
Mahwah, New Jersey   London

Copyright © 2002 by Lawrence Erlbaum Associates, Inc.

All rights reserved. No part of this book may be reproduced in any form, by photostat, microform, retrieval system, or any other means, without prior written permission of the publisher.

Lawrence Erlbaum Associates, Inc., Publishers
10 Industrial Avenue
Mahwah, NJ 07430

Cover design by Kathryn Houghtaling Lacey

Library of Congress Cataloging-in-Publication Data

The psychology of science text comprehension / edited by José Otero, José A. León, Arthur C. Graesser.

    p. cm.

Includes bibliographical references and index.
ISBN 0-8058-3874-0 (cloth : alk. paper)
1. Science—Study and teaching—Psychological aspects.
    2. Science—Textbooks. I. Otero, José. II. León, José A.
    III. Graesser, Arthur C.
Q181 .P77   2002
501'.9 —dc21

2001040699
CIP

Books published by Lawrence Erlbaum Associates are printed on acid-free paper, and their bindings are chosen for strength and durability.

Printed in the United States of America
10 9 8 7 6 5 4 3 2 1

A mis padres, José y Georgina (J.O.)
A mi familia (J.A.L)
To my wife, Nancy (A.G.)

Contents

Preface   xi

1   Introduction to the Psychology of Science Text   1
    Comprehension
    Arthur C. Graesser, José A. León, and José Otero

PART I: THE FUNCTIONS, CONTENTS, AND DESIGN OF SCIENCE TEXTS

2   Toward a Functional Analysis of Scientific Genres: 19
    Implications for Understanding and Learning Processes
    Susan R. Goldman and Gay L. Bisanz

3   The Characteristics of Well-Designed Science Textbooks   51
    Marilyn J. Chambliss

4 Visual Imagery in School Science Texts   73
    Isabel Martins

5 Generating and Understanding Qualitative Explanations   91
    Stellan Ohlsson

PART II: BASIC COGNITIVE REPRESENTATIONS AND PROCESSES IN TEXT COMPREHENSION

6 Comprehension and Memory of Science Texts: Inferential   131
    Processes and the Construction of a Mental Representation
    *Paul van den Broek, Sandra Virtue, Michelle Gaddy
    Everson, Yuhtsuen Tzeng, and Yung-chi Sung*

7 Understanding Causality and Temporal Sequence in Scientific   155
    Discourse
    José A. León and Gala E. Peñalba

8 Situation Models as Retrieval Structures: Effects   179
    on the Global Coherence of Science Texts
    Isabelle Tapiero and José Otero

9 Predictive Inferences in Scientific and Technological Contexts   199
    Pascale Maury, Olga Pérez, and José A. León

10 Situated Regulation of Scientific Text Processing   223
    Marianne Elshout-Mohr and Maartje van Daalen-Kapteijns

PART III: COMPREHENSION MONITORING

11 Metacomprehension of Science Text: Investigating   255
    the Levels-of-Disruption Hypothesis
    *John Dunlosky, Katherine A. Rawson, and Douglas J.
    Hacker*

12 Noticing and Fixing Difficulties While Understanding   281
    Science Texts
    José Otero

13 Updating Mental Representations During Reading 309
Scientific Text
Herre van Oostendorp

PART IV: COORDINATING MULTIPLE INFORMATION
SOURCES AND MEDIA

14 Using Illustrations to Promote Constructivist Learning 333
From Science Text
Richard E. Mayer

15 Understanding Machines From Multimedia and Hypermedia 357
Presentations
Mary Hegarty, N. Hari Narayanan, and Pam Freitas

16 Toward an Integrative View of Text and Picture 385
Comprehension: Visualization Effects on the Construction
of Mental Models.
Wolfgang Schnotz, Maria Bannert, and Tina Seufert

17 "Mining for Meaning:" Cognitive Effects of Inserted 417
Questions in Learning From Scientific Text
Jean-François Rouet and Eduardo Vidal-Abarca

Author Index 437

Subject Index 453

Preface

Science textbooks play an important role in science education. However, surprisingly few studies have been conducted on science text comprehension by discourse researchers. This book grew out of a conviction that science text comprehension is an important, albeit relatively neglected, area in psychological research. We believe that this collection of chapters contributes to filling this hole in the literature on text comprehension.

One distinctive characteristic of this book is the adoption of theories and research in discourse processing to understand how science texts are comprehended and how they should be designed. Contributions from the field of discourse processing are fortified by research in education and cognitive science more generally, although one of our persistent observations is that these fields are remarkably isolated from one another. Part of the purpose of this edited volume is to build bridges between these fields.

The idea of this book grew out from a small seminar on science text comprehension that we organized in Cuenca, Spain, in December 1998. It was supported by the Universidad Autónoma de Madrid, the Universidad de Alcalá, and the Universidad Internacional Menéndez y Pelayo. The goals and scope of the book were refined in discussions that took place in some enjoyable moments—frequently around glasses of both Spanish and American wine together with Art Graesser's preferred tapa: *boquerones en vinagre*.

Some of the contributors to this book attended the Cuenca Seminar, but we were fortunate enough to gather an additional set of valuable authors. Thus, we believe that the book presents a good sample of the work on comprehension and design of science texts that is being conducted both in Europe and the United States.

This project was partially supported by Grant PB98-0711 of the Ministry of Education and Science, Spain awarded to José Otero, and partially support by Grants PB97-0040 and PS95-444 awarded to José A. León by the same Ministry of Education and Science. Additional support came from grants awarded to Art Graesser by the National Science Foundation (SBR 9720314) and the Office of Naval Research (N00014-98-1-K-0110).

Introduction
to the Psychology
of Science Text
Comprehension

Arthur C. Graesser
University of Memphis

José A. León
Universidad Autónoma de Madrid

José Otero
Universidad de Alcalá

It is hardly a secret that students find most science texts very difficult to comprehend and that there are several reasons for these difficulties. The text is loaded with technical terms that need to be deciphered and memorized. There are complex mechanisms with multiple components, attributes of components, relations between components, and dynamic processes that flow throughout the system. Scientists frequently use a mathematical language, with symbols and formulas that are difficult to ground in everyday experience and that often require extreme precision. It is virtually impossible to form a mental image of some of the mechanisms without distorting the integrity of the system. Moreover, textbook authors often do not provide enough cues for readers to create coherent representations of information in science texts.

The problems are especially important for readers with poor scientific knowledge. In fact, all of the difficulties are exacerbated by the fact that most students have minimal background knowledge about science and therefore need to build an understanding nearly from scratch. Or, alternatively, they have *incorrect* knowledge that interferes with the scientific concepts and principles presented in textbooks. And of course, the complexity of scientific theories is increasing dramatically, year by year. As a consequence of all this, students frequently develop negative epistemic attitudes toward science texts and think of them as containing incomprehensible information. These attitudes negatively influence their text-processing strategies, in a continuing downward spiral.

All of these difficulties explain why reading science textbooks is difficult and why it has become difficult to entice students to major in science. The process of learning science is a challenge. Reading scientific text is a struggle that takes effort and concentration. Science texts are not a quick read.

School systems have periodically tried to meet the challenge by adopting radical pedagogical approaches. For example, the "physics first" approach reverses the order in which the different sciences are delivered in the school curriculum. The traditional order has been biology, then chemistry, then physics. The reason for this ordering allegedly is that biology has a high load on memory, but few exceptionally difficult conceptualizations that require a high IQ to master. So students keep busy memorizing parts of the anatomy and detailed taxonomies of animals and plants with exotic, lengthy Latin expressions. The utility of mastering precise genus and species labels is not exactly obvious and is rarely integrated with a deeper understanding of biology, but it does have a good side effect of promoting memorization and organization skills. Most of the fundamental mechanisms in biology are easier to grasp than those mechanisms in the sister sciences, so it makes sense to place biology earlier in the curriculum. In contrast, physics has the opposite profile: It is low on memorization and its key conceptualizations are difficult to master. Therefore, physics should come late. The problem with this curriculum plan is that students with a talent for science get turned off by all of the memorization in biology. A good scientific mind prefers to ask questions, generate hypotheses, play "what-if" games, experiment, test hypotheses, struggle with conflicting results, and become engaged in a host of other forms of reasoning and problem solving. Many scientific minds get turned off by a heavy dose of memorization, so unfortunately they never go into science. The physics-first approach tries to fix this problem by reversing the order of sciences in the curriculum: physics, then chemistry, then biology. So students quickly get started with a physics lab where they can experiment and build an inquiring scientific mind. The essence of the scientific mind is cultivated early and is not clouded by a horrendous exercise of memorization. The effectiveness of the physics-first approach is currently being evaluated, but some reports suggest that it significantly increases the number of science majors.

Another radical method of pedagogy has entirely discontinued science textbooks in the classroom and laboratories. The vision is to get the students to actively experiment in the laboratory, to build inquiring minds, and not to have them accept the textbook knowledge as gospel. This "delete the textbook" approach is perhaps more appealing when literacy levels are extremely low and the quality of textbooks is extremely poor. However, many researchers have been skeptical of the removal of the textbook from the science curriculum. There are times when students need to spend hours concentrating on textbook content until they master the difficult core concepts and mechanisms in a science, without getting distracted by the mundane practices of assembling equipment, collecting observations, and recording numbers in tables and charts. The key challenge is to arrange the learning environment so that the right text is available to the right student at the right time.

Nevertheless, the primary inspiration of this edited book does not really lie in the arena of science curriculum reform. Most of the authors in this book are researchers in cognitive science, discourse processing, and education who are building models of text comprehension. Our goal is to understand how children and adults construct meaning representations while they read and study texts. We develop theoretical models of the comprehension process and test the predictions of the model by collecting empirical data from readers. Some of the data tap the process of comprehension while text is read *online* (i.e., during reading). Examples of online measures include think-aloud protocols, sentence-reading times, the time to name test words aloud, and the timing and patterns of eye movements. Other data involve *off-line* measures that tap the result of comprehension, several minutes, hours, or days after comprehension is finished. Examples of off-line measures are recall tests, recognition tests on words or sentences, summaries of texts, question answering, and ratings of the importance of text constituents. A good theoretical model of comprehension can accurately account for rich patterns of data that include both online and off-line measures.

There are several reasons why science texts have attracted the attention of the comprehension researchers in this volume. One salient reason is that we can investigate comprehension under conditions in which comprehension is extremely difficult. As discussed earlier, scientific texts are difficult to understand at a deep level so these texts provide an interesting test case when the challenges of comprehension are pushed to the limit. Early research on comprehension focused on folktales, stories, everyday scripts, and other forms of narrative discourse that are easy to comprehend—the other end of the continuum on comprehension difficulty (Bruner, 1986; Graesser, Singer, & Trabasso, 1994; Mandler, 1984; Schank, 1999). Narrative is easy to comprehend because the content is very similar to the setting, actions, events, and social world we experience in everyday life. However, researchers in discourse comprehension have advocated moving from an emphasis on the study of narratives toward programmatic research on exposition (Lorch & van den Broek, 1997). That includes the development of theories of the structure and processing of science texts.

A second reason to study scientific texts is that there are more individual differences in comprehension processes among readers. Readers dramatically vary in their knowledge of the subject matter, their cognitive strategies of coping with exceptionally difficult content, their criteria in what it means to comprehend, and their motivation to persevere in mastering the science content. A good comprehension of scientific discourse fundamentally requires an excellent domain of highly specialized language, discourse, and world knowledge (Lemke, 1990; McKeown, Beck, Sinatra, & Loxterman, 1992; Means & Voss, 1985). In contrast, there is more uniformity among adult readers when they comprehend narrative text, at least narratives that do not have sophisticated literary forms (Graesser, Kassler, Kreuz, & McLain-Allen, 1998).

A third reason for investigating science texts is that the content of the material is useful for the readers to master. The content is not arbitrary or trivial, as in the case of much of the text materials that are written by experimental psychologists. Promoting science education fits a prominent mission in virtually all countries and cultures. Science textbooks have obviously played an important role in this endeavor. Yager (1983) reported that over 90% of all science teachers in the United States used a textbook 95% of the time. The importance of textbooks as a component of science instruction has also been advocated by other researchers (Chiapetta, Sethna, & Fillman, 1991; Gottfried & Kyle, 1992; Yore, 1991), in spite of the trend to minimize textbooks in some circles in science education.

A fourth reason for studying scientific text is because this genre of text has a distinctive way of organizing and explaining material. It is frequently assumed that coherence and comprehension are closely related. Under most, but not all circumstances, a coherently organized text facilitates the readers' comprehension and subsequent task performance. However, sometimes the text per se is not sufficient for conveying the complex systems in mechanical, biological, or physical systems. The text needs to be enriched by adjunct illustrations, diagrams, tables, figures, photographs, and so on. Furthermore, in this electronic age, there are multimedia, hypermedia, simulation, and other computer technologies that allegedly facilitate more active learning and hopefully deeper comprehension. However, there is very little empirical research on the effectiveness of these nontextual technologies, so this is an important direction for future research.

WHAT IS SCIENCE TEXT?

We intentionally define science text very broadly in this volume. There is a broad definition of science and a broad definition of what falls under the umbrella of a scientific text genre. Regarding a definition of science, we adopt the natural category that is recognized in the National Science Foundation as SMET, which stands for science, mathematics, engineering, and technology. Our definition is compatible with Parker's definition in the *Concise Encyclopedia of Science and Technology* (1994):

> Science ... is characterized by the possibility of making precise statements which are susceptible of some sort of check or proof. This often implies that the situations with which the special science is concerned can be made to recur in order to submit themselves to check, although this is by no means always the case. There are observational sciences such as astronomy or geology in which repetition of a situation at will is intrinsically impossible, and the possible precision is limited to precision of description. (p. 1661)

According to Parker, technology is a part of science, as described in the following:

> Technology is a systematic knowledge and action, usually of industrial processes but applicable to any recurrent activity. Technology is closely related to science and to engineering. Science deals with humans' understanding of the real world about them—the inherent properties of space, matter, energy, and their interactions. Engineering is the application of objective knowledge to the creation of plans, designs, and means for achieving desired objectives. Technology deals with the tools and techniques for carrying out the plans. (p. 1876)

The status of mathematics is perhaps on the edge of these definitions and is not directly addressed in this edited volume. However, all forms of science, engineering, and technology embrace some form of mathematics, which perhaps explains its inclusion in the SMET program of the National Science Foundation.

Our definition of the scientific text genre embraces several rhetorical forms and media. There are academic textbooks, scientific journal articles, technical manuals, magazine and newspaper reports tailored for the general public, information brochures for the public, and electronic multimedia on the Web and CD-ROM. The material is prepared by the author with the primary role of the diffusion of new knowledge about science. The chapter in this volume by Goldman and Bisanz presents a large landscape of science texts and their discourse functions. The chapter by Chambliss describes a theoretical framework for designing textbooks that integrate curriculum, instruction, and comprehensibility. Nearly all science texts are in the expository genre because they are written to explain and describe to the reader new content that has a foundation in truth and/or empirical evidence. However, some forms have a layer of persuasion, such as when a researcher is arguing with colleagues that a particular scientific claim is true or a particular scientific theory has merit. Scientific texts may also be in the narrative genre, as in the case of science history. It is widely acknowledged that many texts do not crisply fall into the traditional genre umbrellas of exposition, persuasion, narrative, and description (Brooks & Warren, 1972).

THE PRESENTATION AND PROCESSING OF SCIENTIFIC TEXT

The content of scientific texts has multiple levels of representation, but the most important split is between shallow and deep knowledge. Shallow knowledge consists of explicitly mentioned ideas in a text that refer to: lists of concepts, a handful of simple facts or properties of each concept, simple definitions of key terms, and major steps in a procedure (not the detailed steps). Deep knowledge consists of coherent explanations of the material that fortify the learner for generating inferences, solving problems, making decisions, integrating ideas, synthesizing new ideas, decomposing ideas into subparts, forecasting future occurrences in a system, and applying knowledge to practical situations. Deep knowledge is presumably needed to articulate and manipulate symbols, formal expressions, and quantities, although some individuals can master these skills after extensive practice without deep mastery. Deep knowledge is essential for handling challenges and obstacles because there is a need to understand how mechanisms work and to generate and implement novel plans. Explanations are central to deep knowledge, whether the explanations consist of logical justifications, causal networks, or goal-plan-action hierarchies. It is well documented that the construction of coherent explanations is a robust predictor of an adult's ability to learn technical material from written texts (Chi, deLeeuw, Chiu, & La Vancher, 1994; Coté, Goldman, & Saul, 1998; Graesser, VanLehn, Rose, Jordan, & Harter, in press; Webb, Troper, & Fall, 1995). Some of the chapters in this volume directly address the processes and challenges of constructing coherent explanations of the material (see León & Peñalba; Mayer; Ohlsson).

The representations of texts and pictures can be segregated into the levels of surface code, explicit propositions, mental models, and pragmatic interaction (Graesser, Millis, & Zwaan, 1997; W. Kintsch, 1998). The most shallow level is the *surface code*, which preserves the exact wording and syntax of the explicit verbal material. When considering the visual modality, it preserves the low-level lines, angles, sizes, shapes, and textures of the pictures. The *explicit proposition* representation (often called the *textbase*) captures the meaning of the explicit text and the pictures. A proposition contains a predicate (main verb, adjective, connective) that interrelates one or more arguments (noun-referents, embedded propositions). Examples of propositions are *the cam is between the cylinder and the spring* [BETWEEN (cam, cylinder, spring)], *the singer repaired the computer*] repair(singer, computer)], and *if the cam rotates, the spring contracts* [IF (rotate (cam)), (contract (spring))]. At the deepest level, there is the *mental model* (or *situation model*) of what the text is about. For everyday devices, this would include: the components of the electronic or mechanical system, the spatial arrangement of components, the causal chain of events when the system successfully unfolds, the mechanisms that explain each causal step, the functions of the device and device components, and the plans of agents who manipulate the system for various purposes.

Still another level of representation of scientific texts, related to the situation model but slightly different from it, has been proposed for scientific problems (Nathan, W. Kinstch, & Young, 1992). Good readers create a level of representation called the *problem model* that is built taking into account the formal (mathematical) relations that exist between the elements described in the statement of a problem. For this, a reader needs not only world knowledge, as for building a situation model, but also scientific and mathematical knowledge on the relations between the variables involved in the problem statement. Thus, a student may create an appropriate situation model corresponding to the text that describes a scientific problem, for example, one involving a person sliding down an hemispheric dome. However, the student may be incapable of translating this into scientific concepts and principles, that is, building the problem model. In other words, the student may be unable to represent the situation in terms of the variables and relations needed to describe position and velocity, the forces acting on the person, the types of energy change involved, and the relations among all of the various components.

Finally, there is the *pragmatic communication* level that specifies the main messages that the author is trying to convey to the reader (or the narrator to the audience). Examples of purposes of reading are to explain how to repair equipment, to advertise a product, or to protect someone from a hazardous condition.

The *types* of representations are theoretically different from the *levels*. From the present standpoint, there are several types of knowledge representation affiliated with the explicit propositions and mental models that underlie science texts. Table 1.1 lists some important types of knowledge representations that are prominent in science (Graesser, Gordon, & Brainerd, 1992). Each of these types of knowledge become progressively deeper to the extent that they are more fine-grained (i.e., the grain size has high resolution) and have more complex interconnections among

TABLE 1.1
Important Types of Knowledge Representation for Science Texts

Class inclusion. One concept is a subtype or subclass of another concept.
   For example, a Pentium is-a computer is-a device.

Spatial layout. Spatial relations among regions and entities in regions.
   For example, a pin is-in a cylinder is-in a lock. A spring surrounds a rod.

Compositional structure. Components have subparts and subcomponents.
   For example, a computer has-as-parts a monitor, a keyboard, a CPU, and memory.

Procedures and plans. A sequence of steps/actions in a procedure accomplishes a goal.
   An example is the steps in removing the hard drive in a computer.

Causal chains and networks. An event is caused by a sequence of events and enabling states.
   An example is the sequence of events that lead to a polluted lake.

Agents. Organized sets of people, organizations, countries, and complex software units.
   Examples are organizational charts and client-server networks.

Others. Property descriptions, quantitative specifications, rules.

subcomponents (i.e., there are more relational links and more links that deviate from a strict hierarchy).

Cognitive processes also vary in difficulty. Table 1.2 lists the major types of cognitive processes that were proposed by Bloom (1956) and others nearly 50 years ago. According to Bloom's taxonomy of cognitive objectives, the cognitive processes with higher numbers are more difficult and require greater depth. Recognition and recall are the easiest, comprehension is intermediate, and Classes 4–7 are the most difficult. It is debatable whether there are differences in difficultly among Categories 4–7, so they are often collapsed into one category in most applications of this taxonomy.

The representations and processes in Table 1.2 do not cover all of the theoretical distinctions that are embraced by today's comprehension researchers. As one would expect from any scientific enterprise, the researchers have dissected the representations and processes in rich detail. For example, researchers have contrasted the different memories that operate during comprehension. There are the distinctions between short-term memory (STM), working memory (WM), and long-term memory (LTM), which are quite familiar to anyone who has taken an introductory course in cognitive psychology. Ericsson and W. Kintsch (1995) recently added a

TABLE 1.2
Types of Cognitive Processes

(1) *Recognition.* The process of verbatim identification of specific content (e.g., terms, facts, rules, methods, principles, procedures, objects) that was explicitly mentioned in the text.

(2) *Recall.* The process of actively retrieving from memory and producing content that was explicitly mentioned in the text.

(3) *Comprehension.* Demonstrating understanding of the text at the mental model level by generating inferences, and interpreting, paraphrasing, translating, explaining, or summarizing information.

(4) *Application.* The process of applying knowledge extracted from text to a problem, situation, or case (fictitious or real-world) that was not explicitly mentioned in the text.

(5) *Analysis.* The process of decomposing elements and linking relationships between elements.

(6) *Synthesis.* The process of assembling new patterns and structures, such as constructing a novel solution to a problem or composing a novel message to an audience.

(7) *Evaluation.* The process of judging the value or effectiveness of a process, procedure, or entity, according to some criteria and standards.

layer of complexity by introducing the notion of a long-term-working memory (LT-WM). The contents of STM at any point in time may trigger processing skills in LTM that quickly fetches additional content in LTM. Thus, a person who is highly skilled in memory retrieval for a particular subject matter (e.g., an expert in botany) would appear to have a larger WM for scientific texts on botany because of the expert retrieval skills in LTM for botany. The chapter by Tapiero and Otero reports that this added expertise in a subject matter, and the associated LT-WM, allows the reader to build richer situation models and more globally coherent text representations. In contrast, these advantages in subject matter expertise cannot be explained by the propositional textbase level.

As another example, comprehension researchers have vigorously investigated the process of constructing knowledge-based inferences during the comprehension of scientific texts (Coté et al., 1998; Graesser & Bertus, 1998). Some of the important classes of inferences are presented in Table 1.3. The inferences in Table 1.3 do not exhaust the classes of inferences that comprehension researchers have investigated (see Graesser et al., 1994, for a more complete inference taxonomy), but they do cover the inferences investigated by the authors of this volume. For example, Maury, Pérez, and León investigated the extent to which predictive inferences and goal inferences are constrained by the verbs in the explicit events being read. León and Peñalba compare the explanation-based causal inferences that get constructed in scientific text versus narrative text. Ohlsson proposes that explanations in science are constructed from an assembly of generative relations and explanation schemas. He demonstrates how this is done by analyzing a corpus of naive explanations in the domain of evolutionary biology.

Inferences play a particularly important role in creating coherence in the representations of science texts. Some scientific genres, like those addressed to experts, take for granted an important inferencing activity of readers to fill many deliberate coherence gaps in the explicit textbase. This style is sometimes inappropriately carried over to educational texts. When it happens, it places a large burden on readers who are expected to make inferences, without the fortification of expert world knowledge. Such inferences can be made only by the more able students. Sometimes it is beneficial for knowledgeable readers to receive texts with coherence gaps, and to expect them to fill the gaps with inferences (MacNamara, E. Kintsch, Songer, & W. Kintsch, 1996). However, texts with coherence gaps are detrimental for most readers because of the limitations in their knowledge and processing strategies.

TABLE 1.3

Classes of Inferences that are Relevant to Scientific Texts

(1) *Anaphoric references.* A pronoun or noun-phrase refers to a previous text constituent or to an entity already introduced in the mental model.

(2) *Bridging inferences.* These inferences are needed to semantically or conceptually relate the current sentence being read with the previous content. These are sometimes called backward inferences.

(3) *Explanation-based inferences.* The current event being read is explained by a causal chain or network of previous events and states. These are sometimes called causal antecedent inferences.

(4) *Predictive inferences.* The reader forecasts what events will causally unfold after the current event being read. These are sometimes called causal consequence or forward inferences.

(5) *Goal inferences.* The readers infers that an agent has a motive that explains an intentional action.

(6) *Elaborative inferences.* These are properties of entities, facts, and other associations that are not explained by causal mechanisms.

(7) *Process inferences.* These inferences specify the detailed steps, manner, or dynamical characteristics of an event as it unfolds.

Reader standards

The extent to which readers generate inferences depends on the reader's standards for what it means to comprehend something. Some readers demand a deep comprehension of the material, particularly if they have high subject matter knowledge, high standards, and/or high motivation. Other readers settle for a shallow representation that glosses over potential contradictions within the text and between the text and world knowledge. The process of *comprehension monitoring* determines the depth of comprehension, whether discrepancies or gaps in understanding are detected, and whether readers repair these problems appropriately. These metacognitive regulatory processes are addressed in several chapters in the volume. Dunlosky, Rawson, and Hacker propose that comprehension disruptions may occur at different levels of text representation and that rereading a text has the benefit of addressing more disruption at the deeper mental model. Otero analyzes the regulatory processes that occur when readers find inconsistencies in science texts and attempt to repair the problems. The regulation mechanism is modeled as a constraint satisfaction process in which readers evaluate the coherence of their mental representation of a text with respect to a standard. Inferences are generated if the coherence of the text does not meet the threshold of a standard. Van Oostendorp investigates the process of updating a mental model of a scientific text when it has a clear-cut contradiction.

Deep comprehension and inferences may be facilitated by information sources other than the text per se. A number of chapters explore the impact of pictures, animation, questions and other adjunct information sources on text comprehension. Martins discusses the content and functions of visual images in science textbooks. Schnotz, Bannert, and Seufert propose a model that identifies the mental representations that are created from scientific text versus pictures, including how they are integrated and how they may differ. There are conditions in which a picture can interfere with comprehension, as in the case of simple pictures that have minimal or misleading information. Mayer has systematically investigated how words, pictures, and animations may be effectively coordinated to promote deep comprehension of various physical, mechanical, and biological systems. Hegarty, Narayanan, and Freitas designed and tested the impact of hypermedia on the construction of explanations of how mechanical systems work. Rouet and Vidal-Abarca discuss the impact of adjunct questions and how the question answering process can systematically influence the comprehension of science texts. These adjunct information sources and media are expected to improve in the future, given that we are in the age of bewildering technological advances, including the electronic textbook. However, it is not necessarily true that learning is facilitated by an animation of a mechanical system, a simulation of the mechanism that the learner can interactively manipulate, and embodied exploration of the science world in virtual reality. There is no solid evidence, for example, that animation facilitates learning. Comparisons between linear text and hypertext/hypermedia are similarly unspectacular, if not disappointing.

Once again, one of the central challenges lies in the fact that most readers have very little knowledge of science as a subject matter. As a consequence, the reader is confronted with a situation in which background knowledge base is virtually bankrupt. How does the reader cope with the comprehension task when there is this serious conceptual handicap? According to the chapter by Elshout-Mohr and Daalen-Kapteijns, the reader relies on establishing local coherence at the level of the textbase, and also on the global schemata at the level of world knowledge and rhetorical structure. There is not much hope in constructing a rich mental model without the requisite background knowledge. According to van den Broek's landscape model, the reader tries to construct a coherent meaning representation by activating incoming information, linking it to prior information, and reactivating the old explicit information in a working memory with limited capacity. The reader therefore resorts to systematically crunching on the textbase rather than incorporating many knowledge-based inferences. This, as pointed out previously, results in incoherent scientific text representations, given the scarcity of explicit causal, logical, or mathematical links in scientific textbases.

The research in this book is guided by theories and models of comprehension that have dominated discourse processing, cognitive psychology, and education in recent years. When considering discourse processing, the major theoretical positions are the constructionist theory (Graesser et al., 1994), the construction-integration model (W. Kintsch, 1998), the memory-based resonance models (O'Brien & Myers, 1999), the landscape model (see chap. 6, this volume), and the event-indexing model (Zwaan & Radvansky, 1998). The field of education has proposed several theories that make specific predictions about what improves comprehension and memory for learning material. These include principles of self-explanation (Chi et al., 1994), the dual code hypothesis (Paivio, 1971), and a variety of constructionist theories (Bransford, Goldman, & Vye, 1991; Moschman, 1982). The more interdisciplinary field of cognitive science has offered architectures of computation and knowledge representation that are routinely embraced by various chapters in this volume, such as conceptual graph structures with nodes and relational arcs, schema-based templates, production systems that operate on content in working memory, abstract neural networks, and constraint satisfaction mechanisms. Collectively, these models offer a rich foundation for generating discriminating predictions on patterns of empirical data, whether they involve online measures or off-line measures.

ORGANIZATION OF THE BOOK

This book reports research on the comprehension and production of scientific texts. It is divided into four major parts. Part I (The Functions, Content, and Design of Scientific Texts) provides an overview of the different discourse genre, rhetorical formats, design features, and functions of scientific texts. This part is not limited to printed text, but includes pictures, images, animation, and various other atextual media. Part II (Basic Cognitive Representations and Processes in Text Comprehension) presents theoretical models of text comprehension, as well as empirical tests of the theoretical predictions. Part III (Comprehension Monitoring) focuses on the process of regulating comprehension, which is particularly critical in science comprehension because of the inherent difficulty of the subject matter. Comprehension monitoring is also a fundamental process indeed, but Part III is devoted to the research projects that have focused on this critical process. Part IV (Coordinating Multiple Information Sources and Media) goes beyond the main text and incorporates adjunct sources and media.

REFERENCES

Bloom, B. S. (1956). *Taxonomy of educational objectives. Handbook I: Cognitive domain.* New York: McKay.

Bransford, J. D., Goldman, S. R., & Vye, N. J. (1991). Making a difference in peoples' abilities to think: Reflections on a decade of work and some hopes for the future. In L. Okagaki & R. J. Sternberg (Eds.), *Directors of development: Influences on the development of children's thinking* (pp. 147–180). Hillsdale, NJ: Lawrence Erlbaum Associates.

Brooks, C., & Warren, R. P. (1972). *Modern rhetoric.* New York: Harcourt Brace.

Bruner, J. S. (1986). *Actual minds, possible worlds.* Cambridge, MA: Harvard University Press.

Chi, M. T. H., de Leeuw, N., Chiu, M., & La Vancher, M. (1994). Eliciting self-explanations improves understanding. *Cognitive Science, 18,* 439–477.

Chiapetta, E. L., Sethna, G. H., & Fillman, D. A. (1991). A quantitative analysis of high school chemistry textbooks for scientific literacy themes and expository learning aids. *Journal of Research in Science Teaching, 28,* 939–951.

Coté, N., Goldman, S. R., & Saul, E. U. (1998). Students making sense of informational text: Relations between processing and representation. *Discourse-Processes, 25,* 1–53.

Ericsson, K. A., & Kintsch, W. (1995). Long-term working memory. *Psychological Review, 102,* 211–245.

Gottfried, S. S., & Kyle, W. C. (1992). Textbook use and the biology education desired state. *Journal of Research in Science Teaching, 29,* 35–49.

Graesser, A. C., & Bertus, E. L. (1998). The construction of causal inferences while reading expository texts on science and technology. *Scientific Studies of Reading, 2,* 247–269.

Graesser, A. C., Gordon, S. E., & Brainerd, L. E. (1992). QUEST: A model of question answering. *Computers and Mathematics With Applications, 23,* 733–745.

Graesser, A. C., Kassler, M. A., Kreuz, R. J., & Mclain-Allen, B. (1998). Verification of statements about story worlds that deviate from normal conceptions of time: What is true about Einstein's dreams. *Cognitive Psychology, 35,* 246–301.

Graesser, A. C., Millis, K., & Zwaan, R. A. (1997). Discourse comprehension. *Annual Review of Psychology, 48,* 163–189.

Graesser, A. C., Singer, M., & Trabasso, T. (1994). Constructing inferences during narrative text comprehension. *Psychological Review, 101,* 371–395.

Graesser, A. C., VanLehn, K., Rose, C., Jordan, P., & Harter, D. (in press). Intelligent tutoring systems with conversational dialogue. *AI Magazine.*

Kintsch, W. (1998). *Comprehension: A paradigm for cognition.* New York: Cambridge University Press.

Lemke, J. L (1990). *Talking science: language, learning, and values.* Norwood, NJ: Ablex.

Lorch, R. F., & van den Broek, P. (1997). Understanding reading comprehension: Current and future contributions of cognitive science. *Contemporary Educational Psychology, 22,* 213–246.

MacNamara, D., Kintsch, E., Songer, N. B., & Kintsch, W. (1996). Are good texts always better? Interactions of text coherence, background knowledge, and levels of understanding in learning from text. *Cognition and Instruction, 14,* 1–43.

Mandler, J. M. (1984). *Stories, scripts and scenes: Aspects of schema theory.* Hillsdale, NJ: Lawrence Erlbaum Associates.

McKeown, M. G., Beck, I. L., Sinatra, G. M., & Loxterman, J. A. (1992). The contribution of prior knowledge and coherent text to comprehension. *Reading Research Quarterly, 27,* 78–93.

Means, M. L., & Voss, J. (1985). Star Wards: A developmental study of expert–novice knowledge structures. *Journal of Memory and Language, 24,* 746–757.

Moschman, D. (1982). Exogenous, endogenous, and dialectical constructivism. *Developmental Review, 2,* 371–384.

Nathan, M. J., Kinstch, W., & Young, E. (1992). A theory of word algebra problem-comprehension and its implications for the design of the learning environments. *Cognition and Instruction, 9,* 329–389.

O'Brien, E. J., & Myers, J. L. (1999). Text comprehension: A view from the bottom up. In S. R. Goldman, A. C. Graesser, & P. van den Broek (Eds.), *Narrative comprehension, causality, and coherence: Essays in honor of Tom Trabasso* (pp. 35–53). Mahwah, NJ: Lawrence Erlbaum Associates.

Paivio, A. V. (1971). *Imagery and verbal processes.* New York: Holt, Rinehart & Winston.

Parker, S. B. (1994). *Concise encyclopedia of science and technology* (3rd ed.). New York: McGraw-Hill.

Schank, R. C. (1999). *Dynamic memory revisited.* New York: Cambridge University Press.

Webb, N. M., Troper, J. D., & Fall, R. (1995). Constructive activity and learning in collaborative small groups. *Journal of Educational Psychology, 87,* 406–423.

Yager, R. E. (1983). The importance of terminology in teaching K–12 science. *Journal of Research in Science Teaching, 20,* 577–588.

Yore, L. D. (1991). Secondary science teacher's attitudes toward and beliefs about science reading and science textbooks. *Journal of Research in Science Teaching, 28,* 55–72.

Zwaan, R. A., & Radvansky, G. A. (1998). Situation models in language comprehension and memory. *Psychological Bulletin, 123,* 162–185.

I

The Functions, Contents, and Design of Science Texts

❧ 2 ❧

Toward a Functional Analysis of Scientific Genres: Implications for Understanding and Learning Processes

Susan R. Goldman
University of Illinois at Chicago

Gay L. Bisanz
University of Alberta

In approaching the psychology of science text comprehension, discourse psychologists are examining issues that have proven to be important to comprehension of other kinds of texts. These issues include mechanisms that readers use to construct coherent, sensible meaning from information presented in text, in the visuals accompanying text, and across multiple texts and visuals (e.g., van den Broek, chaps. 6, 15, and 16, this volume). Other important work is focusing on ways to assist comprehension through the design of the texts themselves, or by developing strategies that readers can use to facilitate meaningful processing (e.g., chaps. 3, 10, and 14, this volume). These efforts assume a general text-processing model that asserts that readers build mental representations of information contained in text. Mental representations capture elements of the surface text, of the referential meaning of the text, and of the interpretation of the referential meaning. The latter is often referred to as a model of the situation described by the text (called the *situation model*) and is the aspect of the representation in which prior content knowledge exerts its most powerful influence (cf. Kintsch, 1998; van Dijk & Kintsch, 1983).

The process of constructing mental representations reflects interactions among the surface structure of the text and various aspects of readers' prior knowledge. Prior knowledge includes content knowledge, knowledge of general discourse structure, and specific knowledge of discourse structures used in the content domain (e.g., Goldman, 1997; Goldman & Rakestraw, 2000). In the case of science text comprehension, several kinds of prior knowledge are potentially relevant to building a representation. There is knowledge of the general domain (e.g., biology) and of the specific topic within the domain (e.g., genetic mutation) (Alexander & Kulikowich, 1994). There is also knowledge of the nature of scientific knowledge, and how scientists come to know that knowledge, both of which contribute to coherence criteria. For example, scientists adhere to rules of evidence and argumentation agreed to by the community of scientists (e.g., Dunbar, 1995; Duschl & Hamilton, 1997). Learners must know how to distinguish claims from evidence, conclusions from observations, and justifications from explanations (Driver, Asoko, Leach, Mortimer, & Scott, 1994; Goldman, Duschl, Ellenbogen, Williams, & Tzou, in press; Norris & Phillips, 1994). They must know how to interpret the validity of knowledge claims, a process that involves contextualizing knowledge claims in their sociohistorical context. That is, new knowledge claims need to be related to previous knowledge claims, taking into account the researcher(s), their biases, and the circumstances under which the various claims were established. This process often involves relating information in the current science text to information in other documents (Perfetti, Rouet, & Britt, 1999). Scientific inquiry is essentially a dialectical process in which one grapples with the ideas, thoughts, and reasoning of others often through the medium of written texts.

However, science texts are not a monolithic set of documents, from the perspective of either content or structure. Indeed, there are important distinctions among science texts that are related to the sociocultural role or function they play in our society. Our purpose in this chapter is to distinguish among categories of scientific texts based on the dominant function they were designed to fulfill. These categories have associated forms that reflect differences in function. The differences in form have implications for the interactive processing that occurs when learners attempt to use science texts to accomplish specific purposes. Our functional approach complements efforts on the part of researchers in other disciplines (e.g., rhetoric, science education, communication, and public health) who are trying to understand the roles, functions, and forms of science texts (e.g., Bazerman, 1985; Berkencotter & Huckin, 1995; Craig & Yore, 1996; Einsiedel, 1992; McMahon & McCormack, 1998; Norris & Phillips, 1994; Nwogu, 1991; Swales, 1990; Yeaton, D. Smith, & Rodgers, 1990).

In this chapter we consider the relationship between function and form, and its implications for text processing and the construction of mental representations of the text and the science content that constitutes the situation model. We begin by considering three sociocultural roles, or functions, of scientific communications, and the associated communication forms. These are communication among scientists, the popularization of scientific information for those outside the scientific community, and formal science education. For each, we propose central forms, or genres, and illustrate them. Processing characteristics specific to central genres are outlined and compared. We conclude with a discussion of implications for scientific literacy and the experiences that support its development.

ROLES FOR SCIENCE COMMUNICATIONS AND IMPLICATIONS FOR TEXT GENRE

There are three major roles for the communication of scientific information in our society. The first is communication among scientists; the second is disseminating or popularizing information generated by the scientific community; the third is providing formal education that prepares people to enter the scientific community as well as take their place in society as scientifically literate citizens. These roles serve the needs of different discourse communities, namely scientists, the general public, and students. Within these broadly defined discourse communities, there are smaller discourse communities, differentiated by a variety of sociocultural dimensions, for example, scientific fields, nonscientific occupations, or age/level in school, respectively. In general, discourse communities share a common set of norms for interacting with one another, common goals, and a language that marks the community as separate from other groups (Gee, 1992; Swales, 1990).

Members of a discourse community define the ways in which they communicate, including oral and written forms (e.g., in science, oral presentations at scientific conferences, journal reports of experimental data). Readers and writers within those discourse communities create and adhere to these definitions. One task for newcomers to a community is learning these forms (Gee, 1992; Lave & Wenger, 1991). These specialized forms of communication are what we refer to in the present context as genre. Our use of the term genre draws heavily on the role of the discourse community in defining and using the genres. According to Swales (1990), definitions of genre in fields as diverse as folklore, literary studies, linguistics, and rhetoric take a common stance with respect to the treatment of genre. Drawing on these traditions and Swales' working definition of genre, we emphasize the following definitional features of genre. A genre is a class of communicative events with shared purposes and goals. Genres are situated within discourse communities and are created and often labeled by the members of those communities. These labels provide windows into the norms of the community (Berkenkotter & Huckin, 1995). Genres establish and extend the community's rhetorical goals and social actions. Some genres are more central to accomplishing the goals of the community than others. Furthermore, within a genre, "exemplars or instances of genre vary in their prototypicality" (Swales, 1990, p. 49). For example, within the context of formal education, the textbook is a central genre but some textbooks are more prototypical than others.

Various communities of practice (Lave & Wenger, 1991) are associated with each of the functional roles of scientific information in society. For our purposes, communities of practice comprise the discourse communities whose members consensually agree upon the genres of their communities. Scientists themselves govern the genre of communication among scientists. Genres of popularization and dissemination are defined largely by communities of practice associated with the media and publishing industry (e.g., journalists, technical writers, and newscasters). The dominant genre of formal education is the textbook. This genre is shaped by the textbook-publishing industry, in the context of curricular standards set by governments and policy debates about curricular reform that can involve scientists and educators. Scientists and educators can also serve as industry consultants or write textbooks. As writers they tend to conform to the structure and content guidelines set out by the publisher. The community of scientists generates the primary scientific literature. Genres and texts written to meet the needs of the general public and of students constitute a secondary literature because the information is drawn from the primary literature.

Genres arise to meet various functions that a community defines as important and evolve in accord with changes in the epistemological orientation of the discipline (Bazerman, 1988; Berkenkotter & Huckin, 1995). We can reasonably expect that the structure for any specific genre has been shaped by the function(s) it is to accomplish for that community, including the audience for whom it is intended. We can also predict that the more the structure-function relationship is known to "users" of the genre, the greater the chances that the genre will serve its intended function. Indeed, students in all fields spend a good bit of their training learning to understand and generate the genres of their fields. Furthermore, the difficulties domain novices experience can be traced, in part, to their lack of understanding of how to use the structure of a genre to guide their comprehension. Research studies indicate that making the structure more explicit or training learners to attend to structure improves their learning (see for discussion Alexander, Kulikowich, & Schulze, 1994; Goldman, 1997; Goldman & Rakestraw, 2000).

Although genres have intended audiences, they may also be used by incidental audiences to accomplish a variety of their own functions. That is, those outside the specific community also have access to many of the communications originally designed for functions within that community. Access for incidental audiences is especially evident for genres originating within the scientific community in an era of mass media, including digital information technologies. Thus, genres designed with a particular structure to accomplish community-specific functions may be accessed by both intended and incidental audiences. Processing issues for incidental audiences will be governed by their purposes and the processing strategies they bring to text. In some cases, processing difficulties will arise for members of incidental audiences because they lack knowledge of the structure-function relationships that are known by members of the intended audience. In other cases, incidental audiences may be able to transfer processing strategies applicable to genres typical of their own communities. In still other cases, members of incidental audiences must develop processing skills that allow them access to genres of other communities. For example, journalists, technical writers, and textbook authors need to develop processing skills for the genres of the scientific community. Otherwise they cannot create the material that disseminates, popularizes, and educates.

In the next sections, we elaborate on the scientific genres that are associated with each of the three major roles for scientific communication, communication among scientists, popularization, and formal education. We describe the prototypical genre used to accomplish these functions and their implications for processing by intended and incidental audiences.

Scientists Communicating With Scientists

As a community of practice, scientists share norms and genres of communicative interactions. The norms include a shared set of values about the nature of knowledge and ways of knowing. They give rise to a variety of genres that reflect agreed upon processes for making knowledge public and establishing knowledge claims. Different genres emphasize different aspects of the scientific endeavor, as illustrated in Table 2.1.

We distinguish two broad groups of genres, formative and integrative. Formative genres document and shape scientists' thinking and reflect the leading edges of scientific fields. They capture the processes of designing and conducting research (e.g., bench notes and research diaries) and the structured content of formal reports of research (e.g., refereed journal articles). Accounts of the research process, such as research diaries, tend to be relatively private in that the writer is the primary intended audience. Presentations, book chapters, and research reports provide the "cutting edge," new knowledge claims of the field. They are intended for a "public" scientific audience and, typically, one whose members work in the same scientific domain and investigate similar phenomena. The authors of theoretical papers, and some review papers, often challenge current conceptions and set out new propositions for the field (cf. American Psychological Association [APA], 1994). Research reports, reviews, and theoretical papers typically bear the "stamp of approval" of the community because they undergo a peer review process or are subject to refutation in public outlets. In an age of specialization and rapid proliferation of research studies, the refereed review article is an increasingly valuable genre for intended audiences in the scientific community, and perhaps even incidental audiences. As noted in the *Publication Manual of the American Psychological Association* (APA, 1994), the function of the review article is clearly "tutorial" (p. 5).

Integrative genres are syntheses of what is widely known and accepted about a particular topic area. In addition, the authors of these genres often suggest new directions, important unaddressed issues, and dilemmas for the discipline to consider (cf. APA, 1994). The intended scientific audience is typically broader than that for formative genres. For example, handbook chapters are often intended for novices in the field and their authors attempt to introduce the area as well as pose critical issues for research and theory.

Understanding and Learning From Research Reports.   Of scientists' various genres, we focus our discussion of processing issues on the research report because it is central to accomplishing a major goal of the science community, the generation of new knowledge claims (Swales, 1990). The research report is essentially a persuasive argument directed at colleagues working in the researchers' field. There are specific conventions on the structure of research reports and the content appropriate to different

TABLE 2.1

Genres of Science Texts

Genres of communication among scientists

   Formative[a]

      Bench notes, research diaries

      Personal communications (oral or written), working drafts

      Institutional presentations (e.g., departmental seminars and colloquia), technical reports

      Chapters in edited books, books

      Refereed conference presentations and posters, invited conference presentations

      Refereed journal articles, including reports of empirical research, critical reviews of a topic area, and theoretical formulations

   Integrative

      Chapters in handbook and advances series

      Refereed review articles

Genres for popularizing scientific information[b]

   Public awareness

      Press releases

      News briefs

      Advertisements or charitable appeals

      Public service messages

      Science fiction

   Public understanding and informal learning

      Feature articles

      Summary reports/critical commentaries

      Autobiographies or biographies

      Special-interest books on specific topics

      Reference books (e.g., encyclopedias, almanacs)

      Pamphlets and other informational documents (e.g., on healthful living practices or detection of dangerous chemicals in the home)

      Special informational Web sites on science topics (e.g., National Geographic)

Formal education and instruction

   Textbooks

continued on next page

TABLE 2.1 (*continued*)

Laboratory workbooks

Training manuals and technical documents

Special educational Websites for specific curricular topics

[a]Within Formative and Integrative categories, genres are listed in an order that reflects degree of peer scrutiny, from least to most. [b]The distinction between genres that serve to raise awareness and those that increase understanding is intended to reflect authors' intended purposes. Obviously, some popularizations are designed to serve both functions (e.g., feature articles).

parts of the structure (Bazerman, 1988; Berkenkotter & Huckin, 1995; Kintsch & van Dijk, 1978; Swales, 1990). These conventions reflect the community's criteria for making and for evaluating new knowledge claims.

The empirical research report consists of three main sections: Introduction, Experiment, and Discussion. The experiment has two main parts: Method and Results. In the multiexperiment research report, the three parts are General Introduction, Experiments, and General Discussion, with each experiment including four parts (introduction, method, results, and discussion). The main goal of the introduction is to set the article in the context of the larger field, establish the credentials of the researcher, and the purpose of the specific work or experiment(s) reported in the article. The experiment(s) constitutes the "guts" of the report and describes how the data were collected and analyzed plus the results of the analyses. Discussion is the section in which researchers embrace their new knowledge claims by highlighting the major findings of the study and how these extend the knowledge base of the field. These are the "contributions to the field" and thereby position researchers in the community of scientists. Finally, researchers establish new territory for themselves when they discuss the implications of their work. (For additional discussion see Berkenkotter & Huckin, 1995; Swales, 1990.) Table 2.2 contains a research report from the journal *Nature* that we have annotated to show these sections. Although it is a "brief communication," it still reflects the canonical research report genre.

Knowledge of the form and function of each section guides both the construction and the comprehension of the research report. Learning the research report genre is one of the requirements of membership in the scientific community. Indeed, to facilitate the learning process for psychologists, the *Publication Manual of the American Psychological Association*

TABLE 2.2

A Brief Illustration of the Research Report Genre

Cognition: Numerical memory span in a chimpanzee

NOBUYUKI KAWAI AND TETSURO MATSUZAWA

Primate Research Institute, Kyoto University, Inuyama, Aichi 484–8506, Japan

(Introduction)

A female chimpanzee called Ai has learned to use Arabic numerals to represent numbers[1]. She can count from zero to nine items, which she demonstrates by touching the appropriate number on a touch-sensitive monitor[2,3], and she can order the numbers from zero to nine in sequence[4-6]. Here we investigate Ai's memory span by testing her skill in these numerical tasks, and find that she can remember the correct sequence of any five numbers selected from the range zero to nine.

Humans can easily memorize strings of codes such as phone numbers and postcodes if they consist of up to seven items, but above this number they find it much harder. This "magic number 7" effect, as it is known in human information processing[7], represents a limit for the number of items that can be handled simultaneously by the brain.

(Method)

To determine the equivalent "magic number" in a chimpanzee, we presented our subject with a set of numbers on a screen, say 1, 3, 4, 6, and 9. She had already displayed close to perfect accuracy when required to choose numerals in ascending order, but for this experiment all the remaining numbers were masked by white squares once she had selected the first number. This meant that, in order to be correct in a trial, she had to memorize all the numbers, as well as their respective positions, before making the first response. Chance levels with three, four, and five items were 50, 13, and 6%, respectively.

(Results)

Ai scored more than 90% with four items and about 65% with five items, significantly above chance in each case. In normal background trials, response latency was longest for the first numeral and much shorter for all the others, indicating that Ai inspected the numbers and their locations and planned her actions before making her first choice. In masking trials, response latency increased only for the choice directly after the onset of masking, but this latency was similar to those recorded in background trials, indicating that successful performance did not depend on spending more time memorizing the numbers.

In one testing session, after Ai had chosen the correct number and all the remaining items were masked by white squares, a fight broke out among a group of chimpanzees outside the room, accompanied by loud screaming. Ai abandoned her task and paid attention to the fight for about 20 seconds, after which she returned to the screen and completed the trial without error.

continued on next page

TABLE 2.2   (*continued*)

(Discussion)

Ai's performance shows that chimpanzees can remember the sequence of at least five numbers, the same as (or even more than) preschool children. Our study and others[8-10] demonstrate the rudimentary form of numerical competence in non-human primates.

(PDF file also included Table 1 Performance in masking trials, which showed the response times and number correct for all trials in normal and masking conditions.)

Supplementary information is available on *Nature*'s World Wide Web site (http://www.nature.com) or as paper copy from the London editorial office of *Nature*.

References

1. Matsuzawa, T. *Nature 315*, 57–59 (1985). Links.

2. Matsuzawa, T., Itakura, S. & Tomonaga, M. in Primatology Today (eds Ehara, A., Kumura, T., Takenaka, O. & Iwamoto, M.) 317–320 (Elsevier, Amsterdam, 1991).

3. Murofushi, K. *Jpn. Psychol. Res. 39*, 140–153 (1997).

4. Tomonaga, M., Matsuzawa, T. & Itakura, S. *Primate Res. 9*, 67–77 (1993).

5. Biro, D. & Matsuzawa, T. *J. Comp. Psychol. 113*, 178–185 (1999).

6. Tomonaga, M. & Matsuzawa, T. *Anim. Cogn.* (in the press).

7. Miller, G. A. *Psychol. Rev. 63*, 81–97 (1956).

8. Rumbaugh, D., Savage-Rumbaugh, E. S. & Hegel, M. *J. Exp. Psychol. Anim. Behav. Process. 13*, 107–115 (1987). Links

9. Brannon, E. & Terrace, H. *Science 282*, 746–749 (1998). Links

10. Boysen, S., Mukobi, K. & Berntson, G. *Anim. Learn. Behav. 27*, 229–235 (1999).

Note: Reprinted by permission. From *Nature* Vol. 403 pp. 39–40 Copyright © 2000 Macmillan Magazines Ltd.

(1994) provides explicit information on what content is to appear in which section, and the format for reporting it.

Interestingly, there are very few empirical studies of scientists reading scientific research articles (see however, Bazerman, 1985; Berkencotter & Huckin, 1995). Drawing on these few studies, and analogous work in the psychology of reading, we discuss considerations for processing research reports. Consistent with prior research on discourse comprehension, prior knowledge of the topic and the purpose of reading the report influence the way in which scientists read and evaluate the research reports. When scientists read reports in their field, studies indicated that they looked for "what's new" in the piece so they could update their own knowledge. They did not read the article sequentially but went to the results and discussion first (Bazerman, 1985; Berkenkotter & Huckin, 1995). On the other hand, when scientists read research reports outside of their field of expertise they tended to read the article more linearly, beginning with the introduction. They reported that their purpose for reading topics not central to their own work was for general intellectual interest (Berkenkotter & Huckin, 1995). Thus, when scientists approach research reports they have different purposes for reading on topics central to the field and for which they have a great deal of prior knowledge as compared to those outside. Using their understanding of the structure of the genre, they adapt their reading strategies to suit their purposes.

Scientists also evaluate the information and knowledge claims they read, especially when it is germane to their own field. Depending again on purpose, scientists may set relatively loose as compared to relatively rigid criteria for coherence and understanding. For example, when scientists are serving as reviewers of research reports, they read with the purpose of "gatekeeping." They want to be sure that published research is sound according to the criteria set by the community. Accordingly, scientists-as-reviewers set high criteria for coherence, including internal consistency, external validity, and the newsworthiness, or importance. In contrast, once a research report is published, scientists-as-readers reported that they paid less attention to methods; they used their knowledge of the review process to essentially assume that if the report made it through the review process, the methods were likely to be sound (Bazerman, 1985; Berkenkotter & Huckin, 1995).

Evaluative criteria also influenced scientists' responses to comprehension problems. In Bazerman's (1985) research with physicists, he found that their strategies for dealing with comprehension difficulties followed a cost/benefit approach. That is, if physicists thought that articles were really worth their time, they worked through the comprehension difficulties; otherwise they did not. Determinations of "worth" relied on judgments about the trustworthiness of the "source" (e.g., scientist-as-author), the reasonableness of the approach, and the sensibility of the assertions (e.g., did they accord with nature?).

The observed differences in scientists' strategies for processing and evaluating research reports are consistent with the formation of a situation model that reflects a rich set of connections among different reports. Perfetti et al. (1999) referred to this as the creation of a document model representation. Elements of a document model reflect the sociohistorical context of the report, including author, time, place, theoretical stance (bias), and standing within the field. Understanding a new research report involves an intertextual process in which the interpretation takes into account the relation between information in the "new" report and information that has appeared in other prior reports by the same or other researchers. From this perspective, scientists reading within their field of specialization already have relatively rich document models, including the "current state" of information in their field as well as the sociohistorical context. These preexisting representations make it possible for them to read findings and discussion sections of reports with no loss of comprehension. However, when they read outside their field they use their knowledge of the report to select those parts of the article (i.e., the introduction, methods) that will provide the scaffolding for them to understand the specific findings.

The issues that confront scientists reading on topics outside their areas of expertise will be exacerbated for both novices within a scientific field and members of incidental audiences for research reports. Both groups have little in the way of prior knowledge that would guide their processing. They are unfamiliar with the structure, the content, and the sociohistorical context of the research. We speculate that they would process the report linearly, have a difficult time separating claims from evidence and observations, and have no basis for evaluating the research. Our speculations are based on work that investigates comprehension of genre intended to popularize or teach scientific content (e.g., Coté, Goldman, & Saul, 1998; Dee-Lucas & Larkin, 1986; Norris & Phillips, 1994) and a single recall study that showed that training on the structure of a research report improved recall for reports presented in the canonical order (Davis, Lange, & Samuels, 1988).

Process Issues for Other Genres and Incidental Audiences. Other genres of communication among scientists tend to be derivative of the research report (Swales, 1990). As such, incidental audiences will face challenges similar to those for research reports with respect to the availability of prior topic and structure knowledge. One exception to this may be those genres that have a more chronological, narrative structure, in particular bench notes and research diaries. Texts in this genre provide documentation of the day-to-day process of doing science. Scientists typically record their thinking about problems and the methods they intend to use to test their hypotheses and conjectures. When these process accounts also relate the personal side of scientific discovery (e.g., the doubts, frustrations, and triumphs involved in personal intellectual struggles), they may be more accessible to novices and incidental audiences (Martin & Brouwer, 1991). Learners might approach texts of this genre for purposes of understanding the "messiness" of science process. In contrast, research reports typically record the "product" of the process. The genres of bench notes and research diaries provide a window into the doing of science.

Popularizing Science for the General Public

A wide variety of genres fill the need to disseminate scientific information to the general public. Much of this information is newsworthy and of interest to the public because it marks an intriguing discovery or has implications for everyday health and well-being (e.g., Einsiedel, 1992; Zimmerman, G. L. Bisanz, J. Bisanz, J. Klein, & P. Klein, 2001). As a class, these genres popularize the information exchanged among scientists, are derived from the primary literature, and appear in diverse media (e.g., newspapers, Web sites, magazines, books, and television). As indicated earlier, journalists and technical writers are the major communities of practice that create the texts that fill these needs. These publications vary in the complexity and depth of information, the ratio of text to visuals, and the emphasis on what is known and how it is known. Such differences reflect assumptions about the intellectual sophistication and information requirements of the intended audiences.

We distinguish two functions of popularizations: raising public awareness of scientific information and increasing public understanding of scientific information. Different genres meet these needs, as outlined in Table 2.1. *Raising public awareness* occurs largely through the media, including the Internet. News briefs are central to raising public awareness. They are generally "reduced" reports of information published in scientific outlets but they conform to journalistic conventions for news reporting (Nwogu, 1991; van Dijk, 1986). These reports can appear in brief or longer formats. In either case, Nwogu referred to them as Journalistic Reported Versions (JRVs) of research articles. The intent of these articles is typically to inform a general audience rather than to persuade a community of peers about the validity of the work. Accordingly, technical details are summarized and simplified (Zimmerman et al., 2001). The elaborateness of the report is determined by pragmatic issues such as space or editorial policy rather than by scientific criteria for knowledge claims. As we discuss later, the brevity typical of these reports has important implications for processing and mental representations.

Advertisements, charitable appeals, and public service announcements also raise public awareness of science. These genres presuppose the validity of the knowledge claims embedded in the communication and *use* scientific information to encourage the public to take particular kinds of actions. Science fiction can also raise public awareness, but in this case authors use scientific information in the service of a story. The dilemma for the reader of this genre of "fiction" is deciding what to believe about the "science" content, just as readers of historical fiction may question the veracity of specific information about place, time, and culture.

Genres for *increasing public understanding* have a didactic or instructional intent. They differ from genres that raise awareness in that they attempt to support informal learning by providing information sufficient for the public to achieve an understanding of the scientific concepts, phenomena, or processes that are discussed. As such they contain more extensive science content. Part of the author's task in writing these communications is to be explicit about criticisms, alternative viewpoints, and other information that readers should take into account when interpreting the information (cf. Conrad, 1999). A variety of diverse genres may enhance public understanding, depending on how they are used by readers (see Table 2.1). The result is that for these genres the structural conventions and labels are less stable, consistent, and informative in terms of guiding processing than the genres discussed previously.

Frequently, within a "public understanding" genre, texts are tailored to different subgroups of the general public. Some are geared for specific age groups such as preschool children, teenagers, or adults. The content of these texts varies and may include definitions of science concepts, descriptions of processes and models of scientific phenomena, explanations of research designs and procedures, and personal accounts of scientific discoveries and theories. Autobiographical or biographical accounts of the discovery process are particularly interesting because they appear as first-person narratives and contrast with the objective voice of most other forms of scientific communication (Martin & Brouwer, 1991). Increasingly, various organizations dedicated to the enhancement of scientific understanding are creating Web sites that provide access to a variety of didactic material, including text, static and dynamic visuals, and graphics. Greater and more convenient accessibility to such materials provides new and ubiquitous opportunities for the occurrence of informal science learning and research on these processes.

Journalistic Reported Versions of Research Reports. Of the various genres intended to meet the public's need to know about science, we focus the remainder of our discussion on the JRV. Derived as it is from research reports written and read by professional scientists, this genre illustrates the transformations that occur when reporters convey the same content through a different medium for different readers with different purposes. It is central among the popularization genres because it is pervasive and because it has the potential to serve both functions of popularizations. For example, in both brief and longer versions, the JRV can raise public awareness of research findings at the cutting edge of science that could enhance personal, professional, and public decisions. Examples are findings on Viagra, global warming, genetically modified foods, and life on Mars. Heightened awareness can motivate readers to view reports of new and important studies as invitations to further reading that could shape new understandings and opinions. In contrast, readers who do not understand the tentative nature of the professional genre from which this type of news report derives could leave the news report with illusions of understanding. Such illusions should be of concern to scientists and science educators because they can quickly lead to public disenchantment with science as contradictory knowledge claims subsequently make the news (cf. Fitzpatrick, 1999). Space does not permit us to consider processing issues for other genres of popularization. However, several chapters in this volume are concerned with such documents (e.g., chaps. 7, 8, 13, 14, and 16, this volume).

Understanding and Learning from Journalistic Reported Versions of the Research Report. Journalists face several challenges in transforming the primary research literature into research reports that conform to journalistic genres. The first challenge is identifying important, credible, and newsworthy research reports (Wright, 1998). Elite peer reviewed journals (e.g., *Science, Nature, New England Journal of Medicine, Lancet*) provide a natural source of potential news stories because they offer the safety net of peer review and their prestige suggests that the findings reported are important or at least potentially important (Conrad, 1999). Journalists also often rely on conference presentations because these represent "up to the minute" findings that may be particularly provocative.

A second challenge for journalists is reader engagement (e.g., Nwogu, 1991). The "information market" is one of high competition for readers' attention. JRVs need to attract and sustain readers' interest throughout the article. To do so, journalists frequently enlist science experts other than the researchers to comment on the findings, especially if there is something controversial or more than one point of view on the results (Conrad, 1999). A third challenge is presenting the scientific information in a way that is consistent with the prior knowledge and reading skills of the intended audiences. At the same time, the structure of the JRV needs to conform to the news article (van Dijk, 1986), as mentioned earlier. Although reporters get the by-line, meeting these multiple challenges requires the collective and cooperative activity of journalists, scientists, editors, and their perceptions of the intended audiences (e.g., Conrad, 1999). The process results in news reports of research that lack the jargon and many of the qualifications found in research reports (Dubois, 1986, reported in Swales, 1990).

Table 2.3 illustrates the transformation of a research report into a JRV for the *Nature* article (Table 2.2). The text of the article is in the first column and the corresponding sections of a generic news report in the second column. In addition to removing all of the technical information, the JRV reflects a significant reordering of the information from the canonical sequence shown for the research report version. The JRV begins with a headline that highlights an unusual event, presumably to attract readers' attention. The lead reports the main event, in this case the finding that makes the article news and worthy of the readers' attention. Only after this has been established is the background of the study conveyed. The middle of the article conveys additional details of the method and results of the study. Finally, the JRV replaces the original discussion of the study by connecting the findings to work of two other researchers who comment on the consequence or importance of the finding. Nwogu (1991) found that the transformation of the research report into the JRV was fairly consistent across popularizations of 15 medical studies. A consistent set of nine rhetorical moves, that is, segments of text with specific associated content, occurred in fairly schematic order, with Moves 1 and 2 occurring first, 8 and 9 last, and varied ordering for the medial moves. The third column in Table 2.3 shows these moves for the chimpanzee JRV. The lead sentence accomplishes both Moves 1 and 2 by highlighting the main finding and hooking the reader by connecting the finding to an ability most of the general public probably does not attribute to chimpanzees. The "middle" of the article provides related research, the purpose of the current research, the procedures, and the results. The final two segments explain the finding and its implications. Because the study involved a single subject, missing from this particular JRV were features of the research design (Move 6), such as how subjects were assigned to treatments.

The information that is included and highlighted by the typical ordering of the information in JRVs constrains the reasoning and evaluation processes open to readers. For example, the inclusion of related research is relatively rare in JRVs yet it is an essential element of research reports (e.g., Nwogu, 1991; Zimmerman et al., 2001). Likewise, information about design and methodology is frequently much reduced or missing in JRVs, although they are well-developed elements of the scientific argument in research reports (e.g., Einsiedel, 1992; Mallow, 1991; Zimmerman et al., 2001). The rarity of

Transformation of Research Report
Chimp — rel. symbol to number.

TABLE 2.3
JRV of *Nature* article

Sentences in JRV	Sections in News Story[a]	Rhetorical Move[b]
From Memory, Chimp gets numbers Right	Headline	
A chimpanzee has shown it can remember the correct sequence of five random numbers—an experiment that adds to the growing evidence that animals have some basic numerical ability. A female chimp tested with the numbers between zero and nine performed about as well as an average preschool child would, researchers at Kyoto University in Japan have found.	Main event	Move 1 and 2: Hooking the reader and highlighting the major research outcome
The Chimp, named Ai, had already demonstrated that she could put five numbers in ascending order when they were scattered across a computer screen.	Background	Move 3: Reviewing related research
But Kyoto researchers Nobuyuki Kawai and Tetsuro Matsuzawa reported in today's issue of the journal *Nature* that they took the experiment a step further.	Details of main event	Move 4: Purpose of the new research
When the chimp touched the first number, the four others were covered up behind small white squares on the screen. She then had to touch the squares in the proper order. Kawai and Matsuzawa said the chimp had to memorize all the numbers to make the right choice.	Details of main event	Move 7: Describing the experimental procedure
The chimp succeeded better than 90% of the time in identifying four numbers in the proper order, and was successful about 65% of the time with five items, far better than chance in each case. Matsuzawa noted that in one testing session, Ai was distracted by a fight among chimps outside the lab, but returned to the screen and completed the trial correctly.	Details of main event	Move 5: Identification of positive results
The study builds on research by Herbert Terrace and Elizabeth Brannon at Columbia University in New York. Brannon said, however, the Japanese research showed stronger evidence of mathematical skill.	Background	Move 8: Explaining the research outcome

continued on next page

TABLE 2.3 *(continued)*

"What is interesting about this work is that they actually trained the chimpanzee to see the relationship between the symbol and the underlying number."	Consequence	Move 9: Stating the implication of the research

Note. From "From Memory, Chimp Gets Numbers Right" (2000). Copyright January 6, 2000 by Associated Press. Adapted by permission of the Associated Press.

[a]These are the categories identified by van Dijk (1986). He segmented the news report into two major sections, the Summary and the News story. The Summary consists of the Headline and the Lead; the News story consists of several categories, including main event, details of main event, background, consequences, and comments.

[b]Rhetorical moves are taken from Nwogu (1991).

related research and the lack of methodological details may reflect the expectations of JRV authors that the general public's purpose in reading is not to evaluate the scientific merit of the findings but to be made aware of new and legitimate discoveries. Indeed, Zimmerman et al. found that the typical JRV about new scientific research was even less detailed than the example in Table 2.3. They noted that the typical, brief JRV was a simple description of a new study described as an isolated event, with some aspects of *who* and *what* described, and sometimes even the geographical *where*. Absent were details about social context that might be correlated with research quality (e.g., quality of the scientific journal or funding agency), details about how the research was conducted, insights into causal mechanisms, information about related research, and comments about the likely significance of findings. Thus, in practice, the reporter writing the JRV is often providing readers with the opportunity to become aware of new research outcomes but not the information necessary to assess the credibility of the findings. Social context information relevant to credibility is typically presented only indirectly (e.g., in the researcher's university affiliation). In meeting the challenges posed by the transformation of research reports into relatively brief news stories, journalists leave the general public with information insufficient to determine the potential significance of these findings.

Processing Journalistic Reported Versions. Although by no means extensive, there is a somewhat larger body of empirical research on reading JRVs than on research reports (e.g., Korpan, G. Bisanz, J. Bisanz, & Henderson, 1997; Norris & Phillips, 1994; Phillips & Norris, 1999; Yeaton et al., 1990; Zimmerman, G. L. Bisanz, & J. Bisanz, 1998). There are a number of studies of variants of the JRV such as those that appear as feature articles in magazines like *Newsweek* and *Discovery*. The research indicates that learning and understanding processes are affected by domain knowledge and knowledge about the epistemology of science. Indeed, prior domain knowledge even predicts readers' interest. For example, Alexander, Kulikowich, and Schulze (1994) found that those undergraduates and graduate students who had greater knowledge of physics also provided higher interest ratings for popular reports about physics than low-knowledge students. Thus, knowledge of relevant content domains in science may help account for individual differences in reader engagement, a potentially important factor in accounting for both what types of science articles are read and what types of mental representations are constructed during reading in everyday contexts (cf. Graesser, Higginbotham, Robertson, & W. R. Smith, 1978).

There is also evidence that high school and university students have severely limited knowledge of the elements of scientific argument. For example, Norris and Phillips (1994) asked students to judge the scientific status of each statement (e.g., causal claim, observation, description of research) and the role of each statement in the chain of scientific argument (e.g., justification, evidence, conclusion) for the sentences in several newspaper and magazine reports. Only half of the students understood the scientific status and the role of statements in the argument being developed. University students have also been shown to perform poorly when asked to recognize appropriate generalizations from health-related research that was reported in newspapers and magazines (Yeaton et al., 1990). In a more direct test of university students' knowledge of information relevant to evaluating a scientific argument, Zimmerman et al. (2001) found that students differed from experts in the emphasis placed on social context information (e.g., funding agency, quality of publication outlet, potential biases of researchers) and related research. In contrast to the students, experts placed high value on social context and related research, informed as they are about the criteria and norms for establishing knowledge claims in the scientific community. Both students and experts emphasized the importance of methodological information.

Perhaps due to limited domain knowledge and knowledge of the elements and form of scientific argument, the general reading public appears to adopt processing orientations that are accepting rather than critical. Phillips and Norris (1999; for related work see, e.g., Klaczynski & Gordon, 1996; Korpan et al., 1997; Kunda, 1987, 1990) identified three processing orientations to text, or "stances" toward understanding popular reports. They noted that readers can position themselves with respect to texts in at least three epistemically different ways. The *critical stance* involves attempting to reach an interpretation that takes into account text information and prior beliefs. These processes that integrate text information and prior knowledge produce a situation model representation. The *dominant stance* allows prior beliefs to overwhelm text information, producing a representation that assimilates new information to existing knowledge frameworks and beliefs (Coté et al., 1998). The *deferential stance* allows the text to overwhelm prior beliefs. This stance may produce momentary "learning" but prior beliefs may subsequently reappear, as research on the persistence of misconceptions or preconceptions suggests (e.g., McCloskey, Caramazza, & Green, 1980). In terms of "ideal" processing stances, the critical stance holds the most promise for longer term learning benefits. However, Phillips and Norris (1999) found that among the high school students they tested, the majority deferred to what they had read in the popular reports of science drawn from newspapers and magazines.

It is also possible that the information presented in JRVs and related genre is insufficient for readers to adopt a critical stance. However, even when social context information was deliberately manipulated to be of high quality, university students did not use it in evaluating popularized versions of research reports (Zimmerman et al., 1998).

In summary, when interacting with popularized reports of scientific research, some of the most well-educated members of the general public (high school students with backgrounds in science and university students) have difficulty (a) differentiating among the various information functions in a scientific argument, (b) recognizing appropriate generalizations of the reported conclusions, (c) considering sociohistorical context and related research, both of which are important to judging the credibility of conclusions, and (d) adopting a critical stance toward the reports. In contrast, reflections on our own "researcher" behavior when reading newspaper accounts of research suggest that practicing scientists frequently adopt a critical stance, suspending acceptance of results for which methodological details are lacking and questioning conclusions and implications drawn from them. Unfortunately, the "scientific literacy" of everyday citizens appears restricted to the acceptance of portrayals in the media. It would be useful to consider what roles journalists and scientists might play in scaffolding more critical and evaluative reading processes.

Formal Education and Instruction

The third important function of scientific communications is in formal education and training settings. Ensuring that citizens are scientifically literate has been an enduring goal of science education throughout much of the 20th century (e.g., Bybee, 1997; DeBoar, 1991, 2000). Definitions of scientific literacy and curricular emphases vary, but three curricular emphases are reflected widely in contemporary educational standards and policy statements: Understanding (a) science content including basic facts, concepts, and processes, (b) the methods and procedures of scientific inquiry, and (c) the connections among science, technology, and society (referred to as STS) (e.g., DeBoar, 1991). Genres arise that reflect such curricular emphases (see Table 2.1). As indicated previously, the dominant genre of formal education is the textbook, supplemented by laboratory workbooks (Chambliss & Calfee, 1989; Glynn & Muth, 1994; Hurd, Robinson, McConnell, & Ross, 1981; Yore, 1991). Textbooks typically emphasize facts, concepts, and processes but may also deal with methods of inquiry and connections among science, technology, and society.

Genres associated with formal education and instruction tend to be focused on well-established science, in sharp contrast to the dynamic, news-breaking qualities of scientific information portrayed in communications among scientists or in the popular press (Bauer, 1992). In training settings, textbooks are augmented by training manuals and technical documents specific to the task(s) for which the learner is being trained. Typically, neither textbooks nor training manuals convey the sociohistorical context of the presented information and they provide limited information about the process by which knowledge claims are made and evaluated. As well, the intended audiences for particular textbooks or manuals are very well defined.

The availability of the Internet is creating possibilities for new genres to emerge in the form of educational Web sites on specific curricular topics and for intended audiences. The capabilities of the Web include exploratory possibilities that far exceed those possible in print media and also bring new challenges to the authors of such materials (Goldman, 1996; Goldman & Rakestraw, 2000; Kamil, Intrator, & Kim, 2000; Reinking, McKenna, Labbo, & Kieffer, 1998). To date, however, textbooks are still the dominant educational genre and we focus our processing discussion on this genre. Many of the issues that arise in learning from textbooks are relevant to learning from material on the Web.

Understanding and Learning from Textbooks. Analyses of American science textbooks indicate that they cover too many topics, use difficult vocabulary, make little contact with students' background knowledge, and do not address commonly held misconceptions (Anderson, 1995; Roseman, Kesidou, Stern, & Caldwell, 1999; Van den Akker, 1998). They also lack logical structures that systematically develop concepts and relate topics to one another in a systematic and meaningful way (Ajewole, 1991; de Posada, 1999; Shymansky, Yore, & Good, 1991). Textbooks present information but overlook the important explanative function of science (Strube & Lynch, 1984). There is an emphasis on what is known but these knowledge claims tend to be divorced from the process of coming to know in science.

To be sure, scientific process is reflected in textbooks and related supplemental materials such as laboratory workbooks. However, the process is frequently presented in an archival fashion by relating sometimes apochryphal stories of previous scientific discoveries. Examples include Newton's discovery of gravity when an apple fell on his head, Archimedes' discovery of the displacement principle when taking a bath, Fleming's serendipitous discovery of penicillin in a Petrie dish that was part of an experiment "gone wrong," and so on. Although laboratory workbooks are for purposes of having students conduct experiments, they are typically designed so students can replicate previously discovered effects or previously established procedures (Lehrer, Schauble, & Petrosino, in press). Students are not investigating authentic problems. Thus the function of textbooks and associated lab activities is largely to transmit scientific truths previously discovered by experts.

Research on comprehension and learning from science textbooks is fraught with findings of the difficulties students have making sense of the information (e.g., Dee-Lucas & Larkin, 1986; Guzetti, Hynd, Skeels, & Williams, 1995; Manzo & Manzo, 1990; Ploetzner & Van Lehn, 1997). Textbooks may even be responsible for students' misconceptions because they use imprecise or inappropriate language to explain concepts (Garnett & Treagust, 1990; Goldman & Duran, 1988; Sanger & Greenbowe, 1997). Indeed, given typical science textbooks, learners are left with few processing options other than trying to memorize "important information," often defined by what will be tested.

In response to difficulties learners encounter with textbook material, there have been a number of efforts to produce more effective comprehension. Some of these approaches emphasize altering the text to improve coherence. Alterations can be made in a number of ways, including making explicit the logical structure of the information and the explanative relations among evidence and claims (e.g., Mayer, Bove, Bryman, Mars, & Tapangco, 1996; McNamara, E. Kintsch, Songer, & W. Kintsch, 1996). Another method is to include in the text explicit refutations of conceptions that learners might hold and that explain how or why they are less preferable than alternative conceptions (Hynd & Guzetti, 1998). Refutational texts have been found to be helpful in dispelling students' misconceptions (Guzzetti, Snyder & Glass, 1992; Guzzetti, Snyder, Glass, & Gamas, 1993). As well, high school students prefer them to nonrefutational texts (Guzzetti et al., 1995). However, refutational texts are not always effective (Otero, 1998), suggesting the need for further research in this area.

Other approaches attempt to connect the text to information the students are familiar with by using analogies (Glynn, Law, & Doster, 1998). However, analogies are a double-edged sword and their insertion in text does not always enhance comprehension (Alexander & Kulikowich, 1994; Glynn et al., 1998; Thiele & Treagust, 1994). To be effective analogies need to create a meaningful bridge from the familiar to the new concept, identify where and how the two are similar and where they are different (Glynn et al., 1998). If the similarities and differences are not made explicit, learners are not likely to understand the analogy appropriately and construct the intended representation of the new concept. Rather, the analogy becomes another incomprehensible, unrelated "bit" of knowledge.

A different approach to learners' difficulties with textbook material is to suggest that they use specific processing strategies that are helpful in increasing sense making. One powerful kind of processing is generating explanations. For both physics and biology textbook material, readers who constructed explanations of the material in the text learned more than those who did not (Chi, Bassok, Lewis, Reimann, & Glaser, 1989; Chi, de Leeuw, Chiu, & LaVancher, 1994). Additional research has demonstrated the self-explanation effect over a range of expository science materials (Chan, Burtis, Scardamalia, & Bereiter, 1992; Coleman, Brown, & Rivkin, 1997; Coté & Goldman, 1999; Coté et al., 1998). Finally, generating questions that attempt to integrate information in the text enhances learning outcomes (King, 1994).

The nature of science textbooks, in combination with studies that have shown ways to improve learning from these materials, indicates that learners need to bring a lot of active processing to the text. They need to be sensitive to text structure cues so they can maximize cues to meaning that are embedded in the text. They also need to actively monitor their understanding so they can identify where the text has not provided explanative relations and where they need to construct them, question, and seek additional information. For science in particular, learners need to process the text with an eye toward identifying what they believe, where it agrees with "so-called" established fact, where it does not, and how discrepancies might be reconciled. In this way, the function of reading in formal science education settings can become one that is connected to the dynamic, dialogic process of scientific investigation, rather than one of memorizing definitions and facts for the test. In summary, readers in formal educational settings need to engage in less memorizing and adopt more active, critical approaches to science texts, more akin to the stance of practicing scientists when reading professional genres.

SUMMARY OF SOCIETAL ROLES AND GENRES OF SCIENTIFIC COMMUNICATION

We have discussed three societal roles for scientific communication and some of their associated genres. The genres are determined by various communities of practice and with specific intended audiences in mind. Authors make assumptions, often implicit, about the genre-specific and science-specific knowledge of the intended audiences. However, as we noted earlier, incidental audiences also have access to all of these genres, especially as the Web makes them more readily available. The different functions with which incidental audiences might approach specific genres is illustrated in Table 2.4 for a selected set of genres.

The degree to which processing for incidental audiences differs from that for intended audiences depends on the extent to which the incidental audience departs from assumptions authors made about the intended audiences. As well, incidental audiences may approach these genres with purposes that are different from the purposes of members of intended audiences. For example, a sixth-grade student may consult an informational pamphlet on the effects of environmental pollution for purposes of identifying toxic waste products that might be found in the home. Suppose the pamphlet contains a boxed list of such items. The student sees the list and gets the information without reading anything else in the pamphlet. In contrast, the home owner who wants to know what to do if she finds toxic waste products in her home is a member of the audience for which the pamphlet was intended. She has to search the text, locate the desired information, and construct meaning from the sentences that appear to be generally relevant to her question. She also has to determine what information is directly relevant to her situation and put just that information into action. Thus, the comprehension demands on the sixth grader are quite a bit less than those on the home owner. The impact of various forms of knowledge on processing is mediated by the functions readers want the texts to fulfill. Scientific communications are functional for readers to the degree that they can meet those purposes.

TABLE 2.4
Societal Functions of Scientific Texts and the Genres That Fulfill These Functions

	Selected Genre					
	Original Research Reports	Bench Notes, Research Diaries	Journalistic Reported Versions	Feature Articles in the Media	Textbooks	Lab Workbooks
Scientists to scientists about science						
Advance knowledge	I	R	P	P	P	P
Document process	R	I	P	P	P	P
Popularizing science advances for public						
Raise awareness	P	P	I	I	P	P
Raise understanding	P	R	R	R	P	P
Educating students about formal science						
Convey content	P	P	P	P	I	R
Support inquiry	P	R	P	R	P	I
Make STS connections	P	P	P	R	I	P

Note. I denotes intended function for the genre. R denotes that the genre can serve this function reasonably well. P denotes relatively poor fit of the genre to the function.

IMPLICATIONS FOR UNDERSTANDING SCIENTIFIC LITERACY AND ITS DEVELOPMENT

We have made the argument for the importance of a functional approach to understanding comprehension processes for scientific communications. Our functional approach takes into account distinctions among various genres of scientific communication on the basis of the situated character of reading. That is, readers approach various science communications with particular purposes and these interact with the text structure and content to determine the kinds of processing and understanding that result.

Furthermore, in considering, at least in passing, a wide variety of genres of scientific communication, we intended to bring to light the central role of reading and writing in science, something that is not emphasized in contemporary science education. At least two factors contribute to this underemphasis. First, reading and writing seem quite implicit in the work of practicing scientists. Scientists may take reading and writing science for granted because they learned these skills in the process of acquiring the norms and values of their community of practice. In fact, the paucity of research by discourse psychologists on scientists and on novices reading professional genres may be attributable, in part, to our own familiarity with and tacit knowledge about reading scientific genres. One result of this implicitness and familiarity, however, is that many scientists may fail to fully recognize the centrality of these skills or be cognizant of the instructional scaffolding necessary to acquire them. Thus recognition, even at the college or university level, of the need for instruction that supports the development of a critical stance toward scientific communications is often overlooked. Second, because textbooks have so distorted the epistemology of science, scientists have tended to advocate for students to be more actively engaged in experimentation and demonstrations. However, in emphasizing the "doing" of science, science educators have tended to downplay the multiple ways in which reading and writing are involved in doing science.

The dominance of the textbook and a lack of focus on the authentic role of reading and writing in science lead to the phenomenon reported by a number of researchers that even high school seniors taking advanced science course have difficulty distinguishing among claims, evidence, and justifications, and misconstrue conclusions and evidence. However, in the digital information age, more and more scientific genres are being accessed by incidental audiences who do not participate in the community of scientists. If the public is to be able to take full advantage of this information personally and professionally, our educational system must begin to provide experiences that will enable the acquisition of processes for understanding, evaluating, and learning from more diverse genres of scientific texts. Making this type of scientific literacy a focal curricular emphasis of our educational system will require policy research, further study of the understanding and learning processes used by intended and incidental audiences for a wide range of genres, as well as studies of the forms of instruction that would make such scientific literacy achievable. Clearly, the study of scientific genres provides a rich and challenging research agenda for discourse psychologists and researchers in other disciplines as we begin a new century.

ACKNOWLEDGMENTS

Preparation of this chapter was made possible, in part, by support from a U.S. Department of Education grant, *Student Achievement Across the Whole Day and Whole Year* (305F60170), a Spencer Foundation grant, *Multiple Texts for Academic Learning*, and a grant from the Social Sciences and Humanities Research Council of Canada, *The Development of Scientific Literacy Skills: Evaluating Reports of Scientific Research in the News and on the Net*. However, the opinions expressed in this chapter are those of the authors and should not be attributed to these agencies.

REFERENCES

Ajewole, G. A. (1991). Effects of discovery and expository instructional methods on the attitude of students to biology. *Journal of Research in Science Teaching, 28,* 401–409.

Alexander, P. A., & Kulikowich, J. M. (1994). Learning from physics texts: A synthesis of recent research. *Journal of Research in Science Teaching, 31,* 895–911.

Alexander, P. A., Kulikowich, J. M., & Schulze, S. K. (1994). How subject-matter knowledge affects recall and interest. *American Journal of Educational Research, 31,* 313–337.

American Psychological Association. (1994). *Publication manual of the American Psychological Association* (4th ed.). Washington, DC: Author.

Anderson, R. D. (1995). Curriculum reform: Dilemmas and promise. *Phi Delta Kappan, 77,* 33–36.

Bauer, H. H. (1992). *Scientific literacy and the myth of the scientific method.* Urbana: University of Illinois Press.

Bazerman, C. (1985). Physicists reading physics: Schema-laden purposes and purpose-laden schema. *Written Communication, 2,* 3–23.

Bazerman, C. (1988). Codifying the social scientific style: The APA publication manual as a behaviorist rhetoric. In J. S. Nelson, A. Megill, & D. N. McCloskey (Eds.), *The rhetoric of the human sciences* (pp. 125–144). Madison: University of Wisconsin Press.

Berkenkotter, C., & Huckin, T. N. (1995). *Genre knowledge in disciplinary communication: Cognition/culture/power.* Hillsdale, NJ: Lawrence Erlbaum Associates.

Bybee, R. W. (1997). *Achieving scientific literacy: From purposes to practices.* Portsmouth, NH: Heinemann.

Chambliss, M. J., & Calfee, R. C. (1989). Designing science textbooks to enhance student understanding. *Educational Psychologist, 24,* 307–322.

Chan, C. K. K., Burtis, P. J., Scardamalia, M., & Bereiter, C. (1992). Constructive activity in learning from text. *American Educational Research Journal, 29,* 97–118.

Chi, M. T. H., Bassok, M., Lewis, M. W., Reimann, P., & Glaser, R. (1989). Self explanations: How students study and use examples in learning to solve problems. *Cognitive Science, 13,* 145–182.

Chi, M. T. H., de Leeuw, N., Chiu, M. H., & LaVancher, C. (1994). Eliciting self explanations improves understanding. *Cognitive Science, 18,* 439–477.

Coleman, E., Brown, A. L., & Rivkin, I. D. (1997). The effect of instructional explanations on learning from scientific texts. *Journal of the Learning Sciences, 6,* 347–365.

Conrad, P. (1999). Uses of expertise: Sources, quotes, and voice in the reporting of genetics in the news. *Public Understanding of Science, 8,* 285–302.

Coté, N., & Goldman, S. R. (1999). Building representations of informational text: Evidence from children's think-aloud protocols. In H. Van Oostendorp & S. R. Goldman (Eds.), *The construction of mental representations during reading* (pp. 169–193). Mahwah, NJ: Lawrence Erlbaum Associates.

Coté, N., Goldman, S. R., & Saul, E. U. (1998). Students making sense of informational text: Relations between processing and representation. *Discourse Processes, 25,* 1–53.

Craig, M. T., & Yore, L. D. (1996). Middle school students' awareness of strategies for resolving comprehension difficulties in reading science. *Journal of Research and Development in Education, 29,* 226–238.

Davis, J. N., Lange, D. L., & Samuels, S. J. (1988). Effects of text structure instruction on foreign language readers' recall of scientific journal articles. *Journal of Reading Behavior, 20,* 203–214.

DeBoar, G. E. (1991). *A history of ideas in science education: Implications for practice.* New York: Teachers College Press.

DeBoar, G. E. (2000). Scientific literacy: Another look at its historical and contemporary meanings and relationship to science education reform. *Journal of Research in Science Teaching, 37,* 582–601.

Dee-Lucas, D., & Larkin, J. H. (1986). Novice strategies for processing scientific texts. *Discourse Processes, 9,* 329–354.

de Posada, J. M. (1999). The presentation of metallic bonding in high school science textbooks during three decades: Science educational reforms and substantive changes of tendencies. *Science Education, 83,* 423–447.

Driver, R., Asoko, H., Leach, J., Mortimer, E., & Scott, P. (1994). Constructing scientific knowledge in the classroom. *Educational Researcher, 23,* 5–12.

Dunbar, K. (1995). How scientists really reason: Scientific reasoning in real-world laboratories. In R. J. Sternberg & J. Davidson (Eds.), *Mechanisms of insight* (pp. 365–395). Cambridge, MA: MIT Press.

Duschl, R. A., & Hamilton, R. J. (1997). Conceptual change in science and the learning of science. In B. Fraser & K. Tobin (Eds.), *International handbook of science education* (pp. 1047–1065). Dordrecht, Netherlands: Kluwer Academic.

Einsiedel, E. G. (1992). Framing science and technology in the Canadian press. *Public Understanding of Science, 1,* 89–101.

Fitzpatrick, S. M. (1999, November) Opinion: What makes science news newsworthy? *The Scientist* [Online], *13*(23). Available: http://www.the-scientist.com/yr1999/nov/opin_991122.html

From memory, chimp gets numbers right. (2000, January 6). *The Tennessean,* p. A5.

Garnett, P. J., & Treagust, D. F. (1990). Implications of research of students' understanding of electrochemistry for improving science curricula and classroom practice. *International Journal of Science Education, 12,* 147–156.

Gee, J. P. (1992). *The social mind: Language, ideology, and social practice.* New York: Bergin & Garvey.

Glynn, S. M., Law, M., & Doster, E. C. (1998). Making text meaningful: The role of analogies. In C. Hynd (Ed.), *Learning from text across conceptual domains* (pp. 193–208). Mahwah, NJ: Lawrence Erlbaum Associates.

Glynn, S. M., & Muth, K. D. (1994). Reading and writing to learn science: Achieving scientific literacy. *Journal of Research in Science Teaching, 31,* 1057–1073.

Goldman, S. R. (1996). Reading, writing, and learning in hypermedia environments. In H. van Oostendorp & S. de Mul (Eds.), *Cognitive aspects of electronic text processing* (pp. 7–42). Norwood, NJ: Ablex.

Goldman, S. R. (1997). Learning from text: Reflections on the past and suggestions for the future. *Discourse Processes, 23,* 357–398.

Goldman, S. R., & Durán, R. P. (1988). Answering questions from oceanography texts: Learner, task and text characteristics. *Discourse Processes, 11,* 373–412.

Goldman, S. R., Duschl, R. A., Ellenbogen, K., Williams, S., & Tzou, C. T. (in press). Science inquiry in a digital age: Possibilities for making thinking visible. In H. van Oostendorp (Ed.), *Cognition in a digital age.* Mahwah, NJ: Lawrence Erlbaum Associates.

Goldman, S. R., & Rakestraw, J. A., Jr. (2000). Structural aspects of constructing meaning from text. In M. L. Kamil, P. Mosenthal, P. D. Pearson, & R. Barr (Eds.), *Handbook of reading research* (Vol. 3, pp. 311–335). Mahwah, NJ: Lawrence Erlbaum Associates.

Graesser, A. C., Higginbotham, M. W., Robertson, S. P., & Smith, W. R. (1978). A natural inquiry into the national inquirer: Self-induced vs. task-induced reading comprehension. *Discourse Processes, 1,* 355–372.

Guzzetti, B. J., Hynd, C. R., Skeels, S. A., & Williams, W. O. (1995). Improving physics texts: Students speak out. *Journal of Reading, 38,* 656–663.

Guzetti, B. J., Snyder, T. E., & Glass, G. V. (1992). Promoting conceptual change in science: Can texts be used effectively? *Journal of Reading, 35,* 642–649.

Guzetti, B. J., Snyder, T. E., Glass, G. V., & Gamas, W. S. (1993). Promoting conceptual change in science: A comparative meta-analysis of instructional interventions for reading education and science education. *Reading Research Quarterly, 28,* 116–161.

Hurd, P. D., Robinson, J. T., McConnell, M. C., & Ross, N. M., Jr. (1981). *The status of middle school and junior high school science*. Louisville, CO: Center for Educational Research and Evaluation.

Hynd, C. R., & Guzzetti, B. (1998). When knowledge contradicts intuition: Conceptual change. In C. R. Hynd (Ed.), *Learning from text across conceptual domains* (pp. 139–163). Mahwah, NJ: Lawrence Erlbaum Associates.

Kamil, M. L., Intrator, S., & Kim, H. (2000). Literacy, literacy learning, and other technologies. In M. L. Kamil, P. Mosenthal, P. D. Pearson, & R. Barr (Eds.), *Handbook of reading research* (Vol. 3, pp. 311–335). Mahwah, NJ: Lawrence Erlbaum Associates.

Kawai, N., & Matsuzawa, T. (2000). Cognition: Numerical span in a chimpanzee. *Nature* [On-line], *403*(6765), 39–40. Available: http://www.nature.com

✓ King, A. (1994). Guiding knowledge construction in the classroom: Effects of teaching children how to question and how to explain. *American Educational Research Journal, 31*, 338–368.

Kintsch, W. (1998). *Comprehension: A paradigm for cognition*. New York: Cambridge University Press.

Kintsch, W., & van Dijk, T. A. (1978). Toward a model of text comprehension and production. *Psychological Review, 85*, 363–394.

Klaczynski, P. A., & Gordon, D. H. (1996). Self-serving influences on adolescents' evaluations of belief relevant evidence. *Journal of Experimental Child Psychology, 62*, 1–23.

Korpan, C. A., Bisanz, G. L., Bisanz, J., & Henderson, J. (1997). Assessing scientific literacy: Evaluation of scientific news briefs. *Science Education, 81*, 515–532.

Kunda, Z. (1987). Motivated inference: Self-serving generation and evaluation of causal theories. *Journal of Personality and Social Psychology, 53*, 636–647.

Kunda, Z. (1990). The case for motivated reasoning. *Psychological Bulletin, 108*, 480–498.

Lave, G., & Wenger, E. (1991). *Situated learning: Legitimate peripheral participation*. New York: Cambridge University Press.

Lehrer, R., Schauble, L., & Petrosino, A. J. (in press). Reconsidering the role of experimentation in science education. In K. Crowley, C. D. Schunn, & T. Okada (Eds.), *Designing for science: Implications from everyday, classroom, and professional settings*. Mahwah, NJ: Lawrence Erlbaum Associates.

Mallow, J. V. (1991). Reading science. *Journal of Reading, 34*, 324–338.

Manzo, A., & Manzo, U. C. (1990). *Content area reading: A heuristic approach*. Columbus, OH: Merrill.

Martin, B. E., & Brouwer, W. (1991). The sharing of personal science and the narrative element in science education. *Science Education, 75*, 707–722.

✓ Mayer, R. E., Bove, W., Bryman, A., Mars, R., & Tapangco, L. (1996). When less is more: Meaningful learning from visual and verbal summaries of science textbook lessons. *Journal of Educational Psychology, 88*, 64–73.

McCloskey, M., Caramazza, A., & Green, B. (1980). Curvilinear motion in the absence of external forces: Naïve beliefs about the motion of objects. *Science, 210*, 1139–1141.

McMahon, M. M., & McCormack, B. B. (1998). To think and act like a scientist: Learning disciplinary knowledge. In C. R. Hynd (Ed.), *Learning from texts across conceptual domains* (pp. 227–262) Mahwah, NJ: Lawrence Erlbaum Associates.

McNamara, D. S., Kintsch, E., Songer, N. B., & Kintsch, W. (1996). Are good texts always better? Interactions of text coherence, background knowledge, and levels of understanding in learning from text. *Cognition and Instruction, 14,* 1–43.

Norris, S. P., & Phillips, L. M. (1994). Interpreting pragmatic meaning when reading reports of science. *Journal of Research in Science Teaching, 31,* 947–967.

Nwogu, K. N. (1991). Structure of scientific popularizations: A genre-analysis approach to the schema of popularized medical texts. *English for Specific Purposes, 10,* 111–123.

Otero, J. (1998). Influence of knowledge activation and context on comprehension monitoring of science texts. In D. J. Hacker, J. Dunlosky, & A. C. Graesser (Eds.), *Metacognition in educational theory and practice* (pp. 145–164). Mahwah, NJ: Lawrence Erlbaum Associates.

Perfetti, C. A., Rouet, J.-F., Britt, M. A. (1999). Toward a theory of documents representation. H. van Oostendorp & S. R. Goldman (Eds.), *The construction of mental representations during reading* (pp. 99–102). Mahwah, NJ: Lawrence Erlbaum Associates.

Phillips, L. A., & Norris, S. P. (1999). Interpreting popular reports of science: What happens when the readers' world meets the world on paper. *International Journal of Science Education, 21,* 317–327.

Ploetzner, R., & VanLehn, K. (1997). The acquisition of qualitative physics knowledge during textbook-based physics training. *Cognition & Instruction, 15,* 69–205.

Reinking, D., McKenna, M., Labbo, L. D., & Kieffer, R. (Eds.). (1998). *Handbook of literacy and technology: Transformations in a post-typographic world.* Mahwah, NJ: Lawrence Erlbaum Associates.

Roseman, J. E., Kesidou, S., Stern, L., & Caldwell, A. (1999). Heavy books light on learning. *Science Books & Films* [On-line], *35*(6). Available: http://www.project2061.org/newsinfo/research/textbook/articles/heavy.htm

Sanger, M. J., & Greenbowe, T. J. (1997). Common student misconceptions in electrochemistry: Galvanic, electrolytic, and concentration cells. *Journal of Research in Science Teaching, 34,* 377–398.

Shymansky, J. A., Yore, L. D., & Good, R. (1991). Elementary school teachers' beliefs about the perceptions of elementary school science, science reading, science textbooks, and supportive instructional factors. *Journal of Research in Science Teaching, 28,* 437–454.

Strube, P., & Lynch, P. P. (1984). Some influences on the modern science text: Alternative science writing. *European Journal of Science Education, 6,* 321–338.

Swales, J. M. (1990). *Genre analysis: English in academic and research settings.* Cambridge, England: Cambridge University Press.

Thiele, R. B., & Treagust, D. F. (1994). An interpretive examination of high school chemistry teachers' analogical explanations. *Journal of Research in Science Teaching, 31*(3), 227–242.

Thiele, R. B., & Treagust, D. F. (1995). Analogies in chemistry textbooks. *International Journal of Science Education, 17,* 783–795.

এ50 &⊹ GOLDMAN AND BISANZ

Van den Akker, J. (1998). The science curriculum: Between ideals and outcomes. In B. J. Fraser & K. G. Tobin (Eds.), *International handbook of science education* (pp. 421–447). London: Kluwer.

van Dijk, T. A. (1986). News schemata. In C. Cooper & S. Greenbaum (Eds.), *Studying writing: Linguistic approaches* (pp. 155–185). Beverly Hills, CA: Sage.

van Dijk, T. A., & Kintsch, W. (1983). *Strategies of discourse comprehension.* New York: Academic Press.

Wright, K. (1998, August). When is a scientific breakthrough really news? Reporters still experimenting with formula. *The Los Angeles Times*; reprinted in the *Edmonton Journal*, p. A15.

Yeaton, W. H., Smith, D., & Rogers, K. (1990). Evaluating popular press reports of health research. *Health Education Quarterly, 17,* 223–234.

Yore, L. D. (1991). Secondary science teachers' attitudes toward and beliefs about science reading and science textbooks. *Journal of Research in Science Teaching, 28,* 55–72.

Zimmerman, C., Bisanz, G. L., & Bisanz, J. (1998). Everyday scientific literacy: Do students use knowledge about social context and methods of research to evaluate news about science? *Alberta Journal of Educational Research, 44,*188–207.

Zimmerman, C., Bisanz, G. L., Bisanz, J., Klein, J., & Klein, P. (2001). Science at the supermarket: A comparison of what appears in the popular press, experts' advise to readers, and what students want to know. *Public Understanding of Science, 10,* 37–58.

❧ 3 ❧

The Characteristics of Well-Designed Science Textbooks

Marilyn J. Chambliss
University of Maryland

Many chapters in this volume focus on issues of text comprehensibility, an essential requirement for well-designed textbook materials. Readers who comprehend a text have a chance at learning from it. Those who fail to comprehend will be left out without substantial intervention from the teacher. However, well-designed textbook materials must be far more than comprehensible. Comprehensibility does not address what students will learn from their reading or how they will be taught. Calfee and I (Chambliss & Calfee, 1998) portrayed textbooks as a device for conveying intellectual ideas. The ideas are the curriculum; the conveyor is instruction.

This chapter presents a theoretical framework for well-designed textbooks that integrates curriculum, instruction, and comprehensibility. By searching for these three textbook characteristics, it is possible to identify clearly distinguishable design features that we could expect to affect students' scientific understanding and learning. The chapter applies the framework to several examples of textbook materials and one trade book. I have added the trade book because current science curricula for elementary school, developed by organizations such as the National Science Resources Center, a cooperative venture of the Smithsonian Institution and the National Academy of Sciences, include very little reading. Any sustained reading that children do in science will have to come from trade books provided by the teacher.

The Curriculum

What is worth teaching in science? Whereas psychology can help us understand how to sequence content in a particular developmental order, it cannot readily address the full array of possible answers to this question. Therefore, I turn to curriculum theorists. Ralph Tyler in his classic, *Basic Principles of Curriculum and Instruction* (1949), proposed five answers. According to Tyler, "essentialists" or "subject specialists" believe that curriculum should come from the design of the knowledge domains themselves. Progressives and child psychologists maintain that the goal of education is to produce well-adjusted adults and that student needs should guide curriculum decisions. Sociologists, aware of the needs of society, argue that curriculum should be based on whatever the pressing societal problems are; the goal of schooling is to produce good citizens. Educational philosophers point to important basic life values as a guide because they see that the goal of education is to produce an ethical populace. Educational psychologists answer that curriculum must be developmentally appropriate; the goal of schooling is to teach something. Tyler proposed that a well-designed curriculum must contain all five. Noting that no curriculum could effectively incorporate everything worthwhile, he suggested that curriculum designers use their philosophy of education and what they know about educational psychology to decide what to include among student needs, society needs, and the domain.

Although schooling must certainly meet student and society needs, the unique contribution of the school is to transmit from one generation to the next the major ideas in the content domains, ideas that in some cases have been evolving for thousands of years. If schools do not make this contribution, no other institution is prepared to take up the slack (Chambliss & Calfee, 1998).

The philosopher Alfred North Whitehead (1974) pictured the mind as searching for patterns wherever they can be found in the chaotic stream of events that make up experience. He saw in schooling the potential "to impart an intimate sense for the power of ideas, for the beauty of ideas, and for the structure of ideas ..." (p. 23). He warned educators, "Do not teach too many subjects, [and] what you teach, teach thoroughly, seizing on the few general ideas which illuminate the whole, and persistently marshaling subsidiary facts round them" (p. 3). The difficulty, of course, arises in choosing the few understandings to teach.

Joseph Schwab, in his essay "Education and the Structure of the Disciplines" (1978) argued that all academic disciplines, including the domains of science, are systematic. Building on the ideas of Auguste Comte, Schwab explained that there are "roughly" two kinds of knowledge: ad hoc knowledge, the practical knowledge that fills a need literally thrust upon a person, and subject matter knowledge, systematic knowledge of the properties and behaviors of a subject matter. According to Schwab, subject matter knowledge developed as people became aware of patterns that cut across the bits and pieces of ad hoc, practical knowledge. Over time, subject matters came to be organized with large, generative ideas subsuming less-encompassing ideas and details, analogous to Whitehead's (1974) notion of a few general ideas to illuminate the whole. The geologist can use a single concept (e.g., the theory of plate tectonics) to understand such diverse phenomena as earthquakes, volcanoes, ocean trenches, and the shape of continents. The biologist can use modern evolutionary theory to describe and explain how organisms as different as plants, animals, protista, and fungi have evolved to their present states through a complex interaction of genetics, physiology and biochemistry, and environmental presses.

Schwab (1978) cautioned against applying discipline structures directly to education, however. Raising a similar concern, diSessa (1993) pointed out that the set of core theoretical ideas in science is often very different from the realm of everyday knowing. Rather than leading to new understanding, these ideas can be confusing to the nonexpert. Most children will not become experts in any science, and even the exceptions will not become experts in more than one or two. Tyler (1949) suggested that subject matter specialists address the following question: "What can your subject contribute to the education of young people who are not going to be specialists in your field?" (p. 26).

Calfee and I proposed that one answer to Tyler's question is to help young people acquire the special lens of the expert (Chambliss & Calfee, 1998). Experts see the world quite differently than novices. Most people watch the sun sinking below the horizon; Copernicus was able to see the earth spinning in space, eclipsing the sun. Whereas the novice delights in the decorative diversity in a botanical garden, the biologist observes plants adapting to variations in soil conditions. Education in this perspective means helping novices acquire the expert's X-ray vision, the connoisseur's sense of taste, the scientist's ability to analyze (Chambliss & Calfee, 1998).

Schwab (1978) acknowledged that it is unrealistic to expect the lay public to extract useful knowledge from a discipline unaided; to acquire an expert lens on their own Therefore, he explained, the curriculum must use practical examples and activities carefully chosen according to the discipline's structure for at least the early years of schooling and models and analogies thereafter. Schwab's recommendations are similar to Whitehead's (1974) admonition that educators persistently marshal subsidiary facts around the small number of illuminatory ideas. The bare bones design in a domain can be used to identify the important ideas and guide the choice of practical examples and activities, models and analogies.

According to these ideas from curriculum theorists, the well-designed textbook would be organized around a small number of illuminatory ideas, the seminal theories, models, or concepts in the domain. It would present many practical examples, activities, models, and analogies to exemplify the illuminatory ideas.

INSTRUCTION

The illuminatory ideas in science are often counterintuitive, so carefully planned instruction becomes particularly crucial. A large collection of studies has explored the everyday understandings that children hold in science. Pfundt and Duit (1991) prepared a bibliography of over 2,000 studies focusing on students' naive understandings about science topics. Some of this work has focused on replacing naive understandings with scientific models. This task is difficult because students are strongly committed to their personal understandings and not likely to replace them with the scientific models presented in science instruction (Champagne, Gunstone, & Klopfer, 1983). Interestingly, carefully crafted text has proven to have a potent instructional effect, which appears to be relatively independent of both scientific demonstrations and student discussion (Guzzetti, Snyder, Glass, & Gamas, 1993; Guzzetti, Williams, Skeels, & Wu, 1997). An important key seems to be whether the text, any accompanying instruction such as demonstrations, or both create cognitive conflict (Guzzetti et al., 1997), an outcome that Guzzetti and colleagues (1993) believed supports Kintsch's (1986) proposal that conceptual change occurs only when learners are surprised or become aware of incongruity. Note, however, that work by Mayer and colleagues (e.g., Mayer, 1985; Mayer, Steinhoff, Bower, & Mars, 1995) suggests that highlighting the underlying causal relationships may be sufficient; that creating cognitive conflict may not always be necessary. Perhaps an important factor is the extent to which readers hold naive preconceptions that conflict with the scientific conception being presented in the text.

Refutational text seems to be singularly powerful in bringing about conceptual change even without accompanying demonstrations, particularly if readers' understanding is assessed after a delay (Guzzetti et al., 1993; Hynd, McWhorter, Phares, & Suttles, 1994). Beginning by presenting the nonscientific model based on everyday experiences, refutational texts demonstrate the limitations of this model, present the scientific model, and point out how it addresses the limitations by applying the model to examples from daily life (Hynd et al., 1994). Note that these text features adhere to a logical order from familiar understandings to new understandings that then are applied to familiar examples. Presumably this order is important in creating cognitive conflict.

Not all readers have been affected equally by refutational text. For example, Alverman and Hynd (1989) noted early on that refutational text seemed to be more effective for poorer and younger readers than for more competent and older readers. They suggested that textual features such as examples and analogies might make a difference. In more recent versions of refutational text, Hynd and colleagues added examples (Hynd et al., 1994), but I am unaware of any work where analogies have been included as well.

Analogies may cause cognitive conflict and surprise in much the same way as direct refutation. Duit (1991) proposed that whenever analogies draw surprising or anomalous connections between the analog and the target, they can be of pivotal importance in conceptual change. For example, Clement and colleagues have helped students understand the counterintuitive notion that a static object, like a table, can exert forces by using a series of analogies, beginning with a hand resting on a spring to a book on a foam pad to a book on a thin flexible board and finally to a book on a table (Clement, 1998; Clement et al., 1987). Of course, it is crucial that the analogy render the unfamiliar familiar (Duit, 1991; Holyoak & Thagard, 1997) and that the analog (a hand resting on a spring; a book resting on a foam pad) be familiar. However, a second important feature of an analogy may well be its surprise value. The similarities between a spring and a table are not immediately obvious to the student with naive understanding.

This work has important implications for instructional text, whether demonstrating the power of refutational text or of analogies to help students acquire the understandings of the scientist. To teach the illuminatory ideas in science, which often are counterintuitive, a well-designed textbook or trade book will clearly explicate scientific ideas and offer examples and analogies to link the familiar to the unfamiliar. Wherever children have firmly entrenched naive understandings, the text will address these understandings, introduce the ideas of the scientist, and explicitly demonstrate how the scientific ideas explain better than the naive understandings. To the extent that young readers can apply these scientific ideas to their understanding of reality, the textbook or trade book will have been a successful instructional tool.

COMPREHENSIBILITY

Other chapters in this book provide a detailed description of the relationship between features in science texts and comprehension. I sketch out a brief overview of three text features that consistently have been shown to affect comprehension and that can easily be identified in textbook or trade book materials: familiarity, structure, and interest. Elsewhere, Calfee and I (Chambliss & Calfee, 1998) provided a more complete discussion of each of these features and applied them to a variety of textbook materials.

The relationship between readers' background knowledge and their success in comprehending a text is well established. *Familiarity* of both vocabulary and text topic can affect school-age children's comprehension. Children have been found to comprehend texts with familiar vocabulary or on a familiar topic better than texts with unfamiliar vocabulary or on an unfamiliar topic (Freebody & R. C. Anderson, 1983). Background knowledge varies with the reader, of course. For a passage to connect with everyone, it must include words, examples, and analogies that touch base with a wide range of everyday experiences. Connecting with reader background knowledge may be more crucial for textbooks than for other types of writing because textbooks have the specific purpose of teaching new knowledge. They can be expected to present content that is intentionally unfamiliar to readers.

The effect of *text structure* on children's comprehension is less clear than the influence of familiarity. To be sure, adult readers seem to comprehend more competently texts whose sentences adhere to canonical text patterns than texts with scrambled sentences (Kintsch & Yarbrough, 1982). Adults also appear to find patterns with strong linkages (e.g., problem/solution; compare/contrast) to support their comprehension better than patterns with weak linkages (e.g., collections) (Meyer & Freedle, 1984). Finally, highlighting the structure in a text may further enhance adult comprehension (Mayer et al., 1995). Work with children suggests that many young readers seem to be so unaware of text structure in exposition that they read all expository texts as if they were disconnected sentences (Englert & Hiebert, 1984; Hare, Rabinowitz, & Schieble, 1989; Kucan & Beck, 1996). However, texts that highlight text structure can affect the comprehension of children and adults comparably. Children's comprehension has been enhanced by introductions and conclusions that summarized the structure (Whittaker, 1992) and headings, explicit topic sentences, and words that signaled structural relationships (e.g., first, then, finally; problem, solution)

(Baumann, 1986; Meyer, Brandt, & Bluth, 1980; Hare et al., 1989; Englert & Hiebert, 1984). It is possible that drawing readers' attention to the structure enables them to utilize it more effectively than otherwise. Because textbooks often require children to wrestle with an organizational pattern and domain content that are both unknown to them, including these features in textbook materials would seem to be particularly valuable.

Interestingness relates to both familiarity and structure and can have a strong effect on comprehensibility (Wade, Buxton, & Kelly, 1999). Adult readers find their interest to be enhanced when texts are optimally informative, neither too familiar nor too unfamiliar (Kintsch, 1980), use examples and analogies to connect with what readers already know (Kintsch, 1980; Sadoski, Goetz, & Fritz, 1993), are well structured or coherent (Duffy et al., 1989; Kintsch, 1980), highlight the structure in the text (Harp & Mayer, 1997), reveal the author's "voice" (Beck, McKeown, & Worthy, 1995), and provide vivid details that can be "pictured" (Sadoski, Goetz, & Rodriguez, 2000; Schank, 1979). When these features are missing, they judge texts to be uninteresting (Wade et al., 1999). The features in texts that adult readers find to be interesting are also the ones that adults are most likely to recall (Wade et al., 1999). Work by Hidi and Baird (1988) showed many of these characteristics to have a positive effect on the comprehension of schoolchildren in the middle years. In contrast, other work suggests that sprinkling uninteresting topics with vivid examples, what researchers have called "seductive details," may have a negative effect on comprehension (Garner, Alexander, Gillingham, Kulikowich, & Brown, 1991; Garner, Gillingham, & White, 1989; Harp & Mayer, 1998), particularly for young readers who recall the seductive details in lieu of the superordinate ideas in the text structure (Garner et al., 1989). It is likely, though, that if readers are interested in the overall topic, they will find the important, illuminating ideas in the text to be more informative than the details, and therefore more interesting (Wade et al., 1999).

Curriculum, instruction, and comprehensibility as I have described them overlap significantly. The textbook or trade book passage that mirrors the underlying structure in a domain will have an inherent coherence that should enhance its comprehensibility. The passage that instructs students by using examples and analogies to link what they understand with the illuminatory ideas in a domain may well be optimally familiar, concrete, and informative, important features of comprehensible text.

CURRICULUM GENRE: EPISTEMIC POTENTIAL

Swales (1990) proposed a text genre model that is useful in analyzing and understanding the influences of curriculum, instruction, and comprehensibility on children's learning from textbooks and trade books. According to the model, genres possess identifiable patterns of structure and content that communities of people develop as they work to complete recurring tasks and fulfill shared purposes. For example, authors craft refutational texts with the purpose of helping students replace naive understandings with scientific models. Ideally, students read refutational texts with the purpose of understanding these models. Refutational texts have epistemic potential, part of a larger class of "curriculum genres" developed to support student knowledge construction (Berkenkotter & Huckin, 1993; Chapman, 1999; Freedman, 1996).

Elsewhere, Calfee and I have described three general types of curriculum genre that fulfill different epistemic purposes: to inform, to argue a point, or to explain. Note that Mayer (1985) likewise distinguished between science text that describes, or informs, and text that explains by highlighting underlying causal models. Informational text, argument, and explanation appear in the writing curriculum (Calfee & Chambliss, 1987). They also appear in science textbooks both in this country (Chambliss & Calfee, 1998) and internationally (Chambliss & Calfee, 1989), and in science trade books (Wong & Calfee, 1988). Of these three purposes, the one that most closely matches refutational text is explanation.

Rhetoricians have described explanation as the only type of writing that has the development of understanding as its *primary* goal, rather than informing, arguing a point, or entertaining (Connors, 1985; Rowen, 1988, 1990). Note, though, that text types can often be embedded within one another. Indeed, to develop reader understanding, well-designed explanations present information, examples, analogies, and models as subexplanations. These subexplanations follow a logical order to form a bridge between readers' current understandings and the new understanding. The goal for the reader is to construct a new understanding by attending to the subexplanations and following the text's logical order (Oatley, 1996).

Refutational texts follow this pattern. They begin with a subexplanation that presents the naive model based on everyday experiences. The first subexplanation is followed by subexplanations that demonstrate the limitations of the naive model, present the scientific model, and point out how it addresses the limitations (Hynd et al., 1994). This logical order is designed to connect with a reader's naive understanding and help the reader replace a naive model with a scientific model.

Imagine a textbook passage with the purpose to explain to fifth graders what causes differences in seasons. The passage might begin, "Many people think that it is hot in the summer because the earth is close to the sun and cold in the winter because the earth is farther away. Actually, in North America, the earth is closer to the sun in the winter than in the summer. Astronomers can show that the real difference is how directly the light waves from the sun hit different parts of the earth during different times of the year." This author is using the first of three structural features in an explanation. The author is moving the reader from the understanding of a novice toward the understanding of the expert through the use of familiar examples, analogies, definitions, or statements juxtaposing novice and expert understandings. Next, the explanation might present the scientific model, chronicling how the earth orbits the sun at an angle and how the light waves strike the earth at different parts of the orbit. The model might be followed by giving steps that children in the class could follow to act out the sun and the orbiting earth using a flashlight. This explanation is demonstrating the second structural feature of explanations. Well-designed explanations have subexplanations. The seasons-are-not-caused-by-distance-from-the-sun discussion is one subexplanation, the scientific model is a second subexplanation, and the flashlight demonstration is a third. Notice that these subexplanations progress from general principles to a specific demonstration. Logical order is the third structural feature of an explanation. Other possible logical orders are specific to general or question/answer chains in which the author raises a question about a phenomenon (How does a thermos work?), provides an answer (thermodynamics), which leads to another question (What is thermodynamics?) and answer (the scientific model involving groups of molecules).

Explanations with these features have epistemic potential as suggested by the work on refutational text (Hynd et al., 1994), the scholarship of rhetoricians (Connors, 1985; Rowen, 1988, 1990), and the analyses of curriculum theorists and philosophers (Schwab, 1978; Tyler, 1949; Whitehead, 1974). Explanation seems to be a curriculum genre that the educational community has developed to help students gain scientific understanding.

In this chapter, I propose that conceiving of explanation as a curriculum genre with the purpose to enhance student understanding integrates scholarship in curriculum, instruction, and text comprehensibility. In the following sections, I analyze four passages designed to explain to fourth and fifth graders the scientific model for how sound travels from its source to its recipient. Scientific models of sound consistently appear in reading materials for the middle grades. "How Sound Travels" (Cooper, Blackwood, Boeschen, Giddings, & Carin, 1985), "How Sound Travels" (Barman et al., 1989), and "How Are Light and Sound Similar and Different?" (Cohen et al., 1989) are passages that I have selected from fourth- and fifth-grade science textbooks. "Sound Waves" (Glover, 1993) comes from a trade book. I focus on how well each passage exemplifies the features of a well-designed explanation. Because two of the passages have identical titles, I refer to Cooper's "How Sound Travels" and Barman's "How Sound Travels" to distinguish between them in the following sections.

USING GRAPHIC ORGANIZERS
TO EVALUATE TEXTBOOKS

How to evaluate the curriculum, instruction, and comprehensibility of textbook passages has been by no means obvious. Analytical techniques developed by psychologists have highlighted important features of text comprehensibility applicable to instructional materials. Whereas some of these procedures have remained at the level of the proposition or idea unit (e.g., Mayer, 1985), others have considered the logical relationships at the top level of passages (e.g., Meyer, 1985). The combination of both approaches has led to an understanding of how relationships among ideas in a text, the text structure, can affect reader comprehension.

For their part, educators have developed algorithms (i.e., readability formulas) that use word frequency (a measure of word familiarity) and sentence complexity (a measure of text structure) to determine a text's ease or difficulty of being comprehended (e.g., Chall & Dale, 1995). None of these techniques has been useful for evaluating either the curriculum or the instruction built into the text or for guiding the writing of well-designed instructional materials (see Armbruster, Osborn, & Davison, 1985, for a discussion of this last issue).

Calfee and I proposed an alternative that relies on a handful of graphics that can be used to characterize text design from the level of entire books to small sections of a few paragraphs (Chambliss & Calfee, 1998). Cognitive psychologists have suggested graphical patterns, particularly semantic networks, hierarchies, and sequential strings, that usefully represent how humans link semantic knowledge (Kintsch, 1998). College freshman composition books present common organizational patterns that authors use to compose well-crafted writing (Calfee & Chambliss, 1987). Graphic/organizers that are especially useful for evaluating textbooks combine these two traditions. Because they display words and statements in meaningful patterns, graphic organizers are an efficient means of clearly communicating large amounts of interrelated content (Tufte, 1990). When content is presented graphically, important information is distinguished from less important details, and relationships are displayed visually rather than explained verbally. As Tufte noted, the well-designed graphic can communicate complex relationships such as comparison, contrast, cause, effect, superordination, and subordination in an eye span, preserving limited human processing resources.

In explanations, a series of subexplanations follows a logical order, and this structure can be depicted graphically. The structure of each subexplanation also can be graphically represented. For example, in Cooper's "How Sound Travels," one subexplanation chronicles the model of sound waves from the initial vibrations to the transfer in energy from air molecule to air molecule that eventually reaches someone's ear, whereas another subexplanation describes matter as being composed of molecules. Because the relationships in these two subexplanations are quite different, their graphic representations also differ.

Figures 3.1 and 3.2 are based on my analysis of Cooper's "How Sound Travels" (Cooper et al., 1985) and "How Are Light and Sound Similar and Different?" (Cohen et al., 1989). I use these two figures to discuss the analysis of all four passages. At the top of each figure is the explanation's introduction followed by its subexplanations. Along the left-hand margin are the paragraph numbers for each subexplanation. Along the right-hand margin are the subexplanation content characteristics. The figures also record declarative sentences and questions that signal the logical moves in the explanation. These figures only suggest the complete analysis, however. For purposes of this chapter, I have not included any of the content within the graphic representations, greatly condensing the size of each graphic. These condensed figures highlight the underlying structure of an explanation in the sweep of an eye. Without content, however, they do not depict how an explanation presents the scientific model or orders subexplanations to connect a reader's current understandings to a new understanding. To fill in the missing pieces, I describe each explanation's content as I present the analysis.

Analyzing Textbook Passages

Even a cursory glance at Figs. 3.1 and 3.2 reveals differences between Cooper's "How Sound Travels" and "How Are Light and Sound Similar and Different?" Most obvious are differences in structure and logical order as depicted by the introductions, the graphics, and the subexplanation content characteristics in the right-hand margins. Even without much information about content, the representation in Fig. 3.1 depicts a passage that fulfills more of the characteristics of a good explanation than the representation in Fig. 3.2.

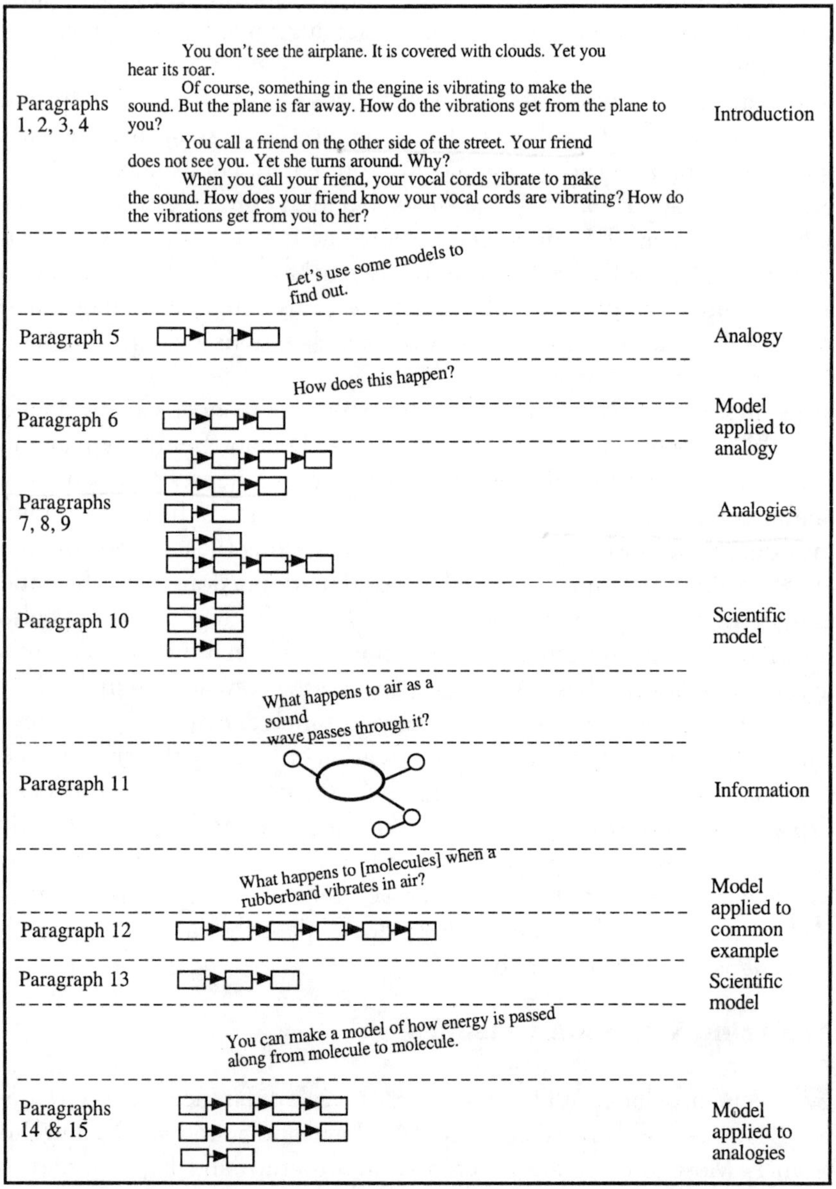

Paragraphs 1, 2, 3, 4 — Introduction

You don't see the airplane. It is covered with clouds. Yet you hear its roar.

Of course, something in the engine is vibrating to make the sound. But the plane is far away. How do the vibrations get from the plane to you?

You call a friend on the other side of the street. Your friend does not see you. Yet she turns around. Why?

When you call your friend, your vocal cords vibrate to make the sound. How does your friend know your vocal cords are vibrating? How do the vibrations get from you to her?

Let's use some models to find out.

Paragraph 5 — Analogy

How does this happen?

Paragraph 6 — Model applied to analogy

Paragraphs 7, 8, 9 — Analogies

Paragraph 10 — Scientific model

What happens to air as a sound wave passes through it?

Paragraph 11 — Information

What happens to [molecules] when a rubberband vibrates in air?

Paragraph 12 — Model applied to common example

Paragraph 13 — Scientific model

You can make a model of how energy is passed along from molecule to molecule.

Paragraphs 14 & 15 — Model applied to analogies

FIG. 3.1. Text analysis graphic for "How Sound Travels" (Cooper et al., 1985, pp. 58–62).

62

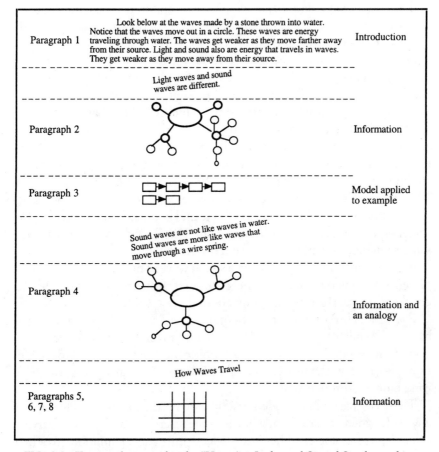

Paragraph 1 — Introduction

Look below at the waves made by a stone thrown into water. Notice that the waves move out in a circle. These waves are energy traveling through water. The waves get weaker as they move farther away from their source. Light and sound also are energy that travels in waves. They get weaker as they move away from their source.

Light waves and sound waves are different.

Paragraph 2 — Information

Paragraph 3 — Model applied to example

Sound waves are not like waves in water. Sound waves are more like waves that move through a wire spring.

Paragraph 4 — Information and an analogy

How Waves Travel

Paragraphs 5, 6, 7, 8 — Information

FIG. 3.2. Text analysis graphic for "How Are Light and Sound Similar and Different?" (Cohen et al., 1989, pp. 198–200).

Cooper's "How Sound Travels" (Fig. 3.1) comes from a fourth-grade general science textbook. The introduction presents two familiar examples to demonstrate the relationship between vibrations and sound and ends with two questions that the passage presumably will answer. Most of the subexplanations are sequential. All subexplanations except the final subexplanation are arranged so that children repeatedly first read a concrete analogy to sound waves or an example of sound and then read a scientific explanation. The logical moves between all but two of the subexplanations are signaled by declarative sentences or subsection titles.

The first subexplanation, Paragraph 5, asks children to imagine tying one end of a rope to a table leg, shaking the free end of the rope back and forth, and watching the other end move. The second subexplanation, Paragraph 6, explains that shaking the rope gives energy to the rope causing it to vibrate. The energy travels along the rope to the other end in waves. The third subexplanation, Paragraphs 7–9, presents two analogies using vibrations in water and one example using a plucked rubber band in air. The fourth subexplanation, Paragraph 10, explains that when a voice calls or an airplane engine roars or a rubber band is plucked, sound waves travel through air. The fifth subexplanation, Paragraph 11, describes matter, including air, as composed of molecules. The sixth subexplanation, Paragraph 12, explains that when a rubber band vibrates in air, it bumps the molecules in the air next to it, which start to vibrate and bump into molecules next to them, and so on. The seventh subexplanation, Paragraph 13, presents the same sequence starting with the energy of a vibrating object that passes from molecule to molecule to form a sound wave. The final subexplanation presents two analogies for how energy transfers from molecule to molecule; checkers and marbles pushing one another.

Even though Barman's "How Sound Travels" is from a fifth-grade textbook, it is similar to Cooper's "How Sound Travels" with only one exception. It uses no analogies, but instead applies the scientific model to familiar examples, such as the movement of bees' wings, the beating of a drum, and wind blowing through trees.

These two passages with identical titles demonstrate the three features of a well-designed explanation. They link the scientific model with everyday examples or analogies. They are divided into subexplanations, each of which presents the model in a somewhat different way. And they follow a logical order, from the more simple and concrete (vibrations causing sound) to the more abstract (molecules passing energy).

"How Are Light and Sound Similar and Different?" (Fig. 3.2) from a fourth-grade textbook differs from the first two passages, both in how it is structured and in the content that it presents. The passage begins with an introduction that refers to a picture at the bottom of the page and likens light and sound waves to waves in water. The introduction concludes with a sentence that notes that light waves and sound waves are different. Only one of the subexplanations is sequential, chronicling the scientific model. All other subexplanations present information organized into either topics and subtopics (a topical net) or a comparison of two subtopics according to three categories (a matrix). The subexplanations follow no obvious logical order. Note, however, that except for the second and third subexplanations, separate subexplanations are linked by declarative sentences or subsection titles.

The first subexplanation, Paragraph 2, describes light waves as similar to waves in water and capable of traveling through empty space. It lists other types of waves, such as microwaves and X rays, and differentiates them from light waves. Finally, it defines wave lengths and relates them to different colors of light. The second subexplanation, Paragraph 3, asks children to imagine a girl slipping a rubber band over a doorknob, pulling the rubber band tight, and plucking it. The plucked rubber band vibrates, which makes the air around it vibrate too. The paragraph explains that sound is made when something vibrates. The air vibrates as it carries sound waves. The third subexplanation, Paragraph 4, describes sound waves as being like a spring. Some parts are close together. A wave travels as parts push together and move apart. It defines wavelengths and relates them to differences in sound. The fourth subexplanation, Paragraphs 5–8, compares light waves and sound waves according to whether they can travel through empty space, the effect of matter on how they move, their speed, and their absorption, reflection, and transmittal. For example, this subexplanation describes light waves as traveling fastest and sound waves as being unable to travel at all through empty space.

The third textbook passage does not clearly demonstrate the three features of a well-designed explanation. It presents only one everyday example, and the analogies using water waves and springs are never used to explain everyday examples of light and sound. It is plausible that these two analogies would not help fifth graders link the familiar with the unfamiliar. Although the text is divisible into subsections, each subsection addresses a different subtopic rather than considering the same scientific model in several different ways. Indeed, only one subsection presents the scientific model. Finally, the subsections do not obviously follow a logical order. It is possible that this passage actually has the purpose to inform (Chambliss & Calfee, 1998) or to describe (Mayer, 1985), rather than to explain.

Analyzing a Trade Book Passage

"Sound Waves" is a short passage from a trade book, and although the book lists no recommended age-levels, the description on the back cover refers to children and young readers. It is reasonable to suppose that a fourth- or fifth-grade teacher would choose this book. Before analyzing what "Sound Waves" covers and how it is structured, I want to describe how its pages are formatted. Each subexplanation is actually a separate text literally boxed off from the other subexplanations. The pages throughout the book resemble articles in popular magazines, such as "The Magnificent Machines That Got Us Here" in Parade Magazine (Levy, 2000). To prepare a graphic for this two-page passage, I identified the top box on the first page as the introduction. Beginning with this box, I placed subexplanations into my graphic by reading them clockwise for each of the two pages.

The introduction presents an analogy that likens the waves that result from flicking a rope to the sound waves that result when a balloon bursts. The remaining subexplanations present two analogies, three examples, and a statement of the scientific model applied to one of the examples. All of the subexplanations chronicle a sequence that begins with a flick, a burst, a knock, a tap, or an explosion that causes waves. In some cases, these are sound waves and in other cases they are analogous to sound waves. The logical relationship between two of the subexplanations is signaled with the heading, "How It Works."

This trade book passage does present a collection of concrete, familiar analogies and examples. It is clearly divided into subexplanations. The subexplanations consistently present the same sequence. In some ways, this passage does connect the understanding of the novice to the understanding of the expert. Note, however, that the version of scientific model that it presents is less abstract (i.e., less "expert") than explanations that chronicle the passing of energy from one molecule to another. Furthermore, there is no evidence of a logical order among the subexplanations. Indeed, the order in which a child would read the subexplanations would be up to the child. The variety of subexplanations and their consistent sequential structures suggest that this passage is intended to be an explanation. The caliber of the model guiding the explanation and the lack of a logical order suggest that children might take away less understanding from this explanation than would be true otherwise.

Evaluating the Four Explanations: Curriculum, Instruction, and Comprehensibility

Which of these four passages best meets the curricular, instructional, and comprehensibility characteristics that I have presented earlier in this chapter? Cooper's "How Sound Travels" and Barman's "How Sound Travels" both present a scientific model and consistently "marshall examples and [analogies] round them" (Whitehead, 1974, p. 3), features of a strong curriculum. Because both passages include familiar examples and analogies as well as explicit statements of the model in a logical order, they meet important instructional qualifications. They include familiar, concrete content, consistent structures, structure signaling, and "surprising" analogies, features of comprehensible text. Both passages have the three hallmark characteristics of the explanation genre.

"How Are Light and Sound Similar and Different?" and "Sound Waves" seem less well designed. To be sure, the two passages present both examples and analogies. However, neither presents a model for sound that is as complete as the model for the first two texts, lacking the hallmark of a strong curriculum. Neither passage presents subexplanations in a logical order, perhaps weakening both instructional potential and comprehensibility. "How Are Light and Sound Similar and Different?" fails to draw explicit connections between its analogies and the phenomena of light and sound and presents inconsistent structures, characteristics that may render it even less comprehensible. Both passages fail to match an explanation genre in important respects.

The purpose of this analysis is to demonstrate an approach for highlighting design differences in science textbooks and trade books. Which of these four explanations would best promote student understanding is both a theoretical and an empirical question even for the two passages that appear to be the better designed. For example, Cooper's "How Sound Travels" uses analogies to present a scientific model that cannot be directly observed. In contrast, Barman's "How Sound Travels" relies heavily on familiar examples where something vibrates and sound co-occurs. To present the causal model, it tells children the causal linkages with no supporting analogies. It is plausible that the analogies in Cooper's "How Sound Travels" would help children understand the abstract aspects of the model better than the examples and telling in Barman's "How Sound Travels." However, even though analogical thinking has been demonstrated in very young children (Holyoak & Thagard, 1997), it is also possible that young readers would have difficulty categorizing the phenomenon of sound traveling from an airplane to a child on the ground and a vibrating rope as "the same kind of thing" (Gentner & Holyoak, 1997), for example. Fourth and fifth graders might be unable to capitalize on the variety of subexplanations built into Cooper's "How Sound Travels." The work on using analogies in science instruction has primarily been conducted with older readers (e.g., Clement, 1998; Clement et al., 1987). Likewise, the patchwork design of the trade book "Sound Waves" seems too incoherent to enhance either comprehensibility or instruction. However, a text with which children have the freedom to pursue their own logic, reading the subexplanations in whatever order they choose, might actually enhance children's understanding. Empirical work contrasting the features in these explanations could help to identify which ones are the most effective for children in the middle grades.

My colleagues and I (Chambliss, 2001) are currently analyzing fourth and fifth graders' responses after reading Cooper's "How Sound Travels"and two similar explanations on echoes and light waves from the same textbook (Cooper et al., 1985). Our aim is to determine which types of subexplanations children find the most appealing and which seem to enhance their understanding best. Across the three texts, most fourth and fifth graders in our study chose concrete examples or direct presentations of a scientific model as the subexplanation that they "liked best."Virtually no children chose the analogies. Those children who chose a subexplanation that explicitly presented the scientific model also demonstrated greater understanding of the model than those who chose examples, whether they were recalling the subexplanation in words or drawing a picture of it. Because Barman's "How Sound Travels" presents examples rather than analogies, it is possible that it would lead to greater understanding among fourth and fifth graders than would Cooper's "How Sound Travels."

CONCLUDING THOUGHTS

Science textbooks in the past have been heavily indicted for being poorly organized, turgid, and uninteresting (T. H. Anderson, Armbruster, & Kantor, 1980; Chambliss & Calfee, 1998; Hurd, Robinson, McConnell, & Ross, 1981). They have neglected to build upon what readers know and believe, launching straightaway into presenting largely counterintuitive causal models (Chambliss & Calfee, 1998). The response in some curriculum materials has been to limit children's reading in science to one or two short passages per curriculum unit (e.g., National Science Resources Center, 1991a, 1991b). Results from research on the positive effects of refutational text suggest that rather than reading virtually no science materials, children should be encountering carefully crafted explanations with the potential to enhance the understandings that they gain from the experiments that they conduct and the scientific activities that they complete. Two of the textbook passages analyzed for this chapter exhibit characteristics of effective explanations. They demonstrate that it is possible to create textbook materials that fit well with scholarship in curriculum, instruction, and comprehension. By "throwing out the textbooks," advice given in the popular press by Jerome Pine, a physicist at the California Institute of Technology (Begley, Springen, Hager, Barrett, & Joseph, 1990), educators may have eliminated a potentially powerful resource. Far better might be the advice to throw out poorly designed textbook materials and replace them with passages that have been carefully crafted to build student understanding.

REFERENCES

Alverman, D. E., & Hynd, C. R. (1989). Effects of prior knowledge activation modes and text structure on nonscience majors' comprehension of physics. *Journal of Educational Research, 83*, 97–102.

Anderson, T. H., Armbruster, B. B., & Kantor, R. N. (1980). *How clearly written are children's textbooks? Or, of bladderworts and alfa* (Reading Education Report No. 16). Urbana: University of Illinois, Center for the Study of Reading.

Armbruster, B. B., Osborn, J. H., & Davison, A. L. (1985). Readability formulas may be dangerous to your textbooks. *Educational Leadership, 42*, 18–20.

Barman, C., Dispezio, M., Guthrie, V., Leyden, M. B., Mercier, S., & Ostlund, K. (1989). *Addison-Wesley Science/Grade 5*. Menlo Park, CA: Addison-Wesley.

Baumann, J. F. (1986). Effect of rewritten content textbook passages on middle grade students' comprehension of main ideas: Making the inconsiderate considerate. *Journal of Reading Behavior, 18*, 1–21.

Beck, I. L., McKeown, M. G., & Worthy, J. (1995). Giving a text voice can improve students' understanding. *Reading Research Quarterly, 30*, 220–238.

Begley, S., Springen, K., Hager, M., Barrett, T., & Joseph, N. (1990, April 9). Rx for learning/There's no secret about how to teach science. *Newsweek*, pp. 150–164.

Berkenkotter, C., & Huckin, T. N. (1993). Rethinking genre from a sociocognitive perspective. *Written Communication, 10*, 475–509.

Calfee, R. C., & Chambliss, M. C. (1987). The structural design features of large texts. *Educational Psychologist, 22*, 357–378.

Chall, J. S., & Dale, E. (1995). *Readability revisited: The new Dale–Chall readability formula*. Cambridge, MA: Brookline.

Chambliss, M. J. (2001, January). *Children as thinkers comprehending arguments and explanations*. Final Report submitted to the Spencer Foundation, Chicago.

Chambliss, M. J., & Calfee, R. C. (1989). Designing science textbooks to enhance student understanding. *Educational Psychologist, 24*, 307–322.

Chambliss, M. J., & Calfee, R. C. (1998). *Textbooks for learning: Nurturing children's minds*. Malden, MA: Blackwell.

Champagne, A. B., Gunstone, R. G., & Klopfer, L. E. (1983). Naive knowledge and science learning. *Research in Science & Technological Education, 1*, 1074–1079.

Chapman, M. L. (1999). Situated, social, active: Rewriting genre in the elementary school. *Written Communication, 16*, 469–490.

Clement, J. (1998). Expert novice similarities and instruction using analogies. *International Journal of Science Education, 20*, 1271–1286.

Clement, J., Brown, D., Camp, C., Kudukey, J., Minstrell, J., Palmer, D., Schultz, K., Shimabukuro, J., Steinberg, M., & Veneman, V. (1987). Overcoming students' misconceptions in physics: The role of anchoring intuitions and analogical validity. In J. D. Novak (Ed.), *Proceedings of the eighth annual meeting of the International Seminar on Misconceptions and Educational Strategies in Science and Mathematics* (pp. 84–97). Ithaca, NY: Cornell University.

Cohen, M. R., Cooney, T. M., Hawthorne, C. M., McCormack, A. J., Pasachoff, J. M., Pasachoff, N., Rhines, K. L., & Slesnick, I. L. (1989). *Discover science/4th grade*. Glenview, IL: Scott, Foresman.

Connors, R. J. (1985). The rhetoric of explanation: Explanatory rhetoric from 1850 to the present. *Written Communication, 2,* 49–72.

Cooper, E. K., Blackwood, P. E., Boeschen, J. A., Giddings, M. G., & Carin, A. A. (1985). *HBJ Science/Orange*. Orlando, FL: Harcourt Brace.

diSessa, A. (1993). Toward an epistemology of physics. *Cognition and Instruction, 10,* 105–226.

✓Duffy, T. M., Higgins, L., Mehlenbacher, B., Cochran, C., Wallace, D., Hill, C., Haugen, D., McCaffrey, M., Burnett, R., Sloane, S., & Smith, S. (1989). Models for the design of text. *Reading Research Quarterly, 24,* 434–457.

Duit, R. (1991). On the role of analogies and metaphors in learning science. *Science Education, 75,* 649–672.

Englert, C. S., & Hiebert, E. H. (1984). Children's developing awareness of text structures in expository materials. *Journal of Educational Psychology, 76,* 65–74.

Freebody, P., & Anderson, R. C. (1983). Effects of vocabulary difficulty, text cohesion, and schema availability on reading comprehension. *Reading Research Quarterly, 18,* 277–294.

Freedman, A. (1996). Genres of argument and arguments as genres. In D. P. Berrill (Ed.), *Perspectives on written argument* (pp. 91–120). Cresskill, NJ: Hampton Press.

Garner, R., Alexander, P., Gillingham, M., Kulikowich, J., & Brown, R. (1991). Interest and learning from text. *American Educational Research Journal, 28,* 643–659.

Garner, R., Gillingham, M., & White, J. (1989). Effects of "seductive details" on macroprocessing and microprocessing in adults and children. *Cognition and Instruction, 6,* 41–57.

Gentner, D., & Holyoak, K. J. (1997). Reasoning and learning by analogy: Introduction. *American Psychologist, 52,* 32–34.

Glover, D. (1993). *Sound and light*. New York: Kingfisher Books.

Guzzetti, B. J., Snyder, T. E., Glass, G. V., & Gamas, W. S. (1993). Promoting conceptual change in science: A comparative meta-analysis of instructional interventions from reading education and science education. *Reading Research Quarterly, 28,* 116–155.

Guzzetti, B. J., Williams, W. O., Skeels, S. A., & Wu, S. M. (1997). Influence of text structure on learning counterintuitive physics concepts. *Journal of Research in Science Teaching, 34,* 701–719.

✓Hare, V. C., Rabinowitz, M., & Schieble, K. M. (1989). Text effects on main idea comprehension. *Reading Research Quarterly, 24,* 72–88.

Harp, S. F., & Mayer, R. E. (1997). The role of interest in learning from scientific text and illustrations: On the distinction between emotional interest and cognitive interest. *Journal of Educational Psychology, 89,* 92–102.

Harp, S. F., & Mayer, R. E. (1998). How seductive details do their damage: A theory of cognitive interest in science learning. *Journal of Educational Psychology, 90,* 414–434.

Hidi, S., & Baird, W. (1988). Strategies for increasing text-based interest and students' recall of expository texts. *Reading Research Quarterly, 24,* 72–88.

Holyoak, K. J., & Thagard, P. (1997). The analogical mind. *American Psychologist, 52*, 35–44.

Hurd, P. D., Robinson, J. T., McConnell, M. C., & Ross, N. M., Jr. (1981). *The status of middle school and junior high school science.* Louisville, CO: Center for Educational Research and Evaluation.

Hynd, C. R., McWhorter, J. Y., Phares, V. L., & Suttles, C. W. (1994). The role of instructional variables in conceptual change in high school physics topics. *Journal of Research in Science Teaching, 31*, 933–946.

Kintsch, W. (1980). Learning from text, levels of comprehension, or: Why would anyone read a story anyway? *Poetics, 9*, 87–89.

Kintsch, W. (1986). Learning from text. *Cognition and Instruction, 3*, 87–108.

Kintsch, W. (1998). *Comprehension: A paradigm for cognition.* Cambridge, England: Cambridge University Press.

Kintsch, W., & Yarbrough, J. C. (1982). Role of rhetorical structure in text structure. *Journal of Educational Psychology, 74*, 828–834.

Kucan, L., & Beck, I. L. (1996). Four fourth graders thinking aloud: An investigation of genre effects. *Journal of Literacy Research, 28*, 259–287.

Levy, D. H. (2000, March 12). The magnificent machines that got us here. *Parade Magazine*, pp. 4–5.

Mayer, R. E. (1985). Structural analysis of science prose: Can we increase problem-solving performance? Part 1. In B. K. Britton & J. B. Black (Eds.), *Understanding expository text* (pp. 65–87). Hillsdale, NJ: Lawrence Erlbaum Associates.

Mayer, R. E., Steinhoff, K., Bower, G., & Mars, R. (1995). A generative theory of textbook design: Using annotated illustrations to foster meaningful learning of science text. *Educational Technology Research and Development, 43*, 31–43.

Meyer, B. J. F. (1985). Prose analysis: Purposes, procedures, and problems, Parts 1 and 2. In B. K. Britton & J. B. Black (Eds.), *Understanding expository text* (pp. 11–64, 269–304). Hillsdale, NJ: Lawrence Erlbaum Associates.

Meyer, B. J. F., Brandt, D. H., & Bluth, G. J. (1980). Use of top-level structure in text: Key for reading comprehension of ninth-grade students. *Reading Research Quarterly, 16*, 72–103.

Meyer, B. J. F., & Freedle, R. O. (1984). Effects of discourse type on recall. *American Educational Research Journal, 21*, 121–143.

National Science Resources Center. (1991a). *Electric circuits.* Washington, DC: Author/Science and Technology for Children.

National Science Resources Center. (1991b). *Magnets and motors.* Washington, DC: Author/Science and Technology for Children.

Oatley, K. (1996). Inference in narrative and science. In D. R. Olson & N. Torrance (Eds.), *Modes of thought: Explorations in culture and cognition* (pp. 123–140). Cambridge, England: Cambridge University Press.

Pfundt, H., & Duit, R. (1991). *Bibliography: Students' alternative frameworks and science education* (3rd ed.). Kiel, W. Germany: University of Kiel.

Rowen, K. E. (1988). A contemporary theory of explanatory writing. *Written Communication, 5*, 23–56.

Rowen, K. E. (1990). Cognitive correlates of explanatory writing skill. *Written Communication, 7*, 316–341.

Sadoski, M., Goetz, E. T., & Fritz, J. B. (1993). Impact of concreteness on comprehensibility, interest, and memory for text: Implications for dual coding theory and text design. *Journal of Educational Psychology, 85*, 291–304.

Sadoski, M., Goetz, E. T., & Rodriguez, M. (2000). Engaging texts: Effects of concreteness on comprehensibility, interest, and recall in four text types. *Journal of Educational Psychology, 92*, 85–95.

Schank, R. C. (1979). Interestingness: Controlling inferences. *Artificial Intelligence, 12*, 273–297.

Schwab, J. J. (1978). Education and the structure of the disciplines. In I. Westbury & N. J. Wilkof (Eds.), *Science, curriculum, and liberal education: Selected essays* (pp. 229–272). Chicago: University of Chicago Press.

Swales, J. M. (1990). *Genre analysis: English in academic and research settings.* Cambridge, England: Cambridge University Press.

Tufte, E. R. (1990). *Envisioning information.* Chesire, CT: Graphics Press.

Tyler, R. W. (1949). *Basic principles of curriculum and instruction.* Chicago: University of Chicago Press.

Wade, S. E., Buxton, W. M., & Kelly, M. (1999). Using think-alouds to examine reader-text interest. *Reading Research Quarterly, 34*, 194–216.

Whitehead, A. N. (1974). *The organisation of thought.* Westport, CT: Greenwood.

Whittaker, A. (1992). Constructing science knowledge from exposition: The effects of text structure training (Doctoral dissertation, Stanford University, 1992). *Dissertation Abstracts International, 53*, 3157A.

Wong, I., & Calfee, R. C. (1988, April). *Informational trade books: A viable alternative to textbooks.* Paper presented at the annual meeting of The American Educational Research Association, New Orleans, LA.

❧ 4 ❧

Visual Imagery in School Science Texts

Isabel Martins
Universidade Federal do Rio de Janeiro, Brazil

Science is, more and more, a matter of public concern and attitudes toward science are regarded as having great impact on patterns of decision making. The communication of scientific ideas to nonspecialists is commonly discussed in the context of the democratization of the access to information, which is needed to inform decisions on both personal and public levels. Scientific information is increasingly and more widely available in museums, popular science magazines, and television programs. Within the school system, recent trends in curriculum development emphasize the need to introduce young students to science as early as possible through the observation and investigation of natural phenomena, drawing on everyday situations. The fact that secondary school clientele is no longer a homogeneous elite with respect to class and gender puts pressure on traditional curricula, which used to focus on the formation of future specialists. Some of these new principles of curriculum organization address issues raised by extensive research about characteristics of learners, their previous knowledge, interests, and needs; about teachers' conceptions of science and of science teaching. Discussions about scientific literacy describe science not only as one of humankind's most important cultural achievement but mainly as a cultural public asset to which everyone should have access.

Images have become more and more pervasive in the textual realizations of the efforts described previously. In this chapter we look at new patterns in science communication to nonspecialist audiences, more specifically those found in modern school science textbooks published in Brazil and in the UK, and discuss the role of visual representations in learning scientific ideas. This discussion draws upon current views on semiotics and science education. Our starting point in semiotics is a grammar of visual design that was developed in the context of a discussion about both the nature and the impact of the increasingly pervasive use of images in western culture communication. From the science education end we start by exploring the inherently visual character of science and the kinds and functions of images in science teaching. By setting up this interdisciplinary framework we move on to analyses of roles, kinds, and functions of images in textbooks as perceived by their target audience of students.

IMAGES, SCIENCE, AND SCIENCE EDUCATION

Images are, in many respects, essential to science. Examples from the history of science include Faraday's construction of the reality of magnetic fields through the visualization of force lines and Watson and Crick's metaphor of a double helix to explain the structure of the DNA molecule. Atoms, continental plates, and the evolution of species are among the abundant examples of entities that are inaccessible to everyday observations but need to be attributed the same reality as visible observable entities. Entities that do not occur together are brought together and displayed visually so that it is possible to see order or relationships between them. The periodic table and tree diagrams illustrating taxonomies of species are examples of these intentional arrangements. Science also requires the visualization of internal structures and component parts of both biological organs and technical artefacts.

The perspective just outlined suggests that representation entails both interpretation and intentionality, a view eloquently illustrated in Olson's (1996) discussions of early visual text produced by historians, natural scientists, philosophers and cartographers in the 16th and 17th centuries. Such attempts to put the "world on paper" do not constitute neutral descriptive mnemonic texts. They reflect particular points of view framed by the possibilities of representation, cultural tools, and icons that are available at a given time.

Not only are images crucial to the conceptualization of scientific ideas, they are also considered to be powerful aids to communicate specialist knowledge to audiences of nonexperts. In fact a great deal of the difficulties experienced by nonspecialists are linked to the so-called language of science. Specific characteristics of scientific texts' grammatical organization, jargon, context-bound terminology, and different connotations acquired by a given lexicon are features of the language of science, which would explain why non-experts feel disconnected or alienated from science. In fact, it is commonplace to equate students' difficulties in understanding science with difficulties understanding, reading and expressing themselves in the language of science. An assumption frequently made, though seldom formally articulated, is that the visual is more transparent a medium than language. Thus images are usually employed to bypass some of the difficulties incurred when communicating science through the verbal mode. A number of recommendations for classroom activities encourage teachers to incorporate graphical representations in their explanations of scientific concepts. Stimuli for students to communicate their own views and understandings through drawings are also based on a view that the visual imposes fewer restrictions to the expression of ideas (Barlex & Carré, 1985). This idea that images would communicate ideas more readily than language is also pervasive among researchers in science education who have used both children's drawings and children's readings of drawings as data in investigations about their conceptual understanding (Driver et al., 1994).

This chapter challenges the view that images can be more readily understood than language. Instead, reading images is treated as a complex situated activity, deeply influenced by principles that organize possibilities of representation and meanings within a culture. Adopting such a stance questions the long-standing privilege dispensed to language as "a full medium of communication, adequate to the expression of everything that needs to be expressed" (Kress, Ogborn, & Martins, 1998, p. 69). Language is considered one of several semiotic modes in acts of communication, each one of which specializes with respect to communicational and representational functions. In this chapter we examine examples from school science textbooks to try and understand better the role played by images, including how they work in cooperation with language, and when they can be seen as more apt than language for a given purpose.

ROLES AND FUNCTIONS OF IMAGES
IN SCHOOL SCIENCE TEXTBOOKS

Even a quick inspection of modern school science textbooks reveals that, more and more often, images and graphical resources are being used. Unlike traditional texts where language predominated, modern textbooks are organized around images. A survey of physics textbooks used in Brazilian courses on basic mechanics over the last five decades has revealed that the number of illustrations per page had increased by a factor of four (Chincaro, Freitas, & Martins, 1999). The modern text combines verbal text displayed visually in tables or shaded boxes with a remarkable variety of graphical forms as diverse as photographs, schematic diagrams, comic strips, and graphs. Among the reasons for that are technological advances in desktop publishing, enhanced possibilities for both creating and capturing images, and the reduction in the costs of color reproduction. However these are not the only and, by no means, the most important issues related to that shift toward the visual. This more widespread use of images in science texts mirrors a pattern, which is observed in advertisement, propaganda, news, that is, in communication more generally. More significant than the increase in the number and variety of images found in those texts are the changes in the relationships between text and image. In traditional texts, the main message was usually in writing and images served the function of illustrating, help with visualization, or simply making the text more interesting or engaging. Illustrations were subordinate to the text. This situation has changed and in modern texts the relationships between written text and image are more complex and serve functions of complementation, comparison, contrast, detail, or elaboration. New relations between text and image have thereafter emerged. Images, which traditionally merely served as illustrations and were used as a way of enlivening the text, become the core text. It is even possible to find examples where the written text only names something that is defined graphically or suggests how the images are to be read and the visual is, in fact, the main mode of communication.

Numerous functions are performed by images in textbooks. A nonexhaustive list includes:

- Orientation, that is, to signal the content to be presented.
- Motivation, or, to catch the reader's attention, interest or curiosity.
- To show how something is done.
- To illustrate an idea or argument.
- To show patterns through organized displays of cases.
- To relate general knowledge to specific examples.
- To move from a macroscopic to a microscopic level of description.
- To establish relationships between the real everyday and the abstract scientific.

These functions and their relationships with principles of curriculum organization help account for the wide variety of kinds of images present in science textbooks nowadays. In Brazil, for example, recent curriculum recommendations suggest the concepts of contextualization or interdisciplinarity (Brasil, 2000) as structural axes for curriculum development. Textbook images are recruited to meet these demands. A photograph, typically found in a primary science textbooks, shows pots and pans made of iron, copper, and aluminum on a kitchen table, and helps bring context to a lesson about materials and their properties, especially those related to their performance in food preparation and to the damaging effects of the ingestion of metal residuals on health. Copies of newspaper excerpts about urban rubbish collection, diagrams showing functional descriptions of a biodigestor, pictures of people being treated for health hazards caused by contamination through chemical rejects are examples of images that are brought together in an interdisciplinary approach of chemical transformations.

Whereas some of these functions fulfill pedagogical goals, others are specifically related to science knowledge itself. Science is a stable and consolidated specialized discourse that influences and shapes ways through which school curricula are organized. There are many functions that can be realized visually. Some possibilities are: definitions, examples, patterns or notations. Even though scientific culture tends to favor knowledge expressed through language, for some concepts (e.g., magnetic fields or the structure of DNA) visualization is crucial for understanding. Also there are images that are specific to science contexts and communicate science knowledge in a quite unique way. One example is the simple pendulum, an exceedingly simple image, stripped off naturalistic features, which is, with very little representational variation, frequently present in science textbooks.

Modern textbooks are also different with respect to the kinds of student activity they encourage. Differently from old-fashioned manuals and reference books, modern textbooks do not simply contain theoretical principles and definitions. More like guides for classroom activity, the modern books pose problems, propose activities, show specific actions involved in the conduction of experiments, and help construct solutions. Thus, apart from the relationships with the text around them and with scientific knowledge itself, images also entail a dimension of relationship with students' activity. Pupil activity can be both physical and intellectual, both inside and outside the classroom environment, including responses by pupils to prompts made in the text.

Another dimension involves rhetorical uses of images. Images can be seen as rhetorical devices, that is as identifiable textual features that relate

introduction

to larger patterns of text organization and perform a number of functions in science texts. These functions include: to convey images of the nature of science and of scientific activity; to construct authority of scientific knowledge and discourse; and to help construct and alter subjectivities. Our analyses discussed how the ways learners are being increasingly portrayed in the textbooks might allow new expectations and attitudes toward a domain of knowledge to be created (Martins et al., 2000). Our data also revealed that, especially in modern British secondary science books, it is quite common to find representations of students actively engaged in some kind of science-related task. These images, which frequently show boys and girls wearing aprons and with their hair tied back manipulating equipment or setting up apparatus in the science classrooms, actually do more than echo the metaphor "pupil as scientist." They relate a set of behaviors that are expected from students in science classrooms (e.g., obeying necessary safety procedures) and characterize the nature of activities they are expected to perform (e.g., conduct experiments). Textbooks also include representations of interaction between participants in classroom activities. In an example drawn from a Brazilian secondary school physics textbook (Guimaraes & Fonteboa, 1997), student and teacher are the main characters of a narrative in the form of comic strips presented throughout the textbook. In the course of their interactions, different patterns of power relations, authority, and hierarchy emerge between them. For instance, there are cases in which it is the student who solves a problem or provides an insightful answer to questions posed. Here images help with telling stories where the student is portrayed as not only observant and creative but also capable of developing and expressing scientifically accepted ideas, in a clear shift of authority relations.

Images have been object of study of in several areas such as psychology, anthropology, cognitive science, semiotics, and media studies (Joly, 1994). Therefore, the science educator's analysis of images benefits from and contributes to a wider discussion that involves several disciplinary domains. More specifically, the potential of images as aids to learning has been established and corroborated by extensive research. For instance, results from the field of cognitive science reveal that pictures are more memorable than their verbal counterparts (Levie, 1987; Levin & Mayer 1993; McDaniel & Pressley, 1987; Paivio, 1971). Another important result is that the addition of illustrations has been shown to improve students' learning from a text (Levie & Lentz, 1982; Levin, Anglin, & Carney, 1987; Schallert, 1980; see also Levin & Mayer, 1993). Educational research has also provided analyses of images in school science texts, which discuss their role in teaching and learning through a number of studies analyzing textbooks and classroom practice. Extensive reviews have documented the nature of the inquiry into the role of images in learning (Filippatou & Pumfrey, 1996; Fleming, 1977, 1979). Strongly influenced by cognitive psychology, work by Goldsmith (1987) proposed an analytical model that deals with image, text, and their interrelationships. From a different perspective Vézin and Vézin (1990) analyzed the use of image from both author's and reader's expectations of images and Duchastel (1980) established basic functions for visual language. In their review, Avgerinou and Ericson (1997) characterized visual literacy as an emergent field of multidisciplinary research. Images have also been analyzed by science educators in the context of science textbook legibility (Kearsey & Turner, 1999) and of comparisons between presentations on paper and on computer screen (Reid & Bevridge, 1986). Children's interpretations about images in their textbooks have also been the object of investigation privileging a number of perspectives, which include affective engagements and aesthetic judgements.

This variety in theoretical standpoints illustrates the complexity of an object of study, the understanding of which involves various aspects from understanding mechanisms of visual perception to discussing the role of symbolic interactions in culture.

GETTING A HANDLE:
THE GRAMMAR OF VISUAL DESIGN

An important contribution was put forward by recent work in the field of social semiotics by Kress and van Leeuwen (1996). According to them, the studies of visual grammar have focused on "rules" and "lexis" and concentrated on "formal, aesthetic description of images, sometimes on the basis of psychology of perception, or sometimes on more pragmatic descriptions, for instance on the way composition can be used to attract the viewer's attention to one thing rather than another" (p. 1). Instead, their aim has been "to provide inventories of the major compositional structures which have become established as conventions in the course of history of visual semiotics, and to analyse how they are used to produce meaning by contemporary image-makers" (p. 1). In their book *Reading Images: The grammar of Visual Design*, the authors argued that visual communication, similarly to other systems of human communication, needs to meet as a requirement three basic demands that reflect aspects of how meaning is made. These demands reflect the fundamental components along which semantic systems are organized as set out by Michael Halliday

(1985): the ideational, the interpersonal, and the textual metafunctions. They require representational systems:

- To be able to represent phenomena and processes of the experiential world, so as to establish a symbolic relation between the representational system (as defined by its particular complex of signs) and aspects of the real world.
- To be able to locate subjects in different structures of social interaction and to account for social relations between participants in communicative acts.
- To enable coherent relations between textual components, and between text and context.

It is from this standpoint that Kress and van Leeuwen (1996) sought to identify underlying structural organizations in images describing how different constituent elements in a picture will combine into meaningful wholes. Similarly to language statements, "visual statements" are best understood as actions on the world, relating social beings to social contexts. The analogy with languages goes further. "Visual forms" are understood against a background of conventions and constraints relating social beings to the social contexts they live in. The sense in which they have used the term *grammar* is fully realized by the following quote: "Grammar goes beyond formal rules of correctness. It is a means of representing patterns of experience .... It enables human beings to build a mental picture of reality, to make sense of their experience of what goes on around them and inside them" (Halliday, 1985, p. 101).

Kress and van Leeuwen's (1996) grammar of visual design addresses both theoretical and practical concerns. As a contemporary development in social semiotics it delves into a discussion of particular modes of representation and their potentials for meaning making in relation to their status and valuation in specific social contexts. They also intended it to be used as a tool for visual analysis providing professionals, for example, educationalists and media specialists, with elements for describing, examining, and investigating the variety of forms and meanings of different visual materials.

Thus Kress and van Leeuwen (1996) developed the bases for a theoretical/descriptive framework of the structural principles of organization of visual representation in Western culture. Through a copious number of examples they showed, for instance, how a left-to-right type of reading usually places a *given* concept on the left and a *new* concept on the right, and how a vertical display organizes models (or the *ideal*) at the top and the *real* at the bottom.

It was possible to observe instances of such patterns among the science textbooks we analyzed. For instance, in one of the examples we have analyzed, different representations of electric circuits, textual and visual, are displayed in table form. The table is itself a structure that allows language elements to be visually displayed so as to emphasize dimensions of comparison and contrast (Lemke, 1998). The vertical organization classifies, in columns, circuits in two types, series and parallel. This organization mirrors a canonical form in teaching electric circuits. Series is usually introduced before parallel. The horizontal organization, in four rows, depicts a split between real (at the bottom) and ideal (at the top), which is realized through a relationship between naturalistic and formal representations. At the bottom we see a hand drawing where wires and bulbs resemble those seen in the laboratory. As we move up, representations become less naturalistic with symbols for batteries, wires, and bulbs being introduced in a circuit diagram. In the row directly above, language is used to explicate the physical arrangement of the bulbs, that is, how bulbs are physically connected. At the top, meaning is encapsulated in an even more abstract type of representation, a linguistic label.

Kress and van Leeuwen (1996) also classified representational structures as narrative or conceptual. Whereas narrative representations portray transitory relationships, conceptual representations depict permanent relationships between (represented) participants.[1] Both structures can be naturalistic or abstract and may co-occur.

Narrative images tell stories. They represent processes and actions that happen along time, such as a block of ice melting or the relative movement of two bodies. Narrative processes can be realized through diagrams showing either boxes linked by arrows, or forms that imply a sequential character like, for example, in comic strips. Gaze is also an important element to convey directionality.

Conceptual structures include classificatory, analytical, and symbolic structures. A classification organizes members of the same class usually in a symmetrical array of images of the same size and kind. This structure allows comparison and contrast between members of the same category. Classifi-

---

[1]Kress and van Leeuwen (1996) preferred the term *participant* to *element* or *object* for two reasons: first, because it conveys a relational character (participants in a semiotic act), and second because it allows a distinction to be made between interactive and represented participants. "The former are the participants in the act of communication—who speak and listen or write and read, make images or view them; the latter are the participants who are the subject of communication, that is, the people, places and things (including abstract 'things') represented in and by the speech or writing or image, the participants *about* whom or which we are speaking or writing or producing images" (Kress and van Leeuwen, 1996, p. 46).

cation also realizes hierarchical relationships between participants. Taxonomies are realizations of classificatory processes. Taxonomies can be *overt* when a "superordinate item," that is, the more general concept of which each individual member could be seen as being related to, is present. But they can also be *covert*, when individual members of the set possesses the same status as each other, and the superordinate item can only be inferred from the similarities and differences that the viewer may perceive in each individual member of the set. Classification structures usually represent participants with respect to their relative position or ranking in a static order. Flow charts and networks are also classification structures, though they allow more flexibility and dynamism. Classifications are of vital importance for science as illustrated by the increased importance attributed in recent years by curriculum planners to activities such as close observation, recording information, sorting into groups, and finding out patterns. Examples of classificatory images in science include consumer–producer pyramids, evolution trees, and sets of materials that share common properties.

Analytical structures relate participants in terms of part–whole relationships. Analytical images involve two kinds of participants: the "carrier" (the whole) and any number of "possessive attributes" (parts). Parts are clearly identified and usually labeled, inside or outside the picture space. Naturalistic representations, like photographs, tend to distract the viewer from the analytical purpose. The plain background, the sparing use of color, the absence of depth, the use of shadow and shades of gray only to help identify the parts, all these invite an impersonal, detached scrutiny. Analytical images are typical of science texts, characterized by their wide use of schematic diagrams in abstract, or idealized, representations. Examples commonly found in science texts in are maps, timelines and charts, diagrams of biological organs, and so on.

Symbolic processes concern what a participant *means* or *is*. Symbolic processes usually involve a *carrier*, whose meaning is established in the relation, and the *symbolic attribute*, the participant that represents the meaning itself. Often symbolic attributes are made salient in the representation, for example, through the use of light or color, being pointed to, or having their size exaggerated.

More important than simply attributing labels to images, these categories of analysis allow one to represent, to discuss, and to make explicit relationships between participants in the image. Furthermore, through examination of structures of representation, they help foreground relationships between the representation and the conceptual domain it relates to. For instance, in a classification it becomes possible to ask about organizing principles or criteria that lie at the bases of class membership. In analytical structures, component parts acquire meaning with respect to their function and their relationship with the whole. Narratives provide the opportunity to analyze processes. This makes them a very important tool for the science educator who is involved in providing opportunities for nonspecialists to construct meanings for scientific entities. For the science teacher, in particular, it provides the necessary resources to talk students through images "in the making," that is, when they are constructed in classroom discourse, revealing motivations behind seemingly arbitrary arrangements.

These basic categories also combine to allow more complex sophisticated structures to emerge. For instance, in the representation of a typical food chain, arrows show the flow of energy/matter throughout the chain, which organizes consumers (at the top) and producers (at the bottom) in a vertical axis. This image can be seen as a classification inside a narrative, portraying patterns of behaviors of the entities involved (one serves as food to the other) and how this behavior organizes them in different classes (producers and consumers).

Another type of combination is the classification of symbolic and analytical structures. In one of the examples we analyzed, a page from a secondary science British textbook, the visual display classified the images, a combination of symbolic and analytical structures, so as to allow the identification of different functional structures within one type of cell by comparison with another type of cell. The page shows, side by side, photographs of a cheek cell and of a pond weed cell as seen through microscope lenses. Directly below each one of these images is an analytical diagram identifying and naming the parts of the animal and plant cell, respectively. The text directly above each one of the photographs draws parallels and points to similarities in the seemingly completely different images. The comparison was made effective through an interaction of language and image on the page. The whole page is about establishing relevant dimensions for contrasting the cheek cell and the pond weed cell. This is done through the vertical parallelism in the layout but also through a strong parallel structure in the written text.

THE STUDENT'S PERSPECTIVE

The principles presented herein have provided the foundations for our research on children's readings of science textbook images. Prior analyses, as described earlier, guided the selection of sets of images, covering a variety of representational features, from a range of books, and these images

were used as prompts in empirical studies about secondary schoolchildren's readings of science images described later (Martins, 1996). The discussion that follows is based on data collected through interviews made
between lessons with pairs of early secondary school students, aged 11 to
14 years old, in the UK. The analyses were informed by classroom observation data, which provided information about relevant contexts of learning
through images that had taken place, for instance, joint efforts by teacher
and students to construct and attribute meaning to a given image (Kress
et al., 1998).

In their accounts students exhibited different levels of engagement in
the activity proposed. They were asked to describe and explain their reading of specific images in the page. A common pattern of reading that we
found among students who were interviewed was labeled *uncommitted
browsing*. Most of students' firsthand comments about the pages involved
references to the images in them and how "nice" they looked, and whether
one "liked" them or not. To judge from these initial reactions, students' first
forms of engagement with these materials happened through an affective
channel. They talked about visual compositions that please the eye and
look attractive. The use of color, the combination of different visual resources, the balance between the amount of text and image were referred to
as features that helped catch the viewer's attention. Color was usually
something that can be played with in order to make a picture look better.
Images are there to be looked at. In a few cases, uncommitted browsing developed into a more critical analysis.

In other cases images were more thoroughly scrutinized straightaway. For
some students images did not readily communicate anything ("it needs to
be 'read' and interpreted). Color was mentioned again as a key feature that
helped draw attention to specific parts of the image and allowed it to be
"read" and interpreted in a given way. For these students, images were
thought of as intentional manipulations of graphic resources to convey a
message.

Yet another way of engaging with visual information in a text is to talk
about images as resources for learning. According to the students interviewed images had to satisfy two criteria in order to be successful as helpful
resources: to be memorable and to match self-perceived reading competence of the reader. Presence or absence of captions, saturation of colors,
and the amount of lines and arrows linking image to written text were also
used by students as terms of comparison between the images and allowed a
number of them to be deemed, for instance, as containing excessively un-
helpful detail.

Interviews also revealed that images were not considered as isolated entities but related both to other pieces of text in a page and, more generally, to other pieces of knowledge. With respect to this more general context, the research identified two main functions for an image: (a) to emphasize some sort of contrast and (b) to instantiate a theoretical account given earlier.

To take this point further let us refer to a set of images that was presented to the children as a double-spread page of a chapter called "The Earth in Space" in a British secondary science textbook designed for an audience of 14-year-olds. The selected images were, according to Kress and van Leeuwen (1996) categories: a naturalistic classification structure (Christmas shopping in Sydney), a symbolic naturalistic structure (midnight in Spitsbergen), and a narrative-analytical diagram (the seasons).

The first image consisted of a color wide-angle photograph of a busy high street in Sydney at Christmas time. Streets and shops are ornamented with lights and Christmas decoration. People, wearing light clothes, walk by with carrier bags. The photograph was taken during the day and shows plenty of sunlight. There is a piece of text that talks about seasonal changes as "another result of the tilt of the Earth's axis" right next to the picture (Partridge, 1992, p. 7)

The second image was a color photograph, taken from a distance, of the landscape of a village. In the foreground we see a train and railway tracks. Behind the tracks there is a row of houses and the outline of their redbrick roofs is shown against high, snow-peaked mountains that contrast with the light blue sky in the background. The caption in the photograph says, "Spitsbergen at midnight June. At this time of the year the Sun never disappears." (Partridge, 1992, p. 6).

Finally, the third image was a complex diagram typically found in school science textbooks. The drawing is made in a light blue background and shows the earth as a blue sphere with continents outlined in green, crossed by a black line inclined to the right, representing its rotation axis. The letters N and S, at either extreme of the line, indicate north and south. The word *Sun* is written in the center of an ellipsis, which has arrows indicating anticlockwise movement of the earth around the sun, and is labeled *Earth's orbit*. The earth is represented in two different positions in the same drawing: at both extremes of the greater semiaxis of the ellipsis, showing summer and winter on the two hemispheres. A similar version of this image was also drawn in the blackboard by the teacher and copied by students in their notebooks. Two small pieces of text are printed inside the picture space, directly below the representation of the earth. The text compares lengths of days and nights in the northern hemisphere in June (on the left) and in December (on the right) and relates the different lengths of daylight and darkness in summer and winter months to the way the North Pole is facing the sun. (Partridge, 1992).

Broadly speaking there were two main dimensions along which students appeared to operate when trying to make sense of these images. The first dimension has to do with projecting experiential knowledge onto the reading of the image. This knowledge reflects elements of both their everyday culture and their classroom culture. As a result, pictures are read against a background of expectations. For instance, it is experiential knowledge about their local reality, in particular of what the night sky looks like, that is brought to bear on their interpretations of the picture *Midnight in Spitsbergen.*

The fact that the perceived bases for contrast are firmly grounded in cultural aspects is crucial to understand interpretations of the image labeled *Christmas shopping in Sydney.* In this case, these aspects relate to both expectations and previous knowledge of how December weather is like in cities at different latitudes. Seasonal changes are also interpreted in terms of the theoretical account provided in the lessons pupils have had on the subject. Thus, Christmas in Britain is equated to "is facing away from the Sun" and the fact that "it gets darker and it's colder" is seen as a consequence of the relative positions of the earth and the sun, a view that is elaborated with the help of a demonstration seen in the classroom involving torches and cardboard. Models, visual metaphors, and analogue relationships were coordinated and articulated so as to generate explanations in terms of theorized entities and to shape students' readings of these images. Thus, there was an identification of elements in the image and aspects of the activity done in class. Yet another interesting possibility for this image is to be read as a demonstration. This possibility depends on imposing meaning on material events (Ogborn et al., 1996). Similarly to what happens in a demonstration, where phenomena are described in terms of a particular theoretical view, the image of a sunny day in Australia in December was read as the consequence of an angle between the earth's axis and the ecliptic.

But there is also knowledge related to the science classroom culture, of which they are a party, and that allows them to identify genres of school science texts, familiar textbook layouts and discursive patterns that are typical of classroom interactions. This type of knowledge may explain why they recognize the picture of the midnight sun as having the function of enlivening the text as opposed to a schematic diagram of the solar system, shown in the same page, which is considered as a piece of knowledge in itself. In fact

function

images are perceived to perform different functions, from enlivening a text by illustrating a case to communicating actual knowledge that must be remembered and learned. The examples of "scientific" images given by pupils included line drawings and diagrams and excluded photographs and comic strips. In general images that are labeled *nonscientific* are usually those that contain humanized characters or high color saturation, that is, images that do not have high scientific modality.

Such perception may, in some cases, be dismissive of images that are not deemed scientific. However, that may lead to a failure in observing other possible intended functions for images apart from simply "making the book prettier." An example may be that of midnight in Spitsbergen. This image offers the potential to generate the need for an explanation by showing what seems to be a paradoxical aspect of reality. But on the whole, students in our sample trivialized the role played by that image, considering it as a superfluous illustration.

The distinction between scientific and nonscientific images also appeared implicitly when students made, on request, drawings of the earth and represented where their own position was on the earth's surface. Pictures they drew were quite similar to those they had seen in their lessons and books, including which specific elements they were supposed to show and how clearly they should be labeled. Elements from a more theorized account of the phenomenon of the seasons, such as the tilted axis, the Poles, the equator, and the Tropics, are explicitly represented, whereas features that do not play a part in the explanation (e.g., the continents, are only outlined or not represented at all. Their drawings are similar to analytical diagrams and show labeled parts. Moreover, the description of the image usually combines hand gestures and oral remarks listing the features of the image; for example, pointing is linked to labeling.

Another dimension relates to perceiving and establishing relationships at both intra- and intertextual levels. Students easily perceive the continuity in the pattern established in the larger scale text. The fact that the contents in a page have an underlying textual coherence, which is ultimately grounded in conceptual coherence, is not foreign to students. Students' descriptions of a given image often integrate and relate to readings of other images they have seen earlier.

All of the aforementioned suggests that meaning and significance of an image are to be found in their actual and their potential use in learning activities. Most of the classwork is indeed directed to instilling knowledge in images. To a greater or lesser extent, classroom work is motivated by the need to construct meaningful links between phenomena and their repre-

sentations in a continual movement in which several modes operate in coordination, mediating accounts and redescribing phenomena.

IMPLICATIONS FOR RESEARCH AND EDUCATION

The studies described earlier reveal, notwithstanding in a preliminary form,
products that result from a dialogue between two disciplines that do not
possess a long-standing tradition of collaboration. It is an exciting point of
departure, with both science education and semiotics pointing to better understanding the roles of visual representations in meaning making.

This chapter identifies and documents new ways textbooks are structured and address students. These pose fundamental questions for researchers in science education. First the transition from a language-based
text to a visual-based text should be examined in the context of contemporary curriculum recommendations, which, apart from developing students'
conceptual knowledge, seek to value their interests and to stimulate their
curiosity about science and its relationships with technology and society. It
is worth inquiring which assumptions are being made about readers, their
interests and needs for information, and their relationships with science
knowledge. Furthermore, it is worth inquiring about the relationships between these assumptions and the vast amount of information that is available on students' alternative conceptions in and about science as already
established by science education research.

Our results suggest that students engage in reading images in their science textbooks in a variety of ways. These ways reflect different roles and
different levels of commitment with the need for making sense of a given
image. Students' readings also seem to indicate that they are capable of perceiving the manipulation of visual elements in science texts and of seeing
discourse as intentionally organized. These results have the potential to
pave the way to recommendations seeking to enable students to be more
critical readers. Analyses of this kind could also help raise awareness about
different possibilities, styles, and strategies for explaining science, and enable teachers to think more critically about the materials they use.

Both empirical and theoretical investigations are, nonetheless, needed
at this stage. Matters to be explored by research include the issue of the
"aptness" of different semiotic modes, how they specialize for different purposes, the relationships between such specializations, and the potentials of
each mode. These also include gathering more information about roles and
functions of visual representations in other contexts and educational reali-
ties, and about readers' different possibilities of engagement with the text. It

is also urgent to develop and systematize methodological approaches to deal with methods and techniques needed to analyze visual information, including the issue of using the visual mode in contexts of knowledge elicitation.

ACKNOWLEDGMENTS

The research reported in this chapter draws on the work by the project "Visual communication in learning or science in," jointly directed by Jon Ogborn and Gunther Kress at the Institute of Education, University of London and funded by the Economics and Social Research Council (ESRC). The research is being extended with the support of the Fundação Carlos Chagas de Amparo a Pesquisa do Rio de Janeiro (FAPERJ), in Brazil.

REFERENCES

Avgerinou, M., & Ericson, J. (1997). A review of the concept of visual literacy. *British Journal of Educational Technology, 28,* 280–291.

Barlex, D., & Carré, C. (1985). *Visual communication in science.* Cambridge, England: Cambridge University Press.

Brasil. (2000). *Parâmetros curriculares nacionais.* Brasília, DF, Brasil; Ministério da Educação.

Chincaro, A., Freitas, C., & Martins, I. (1999, September). *Tipos e funções de imagens em livros didáticos de Ciências.* Paper presented at Atas do II Encontro de Pesquisa em Educação em Ciências, Valinhos, SP, Brazil in CD-ROM.

Driver, R., Aquires, A., Rushworth, P., & Wood-Robinson, V. (1994). *Making sense of secondary science.* London: Routledge.

Duchastel, P. (1980). Rôles cognitifs de l'image dans l'apprentissage scolaire. *Bulletin de Psychologie, XLI* (386), 668–671.

Filippatou, D., Pumfrey, P. (1996). Pictures, titles, reading accuracy and reading comprehension: A research review (1973–95). *Educational Research, 38,* 259–291.

Fleming, M. (1977). The picture in your mind. *AV Communication Review, 25,* 43–61.

Fleming, M. (1979). On pictures in educational research. Instructional Science, 8, 235–251.

Goldsmith, E. (1987). The analysis of illustration in theory and practice. In D. M. Willows & H. A. Houghton (Eds.), *The psychology of illustration: II. Instructional texts* (pp. 53–85) New York: Springer Verlag.

Guimarães, L. A., & Fonte Boa, M. (1997). *Física para o Segundo Grau* [Physics for secondary school]. São Paulo: Harbra.

Halliday, M. A. (1985). *An introduction to functional grammar.* London: Edward Arnold.

Joly, M. (1994). *Introduction a l'analyse de l'image* [An Introduction to the Analysis of Images]. Paris: Nathan Editions.

Kearsey, J., & Turner, S. (1999). How useful are the figures in school biology textbooks? *Journal of Biological Education, 33,* 87–94.

Kress, G., Ogborn, J., & Martins, I. (1998). A satellite view of language: Some lessons from science classrooms. *Language Awareness, 7,* 69–89.

Kress, G., & van Leeuwen, T. (1996). *Reading images: The grammar of visual design.* London: Routledge.

Lemke, J. (1998). Multiplying meaning: Visual and verbal semiotics in scientific texts. In J. R. Martin & R. Veel (Eds.), *Reading science,* (pp. 87–113). London: Routledge.

Levie, W. H. (1987). Research on pictures: A guide to the literature. In D. M Willows & H. A. Houghton (Eds.), *The psychology of illustration: I. Basic research* (pp. 1–50). New York: Springer Verlag.

Levie, W. H., & Lentz, R. (1982). Effects of text illustrations: A review of research. *Educational Communication and Technology Journal, 30,* 195–232.

Levin, J. R., Anglin, G. J., & Carney, R. N. (1987). On empirically validating functions of pictures in prose. In D. M. Willows & H. A. Houghton (Eds.), *The psychology of illustration: I. Basic research* (pp. 51–85). New York: Springer Verlag.

Levin, J. R., & Mayer, R. E. (1993). Understanding illustrations in text. In B. Britton, A. Woodward, & M. Binkley (Eds.), *Learning from textbooks: Theory and practice.* Hillsdale, NJ: Lawrence Erlbaum Associates.

Martins, I. (1996). *The earth in space: Children as readers and as makers of scientific images.* Paper presented at I Domains of Literacy Conference. Institute of Education, University of London.

Martins, I., Mortimer, E., Osborne, J., Tsatsarelis, C., & Jimenez Aleixandre, M. P. (2001). Rhetoric and science education. In H. Behrendt, H. Dahncke, R. Duit, W. Gräber, M. Komorek, A. Kross, & P. Reiska (Eds.), *Research in science education—Past, present, and future* (pp. 189–198). Dordrecht, Netherlands: Kluwer Academic.

McDaniel, M. A., & Pressley, M. (Eds.). (.1987). *Imagery and related mnemonic processes: Theories, individual differences and applications.* New York: Springer Verlag.

Ogborn, J., Kress, G., Martins, I., & McGillicuddy, K. (1996). *Explaining science in the classroom.* London: Open University Press.

Olson, T. L. (1996). *The world on paper: The conceptual and cognitive implication of reading and writing.* Cambridge: Cambridge University Press.

Paivio, A. (1971). *Imagery and verbal processes.* Hillsdale, NJ: Lawrence Erlbaum Associates.

Partridge, T. (1992). *Starting science* (Book 3). Oxford, England: Oxford University Press.

Reid, D., & Bevridge, M. (1986). Effects of text illustration on children's learning of a school science topic. *British Journal of Educational Psychology, 56,* 294–303.

Schallert, D. L. (1980). The role of illustrations in reading comprehension. In R. J. Spiro, B. C. Bruce, & W. F. Brewer (Eds.), *Theoretical issues in reading comprehension: Perspectives from cognitive psychology, linguistics, artificial intelligence, and education.* Hillsdale, NJ: Lawrence Erlbaum Associates.

Vézin, J. F., Vézin, L. (1990). *Illustration, schématisation et activité, interprétative* [Illustration, schematization and interpretive activity]. Bulletin de Psychologie, XLI, (386), 655–666.

❧ 5 ❧

Generating and Understanding Qualitative Explanations

Stellan Ohlsson

The University of Illinois at Chicago

Science has a double impact on the human condition. On the one hand, science forms the intellectual basis for technology and thereby extends the range of human action. On the other hand, it reveals to us the way the world works and thereby increases our understanding.

Science carries out the second of these functions by providing us with explanations for otherwise puzzling phenomena and events. The act of generating an explanation is central to the work of professional scientists. It also plays an important role in science education, because the ability to generate an explanation is often taken as a diagnostic sign that a concept or theory has been acquired (Krupa, Selman, & Jaquette, 1985). Understanding explanations generated by others is of course a frequently occurring task for the working scientist, the science learner, and the educated layperson reading about the latest advances in the Sunday newspaper.

Systematic analysis of explanation began with Hempel and Oppenheimer's (1948) now classical claim that an explanation is a deductive argument, a claim that has faded into the background as philosophers have come to emphasize semantic models (Suppe, 1989; P. Thompson, 1989), causal relations (Salmon, 1984, 1998; Sosa & Tooley, 1993) and explanatory practices (Kitcher, 1993). Artificial Intelligence researchers realized early on that expert systems ought to explain their conclusions to their users (Clancey & Shortliffe, 1984) and research in computational linguistics (e.g., Moore & Paris, 1993) and intelligent tutoring systems (e.g., Buchanan, Moore, Carenini, Forsythe, Ohlsson, & Banks, 1995) is aimed at providing computer systems with this capability. To psychologists and educational researchers, explanation is an activity that engages a variety of cognitive processes (C. A. Anderson, Krull, & Weiner, 1996; Graesser & Hemphill, 1991; Krull & C. A. Anderson, 1997; Leake, 1992; Leddo & Abelson, 1986; Ohlsson, 1993; Ohlsson & Hemmerich, 1999; Schank, 1986a, 1986b). In particular, explanatory inferences are crucial for understanding both narrative and expository texts (Graesser, Singer, & Trabasso, 1994; Langston & Trabasso, 1999; Trabasso & van den Broek, 1985). Whether students engage in explanatory activities can determine their success in solving physics problems (Chi, DeLeeuw, Chiu, & LaVancher, 1994; VanLehn & Jones, 1986). Recently, cognitive scientists have turned their attention to the relations between explanation and conceptual combination (Johnson & Keil, 2000) and between the explanations of scientists and everyday explanations in adults and children (Brewer, Chinn, & Samarapungavan, 2000; Gopnik, 2000; Wilson & Keil, 2000).

In spite of these efforts, central questions about the generation and understanding of explanations remain unanswered. What is an explanation? What is the difference between explanations and other types of epistemic discourse such as descriptions and arguments? What are the knowledge structures that underlie explanatory competence? How—by what processes—are such structures applied in the generation and understanding of explanations?

The answers to these questions are important to educators and textbook authors, because one of the functions of science textbooks is to present scientific explanations in a readable and comprehensible manner. Students are expected to read and understand the standard explanations for rainfall, the seasons, biological evolution, geological erosion, and so on. A textbook can present any one of these explanations in many different ways. A better understanding of the act of explaining and the associated cognitive processes can help the textbook writer negotiate the space of possible presentations.

The purpose of this chapter is to put forward a hypothesis about what type of cognitive entity an explanation is and to sketch a model of the cognitive processes involved in the generation and understanding of explanations, with special focus on qualitative explanations in everyday life and in elementary science. The model assumes that the processes involved in the generation and understanding of explanatory discourse are closely related. More precisely, the model assumes that a student cannot fully understand an explanation unless he or she could, in principle, have generated that explanation. The processes involved in generation and understanding are the same, although they are employed differently in the two cases. The model has not yet been implemented in a computer simulation nor subject to strict experimental tests, but even in its current informal stage it provides a useful framework for the analysis of qualitative explanatory discourse.

Evolutionary biology is a rich source of examples of qualitative explanations. The basic question in this domain is, *why did species X evolve trait Y?* or, *how did species X acquire trait Y?* I refer to this as *the phylogenetic question*. There are other types of questions in evolutionary biology; for example, *why is species X distributed geographically in the way it is?* I do not deal with those other questions in this chapter (see Kitcher, 1993, for an extensive discussion of question types in evolutionary biology).

The natural approach to answering the phylogenetic question is to tell a genetic story, a sequence of events through which the relevant trait emerged. To investigate what kind of phylogenetic stories biology novices tell, two groups of undergraduate psychology students, 50 from the University of Pittsburgh and 95 from The University of Illinois at Chicago, were given sheets of paper with a version of the phylogenetic question written across the top and asked to write down their answers. The Pittsburgh participants were asked why dinosaurs became so large and how birds developed flight, whereas the Chicago participants were asked those two questions, plus how tigers got their stripes. Both groups were told that they were free to make plausible assumptions about factual issues (e.g., the climate millions of years ago) and that their task was to invent an explanation that seemed reasonable to themselves. They were given no help or instruction. The two sets of explanations they generated are referred to as *the Pittsburgh corpus* and *the Chicago corpus*. In the following, I draw upon this database to illustrate the theoretical concepts.

THE NATURE OF EXPLANATION

What Are Explanations?

Explanations are answers to questions, particularly questions about why an event happened, why something is the case, and how a particular state of affairs came about or why it persists. Why is water transparent? Why is the egg of the Kiwi bird so large? Why is ocean water salt when lake water is not?

Why did the dinosaurs die out? Why did the Titanic sink? Why are there seasons? Schank (1986a, 1986b) introduced the convenient term *explanation question* to refer to questions of this sort.

When someone explains something to somebody else, the explanation naturally takes the form of a discourse, either speech or text. There are two reasons why we cannot identify the explanation with the discourse. First, one and the same explanation can be stated in different ways. For example, the obvious explanation why an ice cube melted on hot day can be expressed by saying *the temperature was too high, the air was hot,* or any one of the many possible variations of these formulations. These different linguistic forms express the same explanation. Hence, the explanation itself is not identical to any one of those formulations.

Second, explanations are not necessarily communicated to anybody. Consider a scientist who strives to understand a pattern in his or her data. Suppose he or she hits upon a satisfying explanation, but never writes it down nor says it to anybody. (Perhaps the scientist is worried that others will not believe the explanation and think him or her crazy for suggesting it.) This is no doubt a rare event, but there is nothing in the nature of explanation that prevents it from happening. Explanations are perhaps communicated more often than not, but this is a contingent fact about the contexts in which people strive to explain and not a necessary or intrinsic feature of the act of explaining. Hence, explanations cannot be identified with their overt expressions.

These two observations are familiar in the cognitive sciences and there is a standard response: Introduce a distinction between surface structure and deep structure. For purposes of this chapter, I assume that the relevant type of deep structure—the explanation itself—is a propositional knowledge structure in the explainer's memory. An explanatory discourse that expresses that explanation is a particular surface structure, generated from the deep structure through the process of verbalization. Any given deep structure can be expressed in many different surface structures. (This is not the only possible view; see Hilton, 1990, for a treatment that identifies explanations with their expressions in discourse.) For simplicity of expression, the term "explanation" will be used with deliberate ambiguity to refer to either a propositional memory structure or its overt expression in discourse whenever the context shows which meaning is intended.

How Do Explanations Explain?

How do explanations carry out their function? That is, how do they explain? An explanation always refers to some explanatory target. Hempel and

Oppenheimer (1948) introduced the useful term *explanandum* (plural: *explananda*) to refer to that which is to be explained.

I propose that an explanation explains by describing how the explanandum came to be. For example, to explain why the Titanic sank is to describe the relevant sequence of events: the boat was going too fast, the iceberg was not sighted in time, the ship had too much momentum to avoid the iceberg, the collision damaged several sections of the ship below the waterline, and so on. Although this type of genesis is very common, an explanation does not always consist of a causal chain. There are many types of processes by which objects, events, and phenomena came into being. For example, feedback circles cannot be described as causal chains. The central claim is that an explanation describes a genesis (of some kind).

This idea is so important to what follows that it deserves to be enshrined as a principle:

The Fundamental Principle of Explanation: *An explanation explains by describing the genesis of its explanandum.*

According to this view, explanation is a subspecies of description, *contra* attempts by philosophers (Pitt, 1988; Salmon, 1989) and cognitive scientists (Simon, 2000) to distinguish between the two. However, not all descriptions are also explanations, but only those that describe a genesis, that is, how something came to be.

The feeling of understanding that accompanies an explanation derives from the fact that once we have understood and internalized the explanation, we have acquired the ability to think through—reenact in the mind's eye—the process by which the explanandum came about. Some scholars define explanation in terms of this effect on the recipient. For example, Wilson and Keil (2000) characterized an explanation as "*an apparently successful attempt to increase the understanding*" of some phenomenon (p. 89. italics in original). Similarly, according to Brewer et al. (2000) "an explanation provides a conceptual framework (...) that leads to a feeling of understanding in the reader" (p. 280). Both characterizations imply that a putative explanation that fails to enlighten its intended recipient thereby ceases to be an explanation. In contrast , the account proposed here locates explanation-hood in a particular type of content. The question of the effects of a particular explanation on a particular recipient (does it produce understanding or not?) is to be settled empirically. In a later section, I discuss examples of bona fide explanations that fail to explain.

Types of Explananda

It is useful to distinguish between different types of explananda. First, there are *unique events*. The sinking of the Titanic illustrates this category. Unique events happen at a particular place and at a particular time. Second, there are *recurring events*. For example, consider rain. Each rainfall is a unique event, but "rain", when used without reference to time or place, refers to an event type.

The answer to a question like, *why did the Titanic sink?* differs from the answer to a question like, *why does it rain?* in crucial respects. In the case of the Titanic, the explanation has to mention the specifics of that particular catastrophe: the design of the ship, the details of the collision with the iceberg, and so on. It would not suffice to say that when boats become filled with water, they sink.

In the case of rain, the situation is the opposite. To explain why it rains, it is not sufficient to point to the specifics of any particular rainfall such as the particular humidity and temperature at a particular time and in a particular place. Instead, an explanation for the recurrence of rain has to specify the conditions that characterize rainfalls in general. These include a combination of high humidity and a decrease in air temperature. When explaining a unique event, we seek the specifics; when explaining an event type, the generalities.

Unique and recurring events do not exhaust the list of possible types of explananda. Explanation questions can also refer to *transient states* (why do I have a cold?), *permanent states* (why does the moon lack an atmosphere?), *regularities* (why is materia conserved in chemical reactions?) and *absences* (why are there no insects the size of a horse?). However, enough has been said to illustrate that although all explanations describe the genesis of their explananda, explanations nevertheless differ in character depending on the type of explanandum.

Discussion

How general is the concept of an explanation as a description of a genesis? Genetic explanations obviously encompass those explanations that are commonly called "causal" or "mechanistic" as well as some historical explanations. Are all genuine explanations genetic explanations or are there classes of bona fide explanations that fall outside this concept?

Apparent counterexamples are explanations for steady states, e.g., the fact that the moon orbits the earth. In this case, the centerpiece of the explanation is the force that acts on the moon, not the story of how the moon was captured by the gravitational field of the earth in the first place.

However, merely mentioning the force of gravity is not in itself explanatory. In our everyday experience, gravity makes objects fall down, not stay aloft. Hence, the concept of gravity becomes explanatory vis-à-vis the moon's orbit only if it is coupled with a description of the relevant dynamics: The moon is moving in such and such a way and its inertia operates in such and such a way, but because gravity has such and such effects, we get the result that the moon stays in orbit. This dynamic story, I claim, is a description of a genesis. It describes how the moon's orbiting behavior is generated anew at each moment in time.

Other apparent counterexamples are explanations that subsume particular events or event types under general scientific laws without providing a genesis. Salmon (1990, p. 183) has discussed two different explanations for the fact that a balloon moves forward in an airplane cabin during take-off, in contradiction to the intuition that objects are thrown backward. His first explanation focuses on how the inertia of air molecules affects the distribution of air pressure in the cabin when the plane starts moving and how the resulting pressure differential and the collisions between air molecules and the balloon produce the unexpected movement of the latter. His second explanation subsumes this phenomenon under the Einsteinian principle that gravity and acceleration are, in some sense, the same: The balloon moves upward, that is, in the opposite direction of dense objects, under the influence of gravity, so it moves in the opposite direction of dense objects under the influence of acceleration. When the airplane accelerates, dense objects move backward, so the balloon moves forward.

The first of these two putative explanations is a genetic explanation. It describes the successive events that cause the balloon to move forward. The second, I claim, is not an explanation. The statement that gravity and acceleration are the same might be true, but it provides no insight into the balloon's behavior. Our intuitions about this are stronger with respect to simpler examples of subsumption. If someone asks, *Why is it snowing today?* it is not explanatory to answer, *It always snows here this time of the year.* Similarly, to say that all pieces of wood float on water is not an explanatory answer to the question of why a particular piece of wood floats. I believe that this point is general: Subsumption under a general principle is a legitimate and sometimes useful cognitive operation but it is distinct from explanation; see Brewer et al. (2000, p. 293) for a similar point.

There are two other types of discourse that are often called explanations but that fall outside the scope of genetic explanations. They are often called intentional explanations and formal explanations.

An explanation for why a person carried out a particular action typically refers to that person's intentions and beliefs. Why did John mail Bill a birthday card? Perhaps because John intended to make Bill glad and he believed that a card would have this effect. Explanations that refer essentially to intentions have unique features and raise special questions (see, e.g., Dretske, 1988; Leddo & Abelson, 1986; Taylor, 1980).

Intentional explanations are closely related to explanatory inferences generated in the course of reading. Research on the comprehension of narrative texts has established that readers strive for coherence and that they engage in certain types of bridging inferences in order to connect one part of a text with another (Graesser, Singer, & Trabasso, 1994). We can distinguish between two types of explanatory activity during reading. First, readers often have reasons to ask themselves, *why is the author saying this?* That is, what was the author's intention or purpose in including such and such piece of information? Second, readers of narrative texts often have reason to explain to themselves why the characters in a story are acting or speaking the way they do. Because story characters are the creations of authors, these two types of explanatory inferences are closely related. Both are species of intentional explanation. Intentional explanations are not discussed further in this chapter.

Formal explanations also constitute a special case. An explanation for why a particular algebraic formula is correct consists of a proof that derives that formula from other, previously accepted formulas. Although providing such a proof is frequently referred to as explaining the formula, this usage is not consistent with how the term "explanation" is used in this chapter. Proofs establish correctness. They do not describe a genesis. In fact, ideal entities like mathematical formulas do not have a genesis in the same sense as natural objects and events (Ohlsson, 2000), so they cannot be explained in the same sense. Hence, the cognitive processes involved in understanding proofs are not necessarily similar to those involved in understanding qualitative scientific explanations. Formal explanations are not discussed further in this chapter.

In summary, an explanation is a description of the genesis of its explanandum. Hence, explanations are descriptions, but descriptions characterized by a special type of content. Although analyses of particular examples cannot prove that all qualitative explanations are genetic explanations, I believe this to be true. A putative explanation either describes the genesis of its explanandum, or else it is not, in fact, explanatory. Apparent counterexamples are either only apparent (e.g., explanations of regularities) or else not bona fide explanations (e.g., subsumptions). Intentional explanations and formal explanations are qualitatively different from genetic explanations and they do not explain in the same sense.

EXPLANATORY KNOWLEDGE

The acts of generating and understanding explanations draw upon particular types of knowledge structures. The two most important are generative relations and explanation schemas.

Generative Relations

Relations that attribute the existence of an explanandum to the factor or factors that produced it will here be called *generative relations*. Table 5.1 contains a list of English phrases that express generative relations. No attempt is made to define the class of generative relations formally. Intuitively, a generative relation between X and Y indicates that X was instrumental in making Y happen or come about.

The generative relation that has received most attention from scholars is the relation between cause and effect (Sperber, Premack, & Premack, 1995). Since David Hume, philosophers have worried about how, on what grounds, one might validly infer a causal link, as opposed to mere co-occurrence (Sosa, 1993). In psychology, the empirical question of when people infer causal relations as opposed to mere co-occurrence has been the subject of extensive experimental studies (e.g., Einhorn & Hogarth, 1985). Research on discourse comprehension has shown that the causal structure of narratives is a strong determinant of reading times, memory for events in the text and other behavioral variables (Langston & Trabasso, 1999; Trabasso & van den Broek, 1985). Researchers in Artificial Intelligence have developed systems that infer (Pazzani, 1990) or evaluate (Leake, 1992) causal explanations. In contrast, the theory proposed in the present chapter focuses on the cognitive processes involved in generating explanations from already established or inferred relations.

One might argue that X *causes* Y is the only generative relation and that all other phrases in Table 5.1 are nothing but elliptic descriptions of causal relations. For example, X *created* Y might be represented in semantic memory as X *caused Y to come into existence*. This view is consistent with the centrality of causation in many discussions of explanation (e.g., Wilson & Keil, 2000, pp. 105–106).

TABLE 5.1

Some English Verbs That Express Generative Relations

X allowed Y

X brought about Y

X caused Y

X created Y

X enabled Y

X engendered Y

X forced Y

X gave birth to Y

X gave rise to Y

X generated Y

X lead to Y

X originated Y

X produced Y

X was a sufficient condition for Y

However, componential analyses of lexical concepts such as *cause, create,* and so on are frequently unconvincing and difficult to validate empirically. How would we choose between the analysis of X *created* Y into X *caused to come into existence* and the analysis of X *caused* Y into X *created the conditions for* Y? On pain of circularity, both analyses cannot be valid. Fodor (1998) has recently presented philosophical arguments to the effect that this problem is ill formed, because most lexical concepts are atomic; that is, they lack any componential structure. Finally, some generative relations are not naturally explicated in terms of cause and effect. For example, X *gave birth to* Y does not have the same meaning as X *caused* Y *to be born.* A physician who speeds up the delivery of a baby with a drug can serve as X in the second formulation but not in the first.

The question whether there are multiple generative relations or a single generative relation that appears in many linguistic disguises has to be resolved empirically. In the meantime, I adopt the working hypothesis that there is a repertoire of distinct generative relations. Causation is one of them, but it has no special status.

Generative relations are the atomic building blocks of explanations. A list of the events preceding Y is not in and of itself an explanation for Y. To make it an explanation, we must attribute Y to those preceding events. That is, we have to specify the manner in which the preceding events were instrumental in bringing about Y. This is the central feature that distinguishes explanations from (other types of) descriptions.

Simple explanations use a single generative relation. For example, *it was hot* is one possible answer to the question, *why did the ice cube melt?* This explanation relies on a generative relation that we can symbolize as:

heat → melting,

where the arrow is shorthand for *was instrumental in bringing about.* Many explanations in everyday life are of this single-relation sort: Why did John fail the examination? He did not study enough (ignorance → failure). Why did the car slide off the road? Because the road was slippery (slippery → no road grip). Why is the flight delayed? The weather is bad (bad weather → delayed departure).

For an explanatory discourse to work, that is, to be explanatory, the relevant generative relation must first have been accepted by both the explainer and the explainee. For example, the explanation, *the Titanic sank, because it hit an iceberg* is explanatory for author and readers of this article because we have already accepted

collision → damage

as a valid generative relation. Being accepted, it need not itself be explained. Similarly, to explain why my car did not start this morning by referring to the lack of fuel in the tank one must first know that cars do not run without fuel. Because that relation is indeed part of common sense, the description of my empty fuel tank is a satisfactory explanation. Nothing more need to be said; in fact, the less said, the better.

In contrast, *because he drank a glass of water* is not an explanatory answer to the question, *why did John get sick?* because few people other than sailors believe that drinking water makes you sick. That is, few people accept the putative generative relation

water → disease.

Although *John became sick because he drank a glass of water* has the surface form of an explanation—indeed, the same surface form as *the ice cube melted because the air was hot*—the former is not explanatory. It provides no understanding of how John's ailment came about, because we find no connection between water and disease in our semantic memory. The natural response is, *what do you mean?* or, *how did the water make him sick?* These requests for clarification show that the explanation does not work; that is, it does not produce comprehension of why John became sick. The lack of explanatory power for a particular recipient is a fact about the relation between the explanation and that recipient's background knowledge, not a property of the explanation per se. The very same discourse might be quite explanatory to someone who knows that the stream John drank from is polluted.

I refer to generative relations that have already been accepted before they are used in an explanation as *primitive* with respect to that explanation. The relation *collision causes damage* is primitive in this sense for most people, but *water causes disease* is not. The latter example illustrates that it is possible for the producer and the recipient of an explanation to disagree about which generative relations can be taken as primitive and hence about whether an explanation is explanatory or even comprehensible.

Generative relations are not primitive in any absolute sense but only relative to a particular explanation. Every causal link can, in principle, be analyzed into more fine grained causal interactions. A physicist would have to write many pages to exhaustively explain exactly how a collision causes damage to a material entity like a ship, but an analysis of this sort is not necessary for that relation to be generative. Most of us understand perfectly well that collisions produce damage even though we cannot unpack this relation into interactions between elementary particles. Nor does the proper analysis have to be known by anybody for a generative relation to be explanatory. Statements about collisions fulfilled explanatory functions long before physicists discovered elementary particles. Explanations are frequently constructed by "a skyhook procedure from the top down" (Simon, 2000, p. 35).

If explanations are built out of generative relations, then it ought to be possible to identify which such relations are embedded in students' spontaneous explanations. Furthermore, we ought to be able to hypothesize some context in which the students would have had an opportunity to acquire those relations.

As illustration, consider the following two explanations of the evolution of flight:

> *Before a bird could fly, it was the prey of a carnivorous predator. While running away from its adversary, it would flap its upper appendages, strengthening its muscles over the generations. Eventually, the muscles broadened & one day, while fleeing, the animal (flapping its wings) took flight.* (Subject No. 85, Chicago sample)

Birds began to fly because they needed to get away from predators. They started out running but when they ran, the moved their wings developing the muscles. Eventually they flew from a running start because their wings had strong muscles to use. (Subject No. 98, Chicago sample)

These two discourse samples express the same explanation for the emergence of flight: In their need to escape predators, proto-birds exercised their proto-wings until they became large enough to support flight. Because the explanation is biologically inaccurate, we can be reasonably certain that it was never taught to these students. If so, then it was not retrieved from memory but constructed out of available generative relations in response to the explanation question. It is not difficult to identify the two central relations:

attack → escape;

physical activity → anatomical build-up.

Both of these relations are of course readily available in the popular culture. That escape might be the response to attack is frequently illustrated on movie screens and the fact that activity builds muscle makes the cash registers ring in athletic clubs. The students must have had numerous opportunities to acquire these generative relations. The prevalence of these relations in the surrounding culture helps explain why the two explanations are so similar even though they are free constructions (in the sense of being unresponsive to the biological facts of the matter). The two students drew upon similar repertoires of generative relations.

In short, generative relations are the building blocks of explanations. In order to be an explanation for some explanandum Y, a description of the history of Y must include relations that attribute the appearance of Y to one or more producing factors. A putative explanation is only explanatory for a person P, if P accepts the relevant generative relations. Accepted relations are primitive relative to a particular explanation or explanatory context. A generative relation that is primitive in one explanation E_1 might be the subject of analysis in another explanation E_2, but the existence of such an analysis is not a necessary condition for the relation to fulfill its explanatory function in E_1.

Explanation Schematas

Even though many everyday explanations are based on a single generative relation, most interesting explanations, and almost all explanations in science, are more complicated. They coordinate multiple generative relations. For example, consider the question and answer pair:

Q: *Why was the flight delayed out of Chicago?*

A: *The airplane arrived late due to bad weather in the east.*

This explanation coordinates at least three generative relations: First, that bad weather at an airport can delay a take-off. Second, that late take-off from the point of departure will lead to a late arrival at the destination. Finally, that late arrival of an airplane will lead to a delayed take-off of that airplane. Using the arrow notation, we can summarize this explanation as follows:

bad weather → delayed take-off;

delayed take-off → late arrival;

late arrival → delayed departure.

To most frequent flyers, these generative relations are only too well-known and accepted as primitive in the context of air traffic.

The *bad weather elsewhere* explanation is not an explanation for a unique event, a particular flight that happened once in the history of aviation. Flight delays due to bad weather elsewhere happen all the time, and for each such event the explanation is similar. The only components that differ from instance to instance are the particular locations, flight numbers, arrival and departure times, and so on. All *bad weather elsewhere* explanations share the same structure. That is, they are built out of the same set of generative relations and those relations are coordinated in the same way. The *bad weather elsewhere* explanation is both *complex* (multiple generative relations) and *abstract* (the relations are specified but the relata are not; Ohlsson, 1993).

Similarly, the standard scientific explanation for rain draws upon several generative relations: Sunlight on water causes evaporation, which causes high humidity; wind transports humid air masses to other regions; a drop in temperature causes precipitation. The particular way in which these generative relations are assembled is what makes this description an explanation for rainfall. Like flight delay, rainfall is an event type and all explanations for particular rainfalls share the same structure. The details that vary from instance to instance include the particular locations, specific values for humidity and temperature, and so on.

We can summarize these observations by saying that the *bad weather elsewhere* and the *evaporation-transportation* explanations are not explanations but *explanation schemas,* a concept that plays a central role in many accounts of explanation (Kitcher, 1993; Krull & C. A. Anderson, 1997; Schank, 1986a, 1986b). A schema encodes the structure shared by a set of explanations. The structure is defined by the set of generative relations and the way in which they are combined. A single generative relation is a minimal schema. The concept of an explanation schema implies that explanation types are not merely in the eye of the beholder. That is, similar explanations do not merely look similar to a recipient. They are similar because they are, in fact, generated from one and the same knowledge structure.

In logical terms, particular explanations are instances of their parent schemas. The difference is that an explanation names specific objects or events where the schema has variables. For example, the *evaporation-transportation* schema states that some humid air mass is transported some distance by winds, but a particular explanation for a given rainfall in location L at time t has to fill in the particular air mass, the particular wind and the particular route that air mass was transported before precipitation occurred. Constructing explanation schemas for rain and wind is what meteorologists do; filling in the variables in those schemas is what weather forecasters do.

Explanation schemas are not theories or propositions. Although a particular explanation is subject to the same criteria of correctness as other types of descriptions, the uninstantiated schema is itself neither true nor false (Ohlsson, 1993, 1999). A schema is a recipe for how to construct a particular type of explanation. It does not, by itself, assert anything about the world. In particular, a schema does not assert that any particular event is an instance of itself. For example, the *bad weather elsewhere* explanation does not contain an implicit claim that all flight delays are of this sort; it merely states that this is one type of explanation for flight delay and it may or may not be the correct one in any particular case. Indeed, a schema need not have any instances at all. It is possible to imagine a world in which there is no bad weather and in which the *bad weather elsewhere* explanation consequently has no instances. Even in that world, that schema is not invalid or false, only useless.

The nonpropositional character of schemas is central for a correct account of the relations between multiple schemas for one and the same event type. Alternative schemas are not mutually exclusive in the same sense as alternative theories (Ohlsson, 1993, 2000). A flight that is delayed for some other reason than bad weather (e.g., a tardy pilot), does not prove that the *bad weather elsewhere* schema is invalid, only that the latter does not apply to that particular case. Bad weather and tardy pilot represent two explanation types, both of which are potentially valid with respect to any particular flight delay.

Explanations are mutually exclusive—a given flight is, in fact, delayed for some reason or another—but their parent schemas are not.

There are many different schemas that apply to flight delays, over and above bad weather and tardy pilots: a malfunctioning airplane, management problems, a bomb scare, another airplane blocking the gate, and so on. I suggest that this situation is typical. A person should not be conceptualized as having a single explanation schema for a given explanandum. Instead, a person is likely to possess a *repertoire* of schemas for a given type of event (Ohlsson, 1999).

What repertoire of schemas underpins novice explanations in evolutionary biology? Consider the following three explanations of how the tiger acquired its stripes:

> I would assume that the tiger got its black stripes from some kind of biological cross between lion and black panther. Because of the genetic combination some of the characteristics of black panther blended with some characteristics of the lion's genes. (Student No. 55, Chicago corpus)

[handwritten note: great]

How did this student come up with this biologically incorrect explanation? One possibility is that this student has a *crossbreeding schema*, perhaps acquired in the context of the selective breeding of farm animals, pets, or racehorses. Alternatively, it is possible that the student drew upon a more abstract *blending schema*: Combine two objects to produce a new object with properties that are intermediate between the properties of the two original objects. Opportunities to acquire this schema are abundant in everyday activities involving colors, substances, spices, fashion styles, and so on. The level of abstraction cannot be resolved without additional data.

Another student produced a very different explanation for the stripes of the tiger:

> The tiger was originally all black. After thousands of years, the black color of the tiger's outer body began to fade and continued to fade for generations. The black faded into the stripes we see on the tiger today. Generations from now, we may see no stripes on the tiger. (Student No. 32, Chicago corpus)

This explanation instantiates a *fading schema*: Over time, the strength of a property P spontaneously decreases. This process is quite different from crossbreeding. Once again, it is not clear without further evidence at what level of abstraction this schema is encoded in the student's memory: Does it apply to colors only, or to properties in general? The generative relation that underpins this explanation, the passage of time → disappearance,

is not primitive for biologists (nor for the present author), but daily life provides many instances. A photograph left too long in sunlight is one of them. As a third example, consider the following explanation for tiger stripes:

> *Tigers got their black stripes because of maybe of the environment they lived in. They needed their black stripes to camouflage in their environment.* (Student No. 5, Chicago corpus)

This explanation could be interpreted as an instantiation of the Darwinian schema of natural selection: Variation in stripes leads to differential success in hunting due to the camouflage effect, and hence to differential reproductive success. However, this interpretation assumes that the recorded discourse is abbreviated. In the absence of independent evidence that this student understood the Darwinian theory, we have to consider the possibility that the underlying generative relation directly links needs and anatomical features:

feature X would benefit species S → feature X emerges.

This putative generative relation is famously but controversially rejected as nonprimitive by many biologists. Explanations based on this relation are branded as "teleological" and there is a long tradition of scholarship in biology and philosophy that attempts to understand the specific features of teleological explanations and their proper role, if any, in biology (Mayr, 1982). One aspect of Charles Darwin's accomplishment was to provide a form of explanation for biological evolution that does not involve teleology in any essential way. However, biology novices might nevertheless operate with this generative relation.

Eight Novice Schemas for Evolutionary Biology

The fact that three students generated three qualitatively different explanations for the same explanandum illustrates the existence of multiple schemas that are potentially applicable to the phylogenetic question. To provide a broader view of the novice repertoire in this domain, the two corpora of explanations were coded for eight schemas that were identified in a preliminary scanning of the corpus:

✓1. *Environmentalism.* Traits develop when the environment provides a demand or an opportunity. One student exemplified explanation via environmental demand by saying that the ancestors to birds had to migrate to survive; hence, they had no choice but to develop flight. Another student exemplified explanation via environmental opportunity by saying that dinosaurs had no competition for food, and hence could eat unlimited amounts; that is why they grew so large.

✓ 2. *Survival.* Both the relevant trait and its opposite were once present in the species, but all members without the trait died. One student exemplified this type of explanation by saying that there were once both large and small dinosaurs, but all the small ones were eaten; hence, only large ones remained. (In previous reports, we have sometimes referred to this type of explanation as *static selection.*)

✓ 3. *Creationism.* Animals were created by a deity with the characteristics they have today. For example, dinosaurs were created large so as to flatten the earth in preparation for the coming of humans.

✓ 4. *Training.* Traits are caused by the activity of the organism. For example, birds flapped their proto-wings until they grew large enough to support flight.

✓ 5. *Mutationism.* The trait suddenly appeared in a single organism. For example, due to a random genetic event, one day a bird was born with wings.

✓ 6. *Mentalism.* Animals decide, discover, learn, or are taught new behaviors and traits. For example, a bird discovered that it could fly and taught its offspring.

✓ 7. *Crossbreeding.* Traits arise via interbreeding between species. For example, a black panther and a tiger without stripes mated and produced a tiger with stripes.

✓ 8. *Dissemination.* Organisms with the trait gradually increased in numbers until they replaced those without. For example, in every generation there were more and more tigers with stripes.

There are other types of explanations in the data (e.g., see the fading explanation quoted earlier), but the eight just summarized were selected for coding because the preliminary scan suggested that they occurred repeatedly. All explanations were coded by two coders. The coders were given a definition and two examples of each of the eight explanation types. They went through cycles of coding examples, discussing disagreements and coding additional examples until 85% of their codes were in agreement. They then coded the entire material independently of each other. The author arbitered any remaining disagreements.

The coders were instructed to look for expressions of the eight explanation types, as opposed to classify each answer into a single type. Consequently, an answer could be scored as providing evidence for more than one explanation type.

The frequency of each explanation type in each corpus is shown in Fig. 5.1. To facilitate comparison between the two unequal-sized corpora, the raw frequencies have been converted to proportions. That is, a value of .40 for explanation type X means that 40% of the explanations in the relevant corpus were coded as containing content consistent with that explanation type.

The eight explanation types were applied with varying frequency, but there is a rough correspondence between the two corpora: A type that is frequent in one corpus tends to be frequent in the other corpus also. The distribution in Fig. 5.1 is a distribution of explanations, not of students. Sixty-five percent of the students in the Pittsburgh group and 43% of the Chicago students used two or more explanation types. Creationism, Lamarckianism,

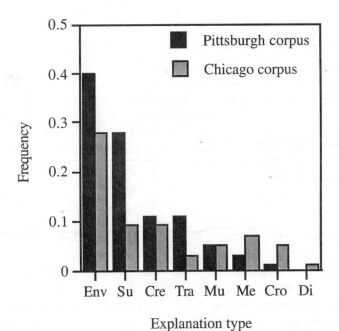

FIG. 5.1. Frequency of eight explanation types in two corpora of novice biology explanations, expressed as proportions of the number of explanations in each corpus. Env = environmentalism; Su = survival; Cre = creationsim; Tra = training; Mu = mutationism; Me = mentalism; Cro = crossbreeding; Di = dissemination.

and teleological thinking are often claimed in the science education literature to be the most common misconceptions of biology novices (Bishop &
C. Anderson, 1990; Brumby, 1984; Demastes, Settlage, & Good, 1995;
Ferrari & Chi, in press; Lawson & L. Thompson, 1988; Samarapungavun &
Wiers, 1997; Settlage, 1994; Tamir & Zohar, 1991). However, the latter two
were not, in fact, dominant in these corpora. In the Pittsburgh corpus, training (Lamarckianism) is fourth from the top in frequency; in the Chicago
corpus, seventh. There are other non-Darwinian explanation types (e.g.,
mutationism, mentalism, crossbreeding) that are as frequent or more frequent. However, the most common type of explanation did indeed link the
organism's needs—as determined by its environment—and the appearance
of anatomical traits to satisfy that need. The central point for present purposes is that the data provide evidence for a repertoire of explanation
schemas in novices who have had no reason to reflect on possible explanations for biological evolution.

Summary

There are two types of knowledge items involved in explanation: generative relations and explanation schemas. A generative relation is a relation that attributes the origin or emergence of some entity Y (object,
event, state of affairs, etc.) to some other entity or factor X. Different
generative relations specify the different manners in which X can be instrumental in bringing about Y. The presence of generative relations is
the central characteristic that distinguishes explanations from other
types of descriptions.

An explanation schema consists of multiple generative relations. A single generative relation is a minimal schema. A schema is a template or a
recipe for how to construct an explanation of a particular type; it is not a
theory. Schemas are not mutually exclusive, even though their instances
usually are. Different instances of a particular event type can have different causal etiologies and hence require different explanations. As a consequence, people typically have a repertoire of alternative schemas for each
common type of event. In particular, the students who participated in our
studies possessed a repertoire of schemas that they see as relevant for explaining the emergence of new behaviors and traits in the course of biological evolution. These schemas are based on generative relations that can
readily be identified and that are prevalent components of contemporary
Western culture. There is no reason to believe the situation is different in
other domains of elementary science.

THE PROCESSES OF EXPLANATION

A known answer to an explanation question can be retrieved from memory and verbalized like any other knowledge structure. Consider a science teacher who repeats the *evaporation-transportation* explanation for rainfall to new groups of students every year. In that case, the explanation is not constructed anew each time but is retrieved from memory. There is no reason to believe that this process operates according to other laws than those of memory retrieval in general: If dormant for any length of time, the probability of retrieval will diminish according to a negatively accelerated function; interference will produce intrusion errors; and so on. Because these processes are not unique to explanation, the case of recalling a previously constructed explanation is not considered further here.

Instead, the following sections focus on the generation of a new explanation in response to an explanation question and on the comprehension of an unfamiliar explanatory discourse generated by someone else. I proceed on the assumption that generation and understanding are closely related. A person cannot understand an explanatory discourse unless he or she could, in principle, have generated that discourse. The key question in both generation and understanding are which generative relations and which explanatory schemas either the producer or consumer of an explanation have available in memory. The presence of a particular generative relation might bias the generation of an explanation; its absence might interfere with understanding. Memory retrieval re-enters the picture in the context of access to the previously learned relations and schemas.

Activating Generative Relations

Consider the following question: Why do squirrels survive in large numbers in city parks, even though other mammals are absent or at least rare? I do not know the correct answer, but a few minutes of reflection generated two possible explanations:

Squirrels, unlike many other small mammals, can find food in city parks. Squirrels are omnivores, so they can feed themselves almost regardless of which types of plants and flowers humans decide to plant in the park. Nuts, if any, are usually not harvested by city dwellers so they are available. Other small mammals might not have this advantage, at least not to the same degree.

An alternative explanation is that squirrels rely on escape as their main defensive strategy. This strategy works in city parks, because the open lawns enable fast running and the trees provide safe havens. Alternative protection strategies do not work as well. For example, it is difficult to hide in a city park, because the bushes are scattered. To stand and fight is also unworkable, because animals that harm or threaten children or pets would soon be removed by the park authorities.

How did I generate these explanations? Not being a biologist, I could not retrieve them from memory. Never having asked myself a question of the general type, *why does species X survive in city parks?* I did not possess a relevant schema. Instead, the question initiated a search through memory for factors that determine the survival of animals. Like other competent adults, I of course know that food and defense are such factors.

Generalizing the example, we can describe the construction of a new single-relation explanation as a form of means–ends analysis: The explanandum is matched against the right-hand side of generative relations in order to identify factors that might produce the explanandum. In this case, the explanandum was survival, so the two relations that matched included:

food → survival;

protection → survival.

Once at least one relevant generative relation has been found, its left-hand side is matched against the facts of the case to verify that it is satisfied. In this case, this led me to consider whether parks provide food for squirrels (but not for other small mammals), and whether parks enable squirrels to defend themselves (better than other small mammals). Once thought of, these possibilities are quickly seen to be plausible, given common sense about parks. In short, single-relation explanations can be generated by matching the explanandum against the right-hand side of generative relations and then matching the left-hand side of those relations to the context of the explanandum.

Assembling Generative Relations

Many explanation questions cannot be answered on the basis of a single generative relation. As soon as we look outside the set of common everyday events, it is unlikely that we already possess a single relation that fully explains the explanandum. If that is the case (and if there is no prior schema that fits), then the generation of an explanation becomes a search through the space of possible combinations of the available generative relations.

As an example of a complex explanation that was almost certainly assembled in response to our explanation question, consider the following answer to the tiger question:

> Originally, tigers or those that are clearly ancestors of today's tigers were bright orange or tan in color. As changes in the earth's axis occurred, places inhabited by tigers such as Burma and Thailand became tropical in climate. Lush flora developed along with a host of other predators that intruded upon land formerly controlled by tigers. As competition increased, certain species developed camouflage and other hunting tactics. Tigers naturally became darker in color, in order to hide from their prey. (Student No. 62, Chicago corpus)

In this explanation, the student begins by linking astronomy and climate:

shift in axis → hotter climate.

We can guess where the student acquired this particular relation: Speculations about links between astronomical events and climate changes have been discussed in the popular science literature. The student then links the hotter climate to plant growth:

hot climate → lush plant growth.

There is little mystery about where this relation comes from. Household plants and movie jungles both illustrate this generative relation. The better supply of plants yields competition:

lush flora → stiff competition.

This is somewhat paradoxical, because lusher flora meant more food. Presumably, the student is using the idea that animals migrated into the area with more abundant food, a subschema with its own acquisition history. Finally, the student claims that the stiffer competition "naturally" generated an anatomical trait that allowed the tiger to deal with it:

stiffer competition → better camouflage.

This is the teleological relation that also shows up in other explanations quoted in this chapter. It provides a direct link, as it were, between an organism's need and transformations in its anatomy that help fulfill that need. It is unlikely that this student was ever taught this particular explanation, but it is likely that he had had multiple opportunities to acquire its components. We can be reasonably certain that he assembled these four generative relations online, as it were, in response to the explanation question.

As a second and amusing example of the assembly of a novel and complex explanation, consider the question, *how could dragons fly with their large bodies and small wings?* Because the dragon is a fantasy creature, the reader is unlikely to have asked him or herself this question. Consider the following answer, proposed in Peter Dickinson's (1979) remarkable book, *The Flight of Dragons*:

> *Dragons were lighter than air flyers. Their big bodies contained a large cavity with hydrogen gas, evolved from the digestive system of the ancestor species. The walls of the cavity consisted of the exposed inner sides of their broad ribs and acid was secreted from glands—originally digestive glands—clustered along the spine. As the acid poured down the exposed ribs, it interacted with the calcium in the rib bones to produce hydrogen gas. When a dragon wanted to descend, it vented some of the gas by burning it via a chemical ignition mechanism located in the throat. That is why dragons breathed fire when descending on their prey.*

This intriguing explanation makes use of well-known and factually correct generative relations from chemistry (acid does interact with calcium to produce hydrogen), physics (bodies that are lighter than air do indeed soar), physiology (digestive glands do secrete acids), and biology (natural selection does indeed tend to assign new functions to old structures). In creating this explanation, Dickinson (1979) had to activate these pieces of prior knowledge and assemble them into this intriguing configuration.

In short, when an explanation question is unfamiliar enough so that no prior schema is sufficient to answer it, a new explanation can be generated by activating (retrieving) and assembling available generative relations. Assembly is a bottom-up process in the sense that the raw materials are the individual generative relations, minimal units, and the outcome is the explanation, a larger structure. Assembly can be conceptualized as a search through the space of possible combinations of individual generative relations, as long as we keep in mind that such a search need not be sequential (Holyoak & Thagard, 1989).

Articulating a Schema

Let us suppose that the explainer already has an explanation schema with a right-hand side that matches the explanandum. In this case, the process of constructing an explanation can be expected to be quite different. What is needed in this case is to work out the application of the relevant schema vis-à-vis the case at hand. I refer to this as *articulating* the schema (Ohlsson, 1992; Ohlsson & Lehtinen, 1997; Regan & Ohlsson, 1999).

At its simplest, the articulation process requires nothing but the replacement of variables with constants. Consider once more the *bad weather elsewhere* explanation for flight delays:

bad weather at X → flight Y delayed at X;

flight Y delayed from X → flight Y delayed arrival at Z;

flight Y delayed arrival at Z → delayed departure from Z.

Suppose that flight ABC123 originates in Pittsburgh, but is showing a delay in taking off from Chicago. To generate an explanation for a delay in flight ABC123 out of Chicago, we substitute ABC123 for Y, Pittsburgh for X, and Chicago for Z, thus creating an instance of the schema that is specific to that particular instance. This process is not complicated and easily accomplished with standard pattern-matching algorithms such as the RETE networks (Forgy, 1982), Mac/Fac (Forbus, Gentner, & Law, 1995), or algorithms for constraint relaxation (Holyoak & Thagard, 1989).

Simple schema articulation is evident in the following series of explanations, all produced by one and the same person (Student No. 73 in the Chicago corpus):

Dinosaur Question:

The explanation for why some species of dinosaurs became so gigantic was due to the diet of most dinosaurs. Most dinosaurs [sic] diet at the time was plants and tree leaves. The problem was that none of the dinosaurs could reach and eat the tree leaves. Through evolution the dinosaurs became gigantic so that they can eat the leaves and mainly for survival.

Tiger Question:

The black stripes on a tiger were necessary for survival. The black stripes on a tiger aids it in camouflaging itself during hunting of other animals. From another animals perspective the black stripes look like tall grass.

Bird Question:

Birds have always been prey to other animals, so through evolution they developed the art to fly as a defense mechanism to get away from their natural predators.

In each case, this student explained the relevant anatomical trait by specifying some way in which that trait increases the animals' probability of survival. What differs from explanation to explanation is merely the type of advantage (longer reach, camouflage, escape). These explanations are articulations of the teleological relation introduced in a previous section: When animals need a trait to survive, that trait emerges.

However, schema articulation is not always that simple. For example, consider the following explanation question: *Why do bacterial diseases become resistant to antibiotics?* This question has a Darwinian answer: A disease is a population of bacteria; when an antibiotic enters the environment of that population, that is, the patient's body, there is a severe selective pressure on that population, and it consequently undergoes rapid evolutionary changes. If there are any bacteria left alive at the end of the so-called cure, those bacteria are highly likely to have higher than average resistance to the antibiotic; when those survivors reproduce, they produce a generation of bacteria that has higher rate of survival through the next dose; this process continues until there is a novel, resistant strain.

To generate this explanation, a person has to articulate the Darwinian explanation schema in unfamiliar ways. First, laypeople without medical training do not usually think of bacteria as animals or organisms. Not everyone knows that bacteria reproduce and pass on their genes to their offspring. Second, it is counterintuitive to think of a person's body as an environment, even though that is what it is for the microbes that live in it. Third, we usually think of evolution as a progressive process that produces positive outcomes: animals that are more complex, better adapted, more intelligent, and so forth. But we naturally think of bacteria becoming resistant to medicine as a negative process. Hence, fusing the two in the mind is also counterintuitive.

Another striking example of a nonobvious articulation of natural selection is Gould's (1991, chap. 7) explanation for why the Kiwi bird lays such a large egg. It turns out that the Kiwi bird, unlike most animal species, is descendent from an ancestor species with a larger body. Something exerted selective pressure toward smaller body size. Furthermore, it turns out that, in general, egg size increases with increasing body size at a slower rate within than across bird species. Consequently, consistent selection in favor of the smallest birds in a bird population will eventually produce a bird species with a disproportionately large egg. This interesting explanation illustrates not only that schema articulation can be a creative process—how many people would have thought of Gould's explanation?—but also that schema articulation sometimes involves complicated interactions between the structure of a schema and domain-specific facts.

Scientific progress can consist precisely in discovering such non-standard articulations of an established explanation schema. It took physicists almost 200 years to work out the more complicated articulations of the Newtonian schema. In the latter, physical phenomena are explained on the basis of changes in velocity and acceleration as a function of the forces material objects exert on each other. The application of this schema to pendulums and planets was relatively straightforward, but articulating it vis-à-vis light and radio waves turned out to be complicated enough to force the development of alternative schemas.

In short, when a suitable schema is available, an explanation can be generated by articulating it, that is, by working out how each of its components is to be instantiated vis-à-vis the problem at hand. In the case of routine explanation, this process requires nothing more than replacing variables with constants. Schank (1986a, 1986b) emphasized that this seemingly simple process can generate creative explanations when the constellation of variable bindings is novel. In more complicated cases, finding the right mapping between the schema and the explanandum can require significant cognitive work (Ohlsson, 1992).

Resolving Conflicts — Choices

If people possess a repertoire of explanation schemas, it follows logically that both generation and understanding of an explanation must involve a process of choice: If there are multiple relevant schemas, which of them will control generation or understanding? Although it is convenient to conceptualize conflict resolution as a separate stage following memory retrieval, the boundary between retrieval and selection is more conceptual than real. People act on what comes to mind.

Memory retrieval has been the subject of intense research over a long period of time and there are multiple competing theories. For present purposes, I adopt the view incorporated into the ACT–R theory (J. R. Anderson & Lebiere, 1998). According to this theory, the activation and utilization of a knowledge structure is controlled by two quantities: *strength*, which is a measure of the structure's past usefulness, and *activation*, which is a measure of its relevance in the current context. Relevance, in turn, is a function of connections to other currently active knowledge structures. The choice of knowledge structure is a probabilistic function of these two quantities. The formal details of the theory can be ignored here (see J. R. Anderson & Lebiere, 1998, chap. 3).

Suppose that each student in the present study possessed a schema repertoire that included at least some of the eight schemas described in previous sections. What will happen when those students encounter our explanation questions?

The questions will cause activation to spread to related knowledge structures and a more or less implicit choice will occur. If there are multiple relevant schemas and if the choice is probabilistic and in part a function of relevance to the specific concepts mentioned in the question, there is no reason to expect a student to be consistent across a series of questions. Instead, we should expect different questions to pull out, as it were, different schemas from the student's memory.

This effect can be illustrated by considering the answers to the dinosaur question produced by Students No. 55, 32, and 5, the three students whose tiger explanations were analyzed in a previous section. First, consider the student who explained the tiger's stripes via crossbreeding. His or her explanation of why the dinosaurs became so large is as follows:

> I think that some species of dinosaurs became so gigantic because of the warm climate. Many other animals back then were gigantic too. I think because of the pleasant temperatures dinosaurs could develop very well. It was the temperature, very cold temperature, that cause dinosaurs to go extinct. Their bodies were mainly dependent of high, warm temperatures. (Student No. 55, Chicago corpus)

In contrast to the crossbreeding explanation that this subject produced for the tiger's stripes (see the previous section), this explanation relies on the putative generative relation:

warm environment → growth in size.

Student No. 32, on the other hand, derived the dinosaur's size from their own behavior:

> Dinosaurs who existed at the period of time had no competition for food source, therefore some species of dinosaur who eat as much food as they want to without any other animal stopping it. This led to the gigantic size of some dinosaurs. (Student No. 32, Chicago corpus)

This explanation is quite different from the *fade from black* explanation that this student produced in response to the tiger question (see previous section). The generative relation used here,

food → body size,

is of course very prevalent in the popular culture. It invariably appears on the front covers of monthly magazines.

Finally, we can compare Student No. 5's teleological explanation for the tiger's stripes (see previous section) with the following competition between the overeating and good environment explanations for the size of dinosaurs:

> Dinosaurs became so gigantic because all that they would eat is water and grass, which there was a lot available. Another reason that they might be gigantic is there were no cars, and therefore no pollution—clean air. Maybe its [sic] because there were no humans around and they were gigantic because there was so much space—no humans, buildings, etc. (Student No. 5, Chicago corpus)

In short, neither of these three subjects produced the same explanation to the tiger question as they did to the dinosaur question. The two explananda, *stripes* and *large body*, do not match the output parts of the same schemas and relations; hence, different knowledge structures win out during conflict resolution.

Probabilistic conflict resolution among items in the schema repertoire is sometimes visible within a single explanation. This is illustrated by the following answer to the dinosaur question by student No. 19 in the Chicago corpus:

> Well, maybe one of the reasons is that the environment that time was different for every species. The gigantic dinosaurs maybe were born with some large genes and that may be why there are some many different types of dinosaurs. The world then was not filled with pollution like today so maybe the environment overall was better for these animals. They could have breathed cleaner air, and that may contribute to the large size of them. There were also a lot of different plants back then that provided the dinosaurs the food. Maybe the ones who didn't get as much food didn't grow as big as the others. There were probably limited amounts of plants around for all those dinosaurs, so maybe the aggressive ones had a better chance of eating more and becoming bigger in size. (Student No. 19, Chicago corpus)

This discourse expresses at least two separate explanations. First, the student proposes that the environment was different in the past. In particular, the air was less polluted and this enabled growth. Second, some dinosaurs ate more than others, so they grew larger. These two explanations draw upon two familiar generative relations:

healthy environment → growth;

large amounts of food → growth;

In addition, there is a hint in the second sentence of a third explanation based on the idea that the large dinosaurs had "large genes." That is, that the large body size was a genetic effect of some kind. However, this idea is not clearly stated.

These generative relations must have been activated more or less in parallel to be so interleaved in the resulting discourse: Sentence 1 states the environmental theme; sentence 2 the genetic theme; sentence 3 returns to the environmental theme; sentence 5 bridges the gap between the environment idea and the food idea. There is no sign that the student regarded these different explanations as incompatible with each other. This is consistent with the idea that schemas are not theories and do not encode beliefs or assertions but are templates for the generation of discourse. The detailed and deliberate processes of evaluation included in the computer model by Leake (1992) appear to be absent from this student's cognition.

In summary, the existence of a repertoire of alternative explanation schemas necessitates an element of choice in the generation of explanations. Current theories of memory retrieval and conflict resolution emphasize the probabilistic nature of these processes. Consequently, there is little reason to expect a person to be consistent in his or her explanations across seemingly similar explanation questions. Different combinations of content words in a question will distribute activation over memory in different ways, and as a consequence different explanation schemas will be chosen to control the generation of the answers to those questions. The two corpora of novice biology explanations analyzed here contain clear examples of such within-individual variations.

Summary

The main processes involved in generating and understanding explanations are summarized in Fig. 5.2. First, the relevant generative relations have to be activated (retrieved). This process can proceed means–ends fashion, by matching the explanandum against the output sides of particular generative relations. For simple explanations that require a single generative relation, matching that relation to the facts of the case is sufficient. This is the routine explanatory activity that characterizes most of everyday life. As Wilson and Keil (2000) emphasized, such single-relation explanations are quite shallow.

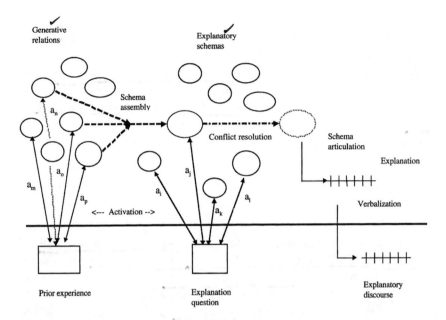

FIG. 5.2.   Cognitive processes involved in explanation.

Second, when a single generative relation is not sufficient, the explainer must assemble multiple generative relations into a new configuration. Both generation and understanding is blocked if the requisite generative relations are not available in memory. Unlike the theory proposed by Krull and C. A. Anderson (1997), the theory proposed here does not identify these basic explanatory relations as necessarily perceptual in nature.

Third, if a particular type of explanation is encoded as a schema, then an explanation can be generated or understood by articulating that schema. At its simplest, schema articulation consists of replacing variables with constants. At its most complex, schema articulation takes a long time, requires creativity, presupposes multiple subschemas, builds on many domain-specific facts, and might result in a Nobel Prize. Understanding a complicated explanation is greatly facilitated by a prior schema for explanations of that type. Unlike the theories of Schank (1986a, 1986b) and Krull and C. A. Anderson (1997), the present theory emphasizes the complexity of the schema articulation process.

Fourth, when more than one schema is potentially applicable to the case at hand, there must follow a process of competition and conflict resolution.

This process is assumed to be probabilistic but influenced by the degree of overlap with the case at hand as well as by past usefulness (J. R. Anderson & Lebiere, 1998).

Finally, there is the process of verbalization by which an explanation—a knowledge representation—is translated into words and communicated to someone else. This process is presumably common to all discourse processes. Nevertheless, what is proposed here is a theory of explanation, specifically, rather than a theory of question answering in general (Graesser & Hemphill, 1991).

Discussion

The account of explanation proposed in this chapter differs from alternative accounts in several respects. First, the present account does not attempt to distinguish between explanations and descriptions. Instead, it claims that explanation is a species of description. Explanations are descriptions characterized by a particular type of content. This view avoids the difficult problem of distinguishing explanation and description that has occupied philosophers over the past five decades (Salmon, 1989).

Second, the present account distinguishes between explaining something and explaining something to somebody else. That is, I claim that explanation is a cognitive kind, a mental process with particular characteristics, alongside decision making, reasoning, remembering, and so on. This is not to deny that explanations typically are communicated, or that attempting to explain something to somebody else might be a good strategy for discovering a good explanation. But it is to deny that explanations have to be communicated, or even expressed in language, to be explanations. The latter assertion is basic to the view advocated in Hilton (1990) and implicit in the treatments by Brewer et al. (2000), and Wilson and Keil (2000).

Third, unlike the accounts by both philosophers (Pitt, 1988; Salmon, 1989) and cognitive scientists (Keil & Wilson, 2000) the present account does not assume that an explanation succeeds. There are explanations that are false and others that fail to explain regardless of truth value. According to the account presented here, this does not prevent them from being bona fide explanations, just as a bad novel is still a novel and a slow racehorse is still a racehorse. In short, "explanation" is not a success word like "achievement" but a label for a natural kind; success is not built into its definition. Philosophical analyses have shown that assuming that an explanation necessarily succeed in explaining leads to serious conceptual difficulties (Pitt, 1988).

Fourth, unlike most of the philosophical, empirical, and formal work on explanation, the present account does not focus on when and how a person infers a generative (causal) relation from experience or from a text. Instead, it assumes that people learn generative relations in a variety of ways and focuses on the processes involved in using them to generate explanations.

Fifth, the present account differs from the schema-based theories by Schank (1986a, 1986b) and others in two respects. It does not assume that explanation schemas are acquired inductively or via analogical learning. Instead, it claims that the repeated assembly of primitive generative relations ultimately leads to the encoding of that assembly as a memory structure in its own right. Explanation schemas are products of constructive, not inductive, processes (Ohlsson & Lehtinen, 1997).

Unlike other schema-based theories, the present account also emphasizes the potential complexity of the schema articulation process. Although many everyday explanations are shallow and trivial instantiations of a single generative relations (the battery is dead, so my car won't start), working out exactly how the slots of a complex schema are to be mapped onto the case at hand is sometimes an intellectually demanding process. Thus, in contrast to claims that scientific explanations and everyday explanations are essentially different (McCauley, 2000) and also in contrast to claims that they are essentially similar (Gopnik & Meltzoff, 1997) (the present theory claims that the explanatory processes of everyday life and of scientists are of the same kind but differ radically in the complexity of the associated articulation processes.)

The development of the present theory has proceeded from the perspective of the person who generates an explanation. A student is perhaps more often in the situation of trying to understand an explanation generated by somebody else. Understanding explanatory discourse requires, I suggest, the same knowledge structures and the same processes as generation.

Unless the person reading or hearing an explanation can access the generative relations out of which an explanation is built, he or she will fail to comprehend it. At the very least, the putative explanation will not be explanatory. As an illustration, consider the following answer by a college student to the question of why the dinosaurs were so large:

> Dinosaurs became so gigantic probably because at that time, the Big Bang had just happened and our solar system was very close together, that is, the planets and the sun were closer back then, than they are [1 word unreadable] Too, the gravity from all the planets and the sun made some species of dinosaurs gigantic. The other species of dinosaurs that were not gigantic came later, when the planets and the sun were farther apart. (Student No. 3, Chicago corpus)

This explanation is based on the generative relation

   strong gravity → large bodies,

which is not primitive for the present author. Although I can understand *the discourse* in the sense of successfully computing the meaning of each successive sentence, I do not understand *the explanation* expressed by that discourse. That is, the discourse provides no insight into the body size of dinosaurs. Due to its absence from my semantic memory, the central relation is itself in need of explanation. How does stronger gravity cause animals to have larger bodies? In short, to understand an explanatory discourse *qua* explanation, the reader or hearer must possess, and be able to access, its constituting generative relations.

There is at least one sense in which understanding an explanation is easier than generating it: Memory access and conflict resolution are considerably facilitated for the reader as compared to the explainer. The content words in an explanatory discourse function as retrieval probes that help activate the relevant knowledge structures. Obviously, it is much easier to access one's knowledge about, for example, the reproduction of bacteria when encountering discourse about that topic than when sitting by oneself and trying to figure out why bacteria become resistant to antibiotics. Nevertheless, generation and understanding are similar in that unless the reader can access the relevant generative relations, not only is he or she incapable of generating an explanation that builds on them, but he or she is also incapable of understanding such an explanation.

Very complicated explanations are probably never generated or understood in a completely bottom-up process. Instead, they are constructed in stages, each stage completing a subassembly. For example, the standard explanation for how the genetic code works requires several pages to state and is very difficult to fully comprehend in a first pass unless one has at least some parts of it (e.g., the shape of the DNA molecule) already encapsulated in prior schemas. To assemble an explanation that consists of dozens of generative relations requires more working memory capacity than is available to most people. They will exit with a partial sense of comprehension, at best. However, if the learner already has an abstract schema for the relevant structure, assimilating or discovering the specifics of the DNA molecule is facilitated (Ohlsson & Regan, 2001).

These observations have one clear implication for educational practice: To make a scientific explanation comprehensible to students, make sure that the students already possess the generative relations that underpin that explanation. This conclusion diverts our attention away from the details of the presentation, the particular words that appear in an explanatory discourse, the syntax of the sentences, the presence of pictures and other features that figure prominently in contemporary discussions of text comprehension (Kintsch, 1998; van Oostendorp & Goldman, 1999). Instead, the present account implies that understanding a qualitative explanation in science is mainly a question of being ready: The learner has to possess the requisite prior knowledge. In addition to improving the presentation of an explanation, a teacher can improve comprehension of an explanation by sequencing the fundamental ideas in the subject matter so that the students have acquired all the relevant generative relations before encountering that explanation.

ACKNOWLEDGMENTS

Preparation of this chapter was supported in part by Grant No. N00014-97-1-0826 from the Cognitive Science Program of the Office of Naval Research (ONR) and in part by Grant BCS-9907839 from the National Science Foundation. Scott Minkoff and Joshua Hemmerich assisted with data collection and analysis.

REFERENCES

Anderson, C. A., Krull, D. S., & Weiner, B. (1996). Explanations: Processes and consequences. In E. Higgins & A. Kruglanski (Eds.), *Social psychology: Handbook of basic principles* (pp. 271–296). New York: Guilford.

Anderson, J. R., & Lebiere, C. (1998). *The atomic components of thought.* Mahwah, NJ: Lawrence Erlbaum Associates.

Bishop, B., & Anderson, C. (1990). Student conceptions of natural selection and its role in evolution. *Journal of Research in Science Teaching, 27,* 415–427.

Brewer, W. F., Chinn, C. A., & Samarapungavan, A. (2000). Explanation in scientists and children. In F. C. Keil & R. A. Wilson (Eds.), *Explanation and cognition* (pp. 279–298). Cambridge, MA: MIT Press.

Brumby, M. (1984). Misconceptions about the concept of natural selection by medical biology students. *Science Education, 68,* 493–503.

Buchanan, B., Moore, J., Carenini, G., Forsythe, D., Ohlsson, S., & Banks, G. (1995). An intelligent interactive system for delivering individualized information to patients. *Artificial Intelligence in Medicine, 7,* 117–154

Chi, M. T. H., DeLeeuw, N., Chiu, M.-H., & LaVancher, C. (1994). Eliciting self-explanations improves understanding. *Cognitive Science, 18,* 439–477.

Clancey, W. J., & Shortliffe, E. H. (1984). *Readings in medical artificial intelligence: The first decade.* Reading, MA: Addison-Wesley.

Demastes, S., Settlage, J., & Good, R. (1995). Students' conceptions of natural selection and its role in evolution: Cases of replication and comparison. *Journal of
Research in Science Teaching, 32*, 535–550.

Dickinson, P. (1979). *The flight of dragons.* New York: Harper & Row.

Dretske, F. (1988). *Explaining behavior.* Cambridge, MA: MIT Press.

Einhorn, H. J., & Hogarth, R. M. (1985). Ambiguity and uncertainty in probabilistic inference. *Psychological Review, 92*, 433–461.

Ferrari, M., & Chi, M. T. H. (1998). The nature of naive explanations of natural selection. *International Journal of Science Education, 20*, 1231–1256.

Fodor, J. A. (1998). *Concepts: Where cognitive science went wrong.* New York: Oxford
University Press.

Forbus, K., Gentner, D., & Law, K. (1995). MAC/FAC: A model of similar-
ity-based retrieval. *Cognitive Science, 19*, 141–205.

Forgy, C. L. (1982). Rete: A fast algorithm for the many pattern/many object pattern matching problem. *Artificial Intelligence, 19*, 17–37.

Gopnik, A. (2000). Explanation as orgasm and the drive for causal knowledge:
The function, evolution, and phenomenology of the theory formation system.
In F. C. Keil & R. A. Wilson (Eds.), *Explanation and cognition* (pp. 299–323).
Cambridge, MA: The MIT Press.

Gopnik, A., & Meltzoff, A. N. (1997). *Words, thoughts, and theories.* Cambridge,
MA: MIT Press.

Gould, S. J. (1991). *Bully for Brontosaurus.* New York: Norton.

Graesser, A., & Hemphill, D. (1991). Question answering in the context of scientific mechanisms. *Journal of Memory and Language, 30*, 186–209.

Graesser, A., Singer, M., & Trabasso, T. (1994). Constructing inferences during
narrative text comprehension. *Psychological Review, 101*, 371–395.

Hempel, C. G., & Oppenheimer, P. (1948). Studies in the logic of explanation. *Philosophy of Science, 15*, 135–175.

Hilton, D. (1990). Conversational processes and causal explanation. *Psychological
Bulletin, 107*, 65–81.

Holyoak, K., & Thagard, P. (1989). Analogical mapping by constraint satisfaction.
Cognitive Science, 13, 295–355.

Johnson, C., & Keil, F. C. (2000). Explanatory knowledge and conceptual combination. In F. C. Keil & R. A. Wilson (Eds.). *Explanation and cognition* (pp.
327–359). Cambridge, MA, US: The MIT Press.

Keil, F. C., & Wilson, R. A. (Eds.). (2000). *Explanation and cognition.* Cambridge,
MA: MIT Press.

Kintsch, W. (1998). *Comprehension.* Cambridge, England: Cambridge University
Press.

Kitcher, P. (1993). *The advancement of science.* New York: Oxford University Press.

Krull, D., & Anderson, C. A. (1997). The process of explanation. In *Current Directions in Psychological Science, 6*, 1–5.

Krupa, M., Selman, R., & Jaquette, D. (1985). The development of science explanations in children and adolescents: A structural approach. In S.
Chipman, J. Segal, & R. Glaser (Eds.), *Thinking and learning skills: Research
and open questions* (Vol. 2, pp. 427–455). Hillsdale, NJ: Lawrence Erlbaum
Associates.

Langston, M., & Trabasso, T. (1999). Modeling causal integration and availability of information during comprehension of narrative texts. In H. van Oostendorp & S. R. Goldman (Eds.), *The construction of mental representations during reading* (pp. 29–69). Mahwah, NJ: Lawrence Erlbaum Associates.

Lawson, A., & Thompson, L. (1988). Formal reasoning ability and misconceptions concerning genetics and natural selection. *Journal of Research in Science Teaching, 25,* 733–746.

Leake, D. B. (1992). *Evaluation explanations.* Hillsdale, NJ: Lawrence Erlbaum Associates.

Leddo, J., & Abelson, R. P. (1986). The nature of explanations. In J. A. Galambos, R. P. Abelson, & J. B. Black (Eds.), *Knowledge structures* (pp. 103–122). Hillsdale, NJ: Lawrence Erlbaum Associates.

Mayr, E. (1982). Teleological and teleonomic: A new analysis. In H. C. Plotkin (Ed.), *Learning, development, and culture* (pp. 17–38). New York: Wiley.

McCauley, R. N. (2000). The naturalness of religion and the unnaturalness of science. In F. C. Keil & R. A. Wilson (Eds.), *Explanation and cognition* (pp. 61–85). Cambridge, MA: MIT Press.

Moore, J. D., & Paris, C. L. (1993). Planning text for advisory dialogues: Capturing intentional and rhetorical information. *Computational Linguistics, 19,* 651–695.

Ohlsson, S. (1992). The cognitive skill of theory articulation: A neglected aspect of science education? *Science & Education, 1,* 181–192.

Ohlsson, S. (1993). Abstract schemas. *Educational Psychologist, 28,* 51–66.

Ohlsson, S. (1999). Theoretical commitment and implicit knowledge: Why anomalies do not trigger learning. *Science & Education, 8,* 559–574.

Ohlsson, S. (2000). Falsification, anomalies and the naturalistic approach to cognitive change. *Science & Education, 9,* 173–186.

Ohlsson, S., & Hemmerich, J. (1999). Articulating an explanatory schema: A preliminary model and supporting data. In M. Hahn & S. Stoness, (Eds.) *Proceedings of the twenty-first annual conference of the Cognitive Science Society* (pp. 490–495). Mahwah, NJ: Lawrence Erlbaum Associates.

Ohlsson, S., & Lehtinen, E. (1997). Abstraction and the acquisition of complex ideas. *International Journal of Educational Research, 27,* 37–48.

Ohlsson, S., & Regan, S. (2001). A function for abstract ideas in conceptual learning and discovery. *Cognitive Science Quarterly, 1,* 243–277.

Pazzani, M. J. (1990). *Creating a memory of causal relationships.* Hillsdale, NJ: Lawrence Erlbaum Associates.

Pitt, J. C. (Ed.). (1988). *Theories of explanation.* New York: Oxford University Press.

Regan, S., & Ohlsson, S. (1999). The impact of abstract ideas on discovery and comprehension in scientific domains. In M. Hahn & S. Stoness (Eds.), *Proceedings of the twenty-first annual conference of the Cognitive Science Society* (pp. 590–594). Mahwah, NJ: Lawrence Erlbaum Associates.

Salmon, W. C. (1984). *Scientific explanation and the causal structure of the world.* Princeton, NJ: Princeton University Press.

Salmon, W. C. (1989). *Four decades of scientific explanation.* Minneapolis: University of Minnesota Press.

Salmon, W. C. (1990). Scientific explanation: Causation and unification. *Crítica, 22,* 3–21.

Salmon, W. C. (1998). *Causality and explanation*. New York: Oxford University Press.

Samarapungavan, A., & Wiers, R. (1997). Children's thoughts on the origin of species: A study of explanatory coherence. *Cognitive Science, 21*, 147–177.

Schank, R. C. (1986a). Explanation: A first pass. In J. Kolodner & C. Riesbeck (Eds.), *Experience, memory, and reasoning* (pp. 139–165). Hillsdale, NJ: Lawrence Erlbaum Associates.

Schank, R. C. (1986b). *Explanation patterns*. Hillsdale, NJ: Lawrence Erlbaum Associates.

Settlage, J. (1994). Conceptions of natural selection: A snapshot of the sense-making process. *Journal of Research in Science Teaching, 31*, 449–457.

Simon, H. A. (2000). Discovering explanations. In F. C. Keil & R. A. Wilson (Eds.), *Explanation and cognition* (pp. 21–59). Cambridge, MA: MIT Press.

Sosa, E. (1993). Davidson's thinking causes. In J. Heil & A. R. Mele (Eds.), *Mental causation* (pp. 41–50). New York: Clarendon.

Sosa, E., & Tooley, M. (1993). *Causation*. Oxford, England: Oxford University Press.

Sperber, D., Premack, D., & Premack, A. (Eds.). (1995). *Causal cognition: A multidisciplinary debate*. Oxford, England: Clarendon.

Suppe, F. (1989). *The semantic conception of theories and scientific realism*. Urbana: University of Illinois Press.

Tamir, P., & Zohar, A. (1991). Anthropomorphism and teleology in reasoning about biological phenomena. *Science Education, 75*, 57–67.

Taylor, C. (1980). *The explanation of behavior*. London: Routledge & Kegan Paul.

Thompson, P. (1989). *The structure of biological theories*. New York: State University of New York Press.

Trabasso, T., & van den Broek, P. (1985). Causal thinking and the representation of narrative events. *Journal of Memory and Language, 24*, 612–630.

VanLehn, K., & Jones, R. (1986). Learning by explaining examples to oneself: A computational model. In S. Chipman & A. L. Meyrowitz (Eds.), *Foundations of knowledge acquisition* (p. 25–82). Boston: Kluwer.

van Oostendorp, H., & Goldman, S. (Eds.). (1999). *The construction of mental representations during reading*. Mahwah, NJ: Lawrence Erlbaum Associates.

Wilson, R. A., & Keil, F. C. (2000). The shadows and shallows of explanation. In F. C. Keil & R. A. Wilson (Eds.), *Explanation and cognition* (pp. 87–114). Cambridge, MA: MIT Press.

II

Basic Cognitive Representations and Processes in Text Comprehension

Comprehension and Memory of Science Texts: Inferential Processes and the Construction of a Mental Representation

Paul van den Broek
University of Minnesota

Sandra Virtue
University of Minnesota

Michelle Gaddy Everson
University of Minnesota

Yuhtsuen Tzeng
National Chung Cheng University

Yung-chi Sung
University of Minnesota

Science texts are a major means of information transmission in our society, in everyday life (e.g., in newspaper and magazine articles) as well as in educational settings (e.g., in text books or scientific articles). It is important to understand how it is that people comprehend such texts, for both theoretical and practical reasons. From a theoretical point of view, it yields insights into complex cognitive processes. These processes include allocation of attention, access of background knowledge, inference-generation, modulation by the reader's goals, and information representation in memory. From a practical point of view, knowing how people understand expository texts, and why they may fail to understand them, is crucial for the development of instructional strategies, for effective text design, and for early diagnosis and remediation of problems of reading and learning.

The focus of this chapter is on the cognitive processes that occur during the comprehension of science texts (and expository texts in general) and on the resulting mental representation of such texts. In the first section, we describe general features of the comprehension processes and representations in reading. These general features are described in the context of a theoretical framework called the Landscape model. In the second section, we focus on expository and science texts in particular. We explore the unique features of science texts and of the processes involved in their comprehension. In the final section, we discuss theoretical and practical implications of the analysis of science text comprehension.

COGNITIVE PROCESSES IN READING

An essential component of successful reading comprehension is the construction of a coherent memory representation of the text (Casteel & Simpson, 1991; Gernsbacher, 1990; Graesser & Clark, 1985; Kintsch & van Dijk, 1978; McKoon & Ratcliff, 1980; van den Broek, 1994). To construct a coherent representation, the reader must interpret each element of the text and identify meaningful connections to other elements in the text and in semantic knowledge. The resulting representation consists of nodes, which capture the elements in or related to the text, and connections, which capture the semantic relations between text elements. Together, these nodes and connections form a network. The more interconnected the representation, the more coherent it is. Indeed, extensive research in comprehension of narratives has shown that texts with a high density of connections are perceived to be more coherent than texts with a low density (Trabasso, Secco, & van den Broek, 1984), that individual text elements with many connections are recalled more frequently and more quickly than elements with few connections (O'Brien & Myers, 1987; Trabasso et al., 1984; van den Broek, Rohleder, & Narvaez, 1996), that the former are deemed more important and included in summaries more frequently than the latter (Graesser & Clark, 1985; van den Broek & Trabasso, 1986), and that connected text elements prime each other more strongly than they prime unrelated elements (O'Brien & Myers, 1987; van den Broek & R. F. Lorch, 1993). We discuss the specific types of relations included in representations of expository texts later. For now, the important points are that successful reading comprehension entails the construction of a coherent mental representation of the text, and that such a representation consists of a network of semantic relations between text elements and between text elements and the reader's background knowledge.

The Identification and Representation of Semantic Relations During Reading

Identifying semantic relations and building a memory representation during reading pose a challenge for the cognitive system of the reader. In order to identify a relation between two informational elements, those elements must be activated simultaneously (i.e., coactivated). Unfortunately, the reader has limited resources in focal attention and working memory (Daneman & Carpenter, 1980; Just & Carpenter, 1992; Miller, 1956; Singer & Ritchot, 1996; Waters & Caplan, 1996; Whitney, Ritchie, & Clark, 1991), so the reader can attend to only a subset of all the elements that potentially could be connected at any one time. Thus, successful reading involves a careful balancing of the need for coherence and the attentional limitations of the human cognitive processing system. Proper allocation of attention becomes crucial to ascertain that the central pieces of information are activated simultaneously, allowing the important connections to be identified and transferred into the developing memory representation of the text.

How is it that readers accomplish this balancing act and what are the cognitive processes involved? Recent theoretical models of text comprehension provide considerable detail in answering these questions (Goldman & Varma, 1995; Kintsch, 1988; Langston & Trabasso, 1998; van den Broek, Risden, Fletcher, & Thurlow, 1996; van den Broek, Young, Tzeng, & Linderholm, 1999). Several of these models are based on research on narrative comprehension, where the text structure is well defined and the cognitive processes are relatively easy to investigate. However, general principles and applicability of these theories pertain to all types of texts (Gaddy, van den Broek, & Sung, 2001). We use one of these models, the Landscape model, to describe the processes involved in comprehension during reading and in the construction of a memory representation in some more detail.[1]

---

[1] A Windows based version of this computational model is available from the first author.

Reading as the Dynamic Fluctuation of Activation. The central premise of the Landscape model is that reading is a cyclical and dynamic process. As the reader proceeds through a text, each consecutive text segment (e.g., phrase, clause, sentence) elicits an array of cognitive processes in the reader. These processes include associative, spread-of-activation processes as well as deeper comprehension processes. As a result of these processes, which we describe in detail later, the contents of the reader's working memory or attention buffer continually change: New text elements become activated, others become deactivated, and yet others increase or decrease in their level of activation. Thus, over the course of reading an entire text, elements fluctuate in their activation, thereby creating a *landscape* of activations. This is illustrated in Fig. 6.1, which depicts the landscape of activations for the expository text in Table 6.1. Along the horizontal, "depth," dimension on the left are listed the major elements of the text.[2] Elements activated from background knowledge also are activated and hence will be part of an individual's landscape of activations, but because these elements are likely to vary across individuals we have not included them in this illustration. The other horizontal, "width," dimension depicts the reading cycles, each corresponding to the reading of a major proposition. Finally, the vertical, "height," dimension indicates the level of activation of each text element.[3] Thus, when read from cycle to cycle Fig. 6.1 describes the patterns of activation as they fluctuate during the course of reading. Cross-sections of the landscape reflect various important properties of the reading process. For example, by following an individual element in the text across reading cycles, one can trace the course of activation of that element during reading. By taking a cross-section at a particular reading cycle, one can identify which elements are activated simultaneously at that cycle. And, by taking a horizontal cross-section at a particular level of activation, one can identify which elements exceed a given threshold of activation and at what cycle they do so. In this fashion the depiction of the reading process as a landscape of fluctuating activations captures important features of the dynamics of reading.

The Construction of an Off-Line Memory Representation. The fluctuating activations form the basis of the construction of a memory repre-

---

[2]Different methods of parsing the text are possible. The processes are independent of the choice of parsing. For this illustration, we have parsed the text into major propositions. In the figures, we use a single word/concept as shorthand notation for each proposition.

[3]Activation levels are relative so any numerical scale can be chosen. For this illustration we have adopted an 8-point scale. Details of what determines the level of activation of a particular element at a particular cycle are given later.

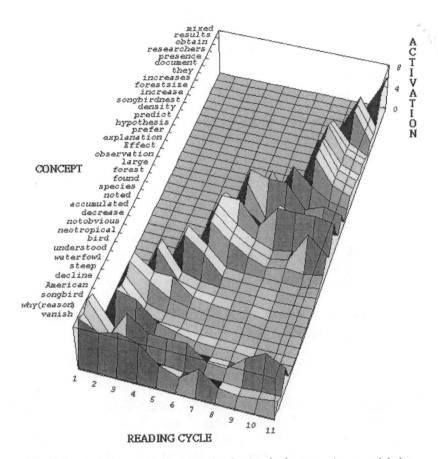

FIG. 6.1.   Landscape of activations for the *Songbird* passage (concept labels are used as shorthand notations for the major propositions in the text; adapted from Gaddy et al., 2001).

sentation of the text. As mentioned, at each reading cycle a cross-section of the landscape of activations shows the different text elements that are activated, to various degrees, at that cycle. When a particular element is activated, the element is added as a node to the episodic memory representation of the text; if the element already is a part of the episodic memory representation, its trace is strengthened. The amount of change in the node strength of a concept is proportional to its activation in the current reading cycle. Furthermore, when two elements are activated simultaneously, a connection between them is built in the reader's episodic memory representation; if a connection already exists, it is strengthened. The amount of change in the

[handwritten margin note: Type clean for]

TABLE 6.1
Example Expository Text Fragment

Why American Songbirds are Vanishing (1)

The steep declines in waterfowl, shoreline birds, and grassland birds over the past several decades generally are well understood (2). What is not as obvious is why forest-dwelling migratory songbirds also are vanishing—especially the so-called Neotropical migrants that breed in northern latitudes but migrate to winter homes in the tropics (3).

As decreases in their populations accumulated (4), it was widely noted that the missing species could still be found in large continuous tracts of forests but not in isolated tracts (5). This observation was dubbed the forest fragmentation effect (6). What possible explanations might be given for the forest fragmentation effect (7)? One simple hypothesis to explain the effect is that they generally prefer larger forest plots as nesting sites and so avoid isolated plots because they tend to be small (8). It is important to note that this hypothesis predicts that the density of these birds' nests in a forest will increase as the size of the forest increases (9). However, when they set about documenting the presence or absence of songbird species in forest fragments of different size (10), researchers obtained mixed and—sometimes—contradictory results (11).

Note. This text was adapted from *Scientific American*. The numbers in parentheses indicate processing cycles.

representational strength of a connection is a function of the activation of each of the constituent elements. The more strongly each is activated in the current cycle, the stronger the ensuing change in connection will be. In this fashion, the memory representation is elaborated, modified, and/or strengthened with each consecutive processing cycle, eventually resulting in a representation of the complete text in memory.

The relation between online processes and memory representation is reciprocal. As is discussed in the next section, the cognitive processes at a particular cycle draw on the episodic memory representation as it has been developed in the preceding cycles. Thus, the fluctuations in activation and the developing memory representation are involved in a dynamic interplay, in which each influences the other over the course of reading.

Sources of Activation and Readers' Standards of Coherence

We have elaborated on this description of the reading process to highlight the central role that activation plays in comprehension. The fluctuating patterns of activation that a reader generates determine the content and structure of the eventual memory representation of the text and related concepts activated in the course of comprehension. Thus, the patterns of activation are at the heart of comprehension. Hence, to understand reading comprehension, it becomes essential to understand the factors that determine the activation patterns.

Sources of Activation. During a cycle, information can be activated from four different sources (van den Broek et al., 1999). A prime source of activation at a particular cycle is, of course, the textual input at that cycle: the sentence that currently is being read. Activation from this source is supplemented by activation from other sources. A second source is the preceding processing cycle. Information that was activated in this cycle may be carried over in working memory into the current cycle, but normally at attenuated levels of activation (Fletcher, Hummel, & Marsolek, 1990; Kintsch & van Dijk, 1978).

The third and fourth sources involve retrieval of information from memory. The third source is the episodic memory representation of the text as it has been constructed over the preceding cycles. Information from this memory representation can be reactivated or "reinstated" during the current cycle. The fourth and final source is the reader's semantic memory or background knowledge. This information may be accessed during reading by means of elaborative inferences that embellish the information given by the text itself (Graesser, Singer, & Trabasso, 1994; Singer, 1994).

Standards of Coherence and the Generation of Inferences. A central factor in determining which sources and what information are accessed at any particular cycle consists of the *standards of coherence* that a reader maintains during reading (cf. van den Broek, Risden, & Husebye-Hartmann, 1995; van Oostendorp, 1994). These standards reflect a reader's knowledge and beliefs about what constitutes good comprehension as well as the reader's specific goals for reading the particular text. Readers use these standards to gauge their comprehension and to determine whether to engage in further comprehension processes, such as a search for additional information from episodic or semantic memory. Readers' standards of coherence can vary as a function of individual differences, reading goals, text types, and so on (Narvaez, van den Broek, & Ruiz, 1999; van den Broek, R. F. Lorch, Linderholm, & Gustafson, in press). Some standards are applied across reading situations, whereas others are adopted under special circumstances. For example, during comprehension of narrative texts, referential and causal coherence are two standards that are almost universally adopted by readers (Graesser et al., 1994; van den Broek, 1990). Consider the following short narrative segment:

1. Joanne was working late.
2. It was raining hard.
3. Joanne left the office building.
4. She locked the door
5. because she did not intend to come back for the rest of the week.
6. The place was quite busy
7. because everyone wanted to get home for dinner.
8. It was a good thing that the elevator had been fixed.
9. As she crossed the parking lot,
10. the wind blew open her folder.
11. The papers got all wet.

To meet the standard of referential coherence, readers must disambiguate referents such as *she* and *her*. By inferring that these words indicate *Joanne*, this task is relatively easy in this simple text. To meet the standard of causal coherence, readers must identify the causal antecedents for the events they encounter in the text. Consider, for example, the event that the papers got all wet. An explanation of this event is readily found by the fact that it was raining hard and that the wind blew open the folder.

The standards sometimes can be met, wholly or in part, by information that is activated currently. Thus, the mention of *she* in the fourth sentence/cycle can be disambiguated by the element *Joanne*, which is likely to be carried over—and remain activated—from the preceding cycle. Likewise, part of the causal explanation for the papers getting wet (11th sentence/cycle) is given in the preceding cycle *The wind blew open the folder.* Often, however, readers must reactivate the information required for attaining coherence. Thus, the mention of *she* in the ninth sentence/cycle is likely to require the retrieval of *Joanne* from the episodic memory representation of the text because no references had been made to Joanne for several cycles. Likewise, a crucial part of the explanation for the papers getting wet (*it was raining hard*, mentioned in the second cycle) needs to be retrieved from episodic memory. Both are examples of reinstatements. If the episodic representation had not contained the required information, readers would need to access their general semantic background knowledge to provide the missing coherence by means of an elaborative inference. The results from a large number of empirical studies—using a variety of measures, such as speed of naming or recognition, reading times, think-aloud frequencies, and so on—show that readers of narrative texts indeed access relevant information in episodic or general semantic memory to make referential and causal inferences (e.g., Bloom, Fletcher, van den Broek, Reitz, & Shapiro, 1990; Casteel, 1993; Gernsbacher, 1990; Suh & Trabasso, 1993; Trabasso & Suh, 1993).

This example illustrates how a reader's standards of coherence direct the generation of inferences and the activation of information from the different sources available to the reader. At each cycle the reader's cognitive system assesses whether the current input has been adequately understood, as measured by his or her standards of coherence. In the simplest case, the information from the current input and information carried over from the preceding cycle together provide the coherence needed and the reader proceeds to the next input cycle. If information from these sources does not establish adequate coherence, the reader can achieve satisfactory comprehension by generating coherence-building inferences. The inferences arise from the (re)activation of information from episodic memory representation and/or from background knowledge. Through these mechanisms, the reader can identify meaningful relations between the currently read information and the remainder of the text.

Cohort Activation.   The inferential processes that we just described are supplemented by a process called cohort activation. Concepts that are activated in the current cycle automatically spread activation to other concepts to which they are associated in the reader's background knowledge or to which they have become related, over the course of reading, in the episodic memory representation for the text. As a result, these associated concepts and elements—the *cohorts* of the currently activated concepts and elements—will be activated (cf. the resonance model: O'Brien & Myers, 1999). Indeed, cohort activation and standards of coherence are interdependent. On the one hand, cohort activation may be instrumental in activating information that is necessary to establish coherence. On the other hand, a reader's standards of coherence dictate how long further cohort activation continues (e.g., whether cohort-activation elements themselves elicit additional cohort activation).

Conclusion.   As a reader progresses through a text, he or she attempts to establish basic coherence. Guided by his or her standards of coherence for each new text segment, the reader at each reading cycle allocates attentional resources to the information that is most likely to yield optimal coherence and understanding. As part of the attempt to meet the standards of coherence, the reader recruits information from memory, either from the available episodic memory representation of the text or from general semantic memory. At each reading cycle, information recruited in this fashion, together with the contents of the currently read text segment itself and any information carried over from the preceding cycle—plus, through cohort activation, associated concepts—creates the overall pattern of activation for that cycle. These fluctuating patterns, in turn, bring about a gradually emerging—and, hopefully, coherent—mental representation of the text as a whole.

COGNITIVE PROCESSES AND COHERENCE
WHILE READING EXPOSITORY TEXTS

As mentioned, the preceding description of the reading process is based mostly on research on narrative texts. Do the same processes apply to reading of expository texts? If so, what types of relations provide the backbone to expository text comprehension? Are the referential and causal connections prevalent, or are there important additional connections? To answer these questions, we walk through an expository text cycle by cycle. At each step, we specify the relations that are identified in the course of good comprehension and we lay out the ensuing patterns of activation. Consider the *Songbird* passage in Table 6.1. This text has been used to illustrate the effects of textual cues on activation patterns (Gaddy et al., 2001). We use it to illustrate the fluctuating activation and inferential processes during expository text reading. Texts can be parsed and provide input to the cognitive system in different ways. For this illustration, the text is divided into clauses/major propositions (cf. Kintsch, 1988; Trabasso, van den Broek, & Suh, 1989), with each constituting a separate input cycle. The numbers inserted in the text indicate the clauses/major propositions. As we proceed through the text, we will identify the relations that readers are likely to infer.

A few preliminary remarks are in order. First, we focus on the intratextual relations but not the information that is imported from the reader's semantic knowledge. Exactly what information is activated from background knowledge depends on the individual reader and on his or her domain knowledge. Rather than make assumptions about readers' background knowledge we simply omit elaborative inferences for the purpose of this illustration. Of course, such information *is* activated in natural reading and *would*, therefore, be included in the activation pattern at each cycle. Second, we assume that researchers can select the level of textual analysis input to the Landscape model, according to their interests and purposes. Following common practice, in this illustration we have parsed each major clause/proposition in its constituent propositions. These are the conceptual units in the analysis.[4] Third, we assume a moderately engaged reader. No doubt it is possible to read the text at a much deeper level of comprehension (i.e., to set much stricter standards of coherence); conversely, there will be readers who process the text at a much more superficial level (i.e., have more lenient standards of coherence). For the present purpose, we assume that the reader employs no special reading strategies, such as trying to anticipate upcoming text or attempting to speculate on an answer to rhetorical questions posed in the text. It would be easy, of course, to modify the landscape to reflect such strategies. Fourth, in line with most models of attention and working memory (Just & Carpenter, 1992; O'Brien & Myers, 1999), concepts are assumed to be activated to different degrees. Thus, activation is not an all-or-nothing phenomenon but rather a phenomenon that has activation values that range from none to complete activation. Further, when a concept receives activation from several sources (e.g., from both carryover and reinstatement from memory), its final activation will equal the larger of the incoming activations.[5]

Reading the Songbird Passage. The input to the first processing cycle of the *Songbird* passage consists of the text contained in the title. The concepts in the title are activated by virtue of the fact that they are explicitly mentioned. Through cohort activation these concepts, in turn, may activate closely associated background knowledge from the reader's semantic memory. Given that this is the first input cycle and that our hypothetical reader employs no special strategies, however, we will assume that no other information will be activated. The resulting activation pattern is depicted in Fig. 6.1. A rudimentary episodic memory representation is constructed with the activated concepts as nodes, related to each other by connections of varying strengths (as a function of the activation levels of each concept).

---

[4]As mentioned before, the level of analysis can be adjusted for the specific purposes or theoretical framework of the researcher. Both more fine-grained and more global levels are possible. For example, more fine-grained analysis would be obtained by ordering the propositions within a cycle in a hierarchy (Kintsch & van Dijk, 1978; Turner & Greene, 1978), with higher propositions being more important—and receiving more activation—than lower ones. To illustrate, in the first cycle of the *Songbird* passage higher order propositions would be that there are songbirds (a) and that they are vanishing (b); lower propositions would be the question "why/what causes this?" and the fact that the songbirds are "American." A more global analysis would be obtained by parsing the text into units larger than major propositions/clauses. For example, entire paragraphs could be used as input units.

[5]In this view activations are not cumulative. This has the advantage that the maximum activation that a concept can receive is what it would receive through explicit mention. We believe this to be a plausible assumption, but it should be pointed out that other assumptions can easily be implemented in the Landscape model.

In the second cycle, the pattern of activation changes in several ways. First, new input results in the activation of novel information and the partial deactivation of concepts from the preceding cycle. Second, the concept *decline* in the input for Cycle 2 is a near synonym to the concept *vanish* from Cycle 1, so the latter concept will receive some reactivation. Activation of *vanish*, in turn, will lead to partial activation of the concepts that have become associated with it during the preceding processing cycle. Third, the phrase *are well understood* may suggest an agent to the reader. However, no agent is specified among the already activated concepts nor is one given in the episodic memory representation of the text so far, so the reader might access his or her semantic knowledge to fill in a referent (e.g., scientists or a government agency). Because the constraints for such an inference are very weak in this case, it is likely that most readers will not make a specific inference. Finally, all activated concepts activate their respective cohorts in the reader's semantic memory. Cohort activation of semantic memory will occur in every cycle, so for brevity's sake we do not repeat this fact for subsequent cycles. For example, the mentioning of three types of birds may activate the more abstract category BIRD (capitalized to indicate that it is a superordinate concept). In summary, the final activation vector in the second cycle consists of the current input, carryover from the preceding cycle, reactivation from the episodic memory representation as constructed in the preceding cycle, and elaboration from semantic memory. This vector will result in modification and updating of the episodic memory representation.

In the third cycle, new input wholly or partially displaces the old activations. The concept *vanish* is reintroduced explicitly and, as a result, *decline* from the preceding cycle will receive activation above simple carryover. Moreover, in Cycles 1 and 2, *vanish* has become associated to the other concepts activated in those cycles so, through cohort activation and through the emerging episodic memory representation of the text, these latter concepts will also receive some activation. Likewise, *songbirds* is repeated from Cycle 1, so all the concepts that have become associated with this concept will receive some activation. The phrase *what is not so obvious* indicates a contrastive relation, leading the reader to search for the antecedent for the contrast—something that *is* obvious. The antecedent is found in the preceding cycle's information that the decline in other, *nonsong* birds is understood. As a result, the concepts *well understood, decline*, and the abstract concept BIRDS will be activated. If readers attempt to maintain spatial or locational coherence, then the specification of *northern latitudes* will reactivate *American* from Cycle 1. Again, through cohort activation, other concepts associated with these reinstated concepts (e.g., the specific other subtypes of birds) will receive some activation as well. Together, all these activations create an entirely new activation pattern, unique to this cycle. This activation pattern, in turn, will transform and update the episodic memory representations for the text that had been constructed in the preceding cycles. The episodic memory representation will be updated accordingly.

We have described reading in the third cycle in some detail to illustrate how the eventual activation pattern reflects multiple processes and multiple sources. Different processes take place in parallel and, moreover, they are intertwined. For example, the activation of *well understood* in order to understand the contrastive *what is not so obvious* is facilitated by the fact that *well understood* was partially available through carryover. Considering that we have discussed only the main components of the reading of three cycles, it is easy to see that tracking the impact of multiple parallel activation processes across an entire text becomes a daunting task. For this reason investigators turn to computational models (e.g., van den Broek et al., 1999).

In the remainder of our illustration, we simplify the description of the activation process by not repeating components that take place in the same fashion at each cycle: activation of the concepts in the input clause/proposition, carryover from the preceding cycle, cohort activation of concepts in semantic and episodic memory, and the updating of the episodic memory representation according to the activation pattern. In our description of the remaining reading cycles, we focus on activation due to coherence-building inferences. Note however that activations due to the other component processes *are* assumed in the following discussion and are incorporated in Fig. 6.1.

In the fourth cycle, the concept *decrease* is a (near) synonym to the concepts *vanish* (Cycles 1 and 3) and *decline* (Cycle 2), so these concepts will be reactivated. The use of the possessive pronoun *their* calls for a referential inference. This inference is easily made by activating *songbirds*. In Cycle 5, *the missing species* constitutes a new concept but the use of the definite article *the* indicates that the concept refers to another, already familiar, concept. The reader will therefore attempt to identify the referent for *the missing species*. Again, *songbirds* (Cycles 1 and 3) provides the referential antecedent, although in this case the inference may be a bit harder because the concept was not mentioned explicitly in the preceding cycle. The phrase *it was widely noted* suggests an agent who does the *noting* so some readers may infer such an agent, either from episodic memory (e.g., the same agent who did the *understanding* in Cycle 2) or from background knowledge. Further, the information in the preceding cycle, carried over into the current cycle, provides a partial explanation for the information in the current cycle: The fact that the decreases accumulated (Cycle 4) enabled the noting of the pattern (depletion of songbird population in isolated tracts but not in continuous tracts) in Cycle 5; put conversely, it is likely that the pattern would not have been detected if the decreases had not accumulated to some critical mass.[6] Recognition of this causal/enabling connection would increase the causal coherence of the text and give the concepts *decrease* and *accumulate* additional activation in cycle 5.

In Cycle 6, the phrase *this observation* elicits several coherence-building processes. The word *this* calls for a referential antecedent, which is found in the information activated in Cycle 5: *it was noted that the missing species could be found in large tracts of forests but not in isolated tracts*. If readers attempt to attain causal coherence, then the information from Cycle 5 required for referential coherence would also provide a causal antecedent for the contents of Cycle 6: If it had not been noted that the missing species could be found in large tracts but not in isolated tracts, then the *forest fragmentation effect* would not have been dubbed. Thus, the major concepts in Cycle 5 receive activation from coherence building referential or causal inferences in Cycle 6. Aside from activation due to coherence building, the concept *forest* from Cycle 5 would receive activation because it is repeated in Cycle 6. This concept would also be activated if readers adopt another standard of coherence, that of spatial location (Zwaan, Langston, & Graesser, 1995). If they do, then *forest* would be activated because it is the location both of the pattern of population decline described in the preceding cycle and of the *forest fragmentation effect*. An interesting phenomenon occurs with the underlining of *forest fragmentation effect*. Underlining and other typographical cues (e.g., headers, italics) are commonly used with the intent to highlight the marked information. Put in terms of activation, the purpose is to encourage the reader to devote extra attention to this information. The effectiveness of cues has been the topic of considerable debate (León & Carretero, 1992; R. F. Lorch, 1989; R. F. Lorch & E. P. Lorch, 1996; see also R. F. Lorch, E. P. Lorch, & Klusewitz, 1995, for a review) but it can be tested easily in the landscape model by simulating reading of the text twice, once with extra activation flowing to typographically marked text and once without such extra activation, and comparing the fit of the resulting representations with comprehension and memory by readers (Gaddy et al., 2001).

Cycle 7 does not provide much new information. However, it focuses the reader's attention toward a causal standard of coherence by raising the

---

[6]This test of a causal relation is called a *counterfactual*: A is considered to cause B if it is the case that, in the circumstances of the text, if A had not happened, B would not have happened either (Mackie, 1980). In text analyses, this test is commonly used to identify causal and enabling relations (see Trabasso et al., 1984, 1989).

question of possible explanations for the forest fragmentation effect. Both the linguistic format (posing a question) and the content (seeking a causal explanation) may prompt the reader to reactivate from episodic memory the other time that he or she read a causal-coherence-based question in the text, namely in the title in Cycle 1. The simultaneous activation of the two questions (from Cycles 1 and 7) may alert the reader to a possible causal chain in the elements in the memory representation of the text: The as-of-yet unspecified answer to the question posed in Cycle 7 causes the forest fragmentation effect described in Cycle 6, which in turn causes the vanishing of songbirds mentioned in the title (and also in Cycle 3). In Cycle 8, both *hypothesis* and *to explain* activate *possible explanations* from the preceding cycle. The phrase *the effect* prompts a referential inference that the effect in question is the *forest fragmentation effect* described in Cycle 7. The pronoun *they* prompts another referential episodic memory inference, namely *songbirds* (directly from Cycle 3 or indirectly through *the missing species* in Cycle 5). The phrase *larger forest plots* and *isolated plots* reactivate their counterparts (and their respective cohorts) processed in Cycle 5. In addition, the combination of concepts in *to explain the effect is that they prefer larger plots* will prompt the reader to explicitly recognize the causal connection between the preference for nesting in large tracts (in Cycle 8) and the pattern of population decrease (Cycle 5) and, possibly, even of the vanishing of songbirds in America (Cycles 1 and 3).

In Cycle 9, the causal connection between size of forest tract and number of nests and songbirds is explicitly mentioned, thereby prompting activation of *the missing species could be found in large tracks of forest* and *missing species could not be found in isolated tracks* in Cycle 5 and of the notion of preference for nesting in large forest plots and avoiding isolated plots (Cycle 8). To achieve referential coherence, the phrase *this hypothesis* activates the referent, namely the hypothesis and its central concepts (*prefer, large plots,* and so on) described in Cycle 8, whereas the phrase *these birds* prompts activation of its referent, namely *songbirds*. The latter referential inference either spans a fairly long distance (from Cycle 3) or is made indirectly via a later cycle in which *songbirds* was activated as part of comprehension or cohort activation. Cycle 9 contains another cue designed to increase activation, namely the phrase *It is important to note that....* As before, if such cues are effective then the landscape of activations should differ between a text with and a text without the cue (Gaddy et al., 2001). In Cycle 10, *songbird, species, forest,* and *size* activate the nodes created for these terms in earlier cycles, and *forest fragments* activates *forest fragmentation effect* mentioned in Cycles 6 and 7. To understand the referent for the phrase *the presence or absence*, readers are likely to note the semantic similarity of the concepts *decline, vanish,* and *decrease.* If so, then these concepts will be reactivated. The concept *they* calls for a referential inference. As before, some readers may infer an agent, either from episodic memory (e.g., the same agent who did the *understanding* in Cycle 2 or 5) or from background knowledge. The fact that *they* (whoever they are) set out to document the possible correlation between songbird presence and forest size is caused by the establishment of the hypothesis in Cycle 9: If there had been no hypothesis predicting such a correlation (Cycle 9), it is unlikely that it would have been considered (Cycle 10). Thus, the concepts central to this hypothesis are activated from Cycle 9. Finally, the linguistic cue *however* indicates a contrast with the information in the preceding cycle, and hence the latter information (i.e., the prediction of increased density of birds' nests with increased forest size) remains activated at a higher level than it would due to carryover alone.

signals

The input in Cycle 11 requires the generation of several inferences. The *obtaining of results* prompts the reader to infer that the results in question originated from the effort to document the absence/presence of the songbird species (Cycle 10). Thus, a causal connection is established between the information in Cycle 10 and the *obtaining of results* in Cycle 11. The *mixed and—sometimes—contradictory* nature of the results, together with the activated information from Cycle 10, is likely to generate the inference that some results indicated that songbirds were more present in large forest fragments whereas others indicated that presence or absence was not related to forest size. It is even possible that readers, at this point, anticipate the contents of upcoming text, whether it is an explicit statement concerning the ambiguous nature of the results or of the implications of such results. Such anticipation involves recruitment of background knowledge from semantic memory and would result in activation of concepts that have not yet been mentioned in the text and, indeed, may never be (see van den Broek, 1990; van den Broek et al., 1995). Finally, in a reverse referential inference, the concept *researchers* may disambiguate the concept *they* from the preceding cycle. This completes the reading of this passage.

Figure 6.1 provides a graphic representation of the fluctuating activations during reading of the *Songbird* passage. For this illustration we have assumed the following activation values for concepts at each cycle:

Explicitly mentioned concept = 5 – 7 (depending on its position in the propositional hierarchy in this cycle)

Reinstatement due to synonym = original value minus 1.

Reinstatement due to the standards of causal/referential coherence, contrastive cues, and superordination = 4.

Reinstatement due to the standard of locational coherence = 2.

Increases in activation due to linguistic markers (e.g., underline) = original value plus 1.

These values are selected on the basis of prior research (Tzeng, Linderholm, Virtue, & van den Broek, 2000; van den Broek et al., 1999). As mentioned previously, it is possible to empirically test for the optimal values and, conversely, one can contrast models with different value settings to test specific theoretical hypotheses about the relative importance of possible sources of activation.

The Mental Representation of the Songbird *Passage.* The fluctuating patterns of activation lead to the gradual construction of a mental representation of the text. Concepts accumulate activation, resulting in representational nodes of varying strengths, and connections between co-occurring nodes are strengthened as a function of the activations of each node involved. The result is a network representation of the entire passage. Examples of the translation of online activations into an off-line representation can be found in van den Broek, Risden et al. (1996) and van den Broek et al. (1999).

A detailed description of the properties of this network would go beyond the space limitations of the current chapter. An illustration of the types of properties captured may be useful however. Figure 6.2 depicts one important property of memory representation—the strength of the connections that each concept has to other concepts in the representation. This figure is based on the application of the Landscape model to the text, using the activations of concepts described in the preceding subsection. The horizontal axis of the figure displays the concepts in the representation, and the vertical axis indicates the total accumulated strength of connections that each concept has to all other concepts. According to the Landscape model, the more highly connected concepts are the most central to the structure and, hence, to the meaning of the text. If we consider those concepts/propositions that have accumulated a total connection strength of 30 or more, we find that these consist of *the songbirds are vanishing, the species is in large forest tracts but not isolated ones*, and the *forest fragmentation effect*. These concepts indeed capture the major information in the text. If we consider concepts/propositions that have accumulated somewhat fewer connection strengths, information about the scientists (or other inferred data-gather-

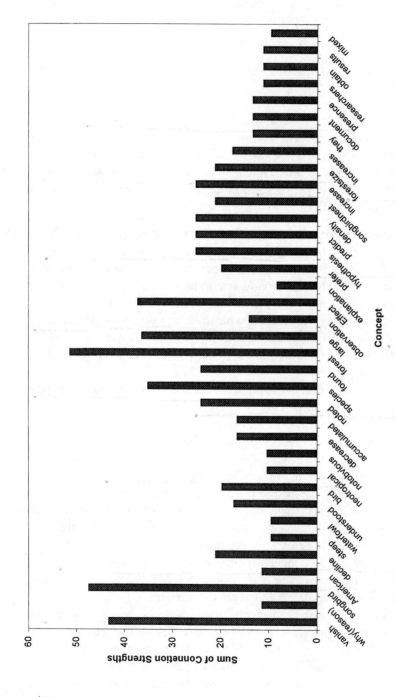

FIG. 6.2. Strengths of connections between concepts in memory representation of the *Songbird* passage (concept labels are used as shorthand notations for the major propositions in the text).

ing agents) is encountered (*they noted, they found*) as is the resulting hypothesis (*the hypothesis predicts that the density of songbirds' nests will increase with forest size*). Finally, in this segment the information about types of birds other than songbirds takes a backseat, as do the *mixed results*. If the text would continue elaborating on the mixed and sometime contradictory results, this information would attain a more prominent place in the overall representation of the text; but for now its importance in the final structure of the text is minor. In summary, connective centrality appears to capture quite well the relative importance of the various propositions in the text. This brief illustration shows how the network captures important aspects of the mental representation that results from the comprehension process. Other important features include the overall memory strengths of individual nodes, the connection between specific concepts, possible clusters of concepts, and so on.

DISCUSSION

In this chapter we have laid out a detailed description of the cognitive processes that take place during reading comprehension and the construction of a mental representation of a text. Our knowledge of these processes is based primarily on investigations of the comprehension of narratives. Comprehension of both narrative and expository texts relies on the same general cognitive processes and architectures, such as limited working memory capacity, long-term and episodic memories, attempts to maintain coherence during reading, the information sources and activation processes available to do so, and the establishment of a memory representation of the text over the course of reading. However, the specific contents of these processes and structures are likely to differ for the two types of text. For example, narrative texts possess a causal-temporal structure that is often more familiar to readers than the logical structure of expository texts (Cote, Goldman, & Saul, 1998). Likewise, the content of narrative texts often deals with topics that also are familiar to readers, such as human relationships or interpersonal problem solving; Expository texts, in contrast, often deal with topics that are novel and hence less familiar to readers. Further, the comprehension of narrative texts appears to rely on readers' attempts to establish certain types of coherence (primarily causal and referential) whereas comprehension of expository texts is likely to involve different types of coherence. As a result of these differences in familiarity with textual structure (e.g., logical, categorical, point-counterpoint), content and standards of coherence, the types of relations that readers identify in different types of text will vary.

This chapter is intended to highlight the relations that are most important in the comprehension of expository texts.

To illustrate how these processes might operate in the comprehension of expository texts, we walked step-by-step through an expository passage and described how the activation of concepts fluctuates as the reader proceeds through the text. Textual cues, inferential processes, properties of the human cognitive system (i.e., limited attentional resources, cohort activation of episodic and semantic memory, the reciprocal relation between episodic representation and activation at each cycle, access to background knowledge, reading goals and standards of coherence) all converge to determine at each point in reading what information will be in the focus of attention. The resulting activation patterns lead to the gradual emergence of a representation of the whole text in episodic memory. This representation constitutes a central component of the reader's understanding of the text.

The step-by-step analyses show that the reading process is extremely complex, even though we simplified matters by not describing at each cycle how cohorts of associated concepts are activated and by only including activated background knowledge at a few points in reading. Even in a short passage like *Songbird*, many inferences are generated. In this context, it is important to note that we have identified only a subset of all the connections that a reader could infer. The subset is based on the assumption of a reader who is only moderately engaged in the reading task, and who attempts to maintain standards of coherence that have appeared to be general across readers and reading tasks. However, readers may adopt different standards of coherence and hence generate different inferences. This would have a direct impact on the patterns of activation and the ensuing representation. The point of the illustration is to show the many sources and processes of activation that together create the patterns of activation.

The illustration also demonstrates that local comprehension processes aimed at simply understanding the information in the current cycle, can go a long way toward establishing global coherence. This is illustrated, for example, by the fact that the activation patterns of the landscape for the *Songbird* passage resulted in a memory representation in which the thematic information was very prominent. Local, bottom-up processes alone will not always yield the overall theme of the text, but this illustration shows that they can lead to a representation that captures a surprisingly large portion of the overall structure of the text.

In addition to providing a theoretical framework for understanding expository text comprehension, the Landscape model provides a powerful methodological tool. As we indicated at several points in the chapter, the model can be used to describe and test specific alternative theoretical ideas. One example is the notion that typographical cues can enhance the activation of the marked concepts. One can generate two landscapes of activation, one with and one without added activation due to the markers, and their accompanying memory representations. We can then test which landscape of activation best predicts the empirical data. A second example involves the creation of landscapes of activation to test which standards of coherence readers do or do not apply. These examples illustrate that the Landscape view of reading comprehension provides a powerful platform for testing theoretical ideas.

Finally, the Landscape view of reading has practical implications. We can compare the activation patterns for different groups of developing readers and identify strategies (for readers or for instructors) that may prevent or solve potential reading problems (van den Broek & Kremer, 2000). One can use the Landscape model to identify locations in a text that are likely to tax the readers' capacities. These analyses, in turn, can be used to revise texts to improve their comprehensibility (Linderholm et al., 2000).

Reading is a very complex process, dependent on the successful convergence of many processes and skills. To understand this process, and why it may go wrong, it is essential to consider all of these processes and skills simultaneously. The Landscape view of reading of expository texts helps us appreciate this complexity and gives us the tools to study the process in detail.

ACKNOWLEDGMENTS

This research was supported by the Golestan Foundation at the Netherlands Institute for the Advanced Study in the Humanities and Social Sciences, by the Guy Bond Endowment for Reading and Literacy, and by the Center for Cognitive Sciences at the University of Minnesota through a grant from the National Institute of Child Health and Human Development (HD-07151). Correspondence concerning this chapter should be addressed to Paul van den Broek, Department of Educational Psychology, Burton Hall, 178 Pillsbury Drive S. E., University of Minnesota, Minneapolis, MN 55455. E-mail: pvdbroek@umn.edu. Tel. (612) 626–1302. Fax (612) 624–8241.

REFERENCES

Bloom, C. P., Fletcher, C. R., van den Broek, P., Reitz, L., & Shapiro, B. P. (1990). An on-line assessment of causal reasoning during comprehension. *Memory and Cognition, 18*, 65–71.

Casteel, M. A. (1993). Effects of inference necessity and reading goal on children's inferential generation. *Developmental Psychology, 29*, 346–357.

Casteel, M. A, & Simpson, G. B. (1991). Textual coherence and the development of inferential generation skills. *Journal of Research in Reading, 14,* 116–129.

Coté, N., Goldman, S. R., & Saul, E. U. (1998). Students making sense of informational text: Relations between processing and representation. *Discourse Processes, 25,* 1–53.

Daneman, M., & Carpenter, P. A. (1980). Individual differences in working memory and reading. *Journal of Verbal Learning and Verbal Behavior, 19,* 450–466.

Fletcher, C. R., Hummel, J. E., & Marsolek, C. J. (1990). Causality and the allocation of attention during comprehension. *Journal of Experimental Psychology: Learning, Memory, and Cognition, 16,* 233–240.

Gaddy, M., van den Broek, P., & Sung, Y. (2001). The influence of text cues on the allocation of attention during reading. In T. Sanders, J. Schilperoord, & W. Spooren (Eds.), *Cognitive approaches to text coherence* (pp. 89–110). Amsterdam: Benjamins.

Gernsbacher, M. A. (1990). *Language comprehension as structure building.* Hillsdale, NJ: Lawrence Erlbaum Associates.

Goldman, S. R., & Varma, S. (1995). CAPping the construction-integration model of discourse comprehension. In C. A. Weaver, S. Mannes, & C. R. Fletcher (Eds.), *Discourse comprehension: Essays in honor of Walter Kintsch* (pp. 337–358). Hillsdale, NJ: Lawrence Erlbaum Associates.

Graesser, A. C., & Clark, L. F. (1985). *The structures and procedures of implicit knowledge.* Norwood, NJ: Ablex.

Graesser, A. C., Singer, M., & Trabasso, T. (1994). Constructing inferences during narrative text comprehension. *Psychological Review, 101,* 371–395.

Just, M. A., & Carpenter, P. A. (1992). A capacity theory of comprehension: Individual differences in working memory. *Psychological Review, 99,* 122–149.

Kintsch, W. (1988). The role of knowledge in discourse comprehension: A construction-integration model. *Psychological Review, 95,* 163–182.

Kintsch, W., & van Dijk, T. A. (1978). Toward a model of text comprehension and production. *Psychological Review, 85,* 363–394.

Langston, M. C., & Trabasso, T. (1998). Identifying causal connections and modeling integration of narrative discourse. In H. van Oostendorp & S. R. Goldman (Eds.), *The construction of mental representations during reading* (pp. 29–69). Mahwah, NJ: Lawrence Erlbaum Associates.

León, J. A., & Carretero, M. (1992). Signals effects on the recall and understanding of expository texts in expert and novice readers. In A. Oliveira (Ed.), *Hypermedia courseware: Structures of communication and intelligent help* (pp. 97–111). New York: Springer-Verlag.

Linderholm, T., Everson, M. G., van den Broek, P., Mischinski, M., Crittenden, A., & Samuels, J. (2000). Effects of casual text revisions on more- and less-skilled readers' comprehension of easy and difficult text. *Cognition and Instruction, 18,* 525–556.

Lorch, R. F., Jr. (1989). Text-signaling devices and their effects on reading and memory processes. *Educational Psychology Review, 1,* 209–234.

Lorch, R. F., Jr., & Lorch, E. P. (1996). Effects of organizational signals on free recall of expository text. *Journal of Educational Psychology, 88,* 38–48.

Lorch, R. F., Jr., Lorch, E. P., & Klusewitz, M. A. (1995). Effects of typographical cues on reading and recall of text. *Contemporary Educational Psychology, 20*, 51–64.

Mackie, J. L. (1980). *The cement of the universe: A study of causation*. Oxford: Clarendon.

McKoon, G., & Ratcliff, R. (1980). The comprehension processes and memory structures involved in anaphoric reference. *Journal of Verbal Learning and Verbal Behavior, 19*, 668–682.

Miller, G. A. (1956). The magic seven, plus or minus two: Some limits of our capacity for processing information. *Psychological Review, 63*, 81–97.

Narváez, D., van den Broek, P., & Ruiz, A. B. (1999). The influence of reading purpose on inference generation and comprehension in reading. *Journal of Educational Psychology, 91*, 488–496.

O'Brien, E. J., & Myers, J. L. (1987). The role of causal connections in the retrieval of text. *Memory & Cognition, 15*, 419–427.

O'Brien, E. J., & Myers, J. L. (1999). Text comprehension: A view from the bottom up. In S. R. Goldman, A. C. Graesser, & P. van den Broek (Eds.), *Narrative comprehension, causality, and coherence: Essays in honor of Tom Trabasso* (pp. 35–53). Mahwah, NJ: Lawrence Erlbaum Associates.

Singer, M. (1994). Inference generation during reading. In M. A. Gernbacher (Ed.), *Handbook of psycholinguistics* (pp. 479–515). New York: Academic Press.

Singer, M., & Ritchot, K. F. M. (1996). The role of working capacity and knowledge access in text inference processing. *Memory & Cognition, 24*, 733–743.

Suh, S. Y., & Trabasso, T. (1993). Inferences during reading: Converging evidence from discourse analysis, talk-aloud protocols, and recognition priming. *Journal of Memory and Language, 32*, 279–300.

Trabasso, T., Secco, T., & van den Broek, P. W. (1984). Causal cohesion and story coherence. In H. Mandl, N. L. Stein, & T. Trabasso (Eds.), *Learning and comprehension of text* (pp. 83–111). Hillsdale, NJ: Lawrence Erlbaum Associates.

Trabasso, T., & Suh, S. Y. (1993). Using talk-aloud protocols to reveal inferences during comprehension of text. *Discourse Processes, 16*, 283–298.

Trabasso, T., van den Broek, P., & Suh, S. Y. (1989). Logical necessity and transitivity of causal relations in stories. *Discourse Processes, 12*, 1–25.

Turner, A., & Greene, E. (1978). Construction and use of a propositional text base. *JSAS Catalogue of Selected Documents in Psychology*. (MS No. 1713), 8, p. 58.

Tzeng, Y., Linderholm, T., Virtue, S., & van den Broek, P. (2000). *The online availability of reading elements: Predictions and evidence from a comprehensive theory*. Manuscript submitted for publication.

van den Broek, P. (1990). The causal inference maker: Towards a process model of inference generation in text comprehension. In D. A. Balota, G. B. Flores d'Arcais, & K. Rayner (Eds.), *Comprehension processes in reading* (pp. 423–445). New York: Academic Press.

van den Broek, P. (1994). Comprehension and memory of narrative texts: Inferences and coherence. In M. A. Gernsbacher (Ed.), *Handbook of psycholinguistics* (pp. 539–588). San Diego: Academic Press.

van den Broek, P., & Kremer, K. (2000). The mind in action: What it means to comprehend during reading. In B. M. Taylor, P. van den Broek, & M. Graves (Eds.), *Reading for meaning* (pp. 1–31). New York: Teachers College Press.

van den Broek, P., & Lorch, R. F., Jr. (1993). Network representations of causal relations in memory for narrative texts: Evidence from primed recognition. *Discourse Processes, 16*, 75–98.

van den Broek, P., Lorch, R. F. Jr., Linderholm, T., & Gustafson, M. (in press). *The effect of readers' goals on the generation of inferences. Memory and Cognition.* Manuscript submitted for publication.

van den Broek, P., Risden, K., Fletcher, C. R., & Thurlow, R. (1996). A "landscape" view of reading (Fluctuating patterns of activation) and the construction of a stable memory representation. In B. K. Britton & A. C. Graesser (Eds.), *Models of understanding text* (pp. 165–187). Mahwah, NJ: Lawrence Erlbaum Associates.

van den Broek, P., Risden, K., & Husebye-Hartmann, E. (1995). The role of readers' standards for coherence in the generation of inferences during reading. In R. F. Lorch, Jr. & E. J. O'Brien (Eds.), *Sources for coherence in reading* (pp. 353–374). Hillsdale, NJ: Lawrence Erlbaum Associates.

van den Broek, P., Rohleder, L., & Narvaez, D. (1996). Causal inferences in the comprehension of literary texts. In R. J. Kreuz & M. S. McNealy (Eds.), *Empirical approaches to literature and aesthetics. Advances in discourse processes* (pp. 179–200). Norwood, NJ: Ablex.

van den Broek, P., & Trabasso, T. (1986). Causal networks versus goal hierarchies in summarizing text. *Discourse Processes, 9*, 1–15.

van den Broek, P., Young, M., Tzeng, Y., & Linderholm, T. (1999). The landscape model of reading: Inferences and on-line construction of a memory representation. In H. van Oostendorp & S. R. Goldman (Eds.), *The construction of mental representations during reading* (pp. 71–98). Mahwah, NJ: Lawrence Erlbaum Associates.

van Oostendorp, H. (1994). Text processing in terms of semantic cohesion monitoring. In H. van Oostendorp & R. A. Zwaan (Eds.), *Naturalistic text comprehension* (pp. 35–56). Norwood, NJ: Ablex.

Waters, S., & Caplan, D. (1996). Processing resource capacity and the comprehension of garden path sentences. *Memory & Cognition, 24*, 342–355.

Whitney, P., Ritchie B. G., & Clark, M. B. (1991). Working memory capacity and the use of elaborative inferences in text comprehension. *Discourse Processes, 14*, 133–145.

Zwaan, R. A., Langston, M. C., & Graesser, A. C. (1995). The construction of situation models in narrative comprehension: An event-indexing model. *Psychological Science, 6*, 292–297.

❧ 7 ❧

Understanding Causality and Temporal Sequence in Scientific Discourse

José A. León
Gala E. Peñalba
Universidad Autonóma, Madrid

Although there exist no universally accepted definitions of causality, it is widely assumed that causal beliefs are essential for human comprehension. The notion of causality is inherent in the very nature of human cognition because knowledge about events implies, among other things, the belief that all events have causes (Noordman & Vonk, 1998). People frequently use rules to assess cause and effect and thus to interpret reality. These rules are applied both in the context of science and in daily life.

The study of causality has attracted the attention of scholars and scientists in such diverse fields as philosophy, psychology, linguistics, statistics, and various experimental disciplines. A formal definition or description of causality that would cover theories from the various disciplines would incorporate the causal cues of covariation, contiguity between cause and effect, and chronological order (Einhorn & Hogarth, 1986; Mackie, 1980; Salmon, 1998). More recently, in different domains such as physics, psychology, or biology, there has been a multidisciplinary debate that inquires how many innate causal modules humans have (Sperber, Premack, & Premack, 1995). Sperber et al. claimed that the existence of cognition in

155

the animal kingdom is an outcome of biological evolution and that cognition has the ability to represent causal regularities so that the organism has some control over its environment.

In psychology, Piaget (1927b), Michotte (1946), and Heider (1944, 1958) began the examination of causal cognition. Following these pioneers came important contributions from the social psychologists who investigated causal attributions in interpersonal and social domains, from the psychologists of reasoning who were interested in general properties of logical causal inferences (Hewstone, 1989; Schustack, 1988), and from the developmental psychologists who examined the types of causal understanding specific to physics, to commonsense psychology, and to innate capacities (Carey & R. Gelman, 1991; Hirschfeld & S. A. Gelman, 1991). A very recent body of research in discourse psychology investigates causal models in text comprehension, causal inferences in narrative discourse, and the knowledge structures that highlight the human intention and causation that explain states, actions, and events (Langston & Trabasso, 1999; Magliano, Baggett, Johnson, & Graesser, 1993; Myers, Shinjo, & Duffy, 1987; Trabasso, Secco, & van den Broek, 1984; Trabasso & Sperry, 1985).

In spite of the central role that causal explanation plays in scientific discourse, its study is underdeveloped when compared with the considerable advances in the study of causality in narrative discourse. Two possible explanations for the comparative neglect of causality in science texts are (a) the diversity of causal relations that occur in science texts and (b) the readers' lack of familiarity with subject matters of science. There remain many important questions about the causal interpretations that are affiliated with science texts. What do we mean exactly by causality? How is causality constructed in the reader's mind? What knowledge structures are needed to recover a causal relation? Are there different ways of understanding causal relations, depending on whether the information is everyday knowledge versus science? Is chronological order an essential component in the generation of a causal relation? Is chronological order important to the understanding of scientific text? When we have clear answers to these questions, we hope to be able to use them to improve understanding in education and the design of textbooks.

In this chapter we analyze a number of features of causality, but focus particularly on the temporal sequence or chronological order of the events in the causal chain. We explore how temporality influences comprehension and the mental representation of scientific texts. The chapter has four sections. In the first, we present a definition of causality that views it as a primary organizational principle of human knowledge. We discuss two modes of cognitive functioning (well-structured story vs. well-formed logical argument), and two genres (narrative vs. scientific). In the second part, we describe some "consequences" of causality in comprehension, discourse processes, and prior knowledge. In the third part, we analyze how temporality influences comprehension and the mental representation; we report some empirical data from a study of causal inferences and from an experimental study in biology. Lastly, we suggest some conclusions about the type of cognitive functioning that seems to dominate comprehension, namely the construction of chronology. This chronological organization prevails in spite of the rhetorical organization of the text.

WHAT IS CAUSALITY?

Here-conceptual events

Causality can be seen in at least three different ways. Following Bunge (1959), causality could be defined as a *category* (corresponding to a causal link), as a *principle* (general causal law), and as a *doctrine* (considering the causal principle as universal and excluding all the other explanatory principles). Here, we take causality to be a category in both the general and the particular sense. On the one hand, there is the general relation that exists between the phenomenon of pollution of rivers and the effects this produces on the fauna and flora. On the other hand, there are the specific details about the pollution of one particular river, such as the Thames River. Causality is synonymous with the causal connections between events that Galileo (1623/1890–1909) described as "a strong and unchanging connection" (Vol. 6, p. 265).

We do not wish to enter the ongoing debates as to whether causality reflects the real world or not, and whether psychological and physical causality are the same construct (Salmon, 1998). We take the position that causality consists of a relation in the domain of mental entities. That is, it refers to conceptual events rather than an objective relationship in reality (Lenzen, 1954). Thus, we include logically and true relations that can be deduced from experience, causal relations deduced from science, and causal explanations that are generated when readers try to explain why the events, states, and actions exist or occur.

We view causality as an ontological property that is inherent in human reasoning. It is a type of relation between ideas that may or may not correspond to some feature in the real world. There are many different regularities in the world that may account for the induction of causal relations. These include covariation, contiguity between cause and effect, necessity and sufficiency, and the temporal sequence of antecedent and consequence

(Einhorn & Hogarth, 1986; Mackie, 1980; van den Broek, 1990b). There is a school of thought in psychology that states that a fundamental constraint on causal reasoning is that causes must precede their effects in time (Hume, 1739–1740/1888, Russell, 1953). For Russell, if there are causes and effects, they should be separated by a finite period of time. Hartmann (1949) claimed that causality means that in the order of events, those that come later are determined by those that occur earlier. Temporal order may be directly observable, such as when someone has an accident and then blood appears in the place of the wound. Even when cues are observed simultaneously or when the order of causality is reversed, we might see blood on our body and infer there must be wound. The natural causal model specifies a temporal direction from causes to their effects.

We believe that causal reasoning is necessary to relate clauses meaningfully and to achieve coherent causal explanations (Langston & Trabasso, 1999; Mackie, 1980). Causal reasoning requires prior knowledge, text, and inferences that consume a nontrivial amount of mental activity. Readers use prior knowledge from long-term memory and working memory, and they integrate this knowledge with the information extracted from the text. Readers build a situation model in order to understand, to interpret, to explain why a consequence could be produced, and to predict a consequence from an antecedent described in the text.

TWO MODES OF THOUGHT AND TWO GENRES

People presumably use rules to assess cause and effect and to interpret reality, both in the context of science and in daily life. Are the foundations of causality different in science and daily life? Is causality different when readers understand narratives versus science texts? Some researchers believe there is a natural way of thinking about causality, a way that parallels the narrative mode of thinking about daily concepts. In contrast, there is an analytical, logical mode that is more appropriate for scientific concepts and context. These two modes of cognitive functioning are correlated with different genres of texts, namely, narrative and expository (Brewer, 1980; Einstein, McDaniel, Owen, & Coté, 1990; Harris, Rogers, & Qualls, 1998; McDaniel, Einstein, Cunay, & Cobb, 1986;). Bruner (1986) put this clearly:

> There are two modes of cognitive functioning, two modes of thought, each providing distinctive ways of ordering experience, of constructing reality. The two (though complementary) are irreducible to one another. Efforts to reduce one mode to the other or to ignore one at the expense of the other inevitably fail to capture the rich diversity of thought. (p. 11).

This author claims that the two modes of cognitive functioning are reflected in a well-structured story versus a well-formed logical argument. The functioning of these two modes differs radically and each could be closely related to two different types of text, narrative versus expository/scientific (see chap. 2, this volume). Following Bruner, one mode, the well-structured story or narrative mode, deals with "good stories, gripping drama, believable and fictional historical accounts" (p. 13). It shows the humans, motives, actions, and problems that we come across in daily life. The narrative mode frequently reflects the time that controls the way we experience events. In contrast, the scientific (well-formed logical argument in Bruner's words) or expository mode attempts to fulfill the ideal of "a formal, mathematical system of description and explanation" (p. 12). Science texts frequently have conceptualizations of ideas, explicitly specified rhetorical *Expository* organization, jargon, context-bound terminology, and technical uses of terms (see chaps. 2 and 4, this volume).

There are several reasons why the types of causality implied in the two modes of cognitive functioning and in the two genres of the text could also be different. One of them claims that the differences appear in the logical proposition "if x, then y," and in the narrative expression "The king died, and then the queen died" (Bruner, 1986). The logical or scientific mode leads to a search for universal truth conditions. Causal network structures prevail. In the narrative mode, in contrast, goal structures prevail and there are connections between events that do not have a strictly causal foundation, as in the case of death and sorrow, or law and death (Bruner, 1986; Graesser & Bertus, 1998). Another possible reason is based on the degree of generalization and the number of observations that are needed to construct a causal explanation. In science, the usual aim is to establish causal generalizations to explain a sample of observations (Hart & Honoré, 1959; White, 1989). But in daily life we normally want to explain single events and cases, which means that the scientific method, with its emphasis on generalization, is not very suitable. A third possible reason is attributed to the structure of the text. Simple oral narratives take on the form of a story grammar and its mental representation, the story schema (Kintsch, 1977; Mandler & Johnson, 1977; Stein & Glenn, 1979; Thorndyke, 1977). Knowledge of a story schema permits the reader to perform the following functions:

- To associate the narrative ideas they encounter in the text with categories such as setting, theme, plot, and resolution (Singer, Harkness, & Stewart, 1997).

- To recognize constituents of a story, such as agent, intention or goal, situation, instrument, that can be considered arguments of actions (Bruner, 1986; Trabasso, van den Broek, & Suh, 1989).
- To identify the temporal sequencing of actions in a script (Schank, 1975). In most narratives, chronology is an important principle for organizing causality. We learn causality by discovering the co-occurrence between causes and effects in the real world, such that the causes precede the effects. This order is not always followed in scientific contexts.

Expository texts and complex narratives, in contrast, are much less predictable in form than simple stories. It has been suggested that the higher level processing of expository texts requires very abstract categories, mechanisms, descriptions, and arguments. These elements, in turn, are organized into abstract structures, such as linear chains and hierarchies, and into rhetorical networks, such as the comparison of two or more elements (Black, 1985).

TEXTS WITH CASUAL RELATIONS AS A BASIC ORGANIZATIONAL PRINCIPLE OF HUMAN KNOWLEDGE

There are some important repercussions that causality has on narrative and expository texts as a consequence of its crucial role in human cognition. This section lists a number of them.

Narrative Text Comprehension

Readers understand an event when they are capable of relating it to other events in a text. One of the most important links is causality. It is not surprising that those who first conducted research on comprehension suggested that causal relationships play an essential role in narrative understanding (Bartlett, 1932; Dewey, 1938; Piaget 1927a, 1927b). Researchers of narrative comprehension in the 1970s shared the assumption that causal representations were central in the comprehension and memory of narratives (Mandler & Johnson, 1977; Rumelhart, 1975; Schank & Abelson, 1977; Stein & Glenn, 1979; Thorndyke, 1977). There were strong associations in memory between narrative events that share a direct causal connection (Trabasso & Sperry, 1985; Trabasso & van den Broek, 1985). There is plenty of evidence that both the strength and the number of causal connections determine the probability of comprehension and recall of the information read (Britton & Graesser, 1996) as well as the level of importance assigned by the reader to the text information (Trabasso & Sperry, 1985; van den Broek, 1988). As a consequence, causal models have been prevalent in psychological studies of narrative comprehension (Graesser, Swamer, Baggett, & Sell, 1996; Langston & Trabasso, 1999; Trabasso et al., 1984; van den Broek, Young, Tzeng, & Linderholm, 1999).

Science Text Comprehension

Causal relation, as a basic organizational principle, is also an explanatory principle, telling us what, how, why, and when the causality occurs. Scientific explanations are often causal (Salmon, 1998; see also chap. 5, this volume) and elicited by posing *why-questions*. That is, when we give scientific explanations, we answer *why* a particular phenomenon occurs. For instance, it is common knowledge that a certain amount of pollution in a river kills some of its fish and plants, and that pollution causes serious problems to nature. These and many others beliefs make up our common sense causal understanding of the natural world, including human beings and their interactions with nature. The characteristics of this system and the way it operates are a matter for scientific debate. That is, we produce scientific discourse with explanations of, for example, *why* pollution occurs, *what* it means, *how* and *when* it takes place, and *what* the consequences are.

Some models and theories in discourse psychology have focused on the psychological mechanisms that underlie the comprehension of causal relationships in these scientific contexts. There have been investigations of the inferences that explain, elaborate, or predict events in causal chains in science (Britton & Black, 1985; Graesser & Bertus, 1998; Millis & Graesser, 1994; see also chap. 6, this volume). Sometimes it is difficult to comprehend the text because of the lack of subject matter knowledge, whereas at other times there is a lack of text coherence. These barriers make it difficult, if not impossible, to link the text causally (McKeown, Beck, Sinatra, & Loxterman, 1992). Expository texts therefore require more intense processing than the narrative texts. Comprehending science discourse requires different kinds of knowledge to form an explanation, such as conceptual and abstract knowledge, mathematical and logical argumentation, and procedural or strategic action.

Graesser and his colleagues developed a model of question answering, called QUEST, to explain readers' responses to questions about expository and narrative texts (Graesser, 1981; Graesser & Clark, 1985; Graesser & Hemphill, 1991; Graesser & Murachver, 1985). Graesser and Hemphill pointed out an important distinction between events and actions in

QUEST's representation model in scientific texts. They claimed that the QUEST model identifies important differences between the question answering procedures of queried events and those of queried actions. In their study, their science texts were sometimes ambiguous as to whether the statements referred to actions or events. Graesser and Hemphill claimed that for readers answering questions about physical systems, causal networks prevail, but in biological and technological systems, goal structures prevail. In other words, whereas in physical science domains the statements clearly referred to events rather than intentional actions, a goal-oriented, teleological ontology was predominant when college students answered why-questions about biological and technological systems.

These results suggest that the causal structures in narrative and scientific texts are not as different as we claimed at the beginning of this chapter. For example, goal structures, an important compositional ingredient of narrative texts, are also found in scientific texts about biology and technology. These results have been confirmed in other studies (e.g., León, Otero, Escudero, Campanario, & Pérez, 1999). León et al. studied the comprehension performance of postgraduates in language and social sciences compared to students in experimental sciences (e.g., physics). The participants answered why-questions about their prior knowledge of physics concepts in two different contexts: naturalistic event (e.g., *why do the stars twinkle?*) and technological events (e.g., *why does a submarine dive?*, or *why do they paint their houses white in Andalusia?*). The principal aim of this work was to analyze how the participants use naive theories of physical (or psychological) causality from their general or specific knowledge to determine "why" each event has occurred. The results showed differences between the two groups in their causal explanations about antecedents. Thus, the elements in the causal chain are seen by the nonexperts as observable events (e.g. water is allowed into the submarine's tanks), whereas the experts preferred to use scientific constructs (e.g., there is a force that acts in a downward direction). Whereas the experts try to identify the center of the causal chain, the nonexperts prefer to look for a functional explanation, asking themselves the question "what for?" (with answers such as *so that the houses will be cooler*), and focusing on goal structures.

It appears that the choice of causal relation depends on prior knowledge (general vs. specific) and context (physical science vs. technology). If this knowledge is specific, then subjects will focus on the nucleus of causal relations, whereas more general knowledge probably produces a more visual and commonsense answer. A physics context would facilitate causal explanations that center on causal logic, whereas a technological context would focus on goals.

CAUSALITY AND PRIOR KNOWLEDGE

Readers have an enormous amount of general and specific world knowledge that is potentially relevant to an understanding of the information in the text. As we have just seen, readers use naive theories of psychological and physical causality to determine "why" each event in a scientific text has occurred. Explanations are found by searching relevant knowledge structures (e.g., scripts, frames, schematas, memory organization packets, etc.) to place an event in an appropriate causal context. Explanations provide causal information regarding reasons, antecedents, and enabling conditions. In many situations, this prior knowledge is so active that it works in contexts where causal explanations are either not necessary or incorrect. For example, adults may give explanations both for occurrences that are normal or can be expected (Lalljee & Abelson, 1983; Read, 1987; Winter & Uleman, 1984), and for those that are unusual or unexpected (Weiner, 1985).

A number of philosophers and psychologists have argued that people use abstract world knowledge that is meaningful for them to guide their causal explanations about new domains (Cheng, 1993; Cheng & Holyoak, 1995; Einhorn & Hogarth, 1986; Holyoak, Koh, & Nisbett, 1989; Mackie, 1980; Waldmann & Holyoak, 1992). Mackie suggested that cause and effect are seen as "differences within a causal field," where cause is understood by the reader from the specific type of background knowledge possessed. Several authors have noted that, depending on the question and the knowledge implied in it, subjects select one factor or another as the cause of an event instead of providing a complete list of factors that may be related to it when offering a causal explanation (Einhorn & Hogarth, 1986; Hesslow, 1983; Hilton & Slugoski, 1986; León & Carretero, 1995; León et al., 1999; Mackie, 1980; McGill, 1989, 1991) Causal fields, then, are compatible with the idea that the prior knowledge of the subjects influences the process of "causal selection."

Another view of causality takes the perspective of the selection of causal explanations. McGill (1991) studied the effects of prior knowledge about possible causes on the selection of causal explanations. One might predict that background effects would be more difficult to produce when the manipulation of the causal background was indirect and when subjects were asked to select their explanations from a list. However, the effect of the causal background did not appear to vary with the type of the response and/or the strength of the manipulation. Thus, the process of causal selection may result from the comparison of the target episode with a contrasting causal background. Causal explanations may indicate as much about types of comparisons people consider most relevant as they do about the factors believed to be related to an event.

Causality is also an important concept in structuring knowledge, so that degrees of expertise in a particular domain are probably related to differences in the organization of causal knowledge. A number of studies have shown that the knowledge of experts is organized differently from that of nonexperts (Adelson, 1984; Chi, Glaser, & Rees, 1982; León & Pérez, 2001; Noordman & Vonk, 1998; Vonk & Noordman, 1992). The knowledge of experts is organized in higher order knowledge structures, at a more abstract level, and according to general categories, laws, and principles. There is some empirical evidence supporting this claim. León and Pérez performed several experiments in order to analyze how domain-related knowledge (in the domain of clinical psychology) influences inferences about clinical diagnosis during text comprehension. Clinical diagnoses were defined as explanatory trait inferences. In order to analyze the time course of clinical diagnosis inferences, experts and novices were compared using a lexical decision and a reading time task. An important conclusion from this work is that the experts' prior knowledge could be shown to be a decisive factor not only in the encoding and generation of the clinical inference, but also in determining when the clinical diagnosis inference is generated. Prior knowledge accelerates the activation of inferences to such an extent that it can transform an inference originally considered off-line into an online one.

There is some evidence that novice subjects in a particular domain acquire knowledge about simple causal relationships in a cause-to-effect direction (Eddy, 1982; Patel & Groen, 1986; Waldmann & Holyoak, 1992), but this pattern may change for more expert subjects who learn more complex tasks. Patel and Groen found evidence for this based on verbal protocols that were obtained during a task involving explanation of medical cases. Whereas the protocols of the novices tended to first suggest diseases and then the symptoms they might produce (following the cause-to-effect direction), experts tended to move directly from symptoms to a diagnosis (following the effect-to-cause direction). A possible explanation is that experts are faster in performing the same basic reasoning process than are novices (León & Pérez, 2001) and they may simply omit the first phase in their protocols. Another possibility is that the reasoning processes in the experts would be restructured in an effect-to-cause direction, due to practice in diagnosing cases.

CHRONOLOGICAL ORDER IN SCIENCE DISCOURSE

In the previous section, we presented some evidence that readers make causal links that depend on their causal model or schema of the situation. In order to find or preserve causal coherence during reading, readers must activate a mental model or schema (in which A causes B) and decide whether its factors and conditions are presented (explicitly or implicitly) in the situation described in the text (Noordman & Vonk, 1998). The reader who has understood the situation in this way has constructed an explanatory, causal mental model. One important example of such a schema would be abstract world knowledge about the basic characteristics of causal relations, such as the fact that causes precede effects. There is empirical evidence that people tend to make links from cause to effect, rather than vice versa (Eddy, 1982; Einhorn & Hogarth, 1986; Tversky & Kahneman, 1980). Tversky and Kahneman found that people estimated that is more likely that a blue-eyed mother will have a blue-eyed daughter than vice versa. These authors interpreted this result as evidence that people often use a directional causal schema.

Usually, in the comprehension of daily events or simple narratives, chronological order is a main criterion to organize causality. As we said, we learn causality by discovering the co-occurrence between causes and effects in the real world, in which causes precede effects. In a scientific context, in contrast, is not always possible to organize causality chronologically. Understanding science often amounts to grasping the meaning of some scientific generalization and using it to explain a specific situation in which the generalization figures (Newton, 1995). Besides this, many scientific explanations reverse the order of causality. They start with the presentation of the problem and then try to answer the question of why the problem has occurred. The reasons why scientific explanations appear in this way could be connected with the complex conceptual analysis needed in order to interpret reality according to scientific principles. This leads to an important question: Does it make a crucial difference whether the information is presented in an antecedent–consequent order or in a consequent–antecedent order?

Perceptually, cause-consequence seems to be more basic than the order consequence-cause. Some authors (e.g., Bruner, 1986; Noordman & Vonk, 1998) have suggested that, if the antecedent–consequent order is more basic, we should prefer to organize our mental model of an event from antecedents to consequences rather than vice versa. In the next section, we describe some results on the way readers generate causal inferences and how they process chronological sequencing in science text.

Research on Causal Inferences

Related to search for global coherence. (handwritten)

Knowledge about the human capacity to understand causal relations is taken from causal inference research. Langston and Trabasso (1999) claimed that causal reasoning about events requires making inferences that relate events described in the narrative text. There have been a number of studies on causal inferences focusing on different questions, such as whether readers make inferences about causes and about consequences in the context of stories (Graesser, Singer, & Trabasso, 1994; Magliano et al., 1993; Trabasso & Magliano, 1996; Trabasso, Magliano, & Graesser, 1999), about antecedent and consequent causal inferences in expository texts (Coté, Goldman, & Saul, 1998; Graesser & Bertus, 1998; Millis & Graesser, 1994; Millis, Morgan, & Graesser, 1990; Singer & Gagnon, 1999; Vonk & Noordman, 1992; see also chap. 9, this volume), about questions on short experimenter-generated textoids (Fincher-Kiefer, 1996; Potts, Keenan, & Golding, 1988; Singer, Halldorson, Lear, & Adrusik, 1992; Singer et al., 1997), and about differences made by text genre (León, Escudero, & van den Broek, 2000; Singer et al., 1997).

Most of these studies have focused mainly on two types of causal inferences: causal antecedents versus consequences. There are a number of different conceptions of causal antecedent inferences: those that are generated when readers connect a sentence with prior text (Magliano et al., 1993; Millis & Graesser, 1994), when they explain why events and actions occur (Graesser et al., 1994), and when they bridge the incoming sentence to the previous passage content via causal chains and networks (Singer et al., 1992, 1997; Trabasso & Magliano, 1996). Causal consequence inferences express outcomes or consequences in which readers predict or forecast subsequent information in the text (Magliano et al., 1993; Millis & Graesser, 1994).

Types (handwritten)

Key (handwritten)

Most of the existing research suggests that causal antecedents are generated online, whereas causal consequences are generated off-line (Graesser, Haberlandt, & Koizumi, 1987; Long, Golding, Graesser, & Clark, 1990; Potts et al., 1988; Singer & Ferreira, 1983). Most of these studies suggest that inferences about causes (antecedent) and goals play an essential role in establishing text coherence (e.g., Black & Bower, 1980; Graesser, 1981; Graesser & Clark, 1985; Singer et al., 1992; Trabasso et al., 1984; van den Broek, 1990a, 1990b) and they are made to explain the events mentioned in the text (Singer et al., 1997). In contrast, inferences about consequences are not made because there are too many possible alternative hypothetical plots that could be potentially foreseen (Graesser et al., 1994). However, there may be special conditions in which causal consequences are generated online when the context allows for only one or two possible outcomes rather than several alternatives (van den Broek, 1990b).

In addition to these effects in narratives, other factors such as prior knowledge and difficulty of the text seem to influence inference making in science text. Here, the status of causal antecedent and consequence inferences is not quite as clear-cut as it was found to be for narrative texts. So, whereas Noordman, Vonk, and Kempff (1992) reported that causal antecedent inferences are not constructed online when readers read very technical text, Singer et al. (1997), in contrast, reported that causal antecedent inferences are constructed, but only when adults are given sufficient time to read the text used in the Noordman et al. study. Similar conclusions appeared with regard to causal consequences. Whereas Millis et al. (1990) reported evidence for online consequence inferences in short expository texts on causal scientific mechanisms, Millis and Graesser (1994) proposed that causal consequence inferences would not occur online.

In general, it is assumed that causal antecedent inferences are made faster than causal consequences. We now offer some reasons supporting the importance of chronological order in this process:

1. Following Graesser and Bertus (1998), if event sequences are usually presented in chronological order, they allow readers to know the past but not the future. Thus, there are constraints on what causal antecedents are plausible. With respect to the future, however, a very large number of scenarios could emerge.

2. Another position is that of Long, Oppy, and Seely (1997). They suggested that the nature of the inferential process is very strongly motivated by a search for global coherence. This suggests the occurrence of "high-level" analytical processes, as opposed to "low-level," pattern-matching processes. Chronological order is important to organize this global coherence. Readers might, then, activate knowledge structures in long-term memory and analyze this information to find causal explanations for the events in the text. In other words, if chronological order helps to preserve global coherence of the text, then the causal antecedent will be facilitated more than the causal consequence. In fact, inferences related to narrative contexts (frequently organized in chronological order) should then be faster than in science texts (where the sequences of event do not follow a chronological order).

Causality and the Order of Information in Science Texts

If the way in which information is expressed were to correspond with the structure of human knowledge, this correspondence would presumably facilitate text processing. Thus, if the order of presentation of an explanation in the text is antecedent-consequent, text processing would be easier. Meyer Viol (1984, cited in Noordman & Vonk, 1998) tested this hypothesis in a narrative context. The experimental text contained a causal relation that was expressed in two different orders. In one condition, the cause sentence ("He had touched the stinging-nettles") preceded the consequence sentence ("His hand itched terribly"). In the other, cause and consequence were reversed ("His hand itched terribly. He had touched the stinging-nettles."). The materials were constructed in such a way that the consequence sentence was indeed a very likely, natural, and predictable consequence of the cause. The results showed that the reading times for the consequence sentences were significantly shorter when preceded by the cause sentences than otherwise.

This same hypothesis was tested for science text (León, Peñalba, Pérez, & Escudero, 2001). Two questions guided our work. Is causal structure, expressed in chronological order, a crucial factor in causal explanations in scientific texts? How does it influence mental representations of readers that differ in their prior knowledge?

Fifty-eight participants took part in this study: 35 were postgraduates in arts and social sciences and 23 were postgraduates in science. A text about pollution in the river Thames from a high school textbook served as a basis for our reading materials. The text described the different factors that had led to the pollution of the river. Two versions were constructed using modifications and explanations made by experts. These texts were analyzed in terms of their causal structure (see Fig. 7.1). One of them had an antecedent–consequent format. This version began explaining the different polluting factors and listed in chronological order the events that led to the final consequence, the death of the river Thames. In the other version, a consequent–antecedent structure was presented, in which the final consequence was presented first in the text, followed by its causes.

In order to examine whether both versions of the text were equally difficult, a preliminary study based on reading times was carried out. The results showed that both text versions were equivalent in reading times. To answer the two questions that guided our work we designed two tasks. A questionnaire was constructed to assess the levels of mental representations (surface code, textbase, and situation model) that the subjects reach as a result of

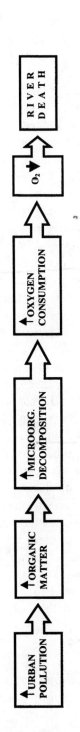

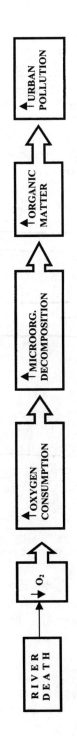

FIG. 7.1.   Partial causal structures of the Thames river text.

the text's causal structure and their prior knowledge. The other task was a causal diagram. Here, we wanted to compare the causal sequences that subjects produced in order to know if one of the causal structures was more common than the other one.

With respect to the mental representations, there were three ANOVAs (analyses of variance), each having a 2 (Group) by 2 (Version) design. The ANOVAs corresponded to three measures that tapped the surface code, the textbase, and the situation model. The results supported the claim that that causal order and prior knowledge do not seem to affect superficial code and textbase representations. However, the data did reveal that readers' prior knowledge could influence the construction of the situation model. In the expert group, the situation model was richer. They included more technical items and more additional information. With respect to the causal diagram, we performed an ANOVA with a 2 (Group) by 2 (Version) by 2 (Type of Links: A-C, C-A) design. We did not find significant differences either in the Group or Version factors. However, there were significant differences in Type of Links factor ($p < .001$). All the subjects made more AC links than CA links in their responses, independently of the text version and group. The interaction between Group × Version was significant ($p < .05$), with the postgraduates in science making more AC links in AC text version than did the postgraduates in arts. The results relating to the causal diagrams analyses indicated that both groups of subjects tended to draw links in an antecedent–consequent direction. This supports the idea that, independently of the causal order in the text, there exists a tendency to follow chronological criteria in the organization of causal chains.

These results agree with other studies (Eddy, 1982; Patel & Groen, 1986; Waldmann & Holyoak, 1992). According to these researchers, people tend to represent directed links from causes to their effects, rather than vice versa, even in situations in which they received effect-information prior to cause-information such as a text with a different causal structure. Although this may not improve comprehension, there is a preference for representing temporal order when readers organize causal explanations. This effect seems to hold not only when there is a single cause and its outcome, but also under conditions involving a single consequence (e.g., the Thames died) and multiple causes (e.g., the different types of pollutions).

CONCLUSIONS

In this chapter we have presented a theoretical framework that puts forward the possibility of two different ways of cognitive functioning that should produce different ways of construing causality: analytic versus chronological. We have described the way causal explanations are found by searching relevant knowledge structures (e.g., scripts, frames, schemata, memory organization packets, etc.) to place an event in an appropriate causal context. Readers activate knowledge structures in long-term memory and analyze this information to find causal explanations described in the text. We have also seen how readers' prior knowledge may have an important role to play in the way causal explanations are selected.

Our study used different ways of organizing text (chronological order or consequent–antecedent structure) to structure a causal explanation in science, and showed that there is a preference for antecedent–consequent order and that this could reflect our "natural" way of thinking. Chronological order improves the construction of a causal model, although this was not shown to affect understanding of science text in subjects who were university graduates. We believe that, despite this preference, other ways of constructing causal links may coexist with it, and may be used depending on factors like type of knowledge (general or specific) and the goals to be achieved (functional, pragmatic, conceptual). So, readers with a general knowledge about the text topic and a specific type of goal (functional or intentional) would build more easily a chronological causal mental structure. In contrast, readers with a good specific knowledge and a conceptual goal would rather build a C-A causal mental structure.

Another factor, the text type (narrative and scientific), may also have something to do with the way the mental model is built. In narrative, it is easy to make a mental model, because the reader has plenty of background knowledge and knows the temporal framework in which the sequence of events is structured. In this case, antecedent causal inferences might be made faster or before those referring to consequences, and there will be more predictive and consequent inferences than antecedent ones (León et al., 2000).

With respect to models of science texts, it apparently takes longer to construct a mental model of an event and a causal explanation. It takes more time to process the features of academic discourse: technicality, abstraction, complexity, and inclusion of expert knowledge. Readers need more explanatory inferences, which are an essential part of the model and which make it possible to construct a situation model for the text. In contrast, forward inferences can be made only when the reader has already built the causal situation model.

Temporal sequence is a solid criterion to organize causal structures in scientific discourse. It may improve both research on causal inferences and the study of scientific text in general. Regarding causal inferences, more evidence is needed about the nature of the inferential processes involved in maintaining global coherence. This point of view requires an exploration of inferential processes as high-level, analytical processes as opposed to low-level, pattern-matching processes. Also, these inferential processes are guided by a search for global coherence. We need to know the role of chronological order in the organization of this global coherence. We believe that causal structure has a direct and consistent impact on the type of inferences generated during comprehension.

The causal structure of science texts following a temporal sequence may have important implications on science text comprehension, especially in students with less prior knowledge. If meaningful learning in science involves the process of actively constructing conceptual relations between new knowledge and existing knowledge, conceptual relations in science must include, among others, the causal and temporal criteria to organize the science information successfully. A well-written scientific text should include information that allows students to familiarize themselves with the conceptual relations that form the basis of scientific expertise and understanding. Therefore, chronologically organizing the causal relations that underlie a scientific explanation is a first step toward achieving this goal.

In closing, the results in the present study (León et al., 2001) show that the methods used to analyze causality, such as question asking or written questionnaires, would be complemented by others, such as causal diagrams. Causal diagrams may be used to assess aspects of text representations that cannot be captured completely in other ways (Oestermeier & Hesse, 2000). In our study we used causal diagrams to assess directionality as well as the richness of the subjects' mental representation of the text content. This kind of task seems to be a promising but still relatively unexplored possibility in the study of processing causal relations.

ACKNOWLEDGMENTS

Preparation of this chapter was made possible by support from the Spanish Ministry of Education and Science Grants DGICYT PB97-0040 and DGICYT PS95-444. We are grateful to Art Graesser, Olga Pérez, Inmaculada Escudero, and Rachel Whittaker for help with the data and for useful comments on the chapter.

REFERENCES

Adelson, B. (1984). When novices surpass experts: The difficulty of a task may increase with expertise. *Journal of Experimental Psychology: Learning, Memory, and Cognition, 10,* 483–495.

Bartlett, F. C. (1932). *Remembering: A study in experimental and social psychology.* New York: MacMillan.

Black, J. B. (1985). An exposition on understanding expository texts. In B. K. Britton & J. B. Black (Eds.), *Understanding expository text: A theoretical and practical handbook for analyzing explanatory text* (pp. 249–267). Hillsdale, NJ: Lawrence Erlbaum Associates.

Black, J. B., & Bower, G. H. (1980). Story understanding as problem solving. *Poetics, 9,* 223–250.

Brewer, W. F. (1980). Literary theory, rhetoric, and stylistics: Implications for psychology. In R. J. Spiro, B. C. Bruce, & W. F. Brewer (Eds.), *Theoretical issues in reading comprehension* (pp. 221–239). Hillsdale, NJ: Lawrence Erlbaum Associates.

Britton, B. K., & Black, J. B. (Eds.). (1985). *Understanding expository text: A theoretical and practical handbook for analyzing explanatory text.* Hillsdale, NJ: Lawrence Erlbaum Associates.

Britton, B. K., & Graesser, A. C. (Eds.). (1996). *Models of understanding text.* Mahwah, NJ: Lawrence Erlbaum Associates.

Bruner, J. (1986). *Actual minds, possible worlds.* Cambridge, MA: Harvard University Press.

Bunge, M. (1959). *Causality. The place of the causal principle in modern science.* Cambridge, MA: Harvard University Press.

Carey, S., & Gelman, R. (Eds.). (1991). *The epigenesis of mind: Essays on biology and cognition.* Hillsdale, NJ: Lawrence Erlbaum Associates.

Cheng, P. W. (1993). Separating causal laws from causal facts: Pressing the limits of statistical relevance. In D. L. Medin (Ed.), *The psychology of learning and motivation* (Vol. 30, pp. 215–264). San Diego: Academic Press.

Cheng, P. W., & Holyoak, K. J. (1995). Complex adaptive systems as intuitive statiscians: Causality, contingency, and prediction. In H. L. Roitbalt & J. A. Meyer (Eds.), *Comparative approaches to cognitive science* (pp. 271–302). Cambridge, MA: MIT Press.

Chi, M. T. H., Glaser, H., & Rees, E. (1982). Expertise in problem solving. In R. J. Sternberg (Ed.), *Advances in the psychology of human intelligence* (Vol. 1, pp. 7–75). Hillsdale, NJ: Lawrence Erlbaum Associates.

Coté, N.; Goldman, S. R., & Saul, E. U. (1998). Students making sense of informational text: Relations between processing and representation. *Discourse Processes, 25,* 1–53.

Dewey , J. (1938). *Logic. The theory of inquiry.* New York: Holt.

Eddy, D. M. (1982). Probabilistic reasoning in clinical medicine: Problems and opportunities. In D. Kahneman, P. Slovic, & A. Tversky (Eds.), *Judgments under uncertainty: Heuristics and biases* (pp. 249–267). Cambridge, England: Cambridge University Press.

Einhorn, H. & Hogarth, R. M (1986). Judging probable cause. *Psychological Bulletin, 99,* 3–19.

Einstein, G. O., McDaniel, M. A., Owen, P. D., & Coté, N. C. (1990). Encoding and recall of texts: The importance of material appropriate processing. *Journal of Memory and Language, 29,* 566–581.

Fincher-Kiefer, R. (1996). Encoding differences between bridging and predictive inferences. *Discourse Processes, 22*, 225–246.

Galileo, G. (1890–1909). Opera: (Florencia Edizione Nationale, 20 vols.). (Original work published 1623)

Graesser, A. C. (1981). *Prose comprehension beyond the world.* New York: Springer-Verlag.

Graesser, A. C., & Bertus, E. L. (1998). The construction of causal inferences while reading expository text on science and technology. *Scientific Studies of Reading, 2*, 247–269.

Graesser, A. C., & Clark, L. F. (1985). *Structures and procedures of implicit knowledge.* Norwood, NJ: Ablex.

Graesser, A. C., Haberlandt, K., & Koizumi, D. (1987). How is reading time influenced by knowledge-based inferences and world knowledge. In B. K. Britton & S. M. Glynn (Eds.), *Executive control process in reading* (pp. 217–251). Hillsdale, NJ: Lawrence Erlbaum Associates.

Graesser, A. C., & Hemphill, D. (1991). Question answering in the context of scientific mechanisms. *Journal of Memory and Language, 30*, 186–209.

Graesser, A. C., & Murachver, T. (1985). Symbolic procedures of question asking. In A. C. Graesser & J. B. Black (Eds.), *The psychology of questions* (pp. 15–88). Hillsdale, NJ: Lawrence Erlbaum Associates.

Graesser, A. C., Singer, M., & Trabasso, T. (1994). Constructing inferences during narrative text comprehension. *Psychological Review, 101*, 371–395.

Graesser, A. C., Swamer, S. S., Baggett, W. B., & Sell, M. (1996). New models of deep comprehension. In B. K. Britton & A. C. Graesser (Eds.), *Models of understanding text* (pp. 1–32) Mahwah, NJ: Lawrence Erlbaum Associates.

Harris, J. L., Rogers, W. A., & Qualls, C. D. (1998). Written language comprehension in younger and older adults. *Journal of Speech, Language and Hearing Research, 41*, 603–17.

Hart, H. L. A., & Honoré, T. (1959). *Causation in the law.* Oxford, England: Claredon.

Hartmann, N. (1949). *Neue wege der ontologic* [New ways of ontology]. Stuttgart: Kohlhammer Verlag.

Heider, F. (1944). Social perception and phenomenal causality. *Psychological Review, 51*, 358–374.

Heider, F. (1958). *The psychology of interpersonal relations.* New York: Wiley.

Hesslow, G. (1983). Explaining differences and weighting causes. *Theoria, 49*, 87–111.

Hewstone, M. (1989). *Causal attribution: From cognitive processes to collective beliefs.* Cambridge, MA: Basil Blackwell.

Hilton, D. J., & Slugoski, B. R. (1986). Knowledge-based causal attribution: The abnormal conditions focus model. *Psychological Review, 93*, 75–88.

Hirschfeld, L. A., & Gelman, S. A. (Eds.). (1994). *Mapping the mind: Domain specificity in cognition and culture.* New York: Cambridge University Press.

Holyoak, K. J., Koh, K., & Nisbett, R. E. (1989). A theory of conditioning: Inductive learning within rule-based default hierarchies. *Psychological Review, 96*, 315–340.

Hume, D. (1888). *A treatise of human nature.* Oxford, England: Oxford University Press. (Original work published 1739–1740).

Kintsch, W. (1977). On comprehending stories. In M. A. Just & P. A. Carpenter (Eds.), *Cognitive processes in comprehension* (pp. 36–62). Hillsdale, NJ: Lawrence Erlbaum Associates.

Lalljee, M. G., & Abelson, R. P. (1983). The organization of explanation. In M. R. C. Hewstone (Ed.), *Attribution theory: Social and functional extensions* (pp. 65–80). Oxford, England: Blackwell.

Langston, M., & Trabasso, T. (1999). Modeling casual integration and availability of information during comprehension of narrative texts. In H. van Oostendorp & S. R. Goldman (Eds.), *The construction of mental representations during reading* (pp. 29– 69). Mahwah, NJ: Lawrence Erlbaum Associates.

Lenzen, V. F. (1954). *Causality in natural science.* Springfield, IL: Thomas.

León, J. A., & Carretero, M. (1995). Intervention in comprehension and memory strategies: Knowledge and use of the text structure. *Learning and Instruction, 5,* 203–220.

León, J. A., Escudero, I., & van den Broek, P. (2000, July). *Genre of the text and the activation of elaborative inferences: A cross-cultural study based on a thinking aloud task.* Poster presented at the 10th annual meeting of the Society for Text and Discourse, Lyon. France.

León, J. A., Otero, J. C., Escudero, I., Campanario, J. M., & Pérez, O. (1999, July). *Levels of causal explanations in psychology and physics domains. An expert/novice study.* Paper presented at the VI European Congress of Psychology, Rome.

León, J. A., Peñalba, G., Pérez, O., & Escudero, I. (2001). *An asymmetry causal model in the comprehension of science texts.* Manuscript in preparation.

León, J. A., & Pérez., O. (2001). The influence of prior knowledge on the time course of clinical diagnosis inferences: A comparison of experts and novices. *Discourse Processes, 31,* 187–213.

Long, D. L., Golding, J., Graesser, A. C., & Clark, L. F. (1990). Goal, event, and state inferences: An investigation of inference generation during story comprehension. In A. C. Graesser & G. H. Bower (Eds.), *The psychology of learning and motivation* (Vol. 25, pp. 89–102). New York: Academic Press.

Long, D. L., Oppy, B. J., & Seely, M. R. (1997). A "global-coherence" view of event comprehension: Inferential processing as question answering. In P. W. van den Broek, P. J. Bauer, & T. Bourg (Eds.), *Developmental spans in event comprehension and representation. Bridging fictional and actual events* (pp. 361–384). Mahwah, NJ: Lawrence Erlbaum Associates.

Mackie, J. L. (1980). *The cement of the universe. A study of causation.* Oxford, England: Clarendon.

Magliano, J. P., Baggett, W. B., Johnson, B. K., & Graesser, A. C. (1993). The time course of generating causal antecedent and causal consequence inferences. *Discourse Processes, 16,* 35–53.

Mandler, J. M., & Johnson, N. S. (1977). Remembrance of things parsed: Story structure and recall. *Cognitive Psychology, 9,* 111–151.

McDaniel, M. A., Einstein, G. O., Cunay, P. K., & Cobb, R. E. (1986). Encoding difficulty and memory: Toward a unifying theory. *Journal of Memory and Language, 25,* 645–656.

McGill, A. L. (1989). Context effects on causal judgments. *Journal of Personality and Social Psychology, 57,* 189–200.

McGill, A. L. (1991). Conjunctive explanations: Accounting for events that differ from several norms. *Journal of Experimental Social Psychology, 27,* 529–549.

McKeown, M. G., Beck, I. L., Sinatra, G. M., & Loxterman, J. A. (1992). The contribution of prior knowledge and coherent text to comprehension. *Reading Research Quarterly, 27,* 78–93.

Meyer Viol, W. P. M. (1984). *Foregrounding and causality in inference making.* Unpublished master's thesis, University of Groningen, Groningen, The Netherlands.

Michotte, A. (1946). *La perception de la causalite* [Perception of causality]. Louvain, France: Editions de l'Institut Supérieur de Philosophie.

Millis, K. K., & Graesser, A. C. (1994). The time course of constructing knowledge-based inferences for scientific texts. *Journal of Memory and Language, 33,* 583–599.

Millis, K. K., Morgan, D., & Graesser, A. C. (1990). The influence of knowledge-based inferences on the reading time of expository text. In A. C. Graesser & G. H. Bower (Eds.), *Inferences and text comprehension* (pp. 197–212). New York: Academic Press.

Myers, J. L., Shinjo, M., & Duffy, S. A. (1987). Degree of causal relatedness and memory. *Journal of Memory and Language, 26,* 453–465.

Newton, D. P. (1995). Support for understanding: Discourse which aids the construction of a functional mental model of causal situations. *Research in Science and Technological Education, 13,* 109–122.

Noordman, L. G. M., & Vonk, W. (1998). Memory-based processing in understanding causal information. *Discourse Processes, 26,* 191–212.

Noordman, L. G. M., Vonk, W., & Kempff, H. J. (1992). Causal inferences during the reading of expository texts. *Journal of Memory and Language, 13,* 573–590.

Oestermeier, U., & Hesse, F. W. (2000). Verbal and visual causal arguments. *Cognition, 75,* 65–114.

Patel, V. L., & Groen, G. J. (1986). Knowledge based solution strategies in medical reasoning. *Cognitive Science, 10,* 91–116.

Piaget, J. (1927a). *La causalité physique chez l'enfant* [The child's conception of physical causality]. Paris: Alcan.

Piaget, J. (1927b). L'explication de l'ombre chez l'enfant [Children's explanations of shadows]. *Journal de Psychologie, 24,* 230–242.

Potts, G. R., Keenan, J. M., & Golding, J. M. (1988). Assessing the occurrence of elaborative inferences: Lexical decision versus naming. *Journal of Memory and Language, 27,* 399–415.

Read, S. J. (1987). Constructing causal scenarios: A knowledge structure approach to causal reasoning. *Journal of Personality and Social Psychology, 52,* 288–302.

Rumelhart, D. E. (1975). Notes on a schema for stories. In D. G. Bobrow & A. Collins (Eds.), *Representation and understanding: Studies in cognitive science* (pp. 211–236). New York: Academic Press.

Russell, B. (1953) *Mysticism and logic: And other essays.* London: Penguin.

Salmon, W. C. (1998). *Causality and explanation.* Oxford, England: Oxford University Press.

Schank, R. C. (1975). *Conceptual information processing.* Amsterdam: North-Holland.

Schank, R. C., & Abelson, R. (1977). *Scripts, plans, goals, and understanding.* Hillsdale, NJ: Lawrence Erlbaum Associates.

Schustack, M. W. (1988). Thinking about causality. In R. J. Sternberg & E. E. Smith (Eds.), *The psychology of human thought* (pp. 92–115). New York: Cambridge University Press.

Singer, M., & Ferreira, F. (1983). Inferring consequences in story comprehension. *Journal of Verbal Learning and Verbal Behaviour, 22,* 437–448.

Singer, M., & Gagnon, N. (1999). Detecting causal inconsistencies in scientific text. In S. R. Goldman, A. C. Graesser, & P. W. van den Broek (Eds.), *Narrative comprehension, causality, and coherence: Essays in honor of Tom Trabasso* (pp. 179–194). Mahwah, NJ: Lawrence Erlbaum Associates.

Singer, M., Halldorson, M., Lear, J. C., & Andrusiak, P. (1992). Validation of causal bridging inferences in discourse understanding. *Journal of Memory and Language, 31,* 507–524.

Singer, M., Harkness, D., & Stewart, S. T. (1997). Constructing inferences in expository text comprehension. *Discourse Processes, 24,* 199–228.

Sperber, D., Premack, D., & Premack, A. J. (Eds.). (1995). *Causal cognition: A multidisciplinary debate.* New York: Clarendon.

Stein, N. L., & Glenn, C. G. (1979). An analysis of story comprehension in elementary school children. In R. O. Freedle (Ed.), *New directions in discourse processing* (pp. 53–120). Hillsdale, NJ: Lawrence Erlbaum Associates.

Thorndyke, P. W. (1977). Cognitive structures in comprehension and memory of narrative discourse. *Cognitive Psychology, 9,* 77–110.

Trabasso, T., & Magliano, J. P. (1996). Conscious understanding during text comprehension. *Discourse Processes, 21,* 255–288.

Trabasso, T., Magliano, J. P., & Graesser, A. C. (1999). Strategic processing during comprehension. *Journal of Educational Psychology, 91,* 615–629.

Trabasso, T., Secco, T., & van den Broek, P. W. (1984). Causal cohesion and story coherence. In T. Trabasso & N. L. Stein (Eds.), *Learning and comprehension of text* (pp. 83–111). Hillsdale, NJ: Lawrence Erlbaum Associates.

Trabasso, T., & Sperry, L. L. (1985). The causal basis for deciding importance of story events. *Journal of Memory and Language, 24,* 595–611.

Trabasso, T., & van den Broek, P. W. (1985). Causal thinking and the representation of narrative events. *Journal of Memory and Language, 24,* 612–630.

Trabasso, T., van den Broek, P. W., & Suh, S. Y. (1989). Logical necessity and transitivity of causal relations in stories. *Discourse Processes, 12,* 1–25.

Tversky, A., & Kahneman, D. (1980). Causal schemas in judgements under uncertainty. In M. Fishbein (Ed.), *Progress in social psychology* (pp. 49–72). Hillsdale, NJ: Lawrence Erlbaum Associates.

van den Broek, P. (1988). The effects of causal relations and hierarchical position on the importance of story statements. *Journal of Memory and Language, 24,* 612–630.

van den Broek, P. (1990a). The causal inference maker: Towards a process model of inference generation in text comprehension. In D. A. Balota, G. B. Flores d'Arcais, & K. Rayner (Eds.), *Comprehension processes in reading* (pp. 423–446). Hillsdale, NJ: Lawrence Erlbaum Associates.

van den Broek, P. (1990b). Causal inferences and the comprehension of narrative texts. In A. C. Graesser & G. H. Bower (Eds.), *Psychology of learning and motivation: Inferences and text comprehension* (Vol. 25, pp. 175–196). San Diego: Academic Press.

van den Broek, P., Young, M., Tzeng, Y., & Linderholm, T. (1999). The landscape model of reading: Inferences and the online construction of a memory representation. In H. van Oostendorp & S. R. Goldman (Eds.), *The construction of mental representations during reading* (pp. 71–98). Mahwah, NJ: Lawrence Erlbaum Associates.

Vonk, W., & Noordman, L. G. M. (1992). Kennis en inferenties bij het lezen van tekst [Knowledge and inferences in reading text]. *Toegepaste Taalwetenschap in Artikelem, 43*, 39–54.

Waldmann, M. R., & Holyoak, K. J. (1992). Predictive and diagnostic learning whithin causal models: Asymmetries in cue competition. *Journal of Experimental Psychology: General, 121*, 222–235.

Weiner, B. (1985). "Spontaneous" causal thinking. *Psychological Bulletin, 97*, 74–84.

White, P. A. (1989). A theory of causal processing. *British Journal of Psychology, 80*, 431–454.

Winter, L., & Uleman, J. S. (1984). When are social judgments made? Evidence for the spontaneousness of trait inferences. *Journal of Personality and Social Psychology, 47*, 237–252.

⊰ 8 ⊱

Situation Models as Retrieval Structures: Effects on the Global Coherence of Science Texts

Isabelle Tapiero
Universite de Lyon II

José Otero
Universidad de Alcalá

Most models of text comprehension assume that readers create a multilevel representation of texts. These text representations in memory are coherent wholes in normal and successful reading. Nonetheless, because texts are processed sequentially, text comprehension requires the integration of information across sentences to create a coherent representation of the entire text. This creates a problem of explaining how the information that is active in short-term memory (STM) from the current sentence is related to the representation of the prior text. This representation should be accessible so that the presently processed information can be tied to the previously read text and thereby create local and global coherence.

Models differ on the analysis of this coherence-building process. There are *local coherence models*, also called minimalist or linear models by van den Broek and Lorch (1993). Examples of local coherence models are those of Kintsch (1988) and McKoon and Ratcliff (1992). These models focus on

Local Coherence

readers' attempts to link each discourse unit with the immediately preceding unit. McKoon and Ratcliff proposed a *minimalist hypothesis* according to which readers create connections between current information and information that is stored in STM. Connections between current information and information retrieved from long-term memory (LTM) are also made, but only when there is a break in local coherence. In several studies, McKoon and Ratcliff illustrated the psychological validity of this minimal processing by showing that inferences to maintain local coherence are generated during comprehension whereas those required for global coherence are not, unless local coherence fails.

On the other hand *global coherence models* assume that readers establish links both between adjacent units and with other units occurring earlier in the text, even when local connections are successfully created (Collins, Brown, & Larkin, 1980; Graesser & Clark, 1985; Graesser, Singer, & Trabasso, 1994; Johnson-Laird, 1983; Kintsch, 1998; Myers & O'Brien, 1998). Theories of mental models belong to this category, as does also the constructionist theory proposed by Graesser et al. The constructionist theory explicitly adopts two hypotheses that are the building blocks for distinctive predictions on the type of inferences generated during comprehension. First, the explanatory hypothesis states that readers try to explain why actions and events are mentioned in a text. This may be done, for example, by generating plausible causal antecedents of an event mentioned in the text. Second, the coherence hypothesis establishes that readers try to construct a coherent representation both at the local and global levels. It implies that readers make not only causal antecedent inferences but also those relative to characters' goals and emotions, as they play a role in the patterns of global story plots and they are necessary to establish global coherence.

According to the constructionist theory readers match current information with information still active in memory as well as with relevant information that is no longer active in memory. As such, this approach emphasizes global coherence: Readers are sensitive to global inconsistencies even when local coherence is maintained. Consistent with this view and in contradiction to the data from McKoon and Ratcliff's (1992) study, O'Brien and Albrecht (1992) showed that readers detect inconsistent information at a global level even when local coherence is maintained. In their experiments, they manipulated the compatibility between information relative to the location of a character in a specific environment and information mentioned earlier in the text. The inconsistent information could be easily integrated locally but not globally. Results showed that when a sentence was globally incoherent, subjects experienced comprehension difficulties even though it was locally coherent. Thus, spatial information not compatible with the initial location of the character was detected despite the maintenance of local coherence.

A study conducted by Huitema, Dopkins, Klin, and Myers (1993) also furnished results contrary to those obtained by McKoon and Ratcliff (1992). Subjects had to read stories that were similar in content to that from McKoon and Ratcliff's experiments. First, a protagonist's goal was mentioned: *Dick ... wanted to go to a place where he could swim and sunbathe.* Then some intermediate sentences were inserted: *... he went to his local travel agent....* Finally the story ended with a description of an action that was compatible (*... and asked for a plane ticket to Florida*) or incompatible (*... and asked for a plane ticket to Alaska*) with the initially stated goal. The authors observed longer reading times when the sentence described an incompatible action compared to an action that was compatible. This increase in reading times presumably can be attributed to the process of readers' accessing the goal information stated initially. These data support the constructionist theory and other theories of comprehension that claim that readers maintain not only local coherence but also global coherence (Graesser et al., 1994; Kintsch, 1998; van Dijk & Kintsch, 1983).

Research on global coherence has focused on narrative comprehension. Our current research extends this research to science texts. In particular, we examine the effect of situation models on the construction of global coherence in a text representation. We then compare this to explanations of global coherence that rely on a passive resonance process (Albrecht & Myers, 1995, 1998; Klin & Myers, 1993; Myers & O'Brien, 1998; Rizzella & O'Brien, 1996). This chapter first reviews the mechanisms responsible for creating global coherence in a text representation. The chapter subsequently focuses on the role of *long-term working memory* (LT-WM; Ericsson & Kintsch, 1995) and on situation models as retrieval structures that enable readers to relate the contents of STM to previously introduced information in a text. We claim that situation models are more efficient retrieval structures than textbases by analyzing the kind of links that exist between tokens in situation models. Finally, the chapter presents some empirical evidence that is consistent with the facilitating effect of situation models for creating global coherence in the representation of science texts.

MECHANISMS FOR BUILDING LOCAL AND GLOBAL COHERENCE

Local and global coherence are created through different mechanisms. Local coherence is especially dependent on textual characteristics (Halliday &

Hasan, 1976; Mann & Thompson, 1986) and is closely related to *cohesion*. Cohesion refers to local connections that are based primarily on textual surface characteristics instead of background knowledge (Graesser et al., 1994). Kintsch and van Dijk's (1978) original model of text comprehension and the subsequent construction-integration model (Kintsch, 1988) include mechanisms to establish local coherence. According to these models, texts are processed in cycles and some propositions are kept in a memory buffer from one cycle to another. Connections may be created between propositions in each cycle and the propositions in the buffer. The default criterion used to link propositions is argument overlap, or common noun-phrase referents that are shared between propositions. However, other criteria can be used for linking propositions, as in the case of two propositions sharing the same place or time (Kintsch, 1998). When a connection to propositions in the buffer is impossible, a search in long-term memory (LTM) is initiated in order to find a connection to other propositions.

The creation of more distant connections necessary to establish global coherence is less dependent on surface cues in the text. Global coherence implies that incoming pieces of information are related to other information in the text that may not be currently active in STM, due to limitations of STM capacity. This process has been conceptualized in various ways: a backward parallel spread of activation (O'Brien & Albrecht, 1992; O'Brien, Plewes, & Albrecht, 1990), a passive resonance process (Albrecht & Myers, 1995, 1998; Klin & Myers, 1993; Myers & O'Brien, 1998; Rizzella & O'Brien, 1996), a passive automatic constraint satisfaction mechanism (Graesser et al., 1994), or an active meaning-seeking process (Graesser et al., 1994). In particular, the resonance model explains the reinstatement of relevant textual and background knowledge by means of a process where traces in STM send signals to all of LTM. Information in LTM that shares features with these traces will be reactivated and brought to STM. Several textual and reader variables may affect the passive resonance process that is responsible for the establishment of global coherence: overlap of features of the target proposition and the previous traces to which it may be related (Albrecht & Myers, 1995; Huitema et al., 1993; Klin & Myers, 1993; Rizzella & O'Brien, 1996), distance in the surface structure between target and previous related traces (Albrecht & Myers, 1995; O'Brien et al., 1990; Rizzella & O'Brien, 1996), and elaboration of the traces (O'Brien et al., 1990).

Albrecht and Myers (1995) examined whether the resonance process contributes to a change in the availability of previously relevant information. In more specific terms, they studied whether a reference to a previously known episode could serve for reactivating information that is relevant to the goal of the previously known episode. In their experiments, each passage described a character motivated by a specific goal. For example, one of the passages dealt with Mary, who had to make an airline reservation before midnight. Two goal conditions were constructed, an unsatisfied and a satisfied goal condition. In the unsatisfied goal condition, Mary was interrupted before she could book a flight because she had to finish a project. In the satisfied goal condition, she was able to complete the booking and then worked on the project. After some filler sentences, the reactivation of previously relevant information was manipulated. In one condition a statement after the filler sentences provided a contextual overlap with the goal of the episode: A direct reference was made to some of the aspects of the context in which the goal was originally introduced (a leather chair). This corresponded to the context reinstatement condition. In another condition (the nonreinstatement condition), the statement did not provide any contextual overlap and did not make any reference to the previous episode. This statement was immediately followed by two target sentences that described the character implied in actions that were inconsistent with the goal previously unsatisfied (going to bed without booking the flight, putting on pajamas). If participants access the goal information and detect the inconsistency, reading times should be longer for target sentences in the unsatisfied goal conditions than in the satisfied goal conditions.

Results indicated that target sentences were read longer in the unsatisfied goal condition but only when the reinstatement sentence contained concepts that were also present in the context of the initial goal. This demonstrated that the contextual cue in the reinstatement sentence served to reactivate information in the goal episode. Albrecht and Myers (1995) explained this outcome by the fact that concepts and propositions derived from the context reinstatement sentence, including the contextual sentence, are combined with the contents in working memory (WM) and send a signal to LTM. The elements of discourse representation that share some features with the signals resonate in response and, in turn, imply that the related propositions, including goal propositions, are activated. Hence, they provide participants with the access to goal information and with the possibility to detect inconsistencies. By contrast, when the contextual cue was absent from the reinstatement sentence, there is no overlap with the goal episode and thus, no way in which this episode can be accessed.

In another study, Albrecht and Myers (1998) examined whether the resonance process is influenced by the amount of elaboration of the contextual cue in memory and by the specificity of the contextual reinstatement sentence. In three separate experiments, subjects had to read 24 stories, each one composed of five sections. Each passage included either an elaborated contextual cue, that is, a noun plus adjective ("leather chair"), or an unelaborated contextual cue, that is, the noun alone. The contextual cues were always presented in the goal section and in the reinstatement sentence. Based on this design, three context conditions were constructed: an adjective–adjective condition that included an elaborated cue in the goal section as well as in the reinstatement sentence, an adjective–noun condition that included an elaborated cue in the goal section but an unelaborated cue in the reinstatement sentence, and finally, a noun–noun condition in which an unelaborated cue was used both in the goal section and in the reinstatement sentence. If it is true that subjects access a proposition related to an unsatisfied goal when reading a target sentence, they should notice an inconsistency, and this should lead to an increase in reading time of the target sentence in the unsatisfied goal conditions. The difference in reading time between the unsatisfied and the satisfied goal conditions was called the "inconsistency effect." According to the authors, when the contextual goal is elaborated by including an adjective, a stronger memory trace ought to be encoded.

An inconsistency effect was observed in the adjective–adjective condition. There were longer reading times for the two target sentences in the unsatisfied goal condition than in the satisfied goal condition. It follows then that the reinstatement of a modifier allows reactivating information of a preceding episode in the text. Results in the noun–noun condition only showed the inconsistency effect for the second target sentence. Thus, when a noun is used as a retrieval cue, this leads to a decrease of the activation level or to a slower construction pace of activation. Finally, in the adjective–noun condition, the inconsistency effect was three times greater for the first than for the second target sentence. This is interpreted as showing that the removal of the adjective from the context reinstatement sentence reduces overlap between traces, weakening resonance.

THE ROLE OF LONG-TERM WORKING MEMORY IN BUILDING COHERENCE IN TEXTS

The resonance model emphasizes the relation between traces in STM and the corresponding cue in LTM. However, more information is brought to STM than the cue resonating in LTM. Other elements of information from the earlier text and world knowledge are reactivated as well. One important aspect of the retrieval process is how much associated information in LTM is also activated. This depends on the relations between the trace and other information in LTM. Ericsson and Kintsch (1995) dealt specifically with this aspect of the reading process when they analyzed the role of the retrieval structures that are necessary for creating coherence in text comprehension. They provided a mechanism for global coherence by postulating a modification of LTM. In particular, aspects of LTM are easily accessible from working memory (WM); they call this long-term working memory (LT-WM). LT-WM is distinguishable from short-term working memory (ST-WM), the more or less passive storage buffer that is routinely adopted in theories of working memory. LT-WM works as an extension of STM for activities that correspond to skilled performance in particular domains. The reader can quickly and skillfully access information from LTM that is triggered by the content in STM.

Ericsson and Kintsch's (1995) proposal is based on experimental evidence regarding skilled memory and also on some unexplained phenomena in text processing. Readers maintain a multilevel representation of the text that is being read in LTM. Relevant parts of this representation should remain accessible so that they could be related to the information that is being processed in a particular moment. Traditionally, this linking process has been explained in terms of the operation of WM. As mentioned before, some information from previously read sentences is kept in a WM buffer. Reading proceeds smoothly as long as the currently processed information can be related to the previous information kept in the buffer. If that is impossible, a time-consuming search in LTM has to be initiated. But this account implies that any disruption of reading that prevents paying attention to WM contents would lead to a loss of information in the buffer. This in turn would cause an impairment of comprehension of the text information that follows. However, this has not been observed to happen. Glanzer and colleagues (Fischer & Glanzer, 1986; Glanzer, Dorfman, & Kaplan, 1981; Glanzer, Fischer, & Dorfman, 1984) have reported empirical evidence that preventing the use of the WM buffer to link propositions from successive learning cycles does not have the expected disrupting effects in comprehension. Thus, it calls for an explanation how readers in this situation are able to connect propositions from one processing cycle to the representation of the previous text. Ericsson and Kintsch proposed that this is done through LT-WM. Readers maintain in the focus of attention a set of propositions corresponding to the sentence being processed at a certain moment. Some of the propositions in ST-WM are linked to other propositions from previous processing cycles kept in LTM, and these serve as cues to retrieve other integrated information that shape a retrieval structure. Propositions that belong to this retrieval structure may be easily accessed in a time interval of about 400 ms. This portion of LTM that is readily available while a text is being processed is called LT-WM.

Building a coherent rep. of a narrative

The concept of LT-WM, together with some extensions of an event-indexing model (see Zwaan, Langston, & Graesser, 1995), enabled Zwaan and Radvansky (1998) to study the stages of situation model construction for narrative texts and for the creation of coherence in the corresponding representation. Three types of situation models were distinguished: the current model, the integrated model, and the complete model. The current model consists in the situation model existing in WM at a certain time t_n, while the reader is processing a sentence or clause. The integrated model at t_n results from the integration of the successive models that were built, one at a time, at times $t_1 \ldots t_{n-1}$. Finally, the complete model is stored in LTM after the narrative is read completely. All of these models consist of a network of nodes that codify the events described and inferred from a story. The links between these nodes correspond to the dimensions considered in the event-indexing model: time, space, causation, motivation, and protagonist.

Building a coherent representation of a narrative consists in relating the current model, kept in ST-WM, to the integrated model that is stored in LT-WM. To carry this out, the traces of the current model are connected to some retrieval cues in the integrated model. According to Zwaan and Radvansky's (1998) account, which mirrors the Ericsson and Kintsch (1995) proposal, the integrated model is the retrieval structure in LT-WM needed to bring information to ST-WM so that coherence could be achieved in the representation of the processed text.

SITUATION MODELS AS RETRIEVAL STRUCTURES AND THE ESTABLISHMENT OF GLOBAL COHERENCE

Coherence in text representations depends on the retrieval structures available in LTM. Textbases and situation models are precisely these retrieval structures in discourse processing (Ericsson & Kintsch, 1995). But the textbase and situation model levels have different relative importance in the text representations that are built by readers. Emphasis on one of the levels may depend on several factors. Characteristics of a reader, such as the amount of relevant world knowledge, may influence the creation of a situation model. Likewise there are a text's characteristics that may facilitate or disrupt the creation of a situation model (Johnson-Laird, 1983), for example, level of specificity and determinacy, that is, the extent to which a description in a text rules out states of affairs in the world, or alternatively is consistent with several of them. Following Johnson-Laird, "models, like images, are highly specific" (p. 157), and "a propositional representation processes in a similar way determinate and indeterminate spatial relations, whereas situation models handle better determinate than indeterminate relations" (p. 158).

Once a text representation has been built, the relative weights of the textbase and situation model have several implications. For example, textbase dominance causes reproductive recall, close to the text that has been read. Situation model dominance causes recall with knowledge intrusions that are prompted by memory structures, such as schemata or scripts.

The relative importance of the textbase versus the situation model has implications on the relative ease with which coherence is established in a text representation. We claim that situation models are more efficient retrieval structures than textbases in creating coherence in text representations. Van Dijk and Kintsch (1983) already pointed out the importance of situation models in creating coherence: "A sequence of sentences can be said to be coherent if the sentences denote facts in some possible world that are related" (p. 150), or "A prerequisite for coherent text representation is the ability to construct a coherent situation model. Without that, memory for text is stored in disjoint bits and pieces ..." (p. 361). Johnson-Laird (1983) made a similar point: "A necessary and sufficient condition for a discourse to be coherent, as opposed to a random sequence of sentences, is that it is possible to construct a single mental model from it" (p. 370).

LINKS IN TEXTBASES AND SITUATION MODELS

During the process of creating coherence (i.e., linking the representation of the currently read sentence with the memory of the read text), two types of connections may be created above the surface level: textbase links and situation model links, as in the process studied by Zwaan and Radvansky (1998). One example of the textbase links are the explicit connections between propositions, including argument overlap. These links also include the coherence relations classified by Van Dijk and Kintsch (1983) and Kintsch (1998) under the headings "direct coherence" and "subordination" (Kintsch, 1998, p. 39). The former are relations explicitly marked by connectives, and the latter correspond to a meaning unit that is a condition of another and indicated by a subordinate clause. These types of relations were considered by Kintsch and Van Dijk (1978) in their initial model of text comprehension. They contribute coherent discourse by creating connections between propositions in a textbase without having built a situation model. For example, a reader may easily relate propositions resulting from two sentences through argument overlap, without having built a corresponding referential representation or situation model. Sometimes there are propositions in the textbase that are unconnected unless one finds a referent for them, that is, unless one builds a situation model. Two objects that are related in a situation in the world may be unrelated in the surface or textbase structure of the text describing that situation. The texts developed by Bransford and Johnson (1972) are well-known examples of this situation:

> If the balloons popped, the sound would not be carried since everything would be too far away from the CORRECT FLOOR. A CLOSED WINDOW would also prevent the sound from spreading....

CORRECT FLOOR and *CLOSED WINDOW* are hardly related by the readers who create a representation emphasizing the textbase, as would be the case for most readers of this text. But these propositions are related in the appropriate situation model. The model might involve a man serenading a woman from a tall building, where a loudspeaker is held at the appropriate height by means of some balloons, and where the closed window is located in the correct floor.

Another example of propositions that may be unconnected in the textbase, but are closely related in the situation model, is that of coreferential noun phrases. *The man standing by the window,* as in an example given by Johnson-Laird (1983), and another noun phrase that may occur in the same paragraph such as *The Portuguese with the Port wine,* may correspond to the same token in a situation model (i.e., they may have the same referent). But they have little relation when one considers their meaning representation in the textbase.

Spatial relations are excellent examples of the difference between links in situation models and links in textbases. Two objects may be close together or far apart in a reader's representation of a text, depending on the constructed spatial situation model. Such a configuration is illustrated clearly in Glenberg, Meyer, and Lindem's (1987) experiment. They gave readers versions of a text including two different sentences: *After doing a few warm-up exercises, John put on his sweatshirt and began jogging;* or alternatively, *After doing a few warm-up exercises, John took off his sweatshirt and began jogging.* After this, both groups of subjects read *John jogged halfway around the lake.* They were then asked if sweatshirt was a word appearing in the story. Subjects who read that John put on his sweatshirt were faster to say "yes" than those subjects who read that John took off his *sweatshirt.* The sweatshirt seemed to be linked differently to the representation of the sentence describing John halfway around the lake, even though the textbase representation of this last sentence should be the same in both cases. There should be links between information units corresponding to *John* (*halfway-around-the-lake*) and *sweatshirt* that are different from those in the textbase.

To summarize, there are two alternative connection possibilities for propositions. First, a proposition may be connected to others at the textbase level, as in the previous example that involved argument overlap. Second, two propositions may not have an explicit connection through textbase links, but they may be related to situation model objects and these referents may be connected through situation model links. This occurs when two propositions share the same time or location, as CORRECT (FLOOR) and CLOSED (WINDOW) in the earlier example. This corresponds to *indirect coherence* in Kintsch's (1998) classification. Indirect coherence would also include other relations that are not always explicitly indicated in texts, such as antecedent–consequent, enablement, and implication relations (Graesser & Clark, 1985).

Therefore, coherence depends on the relations between elements in the retrieval structures used by readers, and these relations may be different in situation models from those existing in textbases. Our central claim is that situation model links are better than textbase links in establishing coherence in texts' representations. And why are we making this claim? There are some characteristics of situation models that point to their advantages (Tapiero & Otero, in press). First, although situation models have been occasionally represented as propositions, as in the case of textbases (Graesser & Clark, 1985; Kintsch, 1998; Tapiero, 2000; Tapiero & Otero, 1999), they are conceived as analogic representations, that is, as structural analogues of the world. The analogue character of situation models implies that there is a parallelism between represented and representing relations. Consequently, relations in the real world should be more faithfully represented in the relations existing in situation models than in the relations existing in textbases.

Second, spatial situation models are similar to images because they have an integrated character; that is, many elements of the represented situation are simultaneously available (Johnson-Laird, 1983). Consequently, there are more conceptual hooks to connect the representation of a sentence being read to previous text information when this is done through a situation model that is used as a retrieval structure, compared to it being done through a textbase. *Note*

AN EMPIRICAL STUDY ON THE ROLE OF SITUATION MODELS AS RETRIEVAL STRUCTURES

We examined the effect of situation models on the global coherence of the representations of science texts. We did this by investigating the detection of *implication* relations in these representations. Implication relations may exist between two objects or tokens in a situation model that correspond to two events or two states described in a text. Examples of implication relations are those that are created through syllogistic reasoning. The generalization *Dancers are sexy* together with the fact that *X is a dancer* imply that *X is sexy* (Graesser & Clark, 1985). Similar relations can often be found in the representations of science texts. The generalization *Viscous drag is proportional to speed* added to the fact *Speed of particle P moving within a viscous fluid is increasing* imply *Viscous drag on particle P is increasing*. In fact, according to the nomological-deductive model, scientific explanation consists in showing that the explanandum is implicated by general laws together with statements about particular facts. For example, the particular orbit traced by Uranus is explained by showing that it may be deduced from Newton's law of gravitation together with facts such as the existence of the sun, and the existence of other planets orbiting in a relative vicinity of Uranus.

Readers who create a globally coherent representation may recognize an implication relation between two propositions that are far apart in the textbase structure. This can be achieved independently of explicitly signaling the implication relation. In fact, these signals are more than often excluded from science texts. For example, one of the texts used in our study (see Table 8.1) contains the following information:

> In the city of Hammerfest, located in the northern of Norway there are months when the sun never rises.... More electricity is necessary to illuminate the streets.

No textbase connection exists between the meanings of these two sentences. However, a reader may relate one to the other through an implication relation: *Sun never rises* → *(No natural light)* → *More electricity is necessary to illuminate the streets*.

Some of the factors affecting the creation of relations necessary for global coherence have been previously discussed. We tested the claim that creating a situation model representation of a text is a powerful way of establishing global coherence. This is because tokens corresponding to information in a text can be easily related within the situation model. In the cited example, a reader may easily relate the absence of sun in the sky with more electricity needed for illuminating the streets when a situation model corresponding to a town at night with streetlights on is constructed. The integrated nature that the situation models share with images may provide simultaneous availability of one element of the situation (no sun in the sky)

TABLE 8.1

Example of Versions of an Experimental Text and Knowledge Text

---

Contradictory, Far, Indeterminate Version

Variations in energy consumption

1. Duration of days and nights is quite different in higher latitudes, near the North Pole, than in lower latitudes. 2. In some places, there are months when the sun never rises. 3. During these months working activity is reduced as well as educational activities. 4. There is less consumption of energy needed for transportation during these months. 5. Several energy requirements change also during this period. 6. The consumption of energy during these months is different from the rest of the year. 7. Less energy is necessary to illuminate the streets. 8. Heating relies on fosil fuels and depends less on electricity.

Noncontradictory, Near, Determinate Version

Variations in electricity consumption

1. Duration of days and nights is quite different in higher latitudes, near the North Pole, than in lower latitudes. 2. In Hammerfest, located in the north of Norway, there are months when the sun never rises. 3. The consumption of electricity during these months is different from the rest of the year. 4. More electricity is necessary to illuminate the streets. 5. During these months working hours are reduced as well as school hours. 6. There is less consumption of fuel needed for cars and public transportation during these months. 7. Several electricity requirements change also during this period. 8. Heating relies on fosil fuels and depends less on electricity.

Specific Knowledge Text: Environmental Conditions Depend on Latitude

---

There are geographical changes that depend on latitude. Regions in higher latitudes have a colder climate than regions nearer the equator. The reason is the different amount of radiation received from the sun. The position of the sun's orbit relative to the earth explains also the important changes of day length in northern latitudes. The sun never sets in places near the North Pole during the summer months of the Northern Hemisphere. The opposite is true during the winter and there is a long period of night. This causes quite different patterns of behavior for the people living there.

General Knowledge Text: Influence of Geographical Variables

Geographical variables have many influences on social and economic characteristics of countries and cities. Climate, for example, depends on variables like latitude, proximity to the sea, or orographical characteristics. It has an important influence on the economy. Climate is an important constraint on the type of agriculture that can be sustained in a country. Climate also affects energy consumption. Other characteristics of a country, like orography, have a decisive influence on transportation. This has an influence on trade, on the communications within a country, and on the relations between neighboring countries.

---

and of another element (increase in electricity consumption of the streetlights). In addition, a reader who builds a situation model will recognize this relation independently of distance in the surface representation or in the textbase.

We conducted a study that compared predictions of a model that assumes that situation models play a critical role in constructing coherence in science texts (i.e., a *referential* model for global coherence) and a model that is based on resonance (i.e., the *resonance model*.) Special texts were designed in which there was an inconsistent implication relation between target information and previous related sentences (memory traces). For example, in the previously discussed text we substituted *there are months when the sun never rises … More electricity is necessary to illuminate the streets* with *there are months when the sun never rises … Less electricity is necessary to illuminate the streets.* Because these two sentences were separated by one or more intervening sentences (depending on experimental condition), the detection of the inconsistency provides a measure of global coherence of readers' representations.

In order to compare predictions of the resonance model with those based on the referential model, four variables were manipulated in the texts: (a) consistency of the implication relation, (b) distance on the surface structure between target information and previously related traces, (c) readers' knowledge about the topic discussed in the text, and (d) level of determinacy of textual information. It was predicted that Variable (b) should affect the resonance process, whereas Variables (c) and (d) should affect the capacity of building a situation model.

Consistency of the implication relation was manipulated as explained earlier. Distance between target and previous related information was manipulated by introducing a different number of sentences between one element of the implication relation and the other (see Table 8.1). In addition, we provided subjects with paragraphs either with specific knowledge on the implication relation or with general knowledge before actually reading the experimental texts. These differences in the specificity of knowledge should independently help in creating an appropriate situation model. For example, the experimental text on the variations of electricity/energy consumption was preceded by a knowledge text dealing with either the influence of latitude on environmental conditions (specific knowledge) or the influence of geographical variables on social and economic characteristics of countries (general knowledge). The construction of a situation model by subjects who lacked the appropriate knowledge is expected to be facilitated in the first case more than the second one. Finally, experimental texts were made more or less determinate in order to differentially affect the creation of a situation model. As an example of the variation in level of determinacy, the original first sentence *In the city of Hammerfest, located in the north of Norway, there are months when the sun never rises* was changed into a less determinate phrase: *In some places, there are months when the sun never rises*.

The four experimental science texts were each eight sentences in length (see Table 8.1 for an example). Each text included an implication relation, as discussed earlier, and it was written in eight versions, depending on manipulations of the variables consistency, distance, and determinacy. There were inconsistent versions (one of the elements of the implication relation was inconsistent with the other) versus consistent versions (the elements of the implication were consistent with each other). There were "near" versions (the sentences related by implication were in the second and fourth places) versus "far" versions (these sentences were in the second and seventh places). There were determinate versions (specific terms were used in the text, as shown previously) versus indeterminate versions (general terms were used in the text). Regarding, the fourth variable, readers' knowledge, each of the experimental texts was preceded by a knowledge text, seven sentences long, that provided readers with either specific or general prior knowledge on the domain of the experimental text. The order of presentation of the experimental texts was counterbalanced between subjects. Three filler texts intercepted the experimental texts.

One hundred volunteers from the University of Lyon 2 (France) participated in this experiment and were randomly assigned to different conditions. Each participant was seated in front of a computer in a soundproof booth. Texts were presented sentence by sentence and each sentence appeared after participants pressed the space bar that allowed us to record reading times. An increase in reading time of the target sentence (the second element in the implicational structure) was taken as evidence of detection of the inconsistency in the implication relation and, consequently, of having created global coherence in the text representation. Several other measurements were made, but we report here only the main results related to coherence in text representations.

An analysis of variance of reading times of the target sentences was conducted. Consistency (consistent vs. inconsistent), readers' knowledge (specific vs. general), and determinacy (determinate vs. indeterminate) were between-subjects variables. Distance (near vs. far) was a within-subjects variable.

No significant main effects for distance or readers' knowledge were found. Determinacy almost was significant ($F(1, 24) = 3.57$, $p < .07$):

Readers took more time to read target sentences when information was de-terminate (M = 7.4 s) than when it was indeterminate (M = 6.6 s). Accord-ing to the results reported later (see Fig. 8.1) this was caused by longer reading times in the inconsistent condition.

A main effect of consistency (F(1, 24) = 24.11, p < .0001) was observed. As expected, subjects in the inconsistent condition had longer reading times (M = 8.0 s) than those in the control condition (M = 5.9 s).

With respect to the second-order interactions, the resonance model would predict longer reading times in the near condition as compared to the far condition when the text is inconsistent. More readers should detect the inconsistency because memory traces would resonate more easily in the near condition. No such pattern in reading times should be expected in the consis-tent condition. However, our analysis failed to show the significant distance x consistency interaction that would be predicted by the resonance model.

A determinacy x consistency interaction did appear (F(1, 24) = 8.41, p < .01) in the direction predicted by the referential model. Subjects took more time to read the target sentence in the inconsistent condition when information was determinate than when it was indeterminate. No differ-ence appeared in the consistent condition (see Fig. 8.1). However, we did not find a readers' knowledge x consistency interaction, against the predic-tion of the referential model.

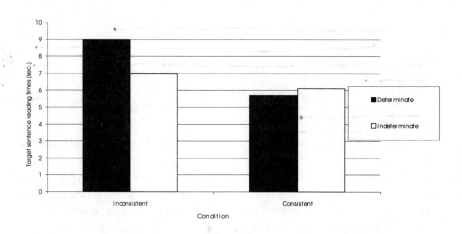

FIG. 8.1. Reading times of the target sentences as a function of condition (consistent vs. inconsistent) and determinacy (determinate vs. indetermi-nate).

Consistent with our argument concerning the role of situation models in establishing coherence, determinacy helped readers to detect the inconsistencies in the implication relations. In the inconsistent version, reading times were significantly longer for subjects who read determinate information; in the consistent version, subjects took the same amount of time to process target sentences in the determinate and indeterminate versions. However, no interaction was found for readers' knowledge and consistency, contrary to our prediction. Reading target sentences after having been provided with specific knowledge on the implication relation did not help to identify the inconsistency. A possible explanation for this may be the inefficacy of the specific knowledge paragraphs in helping readers to create a situation model. The knowledge that readers could obtain from these short paragraphs may have been insufficient to create a situation model representation of the target texts.

CONCLUSION

Global coherence of science texts can be created through situation model links. In this chapter we have argued that situation models are more efficient retrieval structures than are textbases in creating global coherence. The construction of a situation model enables readers to create connections not explicitly stated in the text and independent of textbase connections.

We designed a study to compare the effect of variables that should influence either resonance of a memory trace or a facility to build a situation model. We did not find any effect of distance on the creation of global coherence. This lack of effect contradicts predictions obtained from the resonance model. However, it is consistent with our claim that situation model links play an important role in creating coherence in science texts, independently of resonance processes at the textbase level. One of the variables, determinacy, did have an influence on the detection of inconsistencies. Determinate information helped readers relate the two terms of the implication relation, thereby showing that the creation of a situation model had an influence on global coherence.

Thus, the present study has indicated that recourse to situation models might help readers to build global coherence of science texts. Further research will perhaps clarify the relative importance of the factors that may have an influence on the situation model's construction when students read scientific texts. Lack of relevant knowledge and the difficulties caused by mathematical language (see chap. 1, this volume) are some of the factors that could hinder the construction of situation or mental models of scientific texts.

This study has practical implications for education. It is important to help students create situation models that support coherence in the representations of scientific texts. Connections between distant parts of a text can be easily made when a reader is able to use situation model links. This appears to be a self–sustaining process once put into motion: A situation model helps in creating links among many pieces of information, even those that are distant in the text. These related elements of information, in turn, help create a richer situation model.

ACKNOWLEDGMENT

Preparation of this chapter was partially supported by Project PB98-0711 of DGICYT, of the Ministry of Education, Spain.

REFERENCES

Albrecht, J. E., & Myers, J. L. (1995). Role of context in accessing distant information during reading. *Journal of Experimental Psychology: Learning, Memory, and Cognition, 21*, 1459–1468.

Albrecht, J. E., & Myers, J. L. (1998). Accessing distant text information during reading: Effects of contextual cues. *Discourse Processes, 26*, 87–107.

Bransford, J. D., & Johnson, M. K. (1972). Contextual prerequisites for understanding: Some investigations of comprehension and recall. *Journal of Verbal Learning and Verbal Behavior, 61*, 717–726.

Collins, A. M., Brown, J. S., & Larkin, K. M. (1980). Inferences in text understanding. In R. J. Spiro, B. C. Bruce, & W. F. Brewer (Eds.), *Theoretical issues in reading comprehension* (pp. 385–407). Hillsdale, NJ: Lawrence Erlbaum Associates.

Ericsson, K., & Kintsch, W. (1995). Long-term working memory. *Psychological Review, 102*, 211–245.

Fischer, B., & Glanzer, M. (1986). Short-term storage and the processing of cohesion during reading. *Quarterly Journal of Experimental Psychology, 38A*, 431–460.

Glanzer, M., Dorfman, D., & Kaplan, B. (1981). Short term storage in the processing of text. *Journal of Verbal Learning and Verbal Behavior, 20*, 656–670.

Glanzer, M., Fischer, B., Dorfman, D. (1984). Short term storage in reading. *Journal of Verbal Learning and Verbal Behavior, 23*, 467–486.

Glenberg, A. M., Meyer, M., & Lindem, K. (1987). Mental models contribute to foregrounding during text comprehension. *Journal of Memory and Language, 26*, 69–83.

Graesser, A. C., & Clark, L. F. (1985). *Structures and procedures of implicit knowledge*. Norwood, NJ: Ablex.

Graesser, A. C., Singer, M., & Trabasso, T. (1994). Constructing inferences during narrative text comprehension. *Psychological Review, 3*, 371–395.

Halliday, M. A. K., & Hasan, R. (1976). *Cohesion in English*. London: Longmans.

Huitema, J. S., Dopkins, S., Klin, C. M., & Myers, J. L. (1993). Connecting goals and actions during reading. *Journal of Experimental Psychology: Learning, Memory and Cognition, 19*(5), 1053–1060.

Johnson-Laird, P. N. (1983). *Mental models*. Cambridge, England: Cambridge University Press.

Kintsch, W. (1988). The construction-integration model of text comprehension. *Psychological Review, 95*, 163–182.

Kintsch, W. (1998). *Comprehension: A paradigm for cognition*. Cambridge, England: Cambridge University Press.

Kintsch, W., & van Dijk, T. A. (1978). Toward a model of text comprehension and production. *Psychological Review, 85*, 363–394.

Klin, C. M., & Myers, J. (1993). Reinstatement of causal information during reading. *Journal of Experimental Psychology: Learning, Memory, and Cognition, 19*, 554–560.

Mann, W. C., & Thompson, S. A. (1986). Relational propositions in discourse. *Discourse Processes, 9*, 57–90.

McKoon, G., & Ratcliff, R. (1992). Inference during reading. *Psychological Review, 99*, 440–466.

Myers, J. L., & O'Brien, E. J. (1998). Accessing the discourse representation during reading. *Discourse Processes, 26*(2 & 3), 131–157.

O'Brien, E. J., & Albrecht, J. E. (1992). Comprehension strategies in the development of mental model. *Journal of Experimental Psychology: Learning, Memory, and Cognition, 18*(4), 777–784.

O'Brien, E. J., Plewes, S., & Albrecht, J. E. (1990). Antecedent retrieval processes. *Journal of Experimental Psychology: Learning, Memory, and Cognition, 16*, 241–249.

Rizella, M. L., & O'Brien, E. J. (1996). Accessing global causes during reading. *Journal of Experimental Psychology: Learning, Memory, and Cognition, 22*(5), 1208–1218.

Tapiero, I. (2000). *Construire une représentation mentale cohérente: Structures, relations et connaissances*. [Building a coherent mental representation: Structures, relations and knowledge]. Unpublished manuscript, Habilitation à Diriger des Recherches, University of Lyon 2.

Tapiero, I., & Otero, J. (1999). Distinguishing between textbase and situation model in the processing of inconsistent information: Elaboration versus tagging. In H. van Oostendorp & S. R. Goldman (Eds.), *The construction of mental representation during reading* (pp. 341–365). Mahwah, NJ: Lawrence Erlbaum Associates.

Tapiero, I., & Otero, J. (in press). La estructura interna de los modelos de la situación y la generación de inferencias [The internal structure of situation models and the generation of inferences]. In J. A. Leon (Ed.), *Inferencias y comprensión*. Barcelona: Ediciones Paidos.

van den Broek, P. W., & Lorch, R. F. (1993). Network representations of causal relations in memory for narrative texts: Evidence from primed recognition. *Discourse Processes, 16*, 75–98.

van Dijk, T. A., & Kintsch, W. (1983). *Strategies of discourse comprehension*. San Diego: Academic Press.

Zwaan, R. A., Langston, M. C., & Graesser, A. C. (1995). The construction of situation models in narrative comprehension: An event-indexing model. *Psychological Science, 6,* 292–297.

Zwaan, R. A., & Radvansky, G. A. (1998). Situation models in language comprehension and memory. *Psychological Bulletin, 12,* 162–185.

9

Predictive Inferences in Scientific and Technological Contexts

Pascale Maury
Université de Montpellier III

Olga Pérez
José A. León
Universidad Autónoma de Madrid

It is widely accepted that during text comprehension, readers construct a situation model of what the text is about. This construction relies on making inferences that link the currently read sentence with previously processed text and/or with previous knowledge. Given the complexity of the inference-making process, the phenomenon has been explained from multiple theoretical viewpoints (e.g., Graesser, Singer, & Trabasso, 1994; McKoon & Ratcliff, 1992, 1995). At the same time, some contradictory data have emerged that pose some important questions. These questions address what taxonomy of inferences is ideal, how and when inferences are processed and activated, what context is available to perform inferences, and which of the theories best explains and predicts inference making.

Inference processes are crucial to detect the relations between the various parts of the text, as well as between the text and the reader's world knowledge. Thus, inferences can be divided into two major categories: those that provide coherence among the explicit ideas in the text (such as

199

Backward + forward inferencing

bridging or backward inferences) and those that are not important for establishing coherence (called elaborative or forward inferences). For example, inferences that refer to causal antecedents of explicit events in the text are backward inferences whereas inferences that refer to predicted causal consequences are forward inferences. Both bridging and elaborative inferences are constructed on the basis of the reader's world knowledge of the topics mentioned in the text and on the constraints of the explicit text (Millis & Graesser, 1994). The knowledge-based inferences also play an important role in higher order discourse representations and the referential situation models (Singer, 1994). Although it traditionally has been assumed that elaborative inferences take longer to process than bridging inferences, and also require a greater cognitive load (Fincher-Kiefer, 1992; Haberlandt, 1994; Haviland & Clark, 1974; Keenan, Potts, Golding, & Jennings, 1990; Kemper, 1983), there are violations to this simple generalization. Some elaborative inferences (such as superordinate goals) are generated virtually automatically with little cognitive load (Long, Golding, & Graesser, 1992) and some bridging inferences (such as underspecified anaphoric references) require deliberative processing and impose a high cognitive load (Greene, McKoon, & Ratcliff, 1992).

There are additional unsettled issues about inference processes. First, are the mechanisms by which elaborative inferences are constructed in the situation model constrained or invariant (e.g., Graesser & Bertus, 1998), or are they flexible, malleable, and sensitive to individual differences among *Contreras* readers (e.g., Perfetti, 1994)? Second, are elaborative inferences activated online or are they off-line inferences constructed after comprehension is completed? Some researchers originally believed that bridging inferences are generated online while reading, but some of the available data challenge that simple generalization. There is widespread disagreement over whether elaborative inferences (particularly predictive inferences) are generated online (Fincher-Kiefer, 1992; Graesser et al., 1994) Last, the role of inferences in scientific and technological contexts needs to be assessed in light of the fact that most research has been conducted on narrative contexts) This chapter focuses on these issues from the standpoint of one specific kind of elaborative inference: the predictive inference.

MECHANISMS THAT CONSTRUCT THE SITUATION MODEL

A situation model contains a rich representation of the situation described by the text. It is the content of the microworld that the text is about. This representation is based on explicitly stated information, general and/or specific world knowledge, and inferences and elaborations generated by the reader. A well-established situation model would provide many of the semantic and contextual features necessary for reactivation of relevant information (O'Brien & Myers, 1999). However, the specific process involved in the construction of the situation model is still uncertain. Graesser and Bertus (1998) pointed out two main positions. On the one hand, many authors note that the process of constructing situation models is a time-consuming, strategic activity that has little systematicity and is, therefore, quite variable among readers (Perfetti, 1994; Rayner & Pollatsek, 1989). In this sense, individual differences could help researchers construct better theories of situation model construction. Several studies have focused on different factors that could affect the construction of the situation model and the inferential processing, such as the reader's prior knowledge (León & Pérez, 2001), and the reader's purpose (Noordman, Vonk, & Kempff, 1992). In an expert-novice study, León and Pérez studied the influence of prior knowledge on the time course of one specific type of elaborative inference, the clinical diagnosis inferences. They identified systematic differences between experts and novices, with the experts able to generate such inferences more quickly and reliably. They concluded that clinical diagnosis inferences can be generated online by the experts, but off-line in the case of novices.

On the other hand, some researches assert that some of the mechanisms that construct situation models are as constrained, invariant, and systematic as the mechanisms at the more shallow levels of reading (Graesser & Bertus, 1998). These authors investigated whether the process of generating causal inferences was consistent across adult subjects with different characteristics and cognitive abilities, such as age, working memory span, general world knowledge, reasoning ability, and reading frequency. They collected self-paced reading times for sentences in expository texts on scientific and technological mechanisms. The patterns of reading time data supported the claim that the impact of the inference variables on sentence-reading times was remarkably resilient to individual differences among readers. For example, causal antecedent inferences are constructed more quickly and reliably than predictive causal consequence inferences for both young and old readers, and the magnitude of the processing-time parameters are comparable. Thus, if these cognitive abilities are not affecting the construction of the mental model, the status of these deeper comprehension mechanisms is in principle not qualitatively different from the shallow levels of reading, such as processing of letters, syllables, words, and syntax. Simply put, the stability of the deep comprehension processes is not any different than that of the shallow levels of reading.

TIME COURSE OF PREDICTIVE INFERENCES

Some researchers claim that predictive inferences are not generated during reading (Potts, Keenan, & Golding, 1988; Singer & Ferreira, 1983) or that they are encoded only minimally and temporarily (McKoon & Ratcliff, 1986). Other researchers claim that predictive inferences do not seen to occur online unless: (a) they are highly constrained by the context, (b) they are available from general knowledge, and (c) they have few, if any, alternative consequences or contradictions (Graesser et al., 1994; McKoon & Ratcliff, 1992, 1995; van den Broek, Fletcher, & Risden, 1993).

The class of elaborative inference that has received the most attention is the predictive inference. Predictive inferences are expectations about the likely outcome of an event or action in a particular situation. They are typically characterized by some indication to the reader of "what will happen next." So, in the example given by Potts et al. (1988), *No longer able to control his anger, the husband threw the delicate porcelain vase against the wall,* a predictive inference would presumably be *the vase broke.* Predictive inferences have been classified as *elaborative inferences* (Graesser et al., 1994; Reder, 1980), *forward elaborations* that anticipate information yet to be described in the text (e.g., Graesser & Clark, 1985; van den Broek, 1990; van den Broek et al., 1993), *global inferences* (Fincher-Kiefer, 1992), and *strategic inferences* (McKoon & Ratcliff, 1992). Elaborative inferences are *extratextual* inferences that link prior knowledge of the readers to the current statement.

Research on predictive inferences has produced discrepant results. Whereas a number of studies have indicated that predictive inferences are not drawn online in most circumstances (Fincher-Kiefer, 1993; Magliano, Baggett, Johnson, & Graesser, 1993; Millis & Graesser, 1994; Potts et al., 1988; Whitney, Ritchie, & Crane, 1992), other researchers have reported that predictive inferences can be drawn online (Calvo & Castillo, 1996, 1998; Fincher-Kiefer, 1994, 1995; Keefe & McDaniel, 1993; Millis, Morgan, & Graesser, 1990; Murray, Klin, & Myers, 1993; Potts et al., 1988; Waring & Kluttz, 1998; Whitney et al., 1992). The latter studies suggest that predictive inferences are activated during reading, but with delay and followed by a rapid deactivation stage unless the subsequent text bolsters or recycles its activation. Regarding the time course of predictive inferences, Fincher-Kiefer (1995) and Calvo and Castillo (1996) estimated respectively that a 1,250- or a 750-ms stimulus onset asynchrony (SOA, or time between the onset of the last word in a sentence and the test inference) is necessary to find evidence for predictive inferences. However, Millis, and Graesser (1994) compared a

540- and 1,040-ms SOA condition and observed that causal consequence inferences were not activated in either SOA condition. Moreover, the persistence of predictive inferences in memory is still uncertain. Keefe and McDaniel (1993, Experiment 3) reported that the activation of predictive inferences quickly fades after a short interval filled with a backward counting task. In contrast, Klin, Guzman, and Levine (1999) argued that forward inferences are encoded into reader's situation model because participants' reading times were increased by a sentence that contradicted the to-be-inferred event even after a long intervening filler passage (Klin, Murray, Levine & Guzman, 1999). It must be noted that these authors studied high-predictability forward inferences, consisting of short stories with a character who wants to achieve a superordinate goal.

The majority of past investigations assumed that these inconsistent results are attributable to methodological differences between studies, but it is conceivable that textual and contextual constraints also play a role. If we read that an actress falls off the roof of a 14-story building while shooting a scene, as in the famous example from McKoon and Ratcliff (1986), we suspect that a large number of future scenarios could be evoked and that it reduces the probability of drawing a single predictive inference. That is, in the context of a movie, it may be unlikely that the actress will die and more realistic to infer that the actress will fall down on canvas covers or that she will be safe and sound. Given the wide range of possible predictive inferences in the last example, one would expect that the reader is unlikely to make a time-consuming predictive inference. More generally, the number of alternative consequences for an event in a narrative text strongly depends on the reader's world knowledge and limits of the imagination. In a scientific context, however, the most a reader could drum up for a consequence is one or two predictions. The question that arises, therefore, is whether the conclusions drawn for the predictive inferences in scripted narratives should be generalized to scientific texts.

ELABORATIVE INFERENCES IN SCIENTIFIC AND TECHNOLOGICAL CONTEXTS

The comprehension of most texts imposes demands on the cognitive resources that construct a coherent situation model. When we read a scientific text, this effort is even greater because of the abstract terminology, the inherently complex conceptualizations, the demands of logical or analytical precision, and the need to extract an explanation of the text (Lemke, 1990; León & Slisko, 2000). The scientific discourse is an extremely specific and technical language. Because of that, there are important differences between the situation models for narrative and scientific expository texts. A situation model for a story could refer to the people, the spatial setting, the action and event sequences in the plot, and the mental states of the people in the microworld (Graesser, Millis, & Zwaan, 1997; Graesser et al., 1994; Kintsch, 1998). The situation model for an expository text on a scientific topic would consist of a sketch of the physical components in the scientific system, the event and processes that occur as the system functions, the relations among the entities and events, and the various uses of the system by humans (Graesser & Bertus, 1998; Graesser & Hemphill, 1991; Kieras & Bovair, 1984; Mayer & Sims, 1994).

As already acknowledged, most of the studies on elaborative inferences have concentrated on narrative discourse (Fincher-Kiefer, 1993; Magliano et al., 1993; McKoon & Ratcliff, 1992; van den Broek, 1994). However, most researchers believe that the genre of the text influences the type of inferences drawn as well as the time course of inference generation (León, van den Broek, & Escudero, 1998; Zwaan, 1994). León et al., for example, collected think-aloud protocols on three different genres of text: narrative, expository, and news. The results suggested that the inferences drawn are sensitive to the genre. For example, expository texts have a high density of backward explanations whereas narratives evoked significantly more predictive inferences; the news articles were in between. From another perspective, Graesser (1981) showed that readers make nine times as many inferences in stories as in expository texts. Britton, van Dusen, Glyn, and Hemphill (1990) proposed that readers may not always make the inferences that are needed in expository instructional text, and that the inferences are likely to be costly when they are made. The structure of stories is very conventional in the sense that they can be well represented by a rhetorical grammar and they tap into everyday world knowledge structures that support inferencing (e.g., schemata, scripts, plans, etc.) In contrast, the structure of expositions is much more variable, the subject matter is less familiar, and the content is less predictable, so it is less likely to support inferencing (Bock & Brewer, 1985). These findings support the claim that studies with narratives do not necessarily generalize to other discourse genre. This possibility motivated our research on scientific expository texts.

The class of scientific expository texts is undoubtedly not well defined and uniform. An overview of psychological investigations of scientific text understanding uncovered several subtypes of texts. In Millis and Graesser (1994), all the texts described causally driven event chains in a variety of scientific domains (technological, biological domains and natural science texts describing forces of natural events). In the Dee-Lucas and Larkin study (1988), the passages were definition based or descriptions of the relations among the elements of a machine. The major distinction among these texts concerned the nature of the causality the texts conveyed. Physical causality relates two events by necessary or sufficient causal relations in the material world, for example, "*The chemist heats plastic. Plastic melts* (Teisserenc, 1999; Teisserenc & Maury, 2000). A *teleological* relation between two events occurs when physical causality is coupled with intentionality or goals of animate agents (Graesser & Hemphill, 1991), for example, *Grapes are crushed. Wine is produced.* Grapes are crushed intentionally by a human agent in order to produce wine. So there is a physical causal stance and a goal-oriented stance, where actions are performed for a purpose. We assumed that the intentionality behind actions will enhance the probability of finding evidence for predictive inferences. In contrast, when reading "*The star explodes into a cloud of cosmic debris. The debris floats in space*," it was more difficult to connect causally the two events because they were not designed by a human agent and the causal agent was not explicitly mentioned in the statement.

These distinctions among several types of causality have been well documented in psycholinguistic studies. There are verb categorizations that specify the type of process the verb refers to (François, 1989; Fuchs, 1991). According to François and Denhière (1997), meaning construction for a statement depends on several implicit factors, such as temporal properties of the verb (dynamicity, existence of a change or not), the type of change conveyed by the verb (absolute vs. relative), the presence or not of a causal agent, and the features of the causal agent (animate, semianimate, or inanimate). However, in the research on inferences, only recently has attention been paid to the semantic features of target words and the passages (Magliano & Schleich, 2000; McDonald & Mac Whinney, 1995; McKoon, Greene, & Ratcliff, 1993; Truitt & Zwaan, 1998).

In one recent study, Carreiras, Carriedo, Alonso, and Fernández (1997, Experiment 3) clearly demonstrated that verb tense and aspect systematically influenced the construction of what the text is about. As an example, they had subjects read short paragraphs with two characters introduced by their proper names such as "John was finishing (past progressive) versus had finished (past perfect) his shift when Mary arrived at the restaurant." In these narratives, verb aspect was manipulated (past progressive vs. past perfect forms) to indicate that the action of one of the protagonists had been completed or was currently in progress. The target word was the name of the character whose action could be described either with a past progressive or a past perfect form of the verb (*John* in the previous example). They obtained faster response times to the target character's name when the action was described using the past progressive form because both characters would be in the focus of a scenario-like representation. On the other hand, the use of past perfect form backgrounded the character in the discourse focus. The conclusion to be drawn from this study is that verb aspect determined information accessibility in a text.

Manes Gallo and Bonnotte (1996) reported another example of the interaction between the type of process the verb refers to (state verb, action verb) and the semantic features of the grammatical subject in a sentence (animate, semianimate, inanimate). The participants were instructed to read carefully a series of sentences and to evaluate on a 16-point scale the degree of dynamicity denoted by the verb used in the sentence (state verb, action verb). For instance, the participants judged as more dynamic a sentence like "*the carpenter* (animate) *removed the tiles from the roof*" compared to a similar sentence such as "*the wind* (inanimate) *removed the tiles from the roof.*" However, the semantic features of the grammatical subject (animate, inanimate) did not influence readers' judgment on dynamicity for state verbs (respectively "*the injured person is pale*" vs. "*the sun of winter is pale*").

Consequently, in this chapter, we report two experiments that investigate the activation of predictive inferences as a function of (a) the verbs that define the consequence of the action (transformational change verbs such as to *harden,* to *dry,* to *grow,* to *solidify* compared to destructive change verbs such as to *die,* to *melt,* to *evaporate,* to *explode*) and (b) the semantic features of the predictive sentence (focusing on the agent responsible for the action vs. on the object modified by the action). In the first experiment, we used a lexical decision task in order to measure the activation of predictive inferences. In both experiments, subjects were presented with technological texts (e.g., texts describing paper production, glass manufacturing) and texts describing natural forces (thunder formation, volcano action, cave formation). In the second experiment we used an online sentence verification task in order to assess whether predictive inferences are activated to a greater degree in the texts describing intentional actions of a causal human agent than texts about changes generated through events of natural forces.

EXPERIMENT 1: A LEXICAL DECISION STUDY ON PREDICTIVE INFERENCES

The aim of this experiment was to assess whether the difference already observed between technological texts and texts describing forces of nature mechanisms could be explained by the types of verbs conveyed in the texts (Graesser & Hemphill, 1991). In particular, talk-aloud protocols guided by "what happens next" questions were expected to reveal whether the texts describing forces of nature action were more frequently expressed by destructive change verbs and long-term consequence verbs. If that was the case, then it would be the nature of the verb, rather than the type of domain knowledge, that explains the different profiles of inferences that are generated by texts about technology versus nature. Therefore, we designed this experiment to measure the influence of semantic features of the consequence verb on predictive inferences.

Method

Subjects.   Participants were 46 undergraduate psychology students at the University of Montpellier III (ages 18–24). All of them spoke French as their first language. The 12 male participants and the 10 students with scientific backgrounds were equally split in the two experimental conditions (inference context vs. unrelated context). All participants were tested individually and randomly assigned to one of two context conditions.

Materials. The 12 experimental texts described transformations of material states (solid in liquid, liquid in gaseous) produced by human actions (plastic, glass, paper, leather manufacturing, milk and petrol production) or due to forces of nature action (birth and death of a star, erosion, glacier melting, cave formation, desert formation, volcano action). Original material was presented in French. Specific background knowledge was not necessary to understand the texts because they were constructed from French popular scientific textbooks. The inferential target verbs corresponded to common French verbs that are well known by adult people and were not specific to scientific context. In order to avoid any confusion among the texts, filler passages depicted biological mechanisms (antibiotic action, heart disease, kidney machine functioning, laser action in biology, cellular division mechanisms, blood circulation). Each passage contained two introductory sentences followed by a predictive sentence. An example passage is presented in Table 9.1.

Immediately after the end of some sentences, participants performed a lexical decision task. Talk-aloud protocols based on "what happens next" questions allowed us to select a pool of French verbs. Verbs (rather than nouns) were more frequent answers to express the consequence of an action. Target verbs were destructive change verbs (e.g., to die, to splinter, to melt, to evaporate, to consume, to destroy) versus transformational change verbs (to harden, to grow, to dry, to flatten, to erode, to soften, to solidify); these were 6.8 and 7.1 letters long, respectively. In both cases, the conse-

TABLE 9.1

An Example of Technological Text (Experiment 1)

Introductory Sentences

Plastic is made of artificial resin.

The plastic is delivered in tablet form of different diameters.

Predictive Sentence

The chemist heats the tablet plastic to a high degree.

Comprehension Questions

Factual Question

The chemist:

a. heats the plastic

b. cuts out the plastic

c. injects additive

Inference Question

In the text, tablet plastics

a. evaporate

b. crack

c. become liquid

---

quence of the action led to a modification for the object (it became flat, dry); however, the modified object remained as a single entity with transformational change verbs whereas this entity disappeared as the ice in the glacier-melting text, for instance. Target words were chosen in a way that none of them were specific to scientific context. The filler words were nonverbs and French filler verbs, with both being pronounceable and 7.4 letters long versus 7 letters long, respectively. Type of Text and Change Verbs were both within-subjects factors.

Procedure.   The subjects performed a lexical decision task on the target words following two types of sentence contexts. In the Inference Context, the lexical decision latencies appeared after the sentence that had generated the inference. In the Unrelated Context, lexical decision latencies were collected on the same target verbs but following sentences from a different passage. The delay between the onset of the last word in the predictive sentence and the onset of the lexical target verb (SOA) was 900 ms. Each participant was presented with six filler texts interspersed among the 12 experimental texts. We used a rapid serial visual presentation (RSVP) procedure associated with a word-by-word segmentation. Finally, the readers answered eight comprehension questions and were required to choose as quickly as possible the correct answer among three proposals. An example of factual question (textbase level) and inference question (relevant to the consequence of the action) described in the text are presented in Table 9.1.

Results and Discussion

A mixed analysis of variance (ANOVA) was performed with Context (Inference Context vs. Unrelated Context) as a between-subjects factor and Change verbs (nonverbs, French filler verbs, and destructive verbs, vs. transformational change verbs) and Type of Text (texts describing technological mechanisms vs. texts describing forces of nature actions) as two within-subjects variables. The dependent variable was lexical decision latencies. All lexical decision latencies more than 2 standard deviations from a participant's mean were treated as missing data. This criterion resulted in eliminating the data for two participants.

Table 9.2 presents mean lexical decision latencies. There was a difference of 47 ms between the Inference Context (mean latency: 868 ms) and the Unrelated Condition (mean latency: 915 ms), but this effect was not reliable ($F(1, 44) = 1.33, p = .16$). A significant effect of Type of Text was found, with longer response times for texts describing forces of nature $F(1, 44) = 14.48, p = .001$; mean latencies were respectively 914 ms for the natural science texts and 869 ms for technological texts. This finding suggests that two distinct representations were constructed from the two types of texts (a goal-oriented representation with technological texts vs. a causal chain representation with natural science texts.) In the latter, the consequence verb was only connected with the immediate causal node, whereas in technological texts the consequence verbs were highly connected with the superordinate goal of the text. This distinction was supported by talk-aloud protocols. In the technological texts, a large proportion of readers began their answers by employing infinitive connectives, for example, *"in order to produce plastic goods, it is necessary to heat it"* (see Maury & Blanquer, 1999). Of particular interest was the nearly significant effect of Change verbs, $F(3, 132) = 2.50, p = .06$. A plausible explanation for this finding was that the destructive change verbs were no longer in the discourse focus and the subject needed to reactivate this information in order to make judgments on the lexical decision task.

TABLE 9.2

**Mean Lexical Decision Latencies (in milliseconds)
and Standard Deviations as a Function of Context Type
of Texts and Change Verbs**

	Context Condition			
	Unrelated		Inference	
	Mean	SD	Mean	SD
Technological Texts				
Transformational Change Verbs	901	(183)	805	(118)
Destructive Change Verbs	887	(117)	884	(156)
Natural Science Texts				
Transformational Change Verbs	970	(143)	870	(112)
Destructive Change Verbs	904	(112)	915	(133)

The interaction between Context and Change Verbs was significant, $F(3,132) = 3.66$, $p = .01$. The predictive inferences corresponding to destructive change verbs were probably not activated during reading because of longer response times in the inference context compared to the unrelated context. A reverse pattern was observed for predictive inferences corresponding to transformational change verbs. This finding supported our prediction about the importance of semantic features of the consequence verbs on predictive inference activation. None of the other interactions reached significance; in particular, the Type of Text × Change Verbs interaction was not significant ($F < 1$).

This experiment emphasized the role of intentionality in action on predictive inference activation. The protagonist action appeared to be the core of the situation model constructed from technological texts. However, the content of the situation model in scientific texts, especially natural science texts, remained unclear. Therefore, Experiment 2 was designed to investigate the salience of both the agent and the object in the situation model. Thus, we assumed that the consequence of an action takes the form of an entire proposition, with an agent and a modified object or a schema, rather than a single word. The very nature of the process is captured by the verb that expresses the consequence. The verb critically participates in the mental construction of what the text is about (Magliano & Schleich, 2000).

EXPERIMENT 2: A VERIFICATION JUDGMENT TASK ON PREDICTIVE INFERENCES

To test our prediction, the lexical decision task was replaced by a verification task to measure online activation. The discourse focus was manipulated by varying the grammatical subject of the predictive sentence. For half of the readers, the focus was on the agent action (animate or not), whereas for the other half of readers, the object modified by the action was the grammatical subject of the predictive sentence. The Verification Subject varied in the same way. We predicted that when the Verification Subject did not match the content of the discourse focus, the reader needed to update his or her mental model to answer as quickly as possible. This updating activity should be expressed by longer verification latencies. In natural science texts, the focus on the agent should lead to longer verification times because of the absence of an intentional action whereas shorter response times should be obtained in technological texts.

Method

Participants and Design.   Seventy-five undergraduate participants from Montpellier III University took part in this experiment. They were tested individually and randomly assigned to one of four experimental conditions. Each subject was presented with a total of 20 texts in such a way that each text appeared in the implicit versus the explicit version. Version was a within-subjects variable; there were never more than two consecutive texts in the same version for a participant.

Materials.   The 8 filler texts interspersed among the 12 experimental texts were approximately the same as in the Experiment 1 except that a third introductory sentence was added for each text and 3 of the texts associated with destructive change verbs (erosion, glacier melting, birth and death of a star) were replaced by 3 new texts (champagne production, silk manufacturing, salt production). In this study, we used only transformational consequence verbs as target words and two more filler texts (about digestion and photosynthesis) were constructed. In order to avoid a repetition effect of the consequence verb explicitly mentioned both in the fourth sentence of the explicit version and in the verification statement, we used a synonym of the consequence verb and not the consequence verb itself in the predictive sentence. Original material was presented in French.

Four sets of material were constructed as a function of Text version (implicit vs. Explicit) and the Predictive Subject (a causal agent vs. the object).

An example passage is presented in Table 9.3. The same pattern was adopted for the verification statement. These two factors were combined factorially.

Procedure. Unlike in the Experiment 1, the presentation of the texts was subject paced. Each key press caused the current segment to be erased and the next segment to be presented. The session began with a training text. Immediately after the last segment of the second sentence of the training text had been presented, a verification statement appeared on the screen. Subjects were required to decide as quickly as possible if the sentence is correct or not regarding his or her understanding of the text. Subjects made the yes/no response by pressing a key on a specific keyboard. The same procedure occurred for the experimental texts and the filler texts except that the verification statement was always displayed after the third sentence in the experimental texts. Finally, the subjects completed a final comprehension questionnaire containing one factual question by text and one inference question. For each question, they were to choose the correct response among three alternatives. For instance, in the glass text example, the following propositions were displayed: *When the artisan blows molten glass: a) it grows, b) it retracts, c) it disintegrates.*

Results and Discussion

Comprehension Questionnaire. We conducted an ANOVA on mean comprehension scores and mean response times as a function of two between-subjects factors (the Predictive Subject and the Verification Subject) and two within-subjects factors (Type of Text and Text Version). No

TABLE 9.3
An Example of Technological Text (Experiment 2)

Introductory Sentences
Glass material is mainly composed of silica and soda.
This mixture is heated to a temperature of one thousand degrees.
The artisan takes a drop of molten glass with a rod.
Predictive Sentence
The artisan blows molten glass versus molten glass is blown by the artisan.
Verification Statement (Yes/No Response)
Does the artisan make the glass grow?
Does the glass grow?

significant differences were found between any of these conditions (all $Fs <$ 1). Comprehension scores ranged from 19.2 (out of 24) to 17.3 across conditions (averaged over subjects and texts). However, a three-way interaction was obtained between Version and Predictive Subject × Verification Subject on both the comprehension scores and response times: respectively, $F(1,71) = 5.12, p < .05$ and $F(1,71) = 4.97, p < .05$. Two comments should be made on these results. First, this interaction suggested that error rate and response times were greater in the implicit condition when the predictive sentence and the verification statement both focused on the (object) The subjects focusing on the agent, whatever the Predictive Subject, needed to update their mental model when it came to answering a comprehension question on the object. Second, the absence of a significant difference between technological vs. natural science texts ruled out the possibility that texts describing forces of nature actions were more difficult to understand.

Verification Statement: Response Times and Errors.   We assumed that it is unlikely that elaborative inferences are activated in an all-or-none fashion, so we used the IES (inference encoding score) method to measure the strength of activation for predictive inferences (for more details, see Magliano et al., 1993, and Millis & Graesser, 1994). This IES was calculated as the mean difference between the implicit and the explicit version for the verification times. The higher this difference, the longer the verification times were in the implicit version; therefore, the less the verb expressing the consequence of the action was activated during reading. An ANOVA was computed on IES as a function of the Type of Text (texts describing technological mechanisms vs. texts describing forces of nature actions), the Predictive Subject and the Verification Subject (agent vs. object).

Figure 9.1 shows the activation scores for predictive inferences. The conclusion to be drawn was that predictive inferences were only activated during the reading of texts describing intentional changes, $F(1, 71) = 9.93, p < .01$.

The significant interaction Type of Text × Verification Subject suggested that the agent was more activated in technological texts, $F(1, 71) = 3.72$, $p = .05$. In addition, the amount of activation for the modified object did not differ significantly in technological and natural science texts ($F < 1$). The pattern of errors for the verification statement supported this interpretation. Although a small number of errors have been made (between 20% and 28%), they were less prevalent in natural science texts when the verification statement focused on the agent, $F(1, 71) = 5.16, p < .05$.

The grammatical subject for the predictive sentence did not influence the content of the discourse focus ($F < 1$). Whatever the condition, we ob-

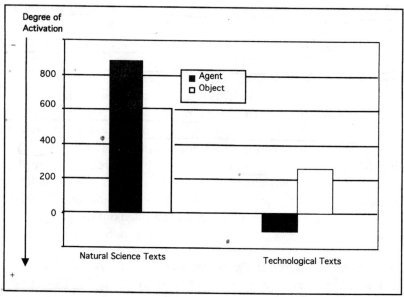

FIG. 9.1. Mean inference encoding score (in milliseconds) as a function of Type of Texts and Verification Subject.

tained shortest response times when the predictive sentence foregrounded the agent, especially in the technological texts with a human agent. The Type of text × Predictive Subject nearly reached significance, $F(1, 71) = 3.01$, $p = .08$. Once again, these data suggested that the salience of the agent varied according to the semantic features of this agent (animate or inanimate in natural science texts). Therefore, it appears that forces of nature did not have agentlike properties. As we predicted, the subjects inferred the consequence of the action performed by the agent and not the consequence relative to a change of state for the object.

→ Even if the discourse focus is on the agent, we cannot rule out the possibility that the passive voice transformation we used when the target sentence began with the object increased response times. In that case, if the interpretation of the passive voice was correct, the object should be foregrounded. We should also obtain a facilitation effect in the response times when the Verification Subject matches the Predictive Subject.

The data presented on Fig. 9.2 addresses the aforementioned questions. As in the case of the questionnaire scores, the three-way interaction reached significance, $F(1, 71) = 3.86$, $p = .05$. Longest response times were obtained in the object-object condition. This suggests that the shortest response times we obtained previously were not due to the passive voice transformation itself but indicated that the agent (animate or not) was in the discourse focus whatever the type of inducing target sentence. This interpretation was strengthened by the shortest response times in the agent–agent condition. The other two cases provide some information about the subject updating mental representation. This updating effect took about 180 ms when the verification statement did not begin with the agent (but with the object affected by the action), but was shorter in the reverse case (about 60 ms in the object–agent condition).

GENERAL CONCLUSIONS

The present study has provided some empirical support for the hypothesis that semantic features influence the generation of predictive inferences in two different types of scientific texts (technological and texts describing natural science forces). This was found when we adopted two different experimental techniques, a lexical decision task and a verification task. Only in the

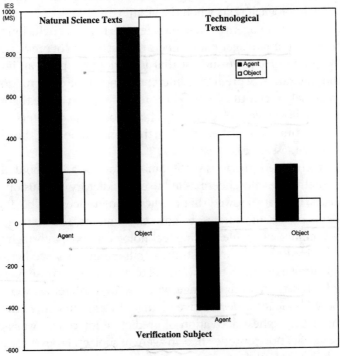

FIG. 9.2.   Mean inference encoding score (in milliseconds) as a function of Type of Texts, Verification Subject, and Predictive Subject.

case of technological texts and under some conditions were the predictive inferences generated online. The results lead us to answer some questions about the three points mentioned earlier: the mechanisms of constructing situational models, the time course of predictive inferences, and the generation of elaborative inferences in scientific and technological contexts.

Regarding the construction of the situation model, our results partially support the notion that semantic features of the predictive sentence and the verb defining the consequence of the action are influencing one of the mechanisms of the construction of the situation model, namely the generation of predictive inferences. In the Experiment 1, we found out that readers' performance was systematically altered by the meaning of the verb, being better for transformational change verbs than for destructive change verbs. This semantic feature therefore affects the activation of predictive inferences. The results from the Experiment 2 suggest that the texts with implicit information were more difficult to understand when both the predictive and verification sentences had an object as a grammatical subject. Thus, the presence of an animate agent could facilitate the understanding of these texts. Regarding the activation of predictive inferences, it was higher in technological texts when the grammatical subject of the verification sentence was an agent. These data lead us to the conclusion that the presence of an animate agent also affects the activation of predictive inferences. Because of that, we suggest that intentionality plays an important role in the generation of predictive inferences and in the construction of the situation model of scientific texts. These results support those theories that claim that shallow levels of reading, such as processing of letters, syllables, words, and syntax, could be affecting the construction of the situation model (e.g., Graesser & Bertus, 1998).

As we mentioned previously, the amount of research about the time course of predictive inferences has led to contradictory conclusions. In our experiments, the data showed that predictive inferences can be drawn online under some circumstances. In both experiments, the inferences were generated online only while reading technological texts, although this was not the case in all the conditions studied. In Experiment 1, predictive inferences were drawn online in technological texts when the consequence verb described a transformational change, whereas these inferences were off-line when the verb meant a destructive change. In Experiment 2, the results suggest that the highest activation of predictive inferences was achieved when the verification sentence had an agent as subject. From these data, we can conclude that both factors, semantic features and the type of text, could be affecting the time course of predictive inferences in technology texts, even transforming an off-line inference into an online one. As some authors pointed out regarding causal consequences inferences (e.g., Graesser et al., 1994, 1997), we also think that the time course of predictive inferences could be influenced by the presence of a character action in order to achieve superordinate goals. In the technological texts used in this study, the reader is able to identify a human agent who acts intentionally in order to achieve a goal, whereas this feature does not appear in natural science texts. This may be one of the reasons why in our experiments predictive inferences were drawn online only in the case of technological texts.

We can draw another conclusion about difference between technological and natural science texts. Experiment 1 showed differences in the activation of predictive inferences for these two science domains, whereas the comprehension data from Experiment 2 indicated that readers understood the two types of texts similarly. Apparently, other factors could be influencing the construction of the situation model rather than the comprehension difficulty. The structure of the information and/or the familiarity of its content could be among these other factors. The presence of a human agent and intentionality could determine a goal-oriented mental representation in technological texts, whereas texts about natural forces lead mainly to causal chain representations (Graesser & Hemphill, 1991). In addition, technological information may be more familiar than the information about natural forces because the former describes mechanisms more tangible to our everyday experiences, and the latter is more related to processes rarely observed directly.

REFERENCES

Bock, J. K., & Brewer, W. F. (1985). Discourse structure and mental models. *New Directions for Child Development, 27,* 55–75.

Britton, B. K., van Dusen, L., Glynn, S. M., & Hemphill, D. (1990). The impact of inferences on instructional text. In A. C. Graesser & G. H. Bower (Eds.), *The psychology of learning and motivation* (Vol. 25, pp. 53–70). San Diego: Academic Press.

Calvo, M. G., & Castillo, M. D. (1996). Predictive inferences occur online, but with delay: Convergence of naming and reading times. *Discourse Processes, 22,* 57–78.

Calvo, M. G., & Castillo, M. D. (1998). Predictive inferences take time to develop. *Psychological Research, 61,* 249–260.

Carreiras, M., Carriedo, N., Alonso, M. A., & Fernández, A. (1997). The role of verb tense and verb aspect in the foregrounding of information during reading. *Memory & Cognition, 25,* 438–446.

Dee-Lucas, D., & Larkin, J. H. (1988). Attentional strategies for studying scientific texts. *Memory & Cognition, 16,* 469–479.

Fincher-Kiefer, R. (1992). The role of prior knowledge in inferential processing. *Journal of Research in Reading, 15*, 12–27.

Fincher-Kiefer, R. (1993). The role of predictive inferences in situation model construction. *Discourse Processes, 16*, 99–124.

Fincher-Kiefer, R. (1994). The effect of inferential processes on perceptual identification. *Discourse Processes, 18*, 1–17.

Fincher-Kiefer, R. (1995). Relative inhibition following the encoding of bridging and predictive inferences. *Journal of Experimental Psychology: Learning, Memory, and Cognition, 21*, 981–995.

François, J. (1989). *Changement, causation, action: Trois catégories sémantiques fondamentales du lexique verbal en français et en allemand* [Change, causation, action: Three fundamental semantic categories of verbal lexicon in French and German]. Unpublished doctoral thesis, Geneva, Switzerland.

François, J., & Denhière, G. (1997). *Sémantique linguistique et Psychologie Cognitive: Aspects théoriques et expérimentaux* [Semantics, linguistics, and cognitive psychology: Theoretical and experimental aspects]. Grenoble, France: Presses Universitaires de Grenoble.

Fuchs, C. (1991). *Les typologies de procès* [Typologies of processes]. Paris: Klincksieck.

Graesser, A. C. (1981). *Prose comprehension beyond the word.* New York: Springer-Verlag.

Graesser, A. C., & Bertus, L. B. (1998). The construction of causal inferences while reading expository texts on science and technology. *Scientific Studies of Reading, 2*, 247–269.

Graesser, A. C., & Clark, L. F. (1985). *Structures and procedures of implicit knowledge.* Norwood, NJ: Ablex.

Graesser, A. C., & Hemphill, D. (1991). Question answering in the context of scientific mechanisms. *Journal of Memory and Language, 30*, 186–209.

Graesser, A. C., Millis, K. K., & Zwaan, R. A. (1997). Discourse comprehension. *Annual Review of Psychology, 48*, 163–189.

Graesser, A. C., Singer, M., & Trabasso, T. (1994). Constructing inferences during narrative text comprehension. *Psychological Review, 10*, 371–395.

Greene, S., McKoon, G., & Ratcliff, R. (1992). Pronoun resolution and discourse models. *Journal of Experimental Psychology: Learning, Memory, and Cognition, 18*, 266–283.

Haberlandt, K. (1994). Methods in reading research. In M. A. Gernsbacher (Ed.), *Handbook of psycholinguistics* (pp. 1–31). San Diego: Academic Press.

Haviland, S. E., & Clark, H. H. (1974). What's new? Acquiring new information as a process in comprehension. *Journal of Verbal Learning and Verbal Behavior, 13*, 512–521.

Keefe, D. E., & McDaniel, M. A. (1993). The time course and durability of predictive inferences. *Journal of Memory and Language, 32*, 446–463.

Keenan, J. M., Potts, G. R., Golding, J. M., & Jennings, T. M. (1990). Which elaborative inferences are drawn during reading? A question of methodologies. In D. A. Balota, G. B. Flores d'Arcais, & K. Rayner (Eds.), *Comprehension processes in reading* (pp. 377–399). Hillsdale, NJ: Lawrence Erlbaum Associates.

Kemper, S. (1983). Measuring the inference load of a text. *Journal of Educational Psychology, 75,* 391–401.

Kieras, D. E., & Bovair, S. (1984). The role of a mental model in learning to operate a device. *Cognitive Science, 8,* 255–273.

Kintsch, W. (1998). *Comprehension: A paradigm for cognition.* Cambridge, England: Cambridge University Press.

Klin, C. M., Guzman, A. E., & Levine, W. H. (1999). Prevalence and persistence of predictive inferences. *Journal of Memory and Language, 40,* 593–604.

Klin, C. M., Murray, J. D., Levine, W. H., & Guzman, A. E. (1999). Forward inferences: From activation to long-term memory. *Discourse Processes, 27,* 241–260.

✓Lemke, J. L., (1990). Talking science: Language, learning, and values. Norwood, NJ: Ablex.

✓León, J. A., & Pérez, O. (2001). The influence of prior knowledge on the time course of clinical diagnosis inferences: A comparison of experts and novices. *Discourse Processes, 31,* 187–213.

León, J. A., & Slisko, J. (2000). La dificultad comprensiva de los textos de ciencias. Nuevas alternativas para un viejo problema educativo [Comprehensive difficulty in science texts. New approaches for an old educational problem]. *Psicología Educativa, 6,* 7–26.

León, J. A., van den Broek, P., & Escudero, I, (1998, December). *Influence of type of text on the activation on elaborative inferences: A cross-cultural study based on a thinking aloud for scientific texts.* Paper presented in the workshop "The Psychology of Science Text Comprehension," Menendez y Pelayo International University, Cuenca, Spain.

Long, D. L., Golding, J., & Graesser, A. C. (1992). A test on the online status of goal-related inferences. *Journal of Memory and Language, 31,* 634–647.

Magliano, J. P., Baggett, W. B., Johnson, B. K., & Graesser, A. C. (1993). The time-course of generating causal antecedent and causal consequence inferences. *Discourse Processes, 16,* 35–53.

✓Magliano, J. P., & Schleich, M. C. (2000). Verb aspect and situation models. *Discourse Processes, 29,* 83–112.

Manes Gallo, M. C., & Bonnotte, I. (1996). On the aim conveyed by verbs in the proposition. *International Journal of Psycholinguistics, 12,* 341–375.

Maury, P., & Blanquer, E. (1999, August). *Predictive inferences and text understanding: Comparison of an "online" lexical decision task with an "off-line" talk-aloud protocol.* Paper presented at the 8th European Conference for Research on Learning and Instruction, Göteborg, Sweden.

Mayer, R. E., & Sims, V. K. (1994). For whom a picture worth a thousand words? Extensions of a dual-code theory of multimedia learning. *Journal of Educational Psychology, 86,* 389–401.

McDonald, J. L., & Mac Whinney, B. (1995). The time-course of anaphor resolution: Effects of implicit verb causality and gender. *Journal of Memory and Language, 34,* 543–566.

McKoon, G., Greene, S. B., & Ratcliff, R. (1993). Discourse models, pronoun resolution and the implicit causality of verbs. *Journal of Experimental Psychology: Learning, Memory, and Cognition, 19,* 1040–1052.

220 ❧ MAURY, PÉREZ, LEÓN

McKoon, G., & Ratcliff, R. (1986). Inferences about predictable events. *Journal of Experimental Psychology: Learning, Memory, and Cognition, 12*, 82–91.

McKoon, G., & Ratcliff, R. (1992). Inferences during reading. *Psychological Review, 99*, 440–446.

McKoon, G., & Ratcliff, R. (1995). The minimalist hypothesis. In C. A. Weaver, S. Mannes, & C. R. Fletcher, (Eds.), *Discourse comprehension: Essays in honor of Walter Kintsch*. Hillsdale, NJ: Lawrence Erlbaum Associates.

Millis, K. K., & Graesser, A. C. (1994). The time course of constructing knowledge-based inferences for scientific texts, *Journal of Memory and Language, 33*, 583–599.

Millis, K. K., Morgan, D., & Graesser, A. C. (1990). The influence of knowledge-based inferences on the reading time of expository text. In A. C. Graesser & G. H. Bower (Eds.), *Inferences and text comprehension* (pp. 197–212). San Diego: Academic Press.

Murray, J. D., Klin, C. M., & Myers, J. L. (1993). Forward inferences in narrative text. *Journal of Memory and Language, 32*, 464–473.

Noordman, L. G. M., Vonk, W., & Kempf, H. J., (1992). Causal inferences during the reading of expository texts. *Journal of Memory and Language, 31*, 573–590.

O'Brien, E., & Myers, J. L. (1999). Text comprehension: A view from the bottom-up. In: S. R. Goldman, A. C. Graesser, & P. W. van den Broek (Eds.), *Narrative comprehension, causality, and coherence : Essays in honor of Tom Trabasso* (pp. 35–53). Hillsdale, NJ: Lawrence Erlbaum Associates.

Perfetti, C. A. (1994). Psycholinguistics and reading ability. In M. A. Gernsbacher (Ed.), *Handbook of psycholinguistics* (pp. 849–894). San Diego: Academic Press.

Potts, G. R., Keenan, J. M., & Golding, J. M. (1988). Assessing the occurrence of elaborative inferences: Lexical decision versus naming. *Journal of Memory and Language, 27*, 399–415.

Rayner, K., & Pollatsek, A. (1989). *The psychology of reading*. Englewood Cliffs, NJ: Prentice-Hall.

Reder, L. M. (1980). The role of elaboration in the comprehension and retention of prose: A critical review. *Review of Educational Research, 50*, 5–53.

Singer, M. (1994). Discourse inference processes In M. A. Gernsbacher (Ed.), *Handbook of psycholinguistics* (pp. 479–516). San Diego: Academic Press.

Singer, M., & Ferreira, F. (1983). Inferring consequences in story comprehension. *Journal of Verbal Learning and Verbal Behavior, 22*, 437–448.

Teisserenc, A. (1999). Causalité et Compréhension de Texte: les caractéristiques sémantiques de l'énoncé peuvent-elles influencer l'activation des inférences prospectives en cours de lecture? [Causality and text comprehension: Did the semantic properties of the text influence the activation of predictive inferences during reading?]. Unpublished manuscript, University of Montpellier III, Montpellier, France.

Teisserenc, A., & Maury, P. (2000, July). *Predictive inferences and text characteristics: Can different types of causality lead to different degrees of activation during reading.* Poster presented at the 10th annual meeting of the Society for Text and Discourse. Lyon, France.

Truitt, T. P., & Zwaan, R. A. (1998). Instrument inferences and verb aspect. *Abstracts of the Psychonomic Society, 2*, 35.

van den Broek, P. (1990). The causal inference maker: Towards a process model of inference generation in text comprehension. In D. A. Balota, G. B. Flores d'Arcais, & K. Rayner (Eds.), *Comprehension processes in reading* (pp. 423–445). Hillsdale, NJ: Lawrence Erlbaum Associates.

van den Broek, P. (1994). Comprehension and memory of narrative texts: Inferences and coherence. In M. A. Gernsbacher (Ed.), *Handbook of psycholinguistics* (pp. 539–588). San Diego: Academic Press.

van den Broek, P., Fletcher, C. R., & Risden, K. (1993). Investigations of inferential processes in reading: A theoretical and methodological integration. *Discourse Processes, 16,* 169–180.

Waring, D. A., & Kluttz, C. (1998). Effects of task on the activation of predictive inferences. *Psychological Reports, 83,* 1287–1296.

Whitney, P., Ritchie, B. G., & Crane, R. S. (1992). The effect of foregrounding on readers' use of predictive inferences. *Memory & Cognition, 29,* 424–432.

Zwaan, R. A. (1994). Effect of genre expectations on text comprehension. *Journal of Experimental Psychology: Learning, Memory, and Cognition, 20,* 920–933.

❧ 10 ❧

Situated Regulation of Scientific Text Processing

Marianne Elshout-Mohr
University of Amsterdam

Maartje van Daalen-Kapteijns
University of Amsterdam

Some cognitive activities are important for all kinds of reading and learning from text, regardless of text type and conditions. Activation of prior knowledge is an example. Prior knowledge is needed for reading and understanding in situations that range from reading narrative texts for pleasure to studying scientific texts for educational purposes (W. Kintsch, 1998). Although the need to activate prior knowledge may be general, the specific regulation strategies applied to activate relevant knowledge may differ for each situation. Alexander, Graham, and Harris (1998) called strategies that are situation-specific *particularized*. We prefer the term *situated*. Situated regulation strategies are regulation strategies that are typically bound to the requirements of the situation in which they occur. We assume that these strategies may represent more general regulation strategies, which the person also uses in other situations. However, they may also incorporate strategic elements that are newly constructed to meet the requirements of the situation.

The present study explored the process of studying text in an ecologically valid situation. We investigated how students in their first year at a university studied scientific texts from an introductory textbook. There were two

223

experimental conditions. Both conditions required the *split focus* that is typical when students study text in an educational context (Goldman, 1997; Locke, 1975). Split focus refers to the fact that students need to focus both on understanding what the text says and on performing operations that produce learning. Our theoretical aim was to understand the strategies that students used to regulate activation of prior knowledge in this split focus situation. We had a more practical aim as well. We wanted to find out why students often process scientific text in ways that teachers regard as shallow rather than deep comprehension (Entwistle & Marton, 1984; Graesser & Person, 1994; Sandberg & Barnard, 1997).

We start with a brief overview of characteristics of readers, texts, tasks, and settings that influence reading and studying text. The second section addresses the issue of self-regulation. In the third section we report an experiment that we conducted and the results that shed informative light on self-regulation mechanisms. The chapter ends with a discussion of what we know about self-regulation while reading and studying text.

VARIABLES THAT INFLUENCE READING AND TEXT STUDYING

Reading and studying text are influenced by characteristics of learners, texts, tasks, and contexts (W. Kintsch, 1998; Otero, 1998). In this section we give examples of these variables.

One obvious category of *learner characteristics* is knowledge, such as world knowledge, vocabulary knowledge, and linguistic knowledge (Anderson & Pearson, 1984; Beck, Perfetti & McKeown, 1982; Coté, Goldman, & Saul, 1998). A second category is skill, such as the skill of making inferences (Schnotz & Ballstaedt, 1996; Walczyk, 1990) and the metacognitive skill of comprehension monitoring (Baker, 1985; Palincsar & Brown, 1984). A third category is attitude, such as personal interest in the reading process (Harmon, 1999), and personal interest in the subject matter conveyed in the text (Hidi, 1990; Schiefele & Krapp, 1996).

There are several relevant *text characteristics*. There are different genre of text. A very broad distinction is between narrative and expository texts, whereas two subclasses of expository texts are scientific journal articles and scientific newspaper articles. The ability to understand narrative texts develops earlier in life than ability to deal with expository texts (Langer, 1986), and scientific texts are notoriously difficult to comprehend (Ausubel, Novak, & Hanesian, 1978; Chinn & Brewer, 1993). Another relevant text characteristic is coherence. Coherence has been defined on the basis of (a) the semantic relatedness of concepts in the text (van Oostendorp, 1994), (b) the syntactic and other forms of linguistic coherence of the propositions (W. Kintsch, 1998; McNamara, E. Kintsch, Songer, & W. Kintsch, 1996), and (c) the structural cohesiveness of the text structure at more global schematic levels (Baker, 1985; Meyer & Rice, 1982).

Task characteristics address the purposes or goals in reading or studying the text. It makes a difference, for instance, whether readers know that they are supposed to detect errors in a text, versus to strive for a meaningful interpretation of the text's content (Markman & Gorin, 1981; Pressley, Van Etten, Yokoi, Freebern, & Van Meter, 1998; Zwaan, Magliano, & Graesser, 1995). Whereas reading goals may be familiar to experienced readers, the goals may be novel and therefore ambiguous to less experienced readers (Schellings & van Hout-Wolters, 1995; Winne & Marx, 1982).

The *context* of reading specifies the physical and social setting of the reading activity. Detecting contradictions in a text is facilitated when the text is presented in a science class setting, versus a language class setting (Garcia-Arista, Campanario, & Otero, 1996; Garner, 1990). It also makes a difference whether text is read in a setting of free reading versus an educational setting (Schellings & van Hout-Wolters, 1995), and whether the setting involves individual versus cooperative reading (Karau & Williams, 1993).

Intriguing patterns of data emerge when researchers investigate interactions among the dimensions of reader, text, task, and context. For example, a paradoxical result has been found in studies on students' learning from expository text in an experimental setting. McNamara et al. (1996) and McNamara and W. Kintsch (1996) manipulated the level of relevant prior knowledge of participants as well as the coherence of the texts. Their studies showed that recall was always better for text with high coherence than with low coherence, for students with both low and high knowledge about the subject matter (such as the functioning of the human heart). This result is quite in line with most of our expectations. The tests that tap deeper levels of comprehension and reasoning had higher scores when low-knowledge readers read texts with high rather than low coherence; this result is once again unsurprising. The paradoxical result was that high-knowledge participants performed better on texts with low rather than high coherence in tests that tap deep comprehension and reasoning. W. Kintsch (1998) offered the explanation that texts should contain coherence gaps in order to stimulate learning. When coherence gaps occur, students are challenged to use available prior knowledge to establish local coherence relations, to figure out the macrostructure of the text, and to elaborate the textual material with what they already know. When coherence gaps are absent, students are not challenged to perform these activities. The combination of a high-coherence text and high background knowledge may induce a "feeling of knowing" or an "illusion of comprehension," which prevents readers from deep processing of the text.

The study that we report in this chapter was motivated by a similar paradox. Why should it be that university students, who are probably proficient readers, are not proficient in studying introductory textbooks? Why do they settle for a shallow comprehension of the material?

REGULATION PROCESSES WHILE READING AND STUDYING TEXT

When defining regulation processes and regulation strategies, it is convenient to distinguish three levels of processing: basic, strategic, and higher order (van Oostendorp & Elshout-Mohr, 1999). At the middle level, there are strategies. There is the strategy of linking text constituents to previous text constituents, another strategy that links nouns to external referents, and yet another strategy that links explicit sentences to the main topics of paragraphs. Strategies are acquired sequences of goal-directed cognitive actions. Good readers are familiar with many strategies. When good readers encounter a text, they have to decide which strategies to use and how to use them. They also have to switch strategies when a selected strategy fails. These strategy changes require the reader to monitor the reading process for successful comprehension and the execution of other higher order processes. Strategies that are frequently employed may become automatized. For example, the process of linking nouns to external referents is a strategy that becomes automatized. Automatized components can be subsumed under the label *basic processes*. Basic-level processes demand little or no conscious attention of the reader and are not under direct command of higher order processes. The relationship between the three levels of processing is a dynamic one (Elshout-Mohr, 1992; Nelson, 1996; van Oostendorp & Elshout-Mohr, 1999). A process that is strategic at one moment of time in a novice reader may become automatized when the reader becomes more proficient. It then becomes a basic process.

In this chapter we investigate text processing by adult readers in a situation that is relatively new for them. The readers potentially recruit processes at basic, strategic, and higher order levels.

When readers are confronted with new types of text, task, and context, they need to reconsider their regulation of prior knowledge activation. The components of these regulatory mechanisms are (a) activation of relevant schemata, (b) monitoring comprehension and learning, and (c) matching prior knowledge and textual information. These components are elaborated in the remainder of this section.

Activation of Relevant Schemata

Domain knowledge about the content of a text helps readers to understand relations among elements within sentences and across sentences in the text. It also helps them to make inferences about the referential meaning (W. Kintsch, 1998). When domain knowledge is lean, readers use other types of prior knowledge. These other forms of knowledge include external cues about the text structure, such as enumeration markers (e.g., first, second, third, etc.) and logical connectors between sentences (however, therefore, because). There is knowledge about conventional expository schemata, schemata that are often used by writers and readers to organize information at a more global level (Baker, 1985; Elshout-Mohr, 1983; Graesser & Person, 1994). Examples of conventional expository schemata are the definition-schema (What does X mean?), the comparison-schema (How is X similar to Y? How is X different from Y?), the instrumental/procedural-schema (What plan or instrument allows an agent to accomplish a goal?), and the causal-schema (Which previous events and states cause an event to occur?). Knowledge of pragmatic principles may also facilitate text processing. One example of pragmatic knowledge is that writers usually monitor common ground and mutual knowledge. If they introduce something new, it should be signaled and embellished with adjectives, phrases, or examples (Graesser, Millis, & Zwaan, 1997).

Activation of prior knowledge occurs at the basic level, at least in part. The activation of prior knowledge is not always relevant to the text and does not ensure successful comprehension, however. Coté et al. (1998) gave readers of 10 to 12 years the task to process an expository text, and to try to understand and remember new information. The children's protocols showed that they made inferences that went beyond the text to create new pieces of knowledge. Their activities included causal reasoning, implications, analogies, comparisons, evaluation, examples, and relevant associations to prior experience. The children made frequent use of self-explanations as a comprehension strategy. Self-explanation generally fosters understanding of difficult text (Chi, de Leeuw, Chiu, & LaVancher, 1994; E. Kintsch & W. Kintsch, 1996). Close inspection of the recall protocols revealed that the children were not aware that the kind of explanations that are required to make sense of the expository text are different from those that are required to make sense of narrative text. A much wider variety of relations is required to successfully link informational units in expository text. Because familiarity with those relations is gained later in children's development, the children simply lacked sufficient knowledge to construct appropriate self-explanations. The children also were not consistent in the use of external cues of the text structure and logical connectors between sentences. In view of the children's deficits in monitoring comprehension of expository text, there is ample room for helping children improve comprehension with suitable comprehension training. For example, King (1994) showed that children of the same age (fourth and fifth graders) can be taught successfully to use "memory questions" and "thinking questions" while studying expository texts. An example of a "thinking question" is *How does … tie in with … that we learned before?* The procedure in which the students were trained to use thinking questions made them familiar with, for instance, the difference between a description and an explanation. The training promoted construction of complex knowledge, in the form of inferences and explanations, which enhanced what was learned from the texts.

In our study, students were asked to read scientific texts. In order to regulate the reading process, students need a rough idea about the sort of reasoning that is typical for the scientific field, the sort of questions asked, and the sort of evidence sought (Hallden, 1986; Voss, 1996). Without any guidance, they would not have a sufficient foundation for comprehending an introductory textbook. Graesser and Person (1994), for example, investigated the questions asked by college students in tutoring sessions on research methods. The results revealed that students partially self-regulated their learning by identifying knowledge deficits and asking questions to repair them. However, the results also revealed that a comparatively small percentage of the questions were deep, sophisticated questions that penetrated the inherent complexity of the material. Apparently, the level of understanding that is required for asking deep questions was seldom reached. Given the available research, the students in our study were given some adjunct study tasks.

Monitoring Comprehension and Learning

Baker (1985) identified seven aspects of the comprehension process that require monitoring and regulation during reading. These are lexical aspects (understanding of individual words), syntactic aspects (grammaticality of words or groups of words), propositional cohesiveness (integration of adjacent propositions in the text), external consistency (congruence between text information and what is already known), internal consistency (congruence between pieces of information within the text), structural cohesiveness (integration of individual propositions within the main theme of the text), and information completeness (clarity and completeness of information, especially regarding instructions to carry out a task). In each new situation, readers have to decide which aspects they need to monitor in particular, and how strictly this monitoring has to be carried out.

Van Oostendorp (1994) investigated monitoring in an experimental situation. He used target sentences, such as: *The cat caught a mouse in the kitchen* and *The cat seized a mole in the field*. Each target sentence was followed by a verification sentence such as *Cat has claws*. Participants had to respond "True" or "False" to the verification sentences. Reaction times were recorded after both the target sentence and verification sentence. The central research issue was how participants monitor whether they have processed a target sentence deeply enough to be prepared for the verification sentence. In other words, to what extent do readers decide that they need to embellish the internal representation of the target sentence by additional inference processes?

The main finding of van Oostendorp (1994) was that participants considered the perceived semantic relatedness of the concepts in the target sentence as dimension for comprehension monitoring. When the semantic relatedness met or exceeded a criterion value (the standard), the subjects assumed that the semantic cohesion of the textbase was sufficient to answer the verification question and that no further inferences were needed. When the semantic relatedness was not up to the standard, inference generation continued. The empirical evidence consisted of two parts. First, when the semantic relatedness of the content was high, the sentence was read faster than when the semantic relatedness was low. For instance, in the sentence *The cat caught the mouse in the kitchen* the semantic relatedness of the concepts (i.e., cat, mouse, and kitchen) was higher than in the sentence *The cat seized the mole in the field* (cat, mole, and field); the former sentence was read faster than the latter sentence. Second, readers made more inferences when the semantic relatedness was low than when the semantic relatedness was high. For instance, the probability that readers made the inference that *Cat has claws* was higher in the sentence about the cat, the mole, and the field than in the sentence about the cat, the mouse, and the kitchen.

Regulation by means of a standard resulted in predictable variations among sentences in processing time. Inference generation was guided by the criterion value on the semantic relatedness dimension. When the standard was not yet reached, inferencing continued. When the standard was reached, inferencing stopped. A further finding was that the criterion value on the semantic dimension was affected by instruction (van Oostendorp, 1988, 1994). Participants set the standard for semantic relatedness lower or higher, depending on the instruction to read a text either fast or carefully. Setting the standard low encouraged fast processing but at the cost of a low-quality text representation. Setting the standard high had the effect of slowing the process down but constructing a richer text representation.

The monitoring process that van Oostendorp investigated includes three components: (a) The reader sets a standard, a criterion value on a dimension that can be readily assessed, (b) the reader reads a text unit and monitors whether the standard is reached, and (c) the reader takes additional steps if the standard is not reached. We assume that readers are, in general, not aware of the content of the three steps. They may be aware, however, of their task conception, of their need to adapt the reading process to instructions, of the setting, and of their personal goals. Although van Oostendorp's description of the monitoring process was based on a simple verification task, we believe that it has broader applicability.

Matching Prior Knowledge and Textual Information

The use of prior knowledge during reading or studying text involves matching operations. Matching prior knowledge and textual information is not an all-or-none affair, however. Internal representations are not constant but of a probabilistic nature (Whitney, Budd, Bramuci, & Crane, 1995). There can be partial matches rather than exact matches (Anderson, Reder, & Lebiere, 1996). Kamas, Reder, and Ayers (1996) investigated how readers query memory and decide that the relevant information has been found in a sentence verification study. Their premise was that information is never queried in exactly the same form as originally presented and encoded. That means that the matching process must result in partial matches to end up being successful. Instead of examining instances in which partial matching is effective, Kamas et al. examined instances in which the partial-matching process tends to lead people astray. They investigated the Moses illusion. This illusion occurs when readers overlook distortions in statements such as *Moses took two animals of each kind in the Ark.* True or false? Most people immediately respond to the question *How many animals of each kind did Moses take in the Ark?* with the answer *Two.* The illusion is that it was Noah, not Moses, who took animals on the Ark, yet the discrepancy is unnoticed. The readers have the illusion that the sentence matches their prior knowledge. In order to create the illusion, the similarity between the critical term

Moses took 2 animals to the ark.

(Noah) and the distorted term (Moses) must be strong enough. When the distorted term is Nixon instead of Moses the illusion fails to occur. The studies of Kamas et al. showed that the Moses illusion is very robust. Instructions to read carefully or to search for distortions had a modest effect, but did not eliminate the illusion. This finding is compatible with the assumption that human cognition allows partial matching rather than exact matching. Susceptibility to planted errors or illusions, such as the Moses illusion, is a logical consequence of the architecture of cognition.

The effects of partial matching have been investigated in situations in which illusions were expected and in situations where readers studied normal texts in normal settings. We mentioned earlier the study by McNamara et al. (1996) that revealed the illusion of knowing, an illusion that occurred when high-knowledge students studied high-coherence texts. Bazerman (1985) described a similar illusion. When experts in a scientific field read a text quickly, they are susceptible to two failures. On the one hand, they overlook new information that does not fit in their already available schemata. On the other hand, they fail to notice that important information is omitted in the text. Nevertheless, they are confident in determining whether the explicit information contained radically new information and serious omissions.

Schommer and Surber (1986) described an illusion of knowing that appears to be typical for college students. College students were instructed to read easy or difficult texts in conditions that elicited either a deep or a shallow level of processing. Deep processing was elicited by the task to prepare a summary of the passage for a fellow student. Shallow processing was elicited by the task to evaluate whether the average student could understand the passage. After task completion, students rated comprehension of the passage and answered multiple-choice comprehension questions. Illusions of knowledge were defined as cases in which two of the three multiple-choice items were answered incorrectly along with a high rating of comprehension. Illusions of knowledge were greatest with difficult passages and a shallow level of processing. Schommer and Surber concluded that deep processing could diminish the illusion. Deep processing leads to more accurate judgments of what is actually learned (Maki, 1998).

The process of matching prior knowledge with new information occurs, at least in part, at the basic level. Whereas matching is partial rather than exact, the results of the match mechanisms are not necessarily adequate. Strategic and higher order regulation may be needed in many settings. A high-knowledge reader who is aware of the risks involved in superficial reading of simple texts can decide, strategically, to slow down the reading speed in order to detect new information and omissions in the text. The illusions may not disappear with these improved strategies, but undesired effects will presumably be minimized.

Cyclic Processing of Difficult Texts

When texts are difficult, regulation processes may lead to a cyclic processing. Neisser (1976), Hacker (1998), and W. Kintsch (1998) described how readers sometimes pass through a number of cycles to bootstrap their way up in a difficult text. In the cyclic process two interactions can be distinguished. The first interaction is between prior knowledge and the representation of the text meaning. The second interaction is between comprehension and learning. Each cycle consists of the following steps. Readers use prior knowledge to successively understand parts of the new information. Comprehension of these parts leads to learning. This learning is meaningful when the new information is integrated in the person's knowledge base. The acquired knowledge can then be used productively, and influence the processing of the textual information during a second cycle. This leads to new understanding, leading to new learning, and so on. Depending on the number of cycles, comprehension ranges from shallow to deep.

AN EMPIRICAL STUDY ON COMPREHENSION MONITORING

Setting and Purpose of the Study

Students frequently encounter the text-studying situation that we investigated in their first year at university. Consider the combination of student characteristics, text, task, and context. The students are proficient readers, hopefully interested in the text content, but knowledge lean in the domain. The texts are scientific texts of the kind that typically occur in introductory books. Although one might expect that introductory texts are relatively easy to understand, even for novices in the field, there are indications that this is not the case. First, texts in introductory textbooks contain information that is new for the students and this information is discussed from a scientific perspective, which is also new for them (Dall'Alba, 1993). An unfortunate consequence is that powerful study strategies, such as self-explanation, may end up being relatively weak (Coté et al., 1998; Dall'Alba, 1993; Hallden, 1986; Voss, 1996). Thus, self-explanation may be optimally

effective for texts that are at the intermediate points on the continuum between knowledge lean and knowledge rich. *Texts are not complete*

A second reason why introductory texts are difficult is that the information contains a large number of concepts, topics, and issues that are introduced but not sufficiently explained. For example, information about a
new concept would be enriched when the definition is given that states
the relation of the concept with a superordinate concept and with other
aspects of meaning. It would help to have some examples and
counterexamples of the concept. In a more complete representation, the
student understands how the concept is part of the theory or mechanisms
that is conveyed in the text. Unfortunately, completeness is seldom
reached when introductory texts are studied in schools and colleges. A
study by Elshout-Mohr and van Daalen-Kapteijns (1985) with university
students showed that incompleteness is particularly problematic when
students do not know the extent of this incompleteness. Whenever a lack
of understanding occurs, the students hesitate between extended processing of the information given (an endeavor with diminishing returns) or re-
treat to the proposition that the information is so incomplete that it does
not afford full understanding.

A third reason why introductory texts are difficult is that the content
goals are diffuse (Beck, McKeown, & Gromoll, 1989). This diffuseness is
partially a result of the setting and split focus of the task. The main content goal of reading introductory texts is to become familiar with basic
concepts, theoretical principles, and the sorts of reasoning that are used
in the scientific field. The assembled knowledge will be used in future
stages when students become more actively involved in scientific thinking and problem solving. This long-term content goal is fairly diffuse and
remote, however. In the short term, the assembled knowledge is needed
to pass an exam, which typically consists of a mix of multiple-choice
questions and short essay questions. These expectations bring along diffuse content goals as well. Students have to decide for themselves which
information they should rehearse and memorize to pass the tests. Diffuseness of the content goals probably increases the difficulty of introductory textbooks.

The aim of the study is to explore which regulation processes occur
while reading and studying introductory textbooks in college. The results
of the exploration are discussed from the standpoint of theory and practice in education. Our basic research question is straightforward: Does
better understanding of students' regulation strategies lead to new ideas
about how to stimulate deep comprehension of introductory textbooks?

Participants and Conditions

Twenty university students participated in the study. The students studied psychology as a major and received credit points for participation in the experiment. The students were randomly assigned to four conditions. In Condition 1, the participants first read one text (text P) and performed the adjunct task of taking notes (the N-task). In the second part of the session they read a second text (text F) and performed an adjunct task that consisted of two subtasks. The first subtask was to formulate study questions (the Q1-subtask); the second subtask was to evaluate the questions (the Q2-subtask). In Condition 2 the adjunct tasks were reversed. Participants first read text P. They formulated and evaluated study questions about this text (the Q-task). In the second part of the session they read text F and performed the N-task. Conditions 3 and 4 were the same as Conditions 1 and 2, but now the texts were reversed. In Condition 3, participants performed the N-task on text F, followed by the Q-task on text P. In Condition 4, participants performed the Q-task on text F, followed by the N-task on text P. No pre- or posttests were taken.

Materials

The texts were selected from two different introductory textbooks in psychology. Text P was labeled "What Is Social Psychology?" and text F "Frustration." Two passages from the texts are presented in Table 10.1. The texts were in English, a foreign language in which Dutch students are rather proficient. A glossary was added to make sure that the students would not experience translation problems. Participants were free to formulate the study questions and notes in English or Dutch. We knew from earlier research that these conditions facilitate differentiation between superficial and deep processing (Elshout-Mohr, van Daalen-Kapteijns, & Sprangers, 1988). Superficial processing frequently leads to copied English utterances, whereas deep processing frequently leads to Dutch utterances.

The two texts were potentially interesting for the participants. They were also expected to induce the difficulties described with respect to the split focus. The texts contain a lot of information that is new for the students, the source of the information is psychological theory rather than everyday experience, and many topics are incompletely explained.

Procedure

Students were guided through the experiment individually. Before they started to study the first text, the experimenter told them that they would

TABLE 10.1

Two Passages From the Introductory Scientific Text

Passage From Text P: What is Social Psychology?

This becomes our working definition of social psychology: the influences that people have upon the beliefs or behavior of others. Using this as our definition, we will attempt to understand many phenomena. How is a person influenced? Why does he accept influence or, put another way, what's in it for him? What are the variables that increase or decrease the effectiveness of social influence? Does such influence have a permanent effect, or is it merely transitory? What are the variables that increase or decrease the permanence of the effects of social influence? Can the same principles be applied equally to the attitudes of the high-school teacher in Kent, Ohio, and to the toy preferences of young children? How does one person come to like his new sports car or his box of Wheaties? How does a person develop prejudices against an ethnic or racial group? Is it akin to liking—but in reverse—or does it involve an entirely different set of psychological processes?

Passage From Text F: Frustration

No matter how resourceful we may be in coping with problems, the circumstances of life inevitably involve stress. Our motives are not always easily satisfied; obstacles must be overcome, choices made, and delays tolerated. Each of us develops characteristic ways of responding when our attempts to reach a goal are blocked. To a large extent, our responses to frustrating situations determine how adequately we adjust to life.

Frustration occurs when progress toward a desired goal is blocked or delayed. A wide range of obstacles, both external and internal, can interfere with an individual's efforts to reach a goal. The physical environment presents such obstacles as traffic jams, crowded lines at the supermarket, droughts that destroy agricultural crops, and noise that prevents concentration. The social environment presents obstacles in the form of restrictions imposed by other people, which may range from parental denials to broader problems of racial or sexual discrimination.

Sometimes the barriers to goal satisfaction stem from the individual's own limitations. Physical handicaps, lack of specific abilities, or inadequate self-control can prevent an individual from achieving a desired goal. Not everyone can become a skilled musician or pass the examinations necessary to become a physician or a lawyer. If an individual sets goals beyond his or her ability, frustration is apt to result.

A major source of frustration is conflict between two opposing motives. When two motives conflict, the satisfaction of one leads to the frustration of the other. For example, a student may not be able to gain recognition as an outstanding athlete and still earn the grades required to enter law school. Frustration—whether it is the result of environmental obstacles, personal limitations, or conflict—can produce a number of possible consequences. Under circumstances that block or interfere with goal-directed activity feelings of anger may be expressed.

have to think aloud while reading and performing the adjunct tasks. They received a brief training in think aloud (Breuker, Elshout, van Someren, & Wielinga, 1986). In Condition 1, students were invited to study the two-page text P. Their task was to "study the text as if for an exam" and to "take notes that would also be useful to another student studying the same text for the same exam." Students were reminded that notes, in general, should be as "correct, well-organized, and concise as possible." After a brief break, students studied the two-page text F. Their task was "to study the text as if for an exam" and to formulate study questions. It was explained to the students that study questions are "adjunct questions that focus the learner's attention on what needs to be learned." The students wrote down the questions. When they had finished, they were asked to reconsider the study questions. They had to evaluate whether the study questions did indeed focus learners' attention to information that needs to be learned, and they had to answer the questions themselves. If they wanted to, they could use the text to find the answer. They could also revise their questions. Time limits were set at 20 minutes for the first part of the session and 30 minutes for the second part. In Conditions 2, 3, and 4 the procedure was similar. This experimental procedure confronted students with a situation that is very similar to the introductory textbook situation. The setting required split-focus attention and the content goals were diffuse. The main differences were that students had to think aloud and that they performed the adjunct tasks. The think-aloud method has been used successfully in earlier studies on comprehending, monitoring and other regulating processes during reading (Pressley & Afflerbach, 1995; van Daalen-Kapteijns, Elshout-Mohr, & De Glopper, 2001). There is no reason to presume that regulatory aspects of studying are significantly altered when students think aloud. The N- and Q-tasks were given in order to gain comparable information from all participants. Whereas students studying on their own employ different study strategies, such as note taking and underlining, in the experiment the adjunct tasks were uniform for all participants.

The adjunct tasks were selected to induce different levels of text processing. The N-task was selected as a superficial task. It does not necessarily require deep levels of processing because notes can be taken by simply copying fragments from the text (Brown & Day, 1983). The two Q-subtasks were selected as more demanding tasks. In order to perform the Q1-subtask, participants have to think about the referential meaning of the text in relation to prior knowledge that the fellow students would already possess. The Q2-subtask confronted participants even more directly with the fact that study questions should address relevant issues and that attempts to answer the questions should contribute to a person's understanding and knowledge. We included tasks that required different levels of processing in order to facilitate identification of those aspects of the regulation processes that are known to be affected by shallow and deep processing. A third difference between the experimental situation and the real-life introductory textbook situation is that students were not required to memorize information.

Data and Analysis

The think-aloud protocols were transcribed verbatim. In combination with the products, the written notes, and the study questions, these transcriptions formed the data. Examples of written notes and study questions are provided in Table 10.2. They refer to the passage of text P that is presented in Table 10.1. Notes and questions that were made in Dutch were translated for the readers of this chapter. The underlining in the notes was the student's. The word *beliefs* is written in small capitals to indicate that the student wrote this one word not in Dutch, but in English.

The aim of our analysis was to understand and describe the three components of the regulation process, namely (a) activation of relevant schemata, (b) monitoring comprehension and learning, and (c) matching prior knowledge and information given in the text. Our analysis was discovery oriented (Entwistle & Marton, 1984), but there was the working assumption that the students would be proficient readers who attempted to handle the requirements of the situation as well as they could.

TABLE 10.2
Examples of Notes and Study Questions

Notes of One Student

Social psychology. Definition. influence that people have on behaviour or beliefs of others.

  -why do you accept influence

  -which variables increase or decrease influence

  -principles universal?

Three Study Questions by Three Different Students

  1. What is social psychology?

  2. What is social psychology? Give examples.

  3. Give a working definition of social psychology.

Situated Activation of Relevant Schemata

The students were knowledge lean, but activation of available knowledge periodically surfaced in the protocols. We found numerous instances of the use of content knowledge, knowledge about linguistic and syntactic cues, and knowledge about conventional expository schemata and pragmatic principles. For many of the students, we assumed that knowledge was activated and applied at the basic, automatized level. We made this assumption when prior knowledge appeared to affect students' activities, even though there were no indications that conscious activities had taken place. For instance, the collection of notes on the first paragraph of text P showed that students differed in their conception of the main topic. Some students assumed that the topic was *What is social psychology?* whereas other students assumed that it was *In what respects does social psychology differ from general psychology?* The students had different conceptions, but the protocols showed no sign whatsoever of students' awareness of a possible choice between two alternatives. Thus, we concluded that the choice was based on employment of conceptual knowledge at the basic, automatized level.

Linguistic and syntactic signals were also frequently employed at the basic level, but also at the strategic and higher order level. One example was enumeration. It was interesting to see that students in our study interpreted *absence* of enumeration as a signal too. The list of (nine) questions in the first paragraph of text P is not enumerated. With or without conscious awareness, many students interpreted this as a signal that all elements were of equal importance, and that the collection was neither closed nor structured. Students seemed to apply the pragmatic principle that a writer has the option to enumerate or not to enumerate. The alternatives are equally informative. We believe that some students invented this principle on the spot. None of the students decided to elaborate the list or to categorize the questions. They simply selected some questions that met their needs. In the note-taking condition, for example, they copied two or three questions (in abbreviated form). Students who had the idea that the text focused on the discrimination between social psychology and general psychology preferred particular questions, such as the question about prejudice against ethnic and racial groups. Other students simply chose questions that were salient because of their first or last position in the list.

Whereas linguistic and syntactic knowledge primarily contributed to building a coherent textbase, students also used prior knowledge to build a coherent situation model. Being knowledge lean in content knowledge, they relied predominantly on knowledge about conventional expository schemata. Schema-activation occurred at the basic level, and at the strategic and higher order level as well. An example should clarify the distinction. For reasons of readability, we present study questions that students wrote down or considered between the symbols < ... >.

> *Example 1*. The student processed the second paragraph of text F. Betsy (not her real name) read the sentence *Frustration occurs when progress toward a desired goal is blocked*. She concluded: *Ah, a definition. This I might use to formulate a study question* <Give a definition of frustration>. She then read the next sentences, and decided to revise the initial idea. She ended up selecting an alternative expository schema, namely a cause/effect-schema. The reasoning cited from her protocol was: *All sorts of obstacles prevent progress toward a desired goal and this can lead to frustration. So, perhaps my study question should better be* <What causes frustration?>.

Expository schemata were activated to capture the information of entire paragraphs into one coherent whole and to represent multistep reasoning in the textual information. W. Kintsch (1988, 1998) defined a situation model as a representation of the real or imaginary world to which the text refers. The world that the students represented by the use of the expository schemata was a scientific world dominated by definitions and fixed patterns of reasoning. An example of such a pattern is reasoning along the lines of a causal-schema. The schema relates the occurrence of events to preceding events and states. The pattern is conventional in the sense that it is widely used, not only in psychology, but in other disciplines as well. Information that is represented in a causal-schema can be used productively for several purposes. It can be used to write a short reproductive essay about the causes of events, but also to predict the probability that an event occurs in a particular situation and to generate questions about the mechanisms that underlie the relation between events that are causally related. In contrast to the 10- to 12-year-old children in the study of Coté et al. (1998), our students were well aware that the schemata that they had to employ to represent the expository text were different from those in narrative text. Their experience with expository schemata was still limited, however, as is discussed later.

Situated Monitoring of Comprehension and Learning

We adopted two heuristic rules in search of indications that monitoring took place. First, we saw it as a sign of monitoring when students rejected an initial conceptualization of the text's referential meaning. We reasoned that the cue for revising could have been that the initial conceptualization was not up to a certain standard. Second, we saw it as a sign of monitoring when the output quality of students' processing was constant, whereas the input quality was diverse. We reasoned that students probably reached the constant output by monitoring whether a standard was reached. When indications of monitoring were found, the protocols and product were further explored. Earlier in this chapter, monitoring was unfolded into three components: (a) The reader sets a standard, a criterion value on a dimension that can be readily assessed, (b) the reader reads a text unit and monitors whether the standard is reached, (c) the reader takes additional steps if the standard is not reached. Thus, when we found indications of monitoring, we actively searched for information about the standards and criterion values. We also investigated which additional steps were taken when the standard was not reached.

Revisions, probably based on monitoring, occurred repeatedly in all conditions. Example 1, given in the previous section, is an instance of such a revision. The student rejected the original idea that a definition-schema would be appropriate to represent the second paragraph of text F. The student opted for a cause/effect-schema instead. It is interesting to note that students were seldom unique in their revisions. A particular sequence of conceptualizations was often found in several protocols. The sequence in Example 1, for instance, was also found in Example 2.

> *Example 2.* Marc read the first sentence of the second paragraph, and said *Yes, then they are giving a definition … or, … well, then they are saying when frustration occurs. Now I can make a question:* <When does frustration occur?>.

Marc's initial idea was that the first sentence could be conceived as a definition. This idea was quickly rejected, however. We got the impression that students possessed a relatively small repertory of conventional expository schemata, which they used to represent the text and to generate study questions. Also, they seemed to be guided by pragmatic principles and expectations, such as the expectation that a definition will be given when a new concept is introduced. Before we elaborate on the standard that Betsy and Marc used to decide that the definition-schema was less appropriate than the cause/effect-schema, we present another example of monitoring.

In some instances, students worked comparatively long on a text passage. Somehow they did not allow themselves to formulate a particular study question and to proceed to a next paragraph. This is the case in Example 3.

Example 3. Carla worked on the second and third paragraph of text F. She selected as key words *physical, social, and internal,* and then attempted to formulate a study question that would elicit these three key words for a correct answer. We cite from the protocol: *Ehm, in which forms … which environments … ; it is difficult to grasp … to formulate an appropriate question … it would be easier to summarize … ; eh …*. After a while, the subject gave up, unsatisfied.

Apparently Carla was looking for an appropriate conventional expository schema, such as a cause/effect-schema. But why, we asked ourselves, was she not satisfied with a question such as <In which forms does frustration occur?>. What was the standard and what was the criterion value?

After having studied a large number of instances, we induced that the students used a standard that expressed the balance between two components of the text representation: (a) a text-based component and (b) a schema-based component. To explain what we mean by a balance between these components, we refer to a discussion about the relation between the situation model and the textbase by W. Kintsch (1998). Kintsch stated that a totally complete, explicit text describes a complete and adequate situation model. A textbase that tells it all is also a good situation model. Usually, however, texts are incomplete and rely on the comprehender to fill in gaps and make links to prior knowledge. One can discern two components: the text-derived (more or less complete textbase) and the knowledge-derived (more or less complete situation model). Normally, Kintsch said, the two components are balanced, but it may also occur that one of the two dominates the representation of the text. When a reader has no relevant background knowledge or does not employ it while understanding a text, the text representation will be dominated by the textbase. At the other extreme, if rich, relevant background knowledge is available, a good situation model may be obtained at the expense of the textbase. In the introductory textbook situation, the balance between the two components is at risk. Being knowledge lean, students risk to construct text representations that are dominated by the textbase (Schommer & Surber, 1986). They do not possess much relevant domain knowledge. However, they do possess knowledge of conventional expository schemata. Thus, these schemata are used to represent meaningful information about the scientific world to which the text refers. In doing so, however, students must take care that the representation fits the textbase and does not dominate or distort the text-based component of the text representation. Monitoring is needed to control the balance between the text-based component and the schema-based component of the representation.

Unfortunately, we have no objective method to measure the absolute value of the standard that students used in these protocols. Our data are instead qualitative. Two things were evident however. First, the standard was, in general, higher in the Q2-subtask than in the Q1-subtask. Students often rejected a study question that was based on one expository schema, in favor of an alternative. This is illustrated in Example 4.

> *Example 4.* Peter commented on the question that he had written down for the second paragraph of text F. We cite from the protocol: *My question was* <What is frustration? Give a definition> ... *Well, yes, the text attempts to make it clear what frustration is ... or, well ...* (looks through the first two paragraphs of the text) ... *no, that is not exactly what the text attempts ... to make clear what frustration is ... It may be intended but it is not actually done....* The subject then discarded the question, which he himself had proposed, in favor of the alternative question: <When does frustration occur?>.

The second finding about standard setting was that there were individual differences. Whereas Marc and Betsy rejected the definition-schema almost immediately in relation to the second paragraph of text F, Peter only rejected this schema during the Q2-subtask. When Peter looked back in the text, he realized that the definition-schema and the text-based component were not properly balanced. He then opted for an alternative. Martha, who was in a similar situation, chose another solution, which is presented in Example 5.

> *Example 5.* Martha said *My question was* <Give a definition of frustration> ... *Yes, then the student must be able to answer that ...* (reads aloud from the text) that frustration occurs when a desired goal is blocked or delayed.

Although the study question was originally designed to cover the whole paragraph, Martha now focuses on the first sentence. She leaves text-based elements out of the text representation and thus succeeds in keeping the balance at the desired level.

When the standard was not reached, students first tried to repair this situation either by revising the situation model or by altering the textbase. Betsy, Marc, and Peter, in Examples 1, 2, and 4, were fairly representative of attempts to alter the situation model by selection of an alternative expository schema. Martha, in Example 5, provided a rather extreme example of altering the textbase. She simply disregarded a large percentage of the paragraph. This was not unusual, however, as similar examples were found in the protocols of other students. A third reparation activity was the students' use of inadequate expository schemata as a starting point either for the construction of new schemata that would better accommodate the textual information or for the elaboration of the textual information. Carla, in Example 3, attempted to construct a new, appropriate schema. She was very near invention of the cause/effect-schema where she transformed her unfinished question <Which forms … ?> into the unfinished question <Which environments … ?>, but she gave up the attempt. Still, her activities demonstrated that students did not only employ expository schemata that they had available, but also tried to increase their repertory. Schema construction is also demonstrated in Example 6.

Schema construction

Example 6. Gerald summarized the text-based elements: *Eh, well there is the physical environment, social environment, and the individual's own limitations, … and, oh yes, conflict also belongs to this … He* then formulated the study question <How is frustration caused? Name four things and give an example of each situation>.

Gerald eventually used a cause/effect-schema. For the occasion, however, he enriched the schema with elements that are not commonly incorporated in a cause/effect-schema. Gerald referred to *things,* a word that probably indicated that he has not yet learned to reason in terms of causal processes. Although this does not lead to a clear study question, the effort is not wasted. Gerald is well on his way to discover how the conventional cause/effect-schema is used in this text.
Example 7 demonstrates the use of inadequate expository schemata as a starting point for the elaboration of the textual information.

Example 7. Otto performed the Q1-subtask for the second and third paragraph of text F. We cite from the protocol: *So there are two sorts of frustration, physical frustrations, and social … eh … frustrations elicited by the social environment … eh one could say external and internal frustrations. Eh, let me pose the following question* <Name two kinds of frustrations> *… and then I would add for myself the goal that is frustrated or could be frustrated … in order to be sure that I understood the text correctly.* (Otto reads the third paragraph) *… eh … a third kind of frustration is mentioned here, frustration which stems from the individual, so I'll change my question into* <Name three kinds of frustrations>.

Apparently, Otto was not quite satisfied with the classification-schema, which he had activated. This schema was in balance with the two kinds of frustration, but there were more textbase elements to consider, such as the goals that could be frustrated.(Otto's activities to repair the balance were meager, however, and did not lead to deep understanding, or transformation of the schema.)In the end, the classification-schema was maintained and the information in the third paragraph of the text was fitted into it. In general, we had to conclude that the experimental conditions did not stimulate students to make elaborations that go beyond the text. Instead, the protocols showed numerous brief attempts to improve on the balance between the schema-based and the text-based component in the representation of the text, but students readily accepted it when their standard was not reached.

The way in which students handled representations of the text that were unbalanced depended on the task. It was not affected by the text or the position of the task as first or last task in the session. When students worked on a Q-task, the expository schema prevailed, probably because it enabled students to formulate a question. When students worked on the N-task, the text-based component prevailed. It was simple for students to add text-based elements to notes even when they were not quite sure about the meaning of these elements or about the future usefulness of the knowledge that the elements were incorporated in the text. In the case of Gerald (Example 6, e.g.), it would have been relatively easy for him to copy the four "things" (physical environment, social environment, the individual's own limitations, and conflict) in a set of notes and to connect them by arrows to the word frustration. There would have been no need to bring the four causal events and states under one common denominator. In Example 3, Carla shows awareness of the different requirements of the Q- and N-tasks where she says *it would be easier to summarize* (than to formulate an appropriate question). However, notes that are based merely on the textual information contribute to knowledge that is fit only for reproductive, but not for productive use.

Situated Matching of Prior Knowledge and the Information Given

In the introductory textbook situations one kind of matching was prevalent, namely the matching between conventional expository schemata and text-based information. In many occasions students' activities depended on the result of this match. Matching was always partial. Pursuit of exact matching would diminish the usefulness of such schemata, because conventional expository schemata are meant to capture text passages of different content, clarity and completeness. The protocols showed the broad reach of the schemata. Students managed to cover a variety of text passages with a limited number of conventional schemata. The other side of this coin is that the students' representation of the texts and their study questions were often coarse and unsophisticated. This was demonstrated earlier in Examples 1 to 7.

Summary of the Results

Students read scientific text in a split-focus situation, which is normal for the introductory textbook study setting. We investigated the regulation processes during this experience and discovered a number of informative findings. First, we found that students, being knowledge lean, had limited conceptual knowledge to understand the text. They used linguistic and syntactic information, such as external signals, to build a textbase. To build a situation model, they primarily used knowledge about conventional expository schemata. Thus, the students' representation of the introductory text consisted of a text-based component and a schema-based component. Conspicuously absent were knowledge-based elaborative inferences.

Second we found that students' monitoring was geared to the specific demands of the situation. A major concern of the students was to keep a balance between the text-based and the schema-based component of the text representation. We could not measure the criterial balance-value, but we found that this value, the standard, was dependent on instruction. When the standard was not reached, three kinds of repairs were sought. Sometimes students revised the expository schema, which they employed to build the situation model. At other times, students altered the textbase, for instance by disregarding parts of the information given. Finally, students attempted to construct new expository schemata that would lead to a better balance. When repairs failed, the resulting text representation was unbalanced, dominated by either schema-based or text-based elements. When the students had to generate study questions, they preferred to tolerate dominance of the schema-based component. When they took notes, they preferred to tolerate dominance of the text-based component.

Third, we looked at the matching between the text-based and the schema-based component. We found that a limited repertory of schemata was employed to cover very different text passages. Thus, the matching was partial. The consequence was that the text representations were not sophisticated. This was the price that students paid for their endeavor to build text representations that would allow productive use. It also reflected that the students' experience with expository schemata was still limited.

DISCUSSION

Reading is always situated in the sense that the readers, texts, tasks, and setting influence the reading processes. In our study we investigated the interaction between these factors in a particular situation, when introductory textbooks are read and studied. Central in the situated regulation process was the monitoring of the balance between the schema-based and the text-based component of the representation of the scientific text.

The situated nature of a regulation process does not exclude the possibility that similar regulation processes occur in other situations. Other studies on reading, in other situations, have already shown that the balance between different components of the text representation is sometimes precarious. McNamara et al. (1996) and Schommer and Surber (1986) conceptualized illusions of knowing and illusions of comprehension as the result of a disturbed balance between a knowledge-based and a text-based component in the text representation. In those illusions, the interesting part was that disturbances occurred without awareness of the reader. In our study, in contrast, the interesting part was that students were somehow aware of potential disturbances and took an active role in monitoring and maintaining the balance. Regulation processes were presumed to take place at the basic level, but at the higher levels as well. Our explanation for the occurrence of strategic and higher order activities in our study is that the textbook situation is a special one. In this situation, the balance is disturbed so frequently and so seriously that proficient readers gain at least partial awareness of these disturbances. The accompanying adjunct tasks apparently promoted this awareness, because the tasks determined the nature of the generated ideas systematically.

The study sessions in our experiment were relatively short. Nevertheless, we could observe that students learned from experience at two levels. First they learned content knowledge. Second, they constructed expository schemata. In several examples, we demonstrated that students used the texts to detect and construct conventional expository schemata, which were used by the writer. Although their attempts were not completely successful, it is plausible that their repertory increases during real-life textbook studying, because of the enormous amount of practice that students get. It seems a modest estimate that the average page of an introductory textbook contains at least three passages that must be interpreted by employment of an expository schema. If this is correct, a textbook of 400 pages would elicit more than a thousand attempts to activate an appropriate expository schema. We therefore believe that the introductory textbook situation provides ideal conditions for *learning how to learn* (Novak & Gowin, 1984; Resnick, 1987; van Daalen-Kapteijns et al., 2001). Students acquire content knowledge, but perhaps even more important, they construct knowledge about expository schemata that are typical for the scientific field to which they are being introduced. They have to employ a limited repertory of conventional expository schemata in the beginning, but gradually this repertory becomes broader and more domain specific.

From an educational point of view, however, we still have to deal with a paradox. On the one hand, one can be impressed by the fact that students develop a strategy to deal with the special requirements of the introductory textbook situation. On the other hand, the content knowledge gained is not deep by any standard. We believe that the paradox is the result of the fact that the students vacillate between two kinds of superficiality. When they use conventional expository schemata, they represent textual information productively. The price is that their representation is not only schematic, but also inaccurate and coarse. This normal effect of the use of schemata is exaggerated by the fact that the students have limited experience with expository schemata, and have just started to assemble a more adequate repertory. When students avoid this coarseness, by representing the textual information more precisely, they cannot employ prior knowledge schemata. Then, the representation is superficial in a different sense, the sense of being merely fit for reproductive use. We expected students to vacillate between deep and superficial processing. They ended up in fact vacillating between productive and reproductive processing, two types of processing that both lead to superficial products.

In general, people find it counterintuitive that building a coherent textbase of an introductory study text should not necessarily lead to deep knowledge that can be used productively (Sandberg & Barnard, 1997). Indeed, if study texts were totally complete and explicit, the textbase would describe a complete and adequate situation model (W. Kintsch, 1998). In that case, students could be able to build a representation of the text that is *deep* in the two senses of *accurate* and *productive*. Introductory texts, however, are far from complete. Perhaps writers and teachers are the least appropriate persons to judge the completeness and explicitness of introductory texts. These persons are knowledge rich and, because the texts are simple, they are liable to fall victim to the illusion of completeness

(Bazerman, 1985). In order to get an unbiased judgment, judges should be representatives of the intended readers.

Our pragmatic conclusion is that it is not fruitful to give students the advice "to study introductory text deeply," because this advice does not facilitate finding the golden mean between the two kinds or superficiality to which they are doomed in the introductory textbook situation. It may be wiser to combine two measures. First, students should be advised to perform a variety of adjunct tasks, such as taking notes and generating study questions. These activities promote awareness of the precarious balance between the schema-based and the text-based component of the text representation. Second, tutors might encourage students to continue their attempts to maintain the balance, although it may appear tiresome to do so for thousands of introductory text passages. Prolonged effort is needed to achieve content knowledge that allows productive and reproductive use. It is also needed to construct a large and flexible repertory of general and domain-specific expository schemata, a repertory that students must have at their disposal when they have rounded off the introductory phase. In this manner tutors would promote acquisition of content and schematic knowledge prerequisite for deep processing of more advanced and more complete scientific text.

ACKNOWLEDGMENTS

The authors thank the Netherlands Organization for Scientific Research (NWO) for financing the research reported in this chapter. They are grateful for the comments given by the members of the special interest group Higher Cognitive Processes (Hogcog) and for the comments and editorial support given by the editors of this volume.

REFERENCES

Alexander, P. A., Graham, S., & Harris, K. R. (1998). A perspective on strategy research: Progress and prospects. *Educational Psychology Reviews, 10*(2), 129–145.

Anderson, R. C., & Pearson, P. D. (1984). A schema-theoretic view of basic processes in reading. In P. D. Pearson (Ed.), *Handbook of reading research* (pp. 255–291). New York: Longman.

Anderson, R. C., Reder, L. M., & Lebiere, C. (1996). Working memory: Activation limitations on retrieval. *Cognitive Psychology, 30*, 221–256.

Ausubel, D. P., Novak, J. D., & Hanesian, H. (1978). *Educational psychology: A cognitive view.* New York: Holt, Rinehart & Winston.

Baker, L. (1985). Differences in the standards used by college students to evaluate their comprehension of expository prose. *Reading Research Quarterly, 20*(3), 297–313.

Bazerman, C. (1985). Physicists reading physics: Schema-laden purposes and purpose-laden schemata. *Written Communication, 2*, 3–23.

Beck, I. L., McKeown, M. G., & Gromoll, E. W. (1989). Learning from social study texts. *Cognition and Instruction, 6*(2), 99–158.

Beck, I. L., Perfetti, C. A., & McKeown, M. G. (1982). The effects of long-term vocabulary instruction on lexical access and reading comprehension. *Journal of Educational Psychology, 74*, 506–521.

Breuker, J. A., Elshout, J. J., van Someren, M. W., & Wielinga, B. J. (1986). Hardopdenken en protokolanalyse [Thinking aloud and protocol analysis]. *Tijdschrift voor Onderwijs Research, 11*, 241–255.

Brown, A. L., & Day, J. D. (1983). Macrorules for summarizing texts: The development of expertise. *Journal of Verbal Learning and Verbal Behavior, 22*, 1–14.

✓Chi, M. T. H., de Leeuw, N., Chiu, M. H., & LaVancher, C. (1994). Eliciting self-explanations improves understanding. *Cognitive Science, 18*, 439–477.

Chinn, C. A., & Brewer, W. F. (1993). The role of anomalous data in knowledge acquisition: A theoretical framework and implications for science instruction. *Review of Educational Research, 63*, 1–49.

Coté, N., Goldman, S. R., & Saul, E. U. (1998). Students making sense of informational text: Relations between processing and representation. *Discourse Processes, 55*(1), 1–53.

Dall'Alba, G. (1993). The role of teaching in education: Enabling students to enter a field of study and practice. *Learning and Instruction, 3*(4), 299–313.

Elshout-Mohr, M. (1983). Communicatiepatronen: een hulpmiddel bij het bestuderen van studieteksten [Communication patterns: A tool for studying study texts]. *Tijdschrift voor Taalbeheersing, 5*, 1–18.

Elshout-Mohr, M. (1992). Metacognitie van lerenden in onderwijsleerprocessen [Metacognition of learners in educational learning processes.] *Tijdschrift voor Onderwijsresearch, 17*, 273–289.

Elshout-Mohr, M., & van Daalen-Kapteijns, M. M. (1985). Het leren van begrippen in het bijzonder in het eerste stadium van het hoger onderwijs [Concept learning in the first year of higher education]. *Pedagogische Studiën, 62*, 459–470.

Elshout-Mohr, M., van Daalen-Kapteijns, M. M., & Sprangers, M. (1988). The topic-comment technique to study expository text. *Journal of Experimental Education, 56*(2), 83–90.

Entwistle, N., & Marton, F. (1984). Changing conceptions of learning and research. In F. Marton, D. Hounsell, & N. Entwistle (Eds.), *The experience of learning* (pp. 211–242). Edinburgh: Scottish Academic Press.

Garcia-Arista, E., Campanario, J. M., & Otero, J. (1996). Influence of subject matter setting on comprehension monitoring. *European Journal of Psychology of Education, 21*, 427–441.

Garner, R. (1990). When children and adults do not use learning strategies: Toward a theory of settings. *Review of Educational Research, 60*, 517–529.

Goldman, S. R. (1997). Learning from text: Reflections on 20 years of research and suggestions for new directions of inquiry. *Discourse Processes, 23*(3), 357–398.

Graesser, A. C., Millis, K. K., & Zwaan, R. A. (1997). Discourse comprehension. *Annual Review of Psychology, 48*, 163–189.

Graesser, A. C., & Person, N. K. (1994). Question asking during tutoring. *American Educational Research Journal, 31*(1), 104–137.

Hacker, D. J. (1998). Self-regulated comprehension during normal reading. In D. G. Hacker, J. Dunklosky, & A. C. Graesser (Eds.), *Metacognition in educational theory and practice* (pp. 165–192). Mahwah, NJ: Lawrence Erlbaum Associates.

Hallden, O. (1986). Learning history. *Oxford Review of Education, 12*(1), 53–66.

Harmon, J. M. (1999). Initial encounters with unfamiliar words in independent reading. *Research in Teaching of English, 33,* 304–338.

Hidi, S. (1990). Interest and its contribution as a mental resource for learning. *Review of Educational Research, 60,* 549–571.

Kamas, E. N., Reder, L. M., & Ayers, M. S. (1996). Partial matching in the Moses illusion: Response bias not sensitivity. *Memory and Cognition, 24*(6), 687–699.

Karau, S. J., & Williams, K. D. (1993). Social loafing: A meta-analytic review and theoretical integration. *Journal of Personality and Social Psychology, 65,* 681–706.

King, A. (1994). Guiding knowledge construction in the classroom: Effects of teaching children how to question and how to explain. *American Educational Research Journal, 31*(2), 338–368.

Kintsch, E., & Kintsch, W. (1996). Learning from text. In E. de Corte & F. E. Weinert (Eds.) *International encyclopedia of developmental and instructional psychology* (pp. 519–524). Oxford, England: Pergamon.

Kintsch, W. (1988). The role of knowledge in discourse comprehension: A construction-integration model. *Psychological Review, 95,* 163–182.

Kintsch, W. (1998). *Comprehension: A paradigm for cognition.* Cambridge, England: Cambridge University Press.

Langer, J. A. (1986). *Children reading and writing: Structure and strategies.* Norwood, NJ: Ablex.

Locke, E. Q. (1975). *A guide to effective study.* New York: Springer.

Maki, R. H. (1998). Test predictions over text material. In D. G. Hacker, J. Dunklosky, & A. C. Graesser (Eds.), *Metacognition in educational theory and practice* (pp. 117–144). Mahwah, NJ: Lawrence Erlbaum Associates.

Markman, E. M., & Gorin, L. (1981). Children's ability to adjust their standards for evaluating comprehension. *Journal of Educational Psychology, 73,* 320–325.

McNamara, D. S., Kintsch, E., Songer, N. B., & Kintsch, W. (1996). Are good texts always better? Interactions of text coherence, background knowledge and levels of understanding in learning from text. *Cognition and Instruction, 14,* 1–43.

McNamara, D. S., & Kintsch, W. (1996). Learning from text: Effect of prior knowledge and text coherence. *Discourse Processes, 22,* 247–288.

Meyer, B. J. F., & Rice, G. E. (1982). The interaction of reader strategies and the organization of text. *Text: An Interdisciplinary Journal for the Study of Discourse, 2,* 155–192.

Neisser, U. (1976). *Cognition and reality. Principles and implications of cognitive psychology.* San Fransisco: Freeman.

Nelson, T. O. (1996). Consciousness and metacognition. *American Psychologist, 51*(2), 102–116.

Novak, J. D., & Gowin, D. B. (1984). *Learning how to learn.* Cambridge, England: Cambridge University Press.

Otero, J. (1998). Influence of knowledge activation and context on comprehension monitoring of science texts. In D. G. Hacker, J. Dunklosky, & A. C. Graesser (Eds.), *Metacognition in educational theory and practice* (pp. 145–164). Mahwah, NJ: Lawrence Erlbaum Associates.

Palincsar, A. M., & Brown, A. L. (1984). Reciprocal teaching of comprehension-monitoring activities. *Cognition and Instruction, 1*, 117–175.

Pressley, M., & Afflerbach, P. (1995). *Verbal protocols of reading: The nature of constructively responsive reading.* Hillsdale, NJ: Lawrence Erlbaum Associates.

Pressley, M., van Etten, S., Yokoi, L., Freebern, G., & van Meter, P. (1998). The metacognition of college studentship: A grounded theory approach. In D. G. Hacker, J. Dunklosky, & A. C. Graesser (Eds.), *Metacognition in educational theory and practice* (pp. 347–366). Mahwah, NJ: Lawrence Erlbaum Associates.

Resnick, L. B. (1987). *Education and learning to think.* Washington, DC: National Academy Press.

Sandberg, J., & Barnard, Y. (1997). Deep learning is difficult. *Instructional Science, 25*, 15–36.

Schellings, G. L. M., & van Hout-Wolters, B. H. A. M. (1995). Main points in an instructional text, as identified by students and by their teachers. *Reading Research Quarterly, 30*, 742–756.

Schiefele, U., & Krapp, A. (1996). Topic interest and free recall of expository text. *Learning and Individual Differences, 8*(2), 141–160.

Schnotz, W., & Ballstaedt, S.-P. (1996). Comprehension: Teaching and assessing. In E. de Corte & F. E. Weinert (Eds.) *International encyclopedia of developmental and instructional psychology* (pp. 492–497). Oxford, England: Pergamon.

Schommer, M., & Surber, J. R. (1986). Comprehension-monitoring failure in skilled adult readers. *Journal of Educational Psychology, 78*, 353–357.

van Daalen-Kapteijns, M. M., Elshout-Mohr, M., & De Glopper, K. (2001). Deriving the meaning of unknown words from multiple contexts. *Language Learning, 51*, 145–182.

van Oostendorp, H. (1988). *Regulatieprocessen bij tekstverwerking [Regulation processes in text processing]* Unpublished doctoral dissertation. Amsterdam: University of Amsterdam.

van Oostendorp, H. (1994). Processing in terms of semantic cohesion monitoring. In H. van Oostendorp & R. A. Zwaan (Eds.), *Naturalistic text comprehension* (pp. 35–55). Mahwah, NJ: Ablex.

van Oostendorp, H., & Elshout-Mohr, M. (1999). Thinking skills in reading and text studying. In J. H. M. Hamers, J. E. H. van Luit, & B. Csapó (Eds.), *Thinking skills and teaching thinking* (pp. 283–313). Lisse, Netherlands: Swets & Zeitlinger.

Voss, J. F. (1996). Learning and instruction of social sciences. In E. de Corte & F. E. Weinert (Eds.), *International encyclopedia of developmental and instructional psychology* (pp. 572–574). Oxford, England: Pergamon.

Walczyk, J. J. (1990). Relationship among error detection, sentence verification and low-level reading skills of fourth-graders. *Journal of Educational Psychology, 82*, 491–497.

Winne, P. H., & Marx, R. W. (1982). Students' and teachers' views of thinking processes for classroom learning. *Elementary School Journal, 82*, 493–518.

Whitney, P., Budd, D., Bramuci, R. S., & Crane, R. C. (1995). On babies, bath-water, and schemata: A reconsideration of top-down processing in comprehension. *Discourse processes, 20*, 135–166.

Zwaan, R. A., Magliano, J., & Graesser, A. C. (1995). Dimensions of situation model construction in narrative comprehension. *Journal of Experimental Psychology: Learning, Memory, and Cognition, 21*, 386–397.

III

Comprehension Monitoring

❧ 11 ❧

Metacomprehension of Science Text: Investigating the Levels-of-Disruption Hypothesis

John Dunlosky
University of North Carolina at Greensboro

Katherine A. Rawson
University of Colorado at Boulder

Douglas J. Hacker
University of Utah

Self-regulated comprehension involves monitoring and subsequent control processes that occur when an individual is attempting to construct meaning from text (Hacker, 1998). Monitoring involves assessing ongoing comprehension, such as detecting inconsistencies in a text or assessing how well a recently read text was comprehended. Outcomes from monitoring in turn may be used in guiding control processes, such as rereading to clarify an ambiguous point, asking a question to elaborate on text information, or referencing an unknown word. The quality of monitoring and the effectiveness of subsequent control presumably have an impact on the coherence and completeness of an individual's representation of a text and the knowledge contained therein (cf. Thiede, 1999). If an individual does not detect textual inconsistencies, the text representation may lack coherence. For example, students who lack scientific knowledge of the solar system may have difficulties detecting a misconception in a term paper on planetary movements and subsequently may acquire the misconception as fact. If inconsistencies are detected, but subsequent control processes do not resolve them, incoherence will remain. For example, students may possess the requisite scientific knowledge, detect the misconception, but lack the strategies or resources to fix it. Accordingly, understanding the monitoring and control processes that are used in self-regulated comprehension will suggest ways to improve student scholarship.

In the present chapter, we focus on monitoring of comprehension. Although both narrative and expository texts have been used in studies of comprehension monitoring, our present concern is with the latter. In particular, of the various kinds of expository text, we focus mainly on scientific texts. Namely, the texts used in the experiments described in this chapter are scientific texts, which were ideal given that this genre provides difficult reading in which readers are unlikely to have a great deal of relevant world knowledge—at least as compared to narrative texts. Accordingly, comprehension monitoring may be even more critical when students are faced with the challenging task of reading and understanding scientific texts.

Comprehension monitoring may be measured in multiple ways, including eye tracking, think-aloud protocols collected while individuals read, signaling to indicate confusion while reading, detection of errors in text, detection of inconsistencies between a priori knowledge and text content, decisions to reread aspects of texts, and explicit judgments of comprehension difficulty. Of these measures, we focus mainly on explicit judgments of comprehension, which are often referred to as *metacomprehension judgments*. To put our research within a larger perspective, however, we first consider differences among the measures. This consideration of differences provides a richer context for understanding the possible limitations of any one measure.

Measures of comprehension monitoring differ on numerous factors, such as the time lag between reading and measurement, or the degree to which the measures are influenced by control processes. Lag is the interval between when reading occurs and when monitoring of that reading is measured. Eye tracking has a minimal lag, whereas a metacomprehension judgment made after reading a text has a relatively long lag. The other measures tend to fall somewhere between these endpoints, and depending on the specific method, the lag for a given measure may range considerably. For instance, error detection and think-aloud protocols can be solicited while an individual is reading or sometime after reading has occurred. As the lag increases, the more likely the measure will provide an inaccurate estimate of the kind or quality of monitoring that occurred while reading (Ericsson & Simon, 1980). For instance, when readers judge comprehension after reading a lengthy text, they may not remember some of the specific instances during which online monitoring indicated poor comprehension. Thus, metacomprehension judgments may inaccurately estimate the accuracy with which people monitor online comprehension and instead tap other aspects of cognition, such as momentary accessibility of the recently read text or perceived expertise in the topic of the text (for a review, see Maki, 1998).

Another factor that differs among the measures is the degree to which a given measure taps control processes. Consider a task in which students are asked to reread those portions of a science text they do not fully understand. When rereading occurs, we infer that monitoring had occurred. In this case, the occurrence of a control process (i.e., rereading) is an indirect measure of monitoring. However, a difficulty here is that a control process is not necessarily triggered whenever accurate monitoring of comprehension occurs. Students may accurately monitor a difficulty in comprehension but may not reread the passage for any number of reasons, including time constraints, lack of interest, and so on (Son & Metcalfe, 2000). Thus, measures of monitoring that are based on control processes may misrepresent any monitoring that occurs while reading. A general theme here is that we have not yet developed process-pure measures of monitoring. Of course, this constraint is pervasive throughout cognitive psychology. In the present case, although the measures may all share some underlying bases, the various measures tap different aspects of monitoring comprehension. Thus, the variety of possible influences on these measures (and hence what each measure potentially represents) should be kept in mind when interpreting them with respect to how accurately individuals monitor comprehension.

In the remainder of this chapter, we discuss our ongoing efforts to understand metacomprehension judgments. Our more specific goal was to answer the following question, "Why has the accuracy of students' metacomprehension judgments often been so poor?" (See also Weaver, Bryant, & Burns, 1995, for other answers to this question.) Toward this end, we first provide an overview of the literature to establish the standard method and modal outcome from the metacomprehension literature. Next, we discuss our general approach to investigating metacomprehension judgments, which involves integrating theory of metacognitive monitoring with theory of text comprehension. A specific hypothesis is then derived from this approach. Namely, when making metacomprehension judgments, people monitor the products of the online processes of reading and (not) necessarily the processes themselves. This hypothesis provides an answer to our central question and provides insight on how to improve readers' metacomprehension accuracy. The hypothesis is then evaluated with evidence from two experiments, one focusing on the effects of rereading on metacomprehension accuracy and another focusing on the effects of providing advance organizers prior to reading.

Overview of the Literature on Metacomprehension Accuracy

When assessing the accuracy of comprehension monitoring, researchers have used a relatively standard method that independently originated with Maki and Berry (1984) and Glenberg and Epstein (1985). In general, participants read multiple texts, usually anywhere from 4 to 16 texts. Sometime after reading a given text, participants make a metacomprehension judgment, such as predicting how well they will perform on a test over the text material. Finally, a criterion test is administered for each text. Accuracy is then operationalized by an intraindividual correlation between judgments and test performance. That is, for each individual, a correlation is computed between that individual's judgments and subsequent performance across texts. Higher intraindividual correlations indicate higher accuracy, with correlations near zero signifying that the participants have discriminated poorly between what they think they understand about the texts and what they do not understand. Ideally, a student would discriminate perfectly between texts, resulting in a correlation of 1.0. In this case, readers could regulate further study time effectively by focusing restudy on those texts that are less well understood.

Such intraindividual correlations should not be confused with correlations computed across individuals, which have occasionally been reported in the literature (e.g., Magliano, Little, & Graesser, 1993; Walczyk & Hall, 1989). Although both correlations provide indicators of predictive accuracy, the measures do not completely tap the same underlying aspect of predictive accuracy (Dunlosky & Hertzog, 2000). Most important, intraindividual correlations (aka *relative* accuracy) represent an individual's ability to discriminate between the relative comprehension of one text versus another, which we believe better captures the aspects of monitoring relevant to an individual's self-regulated comprehension while reading. Accordingly, our subsequent discussion pertains to only relative accuracy.

The literature on metacomprehension has been reviewed in detail elsewhere (for extensive reviews, see Lin & Zabrucky, 1998; Maki, 1998; Weaver et al., 1995), so we highlight only a few main outcomes from the literature. The most relevant finding with respect to our aims, and the most common one, has been low metacomprehension accuracy, with many estimates of accuracy barely exceeding a correlation of zero. Weaver (1990) reported that the relatively low levels of metacomprehension accuracy could be in part an artifact of including too few questions per text (for an alternative view, see Morris, 1995). However, even research that has incorporated more appropriate measurement has rarely produced high levels of accuracy, let alone manipulations that influence accuracy.

Two exceptions are notable. Metacomprehension accuracy has been greater when letters are deleted from some words of texts than when the words of texts are intact (Maki, Foley, Kajer, Thompson, & Willert, 1990). The effect size here was relatively small, with mean correlations even for deleted-letters text not exceeding .40. Second, for college students, metacomprehension accuracy has been greater when the reading levels of the text approximate the reading level of the students than when the texts are too easy or too difficult (Weaver & Bryant, 1995). This effect is relatively large, with the highest levels of accuracy exceeding .60. However, despite these relatively isolated effects, metacomprehension accuracy has often been typically quite poor. Why might this be the case?

Understanding Metacomprehension Accuracy via Integrating Theories of Metacognitive Monitoring and Text Comprehension

To most effectively answer the question just posed, we advocate an integrative approach to metacomprehension. That is, we propose that a better understanding of metacomprehension accuracy will be achieved by integrating theory of text comprehension with theory of metacognitive monitoring. Arguably, comprehension and metacomprehension processes are closely related, yet theorizing about metacomprehension has largely been grounded in the literature on metacognitive monitoring. For instance, as with other metacognitive judgments, metacomprehension judgments are presumably inferential in nature and can be derived from various cues (e.g., Koriat, 1997; Schwartz, Benjamin, & Bjork, 1998), such as the characteristics of the text, the conditions of reading, or the reader's encoding operations. Somewhat surprisingly, however, relatively few researchers who are interested in metacomprehension have incorporated ideas from research on text comprehension. We discuss some of the most noteworthy exceptions next.

Glenberg, Sanocki, Epstein, and Morris (1987) investigated the influence of kind of test question on predictive accuracy. These researchers argued that "inference verification may be inappropriate for demonstrating [accuracy] because the domain of possible inferences is too broad. Verbatim recognition, it could be argued, may be inappropriate for demonstrating [accuracy] because subjects do not represent the text in a verbatim manner. Instead, the representation may be in the form of propositions, or ideas from the text" (van Dijk & W. Kintsch, 1983, p. 123). Thus, they varied the kind of test question used, considering how the question tapped comprehension. However, they found that accuracy was consistently poor regardless of kind of question (see also Maki, 1995).

Glenberg et al. (1987) also appealed to comprehension research on the nature of mental representations to understand effects of feedback on predictive accuracy. In earlier work, they proposed a feedback hypothesis, according to which participant-generated feedback can be used as a cue for judgments and will improve predictive accuracy. Participant-generated feedback here refers to the outcomes of pretests over the text material (e.g., a recognition test) that occur prior to the metacomprehension judgments. However, in a pilot study in which participants either did or did not receive a pretest before predicting performance, accuracy was no better for the pretest group than for the control group who did not receive feedback from pretests. Although this result was contrary to the feedback hypothesis, Glenberg et al. suggested that "the fault may not be with the notion of feedback, but with implicit assumptions regarding the structure of the cognitive representation of the text" (p. 126).

Based on work by van Dijk and W. Kintsch (1983) and Graesser (1981), Glenberg et al. (1987) had assumed that the representation was "abstract and highly interconnected. In this case, feedback based on testing one part of the representation should be valid for predicting performance based on a different (but connected) part of the representation" (p. 126). Important to note, they pointed out that this assumption of a highly interconnected representation is based largely on research with short, simple narratives and thus may not be an appropriate assumption for metacomprehension research that involves difficult, longer, or more technical scientific text. Accordingly, they modified the feedback hypothesis, stating that feedback is useful "only when the processes and knowledge that generate the feedback are relevant for the future test" (p. 126). Based on this rationale, they developed pretest questions that were either identical, related (paraphrase of the identical question), or unrelated to the criterion test questions. Consistent with the modified feedback hypothesis, identical questions led to moderate levels of accuracy (M correlation coefficient = .40), but related question (M = .08) and unrelated questions (M = .07) did not.

Maki, Jonas, and Kallod (1994) noted that some theories of comprehension involve a monitoring component. Presumably, readers assess their comprehension during reading and make "self-corrections" (i.e., apply control processes) while reading. If so, Maki et al. reasoned that "the ability to make accurate assessments of learning should be related to the ability to comprehend … better comprehenders should be better at assessing how well they have performed on a test over text material" (p. 126). Furthermore, Gernsbacher, Varner, and Faust (1990) have shown that individuals with relatively high scores on the Multi-Media Comprehension Battery have better access to recently comprehended information than do lower scorers. Based on these findings, Maki et al. expected that predictive accuracy would increase with comprehension ability, but they found little evidence for this relationship.

Finally, Weaver and Bryant's (1995) investigation was partly based on Einstein and McDaniel's research (e.g., Einstein, McDaniel, Bowers, & Stevens, 1984), which suggested that narratives and expository texts encourage different kinds of processing. Namely, narratives encourage relational processing, or processing of macropropositions (thematic information). By contrast, expository texts encourage item-specific processing, or processing of micropropositions (details of a text). Based on these findings, Weaver and Bryant hypothesized that individuals reading narratives monitor comprehension of macropropositions. Thus, performance predictions for narratives would be most predictive of thematic questions. By contrast, individuals reading expository text were hypothesized to monitor comprehension of micropropositions, and thus predictions for expository text would be most predictive of detail questions. These expectations were borne out (Weaver & Bryant, 1995, Experiment 1).

These researchers have made notable advances by guiding investigations on metacomprehension with ideas from the literature on text comprehension. In particular, serious consideration of text comprehension led to new, testable predictions that may have otherwise been left unconsidered. Of course, many advances have been made without considering basic research on comprehension, but the synergistic benefits resulting from integrating the two areas seem undeniable. Moreover, given that many frameworks of comprehension do not have well-specified components of monitoring and control that apparently influence text comprehension (e.g., W. Kintsch,

1988; van den Broek, Risden, Fletcher, & Thurlow, 1996), a long-term goal of this integrative approach also includes discovering how metacognitive processes influence comprehension.

In the present chapter, we offer one hypothesis about variables that will influence metacomprehension accuracy that is grounded in current theory about text comprehension and about metacognitive monitoring. Although this hypothesis does not comprise a comprehensive theory of metacomprehension, our hope is that our efforts will provide a step toward attaining the goals previously described.

The Levels-of-Disruption Hypothesis

In developing the *levels-of-disruption* hypothesis, we integrated a cue-based framework of metacognitive monitoring with theory concerning the mental representation of text. This particular hypothesis has three core assumptions. The first two assumptions, which are called the *inference* assumption and the *accuracy* assumption, were taken from cue-based hypotheses of metacognitive monitoring (e.g., Koriat, 1993). The final assumption, called the *representation* assumption, is informed by theory and data from the literature on text comprehension. These three assumptions are described next.

The inference assumption is that metacomprehension judgments are derived from a person's inferences about how various cues are related to comprehension (Maki, 1998). According to the levels-of-disruption hypothesis, a major cue underlying metacomprehension judgments is disruptions of comprehension processes that occur while an individual is reading a text. Many factors may produce processing disruptions, such as unfamiliar words, ambiguous pronouns, absence of critical background information, and so forth. Processing disruptions will also likely occur when an individual is reading difficult scientific texts, which often contain technical terms, descriptions of complicated processes, and highly specialized information. As more disruptions occur, people infer that texts are less well understood.

This specific instantiation of the inference assumption has empirical support. Karabenick (1996) had college students listen to two 8-min passages on environmental issues. While listening to the passages, the students pressed a hand-held button each time that they were confused. After listening to the passages, students then made global ratings about how confusing they found the passages. The students judged each passage separately on a scale from 0 (was very clear to me) to 9 (was very confusing to me). Most important, the number of button presses (which arguably tap online disruptions of understanding) were highly related to the retrospective judgments, with the across-individual correlation between button presses and ratings being .65 for the first passage and .59 for the second. Although different processes may underlie these retrospective judgments and the prospective metacomprehension judgments that are our present focus (e.g., Maki & Serra, 1992; Rawson, Dunlosky, & McDonald, in press), these data suggest that global judgments of comprehension are influenced by online disruptions of text comprehension.

The accuracy assumption is that the accuracy of an individual's metacomprehension judgments is a function of the degree to which the cues that underlie the judgments are predictive of test performance. For instance, readers may infer that the length of each to-be-judged text influences test performance, and hence use this cue when making judgments. If length of text happens to be highly correlated with test performance, then the accuracy of the judgments will be relatively high. In this case, however, length will likely not be correlated with test performance, and hence accuracy will be low (assuming length was the sole contributor to the judgments). In the present context, when differential disruptions in processing across texts are reflected in inference-based judgments and are highly predictive of test performance, then accuracy will be relatively high (for supporting evidence relevant to the accuracy assumption within other domains, see Koriat, 1993; McDonald, 1997). That is, readers will demonstrate high metacomprehension accuracy when their judgments are based on disruptions that are predictive of test performance. In contrast, readers will demonstrate low metacomprehension accuracy when they infer that disruptions hinder text comprehension and yet those disruptions are not predictive.

Finally, the representation assumption, which follows directly from theory of text comprehension, suggests when disruptions are likely to be diagnostic of test performance. Most theories of text comprehension propose that processing may occur at multiple levels of text representation while reading: the lexical level, the textbase representation, and the situation model (for an extensive discussion of these and other levels, see Graesser, Millis, & Zwaan 1997). The representation assumption is that disruptions that occur as an individual constructs different levels of text representation will be differentially predictive of performance on comprehension tests. For instance, the textbase includes propositions that represent explicit text information and their interrconnections (W. Kintsch, 1998). Although a textbase representation may support subsequent retrieval of individual phrases and sentences of the text, this level of representation alone will not necessarily support comprehension of the text. Accordingly, differential disruptions across texts while constructing a textbase representation may not be predictive of performance on comprehension tests across texts. If so, the accuracy of metacomprehension judgments made when texts are mainly being processed at this level will be constrained.

The situation model involves integrating the textbase representation with prior knowledge, and best represents comprehension of the text (Graesser et al., 1997; W. Kintsch, 1994). McNamara, E. Kintsch, Butler-Songer, and W. Kintsch (1996) provided a demonstration of the importance of the situation model. Using a pretest that assessed prior knowledge relevant to the topic of a criterion text (heart disease), they assigned students to a high- or low-knowledge group. All students studied a text on heart disease and were then administered tests that tapped primarily memory for the text (free recall and explicit information questions) or comprehension of the text (problem solving and inference questions). High-knowledge students showed a slight advantage over low-knowledge students on the memory measures but there was a large advantage on the comprehension measures that tapped the situation model (for boundary conditions for these effects, see McNamara et al., 1996). As prior knowledge is a component of a situation model, McNamara et al. concluded that the superior performance of the high-knowledge group was attributable to the successful construction of a situation model.

Because comprehension depends on a well-constructed situation model, differential disruptions across texts while constructing situation models will be relatively predictive of comprehension performance. Thus, if metacomprehension judgments are based on situation-level disruptions (as is expected when texts are being processed at this level), their accuracy will be relatively high. To illustrate, consider a reader who is processing multiple texts on astronomy at the level of the situation model. Many disruptions occur while the individual is reading texts about stars, whereas few disruptions occur while reading texts about planets. According to the inference assumption, the reader's metacomprehension judgments should indicate lower comprehension for the texts about stars than the texts about planets. Moreover, because disruptions likely indicate less complete or less coherent comprehension, performance on comprehension tests would be lower for star texts than planet texts. Thus, the metacomprehension judgments across the texts would be relatively accurate at predicting performance on comprehension tests.

In summary, the hypothesis is that students infer comprehension from disruptions in processing (inference assumption). When these disruptions are highly predictive of test performance, accuracy will be relatively high (accuracy assumption). Finally, when students' reading is aimed at the level of constructing a situation model, processing disruptions across texts are expected to be relatively predictive of performance on comprehension tests. An important point is that students are presumably not judging actual comprehension of the texts when they are reading at the situation level (and in fact, students may not even know what it means to comprehend a text). Instead, metacomprehension accuracy is expected to be high when students are reading at the situation level merely because disruptions of processing are expected to be empirically correlated with test performance.

Effects of Rereading and Advance Organizers on Metacomprehension Accuracy

We briefly review evidence that is relevant to evaluating predictions from the levels-of-disruption hypothesis. One general prediction is that when a person focuses processing at the level of the situation model, metacomprehension accuracy will be greater than when he or she mainly focuses processing at the textbase level. The onus was on us to find conditions that promote constructing situation models of text and then to test whether metacomprehension accuracy was affected. Fortunately, others have already identified two conditions that presumably promote construction of a situation model of text: (a) rereading (Millis, Simon, & tenBroek, 1998) and (b) studying advance organizers before reading (Mayer, 1979). In the remainder of this section, we describe preliminary results from research examining the influence of rereading and advance organizers on metacomprehension accuracy. One straightforward prediction is that accuracy will be greater after rereading (or when advance organizers are used) than when texts are read once.

Rereading and Metacomprehension Accuracy.   Rawson, Dunlosky, and Thiede (2000) reported two experiments on rereading that employed quite different methods. First, the participants were from different universities. Second, the content, difficulty, and number of texts were different. The presentation of texts differed, with Experiment 1 involving sentence-by-sentence presentation and Experiment 2 involving the individual presentation of each entire text. Finally, the metacomprehension judgments were collected with different prompts, which have been shown to influence the accuracy of metacomprehension judgments (Rawson et al., in press). Nevertheless, the substantive outcomes and conclusions from these experiments were the same, so we describe outcomes from only Experiment 2.

Sixty undergraduates were asked to read six expository texts that covered scientific topics (e.g., black holes, blood sugar, genetics, and evolution). Each text contained about 10 sentences (21.2 words/sentence), and the mean Flesch–Kincaid reading level across texts was 11.8. Each text was presented on a computer monitor in its entirety, and students could spend as much time as they wanted reading each one. Thirty students were presented each text only once. After reading all six texts, the students in this group were asked to judge their comprehension of a given text. To collect these metacomprehension judgments, we provided the students with the title of the text and the prompt, "How well do you think you understood the passage whose title is listed above?" Students could respond on a 7-point Likert scale, with 1 = very poorly and 7 = very well. Thirty other students were assigned to a rereading group; they read each text once and then read each again. After all texts had been reread, participants made a metacomprehension judgment for each text. Finally, all students answered six four-alternative multiple-choice questions for each text.

Before describing metacomprehension accuracy, let us first consider the effects of rereading on metacognitive judgments and test performance. For each group, we computed the mean metacomprehension judgment across individuals' mean ratings. The magnitude of the ratings was reliably greater for those who reread texts ($M = 5.98$) than for those who read texts once ($M = 5.12$), $t(58) = 3.53$. For each participant, we also computed the proportion of correct test responses. Mean performance was reliably greater for participants who reread texts ($M = .86$) than for those who read the texts once ($M = .70$), $t(58) = 5.25$. Although test performance and judgments were relatively high, the measures were below ceiling for both groups. Moreover, because these measures were highest for the rereading group, if such high performance constrains accuracy, it will tend to produce outcomes that are inconsistent with our prediction that rereading will improve accuracy.

Metacomprehension accuracy was operationalized as the Goodman–Kruskal gamma correlation between an individual student's judgments across texts and his or her mean test performance for each text (Nelson, 1984). The gamma correlation is a measure of the relative accuracy of the judgments, indicating an individual's success at judging his or her comprehension of one text relative to another. Means across gamma correlations between individual's ratings and performance were computed. (Four participants in the rereading group were dropped from this analysis due to indeterminate correlations.) As predicted, students who reread texts were more accurate (M gamma $= .55$) than were those who read texts once ($M = .19$), $t(53) = 3.06$.

The cumulative frequency distributions shown in Fig. 11.1 permit a more detailed examination of the benefits of rereading. As is evident from this figure, rereading maintained an advantage across all levels of accuracy. Furthermore, the level of accuracy was high as compared to previous research. For instance, the accuracy of about 75% of those rereading texts was .25 or greater, which is relatively substantial in comparison to the average levels of accuracy reported in the metacomprehension literature (cf. Maki, 1998). Moreover, the distribution for those who reread texts reveals that 33% of the individuals who reread texts had gamma correlations of 1.0, which represents perfect relative accuracy of the metacomprehension judgments.

Although the levels-of-disruption hypothesis provides an account for the effect of rereading on metacomprehension accuracy, many alternatives will likely surface allowing competitive evaluation among rival hypotheses.

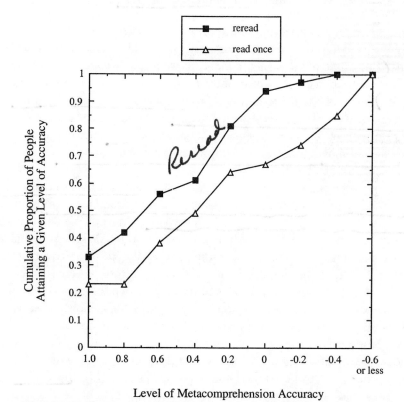

FIG. 11.1.   The cumulative proportion of participants who attained a given level (or higher) of metacomprehension accuracy. Curves are plotted separately for individuals who read texts once and for individuals who reread texts.

We briefly discuss one possibility that currently does not appear successful. In particular, rereading may enhance the reliability of test performance, which in turn could enhance the magnitude of the judgment–test correlation. To evaluate this possibility, we had a group of students read six texts once, make a metacomprehension judgment for each one, reread each text, and then answer test questions. If rereading does not enhance metacomprehension per se but merely increases the reliability of test performance, accuracy for these judgments (made between the reading trials) will be relatively substantial. However, mean accuracy for this group was only +.28, which is reliably lower than the comparable level of accuracy for the rereading group in Rawson et al. (2000). The important point from disconfirming both alternatives is that the rereading effect does not appear to be due to an influence of rereading on comprehension, but instead may be attributed to improving metacomprehension per se.

Advance Organizers and Metacomprehension Accuracy. Rereading appears to improve metacomprehension accuracy, at least in some situations. But what about other conditions that presumably enhance the likelihood that students will process texts at the level of the situation model? Another candidate involves providing advance organizers for students prior to reading to-be-learned material. Although the effects of advance organizers on comprehension are generally small, the literature has consistently shown that they can improve comprehension (for a recent review, see Corkill, 1992).

The purpose of an advance organizer is to activate prior knowledge to increase the likelihood that a learner can better understand new information by relating the new knowledge to prior knowledge (Mayer, 1979). Advance organizers can take a variety of forms, be it an outline, diagram, summary paragraph, or list of key terms. According to Corkill (1992), an advance organizer "should (a) be presented before the to-be-learned material, (b) be in written paragraph form, (c) be written in a concrete fashion, and (d) contain an example that encourages the reader to note the analogous relationship between the ideas in the advance organizer and ideas to come" (p. 63). More generally, an advance organizer describes higher order concepts the reader already understands, which by analogy can be used to more effectively process the to-be-learned material (cf. Mayer, 1979). Research also indicates that advance organizers are most effective when readers paraphrase them prior to reading the to-be-learned material (e.g., Corkill, Glover, Brunning, & Krug, 1988). In an attempt to maximize the potential influence of advance organizers, we constructed our organizers with the

Paraphrase adv org.

aforementioned guidelines in mind and had students paraphrase each advance organizer prior to reading the target text.

Concerning the hypothetical influence of advance organizers, current theory implicates the role of utilizing prior knowledge in understanding to-be-learned material. In discussing the assimilation encoding hypothesis by Mayer (1979), Corkill (1992) noted that an advance organizer "encourages active integration of the new information with prior knowledge … the advance organizer suggests an appropriate cognitive framework into which new information may be assimilated with prior knowledge" (pp. 40–41). Although explicit reference of processing at the level of the situation model was not included in these articles, the correspondence to this idea is evident: Advance organizers presumably influence performance because they help readers integrate explicit textbase representation of the to-be-learned material with existing knowledge. Thus, to the extent that advance organizers increase the likelihood of processing at the situation model, a prediction from the levels-of-disruption hypothesis is that advance organizers will improve metacomprehension accuracy.

To evaluate this possibility, we had individuals read advance organizers prior to reading target materials. Undergraduates were randomly assigned to a single reading ($n = 38$) group or to an advance organizer ($n = 33$) group. Participants were asked to read six critical texts that mainly covered scientific issues (e.g., inventions, intelligence, obesity, and guilt). An advance organizer was written for each text based on the criteria outlined earlier. Each text comprised about 20 sentences (24.4 words/sentence), and the mean Flesch–Kincaid reading level across texts was 13.3. Each advance organizer comprised about 4.5 sentences (15.7 words/sentence), and the mean Flesch–Kincaid reading level across advance organizers was 6.4. A sample advance organizer along with its corresponding text is presented in the Appendix.

Participants in the advance organizer group were told that:

> To help you better understand the texts, you will first study an advance organizer for each text. An advance organizer is a brief paragraph introducing a concept that will help you organize the main ideas contained in a text. The organizer doesn't give you an outline of the text. Instead, it describes a real-world situation that may help you understand the main points of the text. Try to use the advance organizer to help you understand the main points in the text.

They were then presented with a sample advance organizer (corresponding to the sample text) for self-paced study. Participants were also asked to type a paraphrase of the advance organizer in a field on the same screen.

For participants in both groups, computers controlled text presentation and data collection. The sample text was presented one sentence at a time for self-paced study, beginning with the title. Each sentence remained on the screen until participants pressed a button to advance to the next sentence. After the last sentence, a performance prediction was prompted with the text title and the query, How well do you think you will be able to answer a test question over this material in about 20 minutes? 0 (definitely won't be able), 20 (20% sure I will be able), 40 ..., 60 ..., 80 ..., 100 (definitely will be able). Participants next answered the sample test questions.

For the critical trials, order for presentation of the texts was randomized, and the texts were presented as described previously. Participants in the single reading group predicted performance for each text immediately after reading each text. Participants in the advance organizer group read and paraphrased an advance organizer before reading each of the texts. They predicted performance for each text immediately after reading each one. After reading all texts, participants completed the test questions.

Before describing metacomprehension accuracy, first consider the effect of advance organizers on metacomprehension judgments and test performance. We computed the mean across individuals' mean ratings separately for each of the groups. The magnitude of the ratings was less for those who read advance organizers (M = 35) than for those who did not read them (M = 42), $t(69) = 1.77, p = .08$. For each participant, we also computed the proportion of correct test responses. Unfortunately, mean performance was not reliably greater for participants who read advance organizers (M = .45) than for those who did not read them (M = .49), $t(69) = 1.06$. Because test performance is the typical indicator that advance organizers have the presumed influence on the processing of text, one possibility is that our advance organizers did not promote processing at the level of the situation model. If so, the question of whether advance organizers influence predictive accuracy has little bearing on our evaluation of the levels-of-disruption hypothesis, because a precondition of this evaluation is that advance organizers promote situation-level processing. Even so, we were still interested in evaluating predictive accuracy, because if accuracy was enhanced by advance organizers, students may be able to use the organizers to improve their self-regulated learning of text material.

Metacomprehension accuracy was again operationalized as the Goodman–Kruskal gamma correlation between an individual student's judgments across texts and his or her mean test performance for each text.

Means across gamma correlations between each individual's ratings and performance were computed. (Three participants in the advance organizer group and one participant in the control group were dropped from this analysis due to indeterminate correlations.) In contrast to the prediction from the levels-of-disruption hypothesis, students who read advance organizers were not reliably more accurate (M gamma = .42, Mdn = .50) than were those who read texts once (M = .36, Mdn = .43), t(53) = 3.06. Note, however, that the magnitude of the correlations was relatively high for those who read advance organizers, which demonstrates some promise for improving metacomprehension accuracy for students reading science texts.

GENERAL DISCUSSION

The importance of monitoring comprehension during reading has received consistently strong support in recent years (e.g., Pressley & McCormick, 1995). Accurate monitoring of comprehension is a critical step in the self-regulation of reading strategies, which are essential to constructing deeper understanding of texts. But, before we summarily adopt reading strategies that are purported to teach monitoring of science texts, an important question must be answered: "Is highly accurate monitoring even possible?" Results pertaining to the rereading effect described previously provide an optimistic answer to this question, although even rereading failed to produce near perfect levels of predictive accuracy. Moreover, the accuracy of monitoring text comprehension typically is poor. Why? A definitive answer to this question is still out of reach. Nonetheless, the approach that we advocated here—which involves integrating hypotheses of monitoring and text comprehension—promises to generate many testable answers to this question.

Consider our instantiation of this approach offered in the present chapter, which we called the levels-of-disruption hypothesis (Readers' judgments about their own comprehension of a text are presumably inferential in nature) That is, instead of being informed directly by the text representation that underlies comprehension, these judgments are based on various cues. We proposed that disruptions of comprehension that occur while an individual reads allegedly influence metacomprehension judgments. When differential disruptions across texts are predictive of test performance, judgment accuracy is expected to be relatively high. As argued earlier, processing texts at the level of the situation model rather than the textbase level was expected to improve predictive accuracy because under the former conditions disruptions of text processing will be relatively diagnostic of comprehension across texts.

New data presented here were not entirely consistent with a prediction derived from this hypothesis. In particular, advance organizers did not improve metacomprehension accuracy. However, because our advance organizers did not improve comprehension, one could question whether they had increased processing at the level of the situation model for each text; if situation model processing was not more likely after individuals read advance organizers, increases in predictive accuracy would not be expected. Our only indicator of processing at this level was test performance, and the effect of advance organizers on test performance was quite small and in the wrong direction. Thus, perhaps when advance organizers have a demonstrable influence on test performance, metacomprehension accuracy will also be enhanced.

In contrast to the minimal influence of advance organizers, consider the rereading effect. Not only did this effect confirm a prediction from the levels-of-disruption hypothesis, but it has other implications for theory of metacomprehension as well. Perhaps most notable, one cannot entirely discount low accuracy as artifactual, such as if methods typically used in previous research substantially constrained metacomprehension accuracy. Using standard methods, we demonstrated that students can have relatively high levels of metacomprehension accuracy when reading scientific texts (see also, Weaver & Bryant, 1995). But does this rereading effect on metacomprehension accuracy also have educational implications? That is, will improving metacomprehension accuracy via rereading help students to more effectively learn science texts? Certainly, rereading itself may benefit students' test performance (e.g., Barnett & Seefeldt, 1989; Haenggi & Perfetti, 1992). But before we are able to definitively answer this question, three questions need to be considered by those who are interested in future work in this area. In discussing each one, we do not intend to provide definitive answers because none are yet available. Instead, we describe issues and future research that work toward providing answers.

First, students rarely make metacomprehension judgments, so why should improving metacomprehension accuracy matter? This argument is a general dismissal of the applied relevance of metacomprehension research to student achievement. Students may often be reluctant to use strategies that may be of use to them (Garner, 1990). However, if we can discover conditions that produce high levels of accuracy, students may learn to use these judgments in guiding their comprehension and hence will be motivated to use them when the appropriate learning conditions arise. Providing evidence to students that strategies work is an important element in strategy instruction (Pressley, Borkowski, & O'Sullivan, 1985). Thus, if students receive feedback during reading that their judgments are improving comprehension, perhaps they would be motivated to more actively regulate comprehension.

Second, rereading does not always enhance test performance, so why should students care if it enhances metacomprehension accuracy? The potential effects of metacomprehension monitoring on comprehension will be minimized if students are not given the opportunity to use such monitoring in regulating comprehension. The idea here is simply that monitoring can improve comprehension only if an individual is given the opportunity to utilize monitoring (e.g., Thiede, 1999). In the present research, as in most research that has investigated metacomprehension accuracy, students' opportunities to control learning was highly constrained, so any potential benefit of improving accuracy on learning was likely short-circuited. Exploring whether rereading improves regulation of comprehension (via improving predictive accuracy) will fill a major gap in the metacomprehension literature. One avenue that holds particular promise for exploring the issues raised by these first two questions is to incorporate multiple measures of monitoring and control into the same methodological procedure. This approach has provided insight into how individuals self-regulate learning of simple materials and may also elucidate the intricacies of self-regulated comprehension (for reviews, see Son & Metcalfe, 2000; Thiede & Dunlosky, 1999).

And third, will the rereading effect occur under circumstances that are relevant to student scholarship? This is an empirical question, which concerns the boundary conditions for the rereading effect. We note two predictions here—both of which were derived from the levels-of-disruption hypothesis. First, the rereading effect will be absent when a long delay occurs between initial reading and rereading because rereading after a long delay (e.g., a week) does not promote processing at the level of the situation model (Millis et al., 1998). Preliminary evidence is consistent with this prediction (Dunlosky & Rawson, 2000). Second, the rereading effect is expected for expository text (e.g., science texts) but not for narrative text. In contrast to reading expository texts, individuals reading narratives will often have an appropriate knowledge of the discourse form and content to successfully develop situation models even during an initial reading of the texts. If so, rereading will not be expected to improve metacomprehension accuracy. Another situation may also arise in which rereading will not enhance predictive accuracy. In particular, under some conditions, readers can easily repair the processing failures that underlie any disruptions in constructing a text representation. If such repairs are successful, differential disruptions across texts would not be highly predictive of performance on any kind of test. Ironically, rereading may not benefit accuracy for individuals with high levels of knowledge about the content of the target text. These individuals presumably would be constructing a highly coherent and integrated situation model of the text during an initial reading.

Finally, our focus in this chapter was on the levels-of-disruption hypothesis because it led to the rereading effect and remains useful in guiding future research. Note, however, that this hypothesis is currently inadequate as a comprehensive theory because it underspecifies the processes that contribute to metacomprehension accuracy. Evidence from previous research suggests that metacomprehension judgments are based on multiple cues, such as perceived expertise, momentary accessibility, and serial order of text presentation, to name a few. Thus, by focusing exclusively on processing disruptions, the levels-of-disruption hypothesis is unlikely to account for many of the phenomena in the literature. Important modifications to this hypothesis will be motivated by further considering a general cue-based approach to metacomprehension judgments, which offers many empirical questions: "Do some cues always dominate others?" "Do individuals combine multiple cues in making a judgment, or do they typically attend to one, salient cue when judging comprehension?" Answers to these questions will likely be best informed by perspectives that incorporate and integrate theories of text comprehension with theories of metacognition.

ACKNOWLEDGMENTS

We thank Kurt Boneicki for help with constructing advance organizers. Correspondence should be sent to John Dunlosky, P. O. Box 26164, UNCG, Greensboro, NC, 27402-6164, dunlosky@uncg.edu.

REFERENCES

Barnett, J. E., & Seefeldt, R. W. (1989). Repetitive reading and recall. *Journal of Reading Behavior, 21*, 351–361.

Corkill, A. J. (1992). Advance organizers: Facilitators of recall. *Educational Psychology Review, 4*, 33–67.

Corkill, A. J., Glover, J. A., Brunning, R. H., & Krug, D. (1988). Advance organizers: Retrieval context hypotheses. *Journal of Educational Research, 80*, 304–311.

Dunlosky, J., & Hertzog, C. (2000). Updating knowledge about encoding strategies: A componential analysis of learning about strategy effectiveness from task experience. *Psychology and Aging, 15*, 462–474.

Dunlosky, J., & Rawson, K. A. (2000). *Why does rereading improve metacomprehension accuracy? Evaluating the levels-of-disruption hypothesis for the rereading effect.* Manuscript submitted for review.

Einstein, G. O., McDaniel, M. A., Bowers, C. A., & Stevens, D. T. (1984). Memory for prose: The influence of relational and proposition-specific processing. *Journal of Experimental Psychology: Learning, Memory, and Cognition, 10,* 133–143.

Ericsson, K. A., & Simon, H. A. (1980). Verbal reports as data. *Psychological Review, 87,* 215–251.

Garner, R. (1990). Children's use of strategies in reading. In D. F. Bjorklund (Ed.), *Children's strategies: Contemporary views of cognitive development* (pp. 245–268). Hillsdale, NJ: Lawrence Erlbaum Associates.

Gernsbacher, M. A., Varner, K. R., & Faust, M. E. (1990). Investigating individual differences in general comprehension skill. *Journal of Experimental Psychology: Learning, Memory, and Cognition, 16,* 430–445.

Glenberg, A. M., & Epstein, W. (1985). Calibration of comprehension. *Journal of Experimental Psychology: Learning, Memory, and Cognition, 11* (1–4), 702–718.

Glenberg, A. M., Sanocki, T., Epstein, W., & Morris, C. (1987). Enhancing calibration of comprehension. *Journal of Experimental Psychology: General, 116,* 119–136.

Graesser, A. C. (1981). *Prose comprehension beyond the word.* New York: Springer-Verlag.

Graesser, A. C., Millis, K. K., & Zwaan, R. A. (1997). Discourse comprehension. *Annual Review of Psychology, 48,* 163–189.

Hacker, D. J. (1998). Self-regulated comprehension during normal reading. In D. J. Hacker, J. Dunlosky, & A. C. Graesser (Eds.), *Metacognition in educational theory and practice* (pp. 165–191). Mahwah, NJ: Lawrence Erlbaum Associates.

Haenggi, D., & Perfetti, C. A. (1992). Individual differences in reprocessing of text. *Journal of Educational Psychology, 84,* 182–192.

Karabenick, S. A. (1996). Social influences on metacognition: Effects of colearner questioning on comprehension monitoring. *Journal of Educational Psychology, 88,* 689–703.

Kintsch, W. (1988). The use of knowledge in discourse processing: A construction-integration model. *Psychological Review, 95,* 163–182.

Kintsch, W. (1994). Text comprehension, memory, and learning. *American Psychologist, 49,* 294–303.

Kintsch, W. (1998). *Comprehension: A paradigm for cognition.* Cambridge, England: Cambridge University Press.

Koriat, A. (1993). How do we know what we know? The accessibility model of the feeling of knowing. *Psychological Review, 100,* 609–639.

Koriat, A. (1997). Monitoring one's own knowledge during study: A cue-utilization approach to judgments of learning. *Journal of Experimental Psychology: General, 126* (4), 349–370.

Lin, L. M., & Zabrucky, K. M. (1998). Calibration of comprehension: Research and implications for education and instruction. *Contemporary Educational Psychology, 23,* 345–391.

Magliano, J. P., Little, L. D., & Graesser, A. C. (1993). The impact of comprehension instruction on the calibration of comprehension. *Reading Research and Instruction, 32,* 49–63.

Maki, R. H. (1995). Accuracy of metacomprehension judgments for questions of varying importance levels. *American Journal of Psychology, 108,* 327–344.

Maki, R. H. (1998). Test predictions over text material. In D. J. Hacker, J. Dunlosky, & A. C. Graesser (Eds.), *Metacognition in educational theory and practice* (pp. 117–144). Mahwah, NJ: Lawrence Erlbaum Associates.

Maki, R. H., & Berry, S. L. (1984). Metacomprehension of text material. *Journal of Experimental Psychology: Learning, Memory, and Cognition, 10,* 663–679.

Maki, R. H., Foley, J. M., Kajer, W. K., Thompson, R. C., & Willert, M. G. (1990). Increased processing enhances calibration of comprehension. *Journal of Experimental Psychology: Learning, Memory, and Cognition, 16,* 609–616.

Maki, R. H., Jonas, D., & Kallod, M. (1994). The relationship between comprehension and metacomprehension ability. *Psychonomic Bulletin & Review, 1,* 126–129.

Maki, R. H., & Serra, M. (1992). The basis of test predictions for text material. *Journal of Experimental Psychology: Learning, Memory, and Cognition, 18,* 116–126.

Mayer, R. E. (1979). Can advance organizers influence meaningful learning? *Review of Educational Psychology, 49,* 371–383.

McDonald, S. L. (1997). *What underlies the accuracy of predictions of recall for sentences? A competitive evaluation of two hypotheses.* Unpublished master's thesis, University of North Carolina at Greensboro.

McNamara, D. S., Kintsch, E., Butler-Songer, N., & Kintsch, W. (1996). Are good texts always better? Interactions of text coherence, background knowledge, and levels of understanding in learning from text. *Cognition and Instruction, 14,* 1–43.

Millis, K. K., Simon, S., & tenBroek, N. S. (1998). Resource allocation during the rereading of scientific texts. *Memory & Cognition, 26,* 232–246.

Morris, C. C. (1990). Retrieval processes underlying confidence in comprehension judgments. *Journal of Experimental Psychology: Learning, Memory, and Cognition, 16,* 223–232.

Morris, C. C. (1995). Poor discourse comprehension monitoring is no methodological artifact. *The Psychological Record, 45,* 655–668.

Nelson, T. O. (1984). A comparison of current measures of feeling-of-knowing accuracy. *Psychological Bulletin, 95,* 109–133.

Pressley, M., Borkowski, J. G., & O'Sullivan, J. (1985). Children's metamemory and the teaching of memory strategies. In D. L. Forrest-Pressley, G. E. MacKinnon, & T. G. Waller (Eds.), *Metacognition, cognition, and human performance* (Vol. 1, pp. 111–153). Orlando, FL: Academic Press.

Pressley, M., & McCormick, C. B. (1995). *Advanced educational psychology.* New York: Harper Collins.

Rawson, K. A., Dunlosky, J., & McDonald, S. (in press). Influences of metamemory on performance predictions for text. Quarterly Journal of Experimental Psychology.

Rawson, K. A., Dunlosky, J., & Thiede, K. W. (2000). The rereading effect: Metacomprehension accuracy improves across reading trials. *Memory & Cognition, 28,* 1004–1010.

Schwartz, B. L., Benjamin, A. S., & Bjork, R. A. (1998). The inferential and experiential bases of metamemory. *Current Directions in Psychological Science, 6,* 132–137.

Son, L. K., & Metcalfe, J. (2000). Metacognitive and control strategies in study-time allocation. *Journal of Experimental Psychology: Learning, Memory, and Cognition, 26,* 204–221.

Thiede, K. W. (1999). The importance of monitoring and self-regulation during multitrial learning. *Psychonomic Bulletin and Review, 6,* 662–667.

Thiede, K. W., & Dunlosky, J. (1999). Toward a general model of self-regulated study: An analysis of selection of items for study and self-paced study time. *Journal of Experimental Psychology: Learning, Memory, and Cognition, 25,* 1024–1037.

van den Broek, P., Risden, K., Fletcher, C. R., & Thurlow, R. (1996). A "landscape" view of reading: Fluctuating patterns of activation and the construction of a stable memory representation. In B. K. Britton & A. C. Graesser (Eds.), *Models of understanding text* (pp. 165–188). Mahwah, NJ: Lawrence Erlbaum Associates.

van Dijk, T. A., & Kintsch, W. (1983). *Strategies in discourse comprehension.* New York: Academic Press.

Walczyk, J. J., & Hall, V. C. (1989). Effects of examples and embedded questions on the accuracy of comprehension self-assessments. *Journal of Educational Psychology, 81,* 435–437.

Weaver, C. (1990). Constraining factors in calibration of comprehension. *Journal of Experimental Psychology: Learning, Memory, and Cognition, 16,* 214–222.

Weaver, C. A., III, & Bryant, D. S. (1995). Monitoring of comprehension: The role of text difficulty in metamemory for narrative and expository text. *Memory & Cognition, 23,* 12–22.

Weaver, C. A., III, Bryant, D. S., & Burns, K. D. (1995). Comprehension monitoring: Extensions of the Kintsch and van Dijk model. In C. A. Weaver III, S. Mannes, & C. R. Fletcher (Eds.), *Discourse comprehension: Essays in honor of Walter Kintsch* (pp. 177–193). Hillsdale, NJ: Lawrence Erlbaum Associates.

APPENDIX

Advance Organizer for *Intelligence and Measurement*

What is a good athlete? If you asked a bunch of people, you'd probably get a bunch of different answers. Some people would say that a good athlete is a person who wins at several different sports. For them, athleticism equals winning at games. Other people would look at what things you have to be able to do to play those sports well, like running fast, having good eye–hand coordination, and so on. For them, athleticism equals being able to do these things.

Intelligence and Measurement

In 1921, leading investigators in the field of intelligence participated in a symposium, "Intelligence and Its Measurement," sponsored by the *Journal of Educational Psychology*. They defined the title concept, producing almost as many definitions as there were definers, but reached no consensus. One contemporary observer was prompted to quip that intelligence seemed merely to be the capacity to do well on an intelligence test. Now, 60 years later, the situation seems little changed. As Yale's Robert J. Sternberg, an influential cognitive psychologist warns, "If we are to seek genuine understanding of the relationship between natural intelligence and measured intelligence (IQ), there is one route that clearly will not lead us to the heart of the problem and that we must avoid at all costs. This route is defining away (rather than defining) intelligence as whatever it is that the IQ tests measure." The dominant approach followed by researchers attempting to define intelligence has been factor analysis, a statistical method that examines mental ability test scores with an eye to discerning constellations of test scores that are closely related to each other. The underlying thesis is that where a correlation appears among the scores of many people on tests of different mental abilities, a single factor of intelligence must be common to performance on those tests. Charles Spearman, originator of factor analysis, held that two kinds of factors form the basis of intelligence: a general factor and specific factors. Subsequent theorists divided the general factor into two or more subfactors, the two most generally agreed upon being verbal-educational and practical-mechanical abilities. Factor analysis has listed many discrete mental abilities and produced models that show how they combine, but it has not suggested how these abilities work. It has also not been productive in dealing with adaptational ability or practical problem solving. A more recent approach is process analysis, whose thrust is to analyze the processes of test performance rather than the products of test performance. Process analysts, says Dr. Sternberg, do not reject the findings of factor analysis. Rather, they seek "to supplement our understanding of the factors of intelligence with an understanding of the processes that are responsible at least in part for the generation of these factors as sources of individual difference." The counterpart of the factor as a unit of analysis is the component, described by Dr. Sternberg as "an elementary information process that operates upon internal representations of objects or symbols." Componential studies have been subjected to statistical analysis, and the findings have clarified how certain tasks are performed. However, like factor analysis, process analysis has so far provided few insights into practical problem solving and adaptation to real-world environments. Dr. Sternberg hopes that the application of componential analysis to simulations of real-world task performance will contribute to an understanding of how intelligence operates in that area of human activity. Some in the field say that identifying factors and processes is worthwhile, but that doing so will not lead to a definition of intelligence. These critics warn that the models produced by such research may become the basis for some future statement that intelligence is what the models model.

❧ 12 ❧

Noticing and Fixing Difficulties While Understanding Science Texts

José Otero
Universidad de Alcalá, Madrid, Spain

This chapter analyzes the process of noticing and fixing comprehension difficulties that readers encounter in science texts. The term *regulation* of comprehension has been used to describe this process. Regulation refers to the processes used to achieve cognitive consistency in the knowledge elements of a text when they appear to be inconsistent.

Regulation has been studied within different areas of cognitive and social psychology. Perhaps one of the oldest theories of regulation processes to achieve cognitive consistency was Festinger's (1957) cognitive dissonance theory. Dissonance is defined as "a negative drive state which occurs whenever an individual simultaneously holds two cognitions (ideas, beliefs, opinions) which are psychologically inconsistent" (Aronson, 1968, p. 5). The inconsistency does not have to be necessarily logical, but it could arise from incompatible past experiences or incompatible cultural upbringing, for example in situations when an opinion contradicts social conventions or standards. Researchers in this area have studied methods used by individuals to reduce states of dissonance, that is, modes of regulating a situation where inconsistent beliefs are held (Abelson, 1959, 1968a; Adams, 1968; Hardyck & Kardush, 1968; Kelman & Baron, 1968; Read & Miller, 1994).

Regulation has been studied also by researchers interested in the way readers modify situation models (i.e., mental models). According to some theories of text comprehension (Graesser, Millis, & Zwaan, 1997; Just & Carpenter, 1987; Kintsch, 1998; van Dijk & Kintsch, 1983) the situation model is one of the three levels at which texts are represented: It is the referential content of what the text is about. A reader may encounter information that does not fit the model built at a particular moment while processing a text. For example, a reader may run into information that is inconsistent with the situation described in previous passages. There have been periodical investigations of the extent to which readers modify the representation elaborated up to that moment or, alternatively, stick to the existing model (Johnson & Seifert, 1994, 1999; van Oostendorp, Otero, & Campanario, in press; Wilkes & Leatherbarrow, 1988; see also chap. 13, this volume).

Regulation has been investigated in research on comprehension monitoring, within the framework of the *contradiction paradigm*. Typical instances of this research involve subjects reading manipulated texts that contain contradictions. Detecting a contradiction is taken as a sign of adequate monitoring of comprehension. However, it is well known that readers often repair the contradiction themselves (Baker, 1979; Otero & Campanario, 1990) and do not express the difficulty, even when instructed to do so. Thus, researchers in this area have distinguished two components in comprehension monitoring: evaluation and regulation of comprehension. An appropriate evaluation consists in noticing a comprehension problem, whereas regulation refers to the process of repairing the problem once the reader has detected this problem (Baker, 1985b; Otero, 1996; Zabrucky & Ratner, 1986, 1989, 1992). However, the research reported in this chapter suggests that these two phases should not be regarded as independent of each other.

Regulation processes are particularly relevant to science education, especially in relation to the process of *conceptual change*. According to the proponents of the conceptual change approach to science learning, students' preexisting beliefs interact with scientific information provided by teachers or textbooks. These beliefs frequently hinder acquisition of new knowledge. Most of the previous work in this area of research, particularly the work conducted in the field of science education, focused on describing and cataloguing students' inadequate knowledge, rather than analyzing in detail how to transform this knowledge (Rukavina & Daneman,

1996). However, Posner, Strike, Hewson, and Hertzog (1982) proposed a model of conceptual change that underlined students' dissatisfaction with their naive beliefs or theories as a necessary step to learning scientific knowledge. Creating students' dissatisfaction is frequently attempted by creating *cognitive conflict* between external information and the naive knowledge of students. This may be accomplished by providing anomalous data, that is, evidence that contradicts students' naive beliefs. However, it was found that cognitive conflict did not always produce the expected results because students frequently fail to change their beliefs in the face of disconfirming evidence (Burbules & Linn, 1988; diSessa, 1982; Kuhn, 1989). Hence, examining in detail how learners confront their own ideas with anomalous information and the strategies used to cope with these anomalies may clarify the conflicting results (Otero, 1998). There have been studies that analyze the responses of students when they are faced with evidence that confront their beliefs or theories (Chinn & Brewer, 1993; Park & Pak, 1997). Some analyses have focused on variables that may mediate the effect of conflict on conceptual change (Chan, Burtis, & Bereiter, 1997.) The way in which conflict is resolved in science (Darden, 1992) has been a model for many of these studies.

This chapter analyzes the processes enacted when readers encounter inconsistencies in science texts. It presents some elements of a model of the repair processes used by readers who detect inconsistencies between their knowledge and external information (i.e., *external inconsistencies* in the terminology of Baker, 1985b) or between elements of external information (i.e., *internal inconsistencies*).

The forthcoming analysis should not be regarded as a complete model of the regulation of science text comprehension, but rather as a partial approach that attempts to handle the complexity of the regulation process. Two main limitations of this contribution should be pointed out at the outset. First, the model's elements are provisionally represented as sequential steps to avoid excessive complexity (see Fig. 12.1). This assumption is adopted, but some of these processes would probably be carried out in parallel. Second, the model simplifies real situations by ignoring the social factors that influence overt regulatory behavior. For example, research on student questioning has demonstrated the importance of social barriers in question asking, a form of regulatory behavior (Graesser, Person, & Huber, 1992; Karabenick, 1996; van der Meij, 1988). The proposed model assumes an ideal situation in which these barriers are nonexistent.

Some examples that illustrate the model are taken from the artificial, yet relatively simple scientific texts that have explicit and deliberate contradictions. No explanation at the semantic level exists for these contradictions in normal situations. This is the case for many experiments carried out within the contradiction paradigm (Baker, 1979; Markman, 1977, 1979; Otero & Campanario, 1990). Under these settings an adequate regulatory behavior consists of pointing out the contradiction when instructed to do so and rejecting the text as inconsistent. This differs from difficulties found in more

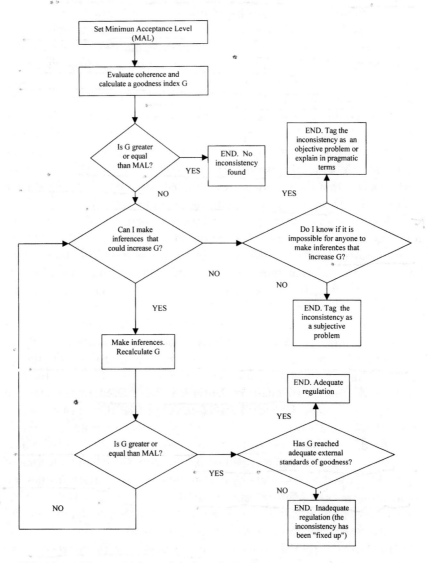

FIG. 12.1.   Elements of a model of regulation.

naturalistic situations, such as those those in school settings, where rejection of the text is an unusual regulatory action. However, many of the regulatory processes that take place in naturalistic settings can be more clearly dissected in experiments that have contradictions in texts.

The elements of the model are presented in the ensuing paragraphs, whereas an overview of the whole process is presented in Fig. 12.1. The essential regulation mechanism is modeled after a constraint satisfaction process in which readers evaluate the coherence of their mental representation of a text according to some standard. If the outcome of this evaluation is unsatisfactory, readers may generate inferences in an attempt to increase coherence above a minimum acceptable level. This is what proficient readers do in normal situations when they find comprehension difficulties in naturalistic texts.   *Standards in eval. of text coherence*

However, in some instances, readers may decide that they are unable to generate these repairing inferences because it is unlikely that there exists any inference that may solve the comprehension problem. This corresponds to the situation in which an expert notices an explicit contradiction in text of the sort that are used in comprehension-monitoring experiments. For example, one of these is depicted in an excerpt reported by Markman (1979): "When it is that dark the fish cannot see anything. They cannot even see colors. Some fish that live at the bottom of the ocean can see the color of their food" (p. 646). In this example, an *objective* comprehension problem would be identified. However, sometimes readers do not believe there is an objective problem with the text. Readers may notice a comprehension problem, but think that they are unable to make any inference that would solve the problem, *but* that someone else, a more knowledgeable reader, would successfully do so. In this case, the outcome is a *subjective* problem. The proposed model takes into account all these possibilities.

COHERENCE IS EVALUATED AS LEVEL OF CONSTRAINT SATISFACTION

Noticing a coherence problem in a text representation is a prerequisite for repairing an inconsistency in the text. The model includes a coherence evaluation stage that calculates a coherence index (G), which represents the coherence or consonance of a text representation in working memory. This is equivalent to the calculation of *goodness* (or *harmony*) in connectionist networks (McClelland & Rumelhart, 1988) or *energy* as defined by Hopfield (1982). Processes of this kind have been proposed when evaluating a parallel constraint network in which many simultaneous constraints have to be satisfied (Britton & Eisenhart, 1993; Lepper, 1996; Read & Miller, 1994; Shultz & Lepper, 1996). Shultz and Lepper, for example, devised a model for reducing cognitive dissonance based on a constraint satisfaction network. The basic units represent cognitions, that is, the subject's beliefs and attitudes. These units differ both in direction and strength. Direction refers to believing that a cognition is true or false, or evaluating it favorably or unfavorably. Strength refers to the degree to which something is believed to be true or is favorably evaluated. The overall consonance of a network, equivalent to goodness, is formally defined as $\sum_i \sum_j w_{ij} a_i a_j$, where the sum is extended over all possible pairs of units, i and j, with activation a_i and a_j, respectively.

Britton and Eisenhart (1993) used a similar approach to analyze the consistency of mental representations of experts and novices who read texts of varying coherence. The authors used a measure based on the degree to which constraints between pieces of information are satisfied in order to evaluate the consistency of mental representations. It was calculated on a network based on Kintsch's (1988) construction-integration model, but the measure is similar to harmony or goodness. The results confirmed the prediction that the harmony of mental representations generated by experts, good readers, and readers of coherent texts is higher than that of novices, poor readers, and readers of less coherent texts. Self-calculation of harmony would enable readers to monitor their comprehension and, should it be low, to generate appropriate repair actions.

However, not all inconsistencies that readers encounter in a text are deemed important enough to be repaired. For example, Coté, Goldman, and Saul (1998) gave informational texts of varying difficulty to a sample of fourth-grade and sixth-grade students, and prompted them to think aloud while reading. They found that one of the most common overt strategies used by the students to solve these problems was ignoring the problem and continue on reading. This insensitivity to inconsistencies may also exist in other scientific tasks, outside of the text-processing domain. Burbules and Linn (1988) investigated students' responses to a contradiction with their expectancies in a scientific task that consisted of predicting how much water would be displaced by objects of varying size, shape, and weight. They found that a change in the face of contradictory evidence is not immediate, but is erratic, and that gains toward the correct interpretation are not accumulative. They pointed out that subjects have "vastly different degrees of tolerance for anomalous results" (p. 74). Also, cultural differences, philosophical traditions, or tacit beliefs about the nature of the world and knowledge may influence readers' reaction to inconsistencies. In a study on cultural differences in dealing with contradictions, Peng and Nisbett (1999) provided contradictory statements to Chinese and American students. The statements had to be rated for plausibility both in a no-contradiction condition (reading only one side of the contradictions) and in a contradiction condition (reading both sides). They found that Chinese students rated significantly higher the less plausible statement in the contradiction condition than in the no-contradiction condition. However, there were no differences between conditions for their American counterparts. This is interpreted as showing that Chinese students may use a heuristic such as "believing that both sides of a contradiction may be right and that the truth lies between the two perspectives" (p. 749).

The model is meant to take into account that readers, faced with dissonant information, have varying degrees of tolerance for inconsistencies (Aronson, 1968; Glass, 1968; Miller & Rokeach, 1968). Such differences are captured by a parameter for consistency, a *minimum acceptance level* (MAL), a value that defines what counts as an inconsistency for a particular reader. A similar parameter (*tolerance level*) has been suggested within the framework of cognitive dissonance theories (Adams, 1968; Glass, 1968) or in text comprehension research. Van Oostendorp (1994) proposed a semantic cohesion monitoring hypothesis to explain differences in the activation of knowledge in text processing; readers monitor the semantic cohesion of a text representation by comparison with internal standards. For that purpose, he provided subjects with sentences that include concepts that had different levels of semantic relatedness. For example, *The cat caught the mouse in the kitchen* has a high relatedness between cat and mouse, whereas *The cat seized the mole in the field* has a low relatedness. He found that readers generate more inferences in the low-relatedness condition than in the high-relatedness condition until reaching the semantic cohesion standard (see also chap. 10, this volume).

Van den Broek, Risden, and Husebye-Hartmann (1994) also suggested a notion that readers employ standards of coherence that influence the inferential activities during reading. The standards of coherence determine whether an adequate causal explanation exists for a presented event, or whether adequate referential coherence has been preserved. In the case where these standards are not met, readers engage in inferential activity to achieve adequate understanding.

Thus, reaction to inconsistencies depends on the relative value of G and MAL. If G is above MAL, a reader will not find any comprehension problem and reading will proceed smoothly. If G falls below MAL, a reader will notice a difficulty. That would not imply an adequate regulation but rather that there is a possibility of moving to the regulation phase. Hence, the possibility of regulation is jointly determined by the coherence index, G, and by the subject's MAL. There are factors influencing the relative value of G and MAL that might explain some inappropriate regulatory behavior, as discussed in the next section.

FACTORS AFFECTING THE RELATIVE VALUE OF G AND MAL

Many studies in the comprehension monitoring literature have shown that subjects of different ages frequently miss inconsistencies between elements of their own knowledge and between this knowledge and external information (Baker, 1979; Markman, 1977, 1979; Markman & Gorin, 1981; Otero & Campanario, 1990). Consequently, evaluation of coherence in these cases fails to yield a G value lower than MAL. There are several reasons for this failure.

First, a reader may represent inconsistent information in such a way that any inconsistency is suppressed *before* having any awareness of it. For example, Otero and Kintsch (1992) used the construction-integration model (Kintsch, 1988) to show that subjects may suppress a text proposition that is inconsistent with another proposition that is highly activated in memory. This is a process carried out during the integration phase, a phase that settles on the appropriate meaning of the processed portion of text. If one of the contradictory propositions (within the network that is being integrated) is highly activated, it may inhibit the other proposition and thereby cause it to vanish. A reader's computation of coherence of such a representation would be inappropriately high because no inconsistency exists: One of the originally contradictory propositions no longer exists in the text's representation.

Second, memory limitations prevent readers from evaluating the coherence of substantial amounts of information and only of a subset of this information is taken into account (Read & Miller, 1994). Although recourse to long-term working memory (i.e. an extension of short-term memory for activities that correspond to skilled performance in particular domains) may partially compensate for these limitations (Ericsson & Kintsch, 1995; see also chap. 8, this volume), readers frequently miss inconsistencies between elements of knowledge, in particular, those corresponding to everyday knowledge. Everyday knowledge is frequently inconsistent, whereas scientific knowledge allegedly is highly consistent (Reif & Larkin, 1991). For example, some Spanish students believe that the earth is closer to the sun in the summer (De Manuel, 1995). They have never noticed the inconsistency of this belief when compared to other knowledge that they probably have, such as *There cannot be summer in two hemispheres at the same time.* The two inconsistent beliefs have never been brought together in working memory at the same time.

Third, the use of different standards to monitor comprehension (Baker, 1985b) may result in values for G that are not below MAL, even for texts that a proficient reader would find unintelligible. For example, young readers are sensitive to disruptions in local coherence caused by lexical problems, but are unaware of violations of global coherence caused by internal inconsistencies (Baker, 1984). Checking for consistency between their own knowledge and information in a text is easier for them than checking for compatibility between text propositions.

In all of these cases, readers are unaware of a coherence problem because of an improper calculation of G and, consequently, would not attempt any regulatory action. An appropriate regulation of comprehension demands (a) an appropriate representation of a text, (b) an evaluation of consistency in a knowledge range that is as wide as possible, and (c) an adequate use of comprehension-monitoring standards. These conditions are not always accomplished, so G is not calculated adequately.

Inappropriate regulatory behavior may be explained also by factors affecting MAL. When MAL is set very low, even poor values of G (i.e., a low computed coherence) would not result in awareness of a comprehension problem.

MAL is a parameter that presumably depends on individual, textual, and contextual variables. For example, MAL is probably affected by variables such as authoritarianism or dogmatism (Miller & Rokeach, 1968), and by personal characteristics like *need for cognition* (Cacioppo & Petty, 1982), the tendency of individuals to engage in and enjoy thinking and understanding. Kardash and Scholes (1996), for example, found a positive relation between need for cognition and drawing accurate, unbiased conclusions from inconclusive, mixed information about the HIV–AIDS relationship. The regulation processes taking place to reconcile inconsistent information seem to be influenced by this personal variable.

MAL may also be related to other textual and contextual variables that have been shown to influence perceived coherence. These variables include expectations about the discourse itself (Roberts, Kreuz, Gilbert, & Bainbridge, 1994), school or subject matter setting (García-Arista, Campanario, & Otero, 1997), or epistemic authority of the information source (Cuerva & Otero, 1996.) For example, a study by Gorman (1986) suggests that MAL decreases in a situation where incoming information is known to have poor quality. In that study, subjects had to discover the rule manifested in a collection of cards, like *Odd and even cards alternate*. Gorman found that errors in incoming data seem to immunize subjects' hypotheses against disconfirmation. When subjects notice unreliability in the incoming information, they are more easily satisfied with the adopted rule even when it contradicts data; that is, they care less for an inconsistent relation between the rule and data. This may be interpreted as a consequence of setting their demand for coherence at a low level; this is captured in the MAL parameter.

To summarize, a value of G representing the coherence of a text's representation is calculated and is subsequently compared to a MAL. G remains above MAL in normal, nonproblematic reading. However, G may be above MAL also in situations where proficient readers are likely to notice comprehension problems. This may be caused by a poor calculation of G, or by an inappropriately low value of MAL. In these cases the difficulty would likely remain unnoticed.

When G is below MAL a reader notices a difficulty and enters the regulation phase. There are two possible paths to follow from there on, which depend on readers' assessment of their capability to make inferences that could increase G. The default situation is a proficient reader who attempts to comprehend an easy text, as in most narratives. The reader notices a problem for the first time, and will probably generate a positive answer. That is, the reader thinks that it is possible to make inferences that solve the comprehension problem. Some models of text comprehension assume that a reader will do that when difficulties are found because of an *effort after meaning* (Graesser, Singer, & Trabasso, 1994). A reader will look for causal relations, for example, that will link events initially perceived as unrelated. When readers believe they can generate inferences that will repair an identified comprehension problem, there will be an attempt to increase G above MAL. This possibility is addressed next. Then I turn to an alternative situation: readers who think that they can not generate inferences that may increase G above MAL.

COHERENCE FALLS BELOW THE MINIMUM ACCEPTANCE LEVEL AND REPAIR INFERENCES ARE POSSIBLE

After having detected a comprehension problem, that is, G below MAL, a reader may think that it is possible to generate inferences that increase G above MAL. An example from a protocol in research conducted by Collins, Brown, and Larkin (1980) illustrates this. The experimental situation included reading the following text: *He plunked down $5 at the window. She tried to give him $2.50, but he refused to take it. So when they got inside she bought him a large bag of popcorn.* A subject initially interpreted the text as referring to someone who was betting at the racetrack. The subject finds an inconsistency between this interpretation and the sentence *She tried to give him $2.50, but he refused to take it.* Thus, an attempt is made to increase the coherence of the representation by making inferences that would solve the inconsistency: *I was trying to integrate that* [She tried to give him $2.50] *into the racetrack hypothesis. And in order to do that I had to believe that the $2.50 was his change and that he refused because it was the incorrect amount, but I was suspicious at that point, because that seemed a little strange; that didn't quite fit in* (p. 389). The reader tries to increase the coherence of the representation but after having recalculated G, the reader finds that it has not increased above MAL. This subject achieves coherence above MAL only after reading the next sentence *So when they got inside....* This reader notices that *she* in the difficult sentence is not the same person who received the money, but a date who wanted to share expenses at a box office. The new anaphoric inference does raise G above MAL for this reader, who judges the regulatory attempt as successful: *... But then I had to reinterpret where the $2.50 had been coming from and it all made sense; it came from his date ...* (p. 389). This process of repair by means of inference generation has been widely studied. Some of this work is described next.

Repair by Means of Correct Inferences

Many authors have analyzed the inferencing activity of subjects who attempt to restore coherence after having detected problems in their representations of external information. One of the first researchers was Abelson (1959, 1968a), who proposed several ways in which subjects may resolve inconsistencies in their belief systems. The first one, known as *denial*, involves ignoring one of the conflicting elements. In *bolstering*, one of the conflicting elements is supported by activation sent from other elements that are introduced. In *differentiation*, one of the elements is differentiated so that one of the parts of the element is no longer inconsistent. *Trascendence* consists of introducing a concept superordinated to the conflicting elements that would resolve the inconsistency. Finally *rationalization* involves introducing elements in the dissonant structure so that an explanation for the dissonant events is obtained (e.g., explaining a bad action in terms of a good goal). In agreement with the underlying constraint satisfaction process, the resolution mode violating the lesser constraints (i.e., the resolution mode involving change of the most vulnerable cognitive element) will be most preferred, whereas the mode that involves "changing the most resistant element [is] the least preferred" (Abelson, 1968b, p. 719).

Mosenthal (1979) studied strategies used by children to resolve internally inconsistent information contained in a story. Five possible strategies were distinguished in this study: to eliminate old or new inconsistent information, to change one piece of information so that it fits the other, to overlook the fact that the old and the new information are related, to explain old–new anomalies in terms of exceptions, and to restructure both old and new information to make them compatible. The preferred strategies for both third-grade and sixth-grade children were, first, to eliminate one of the incompatible statements and, second, to restructure one of the statements by changing the predicate in the corresponding proposition. The least preferred strategy for subjects at both levels was to restructure both inconsistent statements.

Zabrucky (1986) studied recall of new (presented last) and old (presented first) conflicting information for different retention intervals, and the strategies used by readers to maintain factual coherence in this information. When college students read with an integrative goal, old information was recalled less often when it was consistent with new information than when it was inconsistent. The poorer memory of old information was interpreted as a result of strategies of *elimination* (suppression of inconsistent information) and *restructuring* (alteration of part of the inconsistent information to restore consistency). The number of eliminations was much higher than the number of restructurings.

Lightfoot and Bullock (1990) gave a detailed account of regulatory actions, but not in the area of text comprehension. Their study investigated how subjects of different ages made sense of verbal–facial contradictory communications. Subjects tried to regulate their comprehension by operating on the conditions needed for two propositions to stand as contradictory:

1. The two propositions should be mutually exclusive.
2. The two propositions should have the same referent.
3. The two propositions should refer jointly and simultaneously to the referent. (p. 831)

Lightfoot and Bullock classified resolutions that modify the previous three conditions as (a) *content transformations* when the mutual exclusive meanings are negated, (b) *reference transformations* when same referent is negated, and (c) *relational transformations* when the simultaneity of the two propositions is negated. Adults and older children (6th grade) tend to resolve contradictions by relational transformations in the cases where a context was provided for the contradictory communication. Younger children (preschool and 2nd grade) tend to use referential transformations. In the cases where no context was provided, most of the repairs in all age groups involved reference transformations.

There are studies that investigate how subjects generate repair inferences when handling conflicting relations between theory and data. Kuhn, Amsel, and O'Loughlin (1988; see also Kuhn, 1989) studied responses of 6th graders, 9th graders, average adults, and philosophy graduates to theory-discrepant information. Subjects were asked to judge the covariation or noncovariation of information provided on food and susceptibility to colds of a hypothetical group of students. Subjects' theories on this topic were assessed first and they were then asked to evaluate evidence that was sometimes consonant and sometimes inconsistent with their theories. A regulatory action used by 59% of the average adults and similar percentages of the younger subjects was to disregard the evidence provided when it conflicted with their *own* theories on the relation of foods and susceptibility to colds, instead of criticizing the theory provided. For example, when presented a pattern of noncovariation between kind of relish and susceptibility to colds, a ninth-grade student maintained her own theory on the causal influence of mustard: "Yes [it makes a difference]. Mostly likely all the time you get a cold with the mustard. Like there you did [instance 2] and there you did [instance 7]" (Kuhn, 1989, p. 677) She ignored the equal number of cases where mustard was eaten and there were no colds.

In a review study dealing also with the relation of theory and data, Chinn and Brewer (1993) examined the role of anomalous data in knowledge acquisition by analyzing cases from the history of science and results from psychology and education. They proposed a set of possible psychological responses to mismatches between data and theories: (a) to ignore the data, (b) to reject the data, (c) to exclude the data from the domain of the theory, (d) to hold the data in abeyance, (e) to reinterpret the data retaining the theory, (f) to reinterpret the data and make peripheral changes in the theory, and (g) to accept the data and change one theory, possibly by choosing another one.

Researchers interested in the modification of situation models have also explored methods of repairing inconsistencies. Wilkes and Leatherbarrow (1988) presented subjects with a text that included a message at the end that contradicted another statement provided at the beginning. When questioned, the subjects were unable to refrain from making inferences on the basis of the discredited message, even after having noticed the presence of the second contradictory message. Wilkes and Leatherbarrow suggested that the contradiction is stored at the textbase level but it is not incorporated at the situation model level (see Tapiero & Otero, 1999, for a similar interpretation). Johnson and Seifert (1994) reported that "people rarely generate alternative interpretations spontaneously when a correction negates prior information .... If a correction would seriously disrupt [a causal chain], then the need to maintain coherence may override the correction instruction" (p. 1421). These results point toward a conservative stance of readers when they face inconsistencies: No repair inferences are generated when new information contradicts information introduced earlier. However discrepant results have been found in other studies when scientific texts were used (Tapiero & Otero, 1999; see also chap. 13, this volume).

Campanario and Otero (1997) classified the regulatory inferences made by the students who participated in the experiment on comprehension monitoring mentioned earlier (Otero & Campanario, 1990). In that experiment 10th and 12th grade students read paragraphs, about 90 words long, that contained contradictory excerpts such as *Superconductivity consists in the vanishing of electric resistance. Until now it had only been obtained by cooling certain materials to low temperatures near absolute zero ... Until now superconductivity had been obtained by considerably increasing the temperature of certain materials.* Subjects were instructed to read the text and to point out in writing any difficulty that might have arisen and to underline the problematic sentences or words. After recalling the text, they were informed of the contradiction and were asked what had they done about it. Repairs were identified in the written recall and in explanations given to an interviewer. These repairs were classified according to the elements of the propositional schemata (Van Dijk & Kintsch, 1983) that were modified in one or both of the contradictory propositions . There can be transformations of the predicate, arguments, or circumstances of the two contradictory propositions: OB-TAIN[SUPERCONDUCTIVITY, COOL[MATERIALS, TEMPERA-TURE]] and OBTAIN[SUPERCONDUCTIVITY, INCREASE [MATERIALS, TEMPERATURE]]:

> 1. *Predicate transformation.* One of the contradictory predicates is transformed to agree with the other. This transformation could consist of suppressing the modifier of the predicate, as in *I thought that it could be done in both ways* [lowering and increasing temperature] (Student 056). The modifier (*ONLY*) of the predicate of the first contradictory proposition (*OBTAIN[SUPER, COOL[MATERIALS, TEMPERATURE]]*) is disregarded.

2. *Argument transformation*. Arguments in one or both main propositions or subordinated propositions are eliminated or changed. For example, consider the excerpt taken from a student's written recall: *Until now it* [superconductivity] *has only been achieved at very low temperature …There are materials which are also superconductors at high temperature* (Student 031).

The predicate *INCREASE* is assumed to operate on an argument having a different referent (different *MATERIALS*) than the first.

3. *Circumstance transformation*. Time or place is modified in one or both of the propositions. An example of time transformation is *Until now it* [superconductivity] *could be achieved only by lowering temperature to absolute zero. It is now achieved by increasing the temperature of materials* (Student 081). The time circumstance of the predicate *OBTAIN* in the second contradictory proposition is changed from *UNTIL NOW* to *NOW*.

Campanario and Otero (1997) found that change of circumstance was the preferred mode of repair because they accounted for 61.8 % of repairs for 16- and 18-year-old subjects who detected the contradiction. This result is in agreement with the Lightfoot and Bullock's (1990) results. The least preferred repair was a change of predicate (11.8 %), with a change of referent falling in between the two (20.6 %). *Vary in inference*

In summary, readers' inferences in response to inconsistencies are variable and it is difficult to identify clear patterns in these responses. A reason for this may be the inadequacy of the categories that are used in these studies to analyze readers' modification of their initial representation. A more productive approach may be found by examining the processes underlying repair by inference generation. It consists in an attempt to move from a situation of less coherence to another of higher perceived coherence. Different propositions enter in a constraint satisfaction process intended to achieve maximum consistency among elements in a reader's representation. Readers modify an information element on the basis of its individual activation and the influence of the others to which it is connected. These inhibitory or strengthening effects are recognized in studies on the way readers handle text inconsistencies, such as those of Otero and Kintsch (1992) and in the experiments presented by van Oostendorp (chap. 13) in this book.

Repair by Means of Incorrect Inferences

In some of the instances explained earlier, as in the example of Collins et al. (1980), readers who notice a problem are able to take G above MAL by making appropriate inferences. However, there are cases where readers "fix up" comprehension problems by making inappropriate inferences, as judged by experts' standards. For example, in most of the situations considered within the contradiction paradigm, no inference increases the coherence level above that which would be normally considered acceptable. It is difficult to generate an acceptable inference that may explain an explicit contradiction. However, even in that case, subjects generate inappropriate inferences that, in their view, raise coherence to acceptable levels. This outcome can be explained by a low MAL. This is illustrated by some of the results of the previously discussed Otero and Campanario (1990) experiment. One of the texts read by the students in this experiment was the following:

> Neutrinos are particles with nearly zero mass. Their detection is very difficult because they do not react to magnetic or nuclear forces. In order to detect them a great amount of water is necessary, placed in a deep place underground, where it could be free from other radiations. A great amount of water is necessary because neutrinos seldom interact with matter. Several countries have set up neutrino detectors which will be useful in the future. The great facility with which neutrinos are detected makes them very suitable, for example, for the study of cosmic phenomena.

One of the students who noticed the contradiction but did not point it out explained his final interpretation:

> Interviewer: ... you realized that the sentences were contradictory but you did not underline them, why?

> Student C006: It says basically the same [as in the previous Superconductivity text], I mean, that it was difficult before and then they discovered, in some countries, this equipment to detect those tiny values ... neutrinos were detected at great depths ... and I understood that it was easy to detect them at great depths.

The student seemed to be satisfied with the coherence level obtained after making the inappropriate inference *Neutrinos are easily detected at great depths.* Thus taking G above MAL is achieved through appropriate inferences, whenever it is possible, but also through inappropriate ones for those subjects whose MAL is set relatively low. These individuals do not require much to raise G above MAL.

To summarize, after having noticed that G is below MAL, a reader may decide that it is possible to make inferences that would increase G. Appropriate or inappropriate inferences may be generated to raise the coherence level of the new representation (text information + inferences) above the threshold. This will be the newly accepted representation. However the value of G for this final representation may or may not reach required external standards of coherence. The first case corresponds to adequate regulation, that is, a situation where an initial inconsistency is adequately repaired, as in the example provided by Collins et al. (1980). In other instances, as in the neutrinos example, G does not meet external standards of coherence. In this case, regulation is inappropriate because the inconsistency has been incorrectly fixed up.

COHERENCE FALLS BELOW THE MINIMUM ACCEPTANCE LEVEL AND REPAIR INFERENCES ARE IMPOSSIBLE

There are cases in which attempts to increase G above the exigency threshold by making inferences may fail. This is the case of many good readers who find an explicit contradiction in a text, similar to the one previously shown. In this scenario, readers may decide that they are unable to generate inferences that would increase G above MAL, and consequently they will likely stop trying to repair the text representation in this way. Thus, the model includes as the next step taken by these readers, a decision on whether *anybody* could generate an inference that would increase G above MAL. Both the general and specific reader's knowledge may influence this decision. Low-knowledge readers may feel that they are unable to create a coherent representation of inconsistent information, but they do not reject the possibility that someone, more knowledgeable, could achieve it. This reaction is recognized in responses given by subjects who detected the contradiction in the Otero and Campanario (1990) experiment but did not point it out. They did this in spite of the fact that instructions to underline any comprehension problem were clearly posted:

> Interviewer: … *You realized that there were two strange sentences…why didn't you underline them?*
>
> Student 2036: … *when I was reading it I understood it perfectly, but these two sentences seemed strange because one contradicts the other, but I say, since I do not know anything about the subject maybe it is like that … and since I did not understand anything about the subject, so, that is why I did not underline them.*

In another study (Otero, 1987) one student read a text about the speed of light containing the following sentences *The speed of light is the greatest that can ever be achieved …. There exist detailed observations of the behavior of some objects when they surpass the speed of light.* This particular student noticed the problem but she did not point it out, although she had been instructed to do so. Her explanation was *I thought that it was something scientifically established and that there were no errors.*

In the described cases, readers are aware of poor comprehension but it is conceptualized as a *subjective* problem and not as an inconsistency in external information. It is attributed to limitations in one's own comprehension capability because of poor knowledge or other reasons. This would probably be associated with the *deference epistemic stance* described by Phillips and Norris (1999). In their study on reading popular scientific reports, some readers adopted a stance where text information overwhelms readers' beliefs without any attempt to reconcile the two. The situation when students read textbooks may be worse, as textbooks are regarded as sources of knowledge endowed with weighty authority in the classroom (Luke, De Castell, & Luke, 1983).

However, having adequate knowledge may allow subjects to decide that, in addition to being incapable of creating a coherent representation of a text by themselves, there are no conceivable inferences that could be made to solve the problem. This would be the appropriate regulatory behavior in the experimental situations used within the contradiction paradigm. It is difficult to find inferences that could increase the coherence of contradictory statements like those used in the Otero and Campanario (1990) experiment. If a subject decides that it is impossible to increase G above MAL, the inconsistency would be conceptualized as an objective problem that can be explained only in pragmatic terms: A typographical mistake was committed, or the writer had a different purpose in mind, other than communicating true information, violating the quality maxim of the cooperative principle (Grice, 1975). An apparently paradoxical conclusion follows: readers need knowledge to decide that something cannot be understood and to decide that there is an objective problem attributable to the author. This may be one of the reasons behind Miyake and Norman's (1979) finding about knowledge and question asking: "To ask a question, knowing too little is just as disadvantageous as knowing too much" (p. 364).

The effects of instructions and prompting on the detection and reporting of difficulties in texts may be also explained in these terms. Subjects who are warned about the existence of inconsistencies in a text detect more of these inconsistencies than do subjects who are not (Baker, 1985a). In addition to inducing a deeper processing level, these instructions may help readers to decide that the identified inconsistency may not be explained by anyone generating inferences. As such it should be an objective problem. Results like the ones reported by Karabenick (1996) are also consistent with this explanation. He found that students' judgments of comprehension depended on the questions made by colearners: The more questions made by colearners the more a student would externalize his or her confusion. Colearners' questioning enabled students to attribute the source of colearner confusion to the stimulus material that they were attempting to comprehend. In other words, they treated it as an objective problem and not one attributable to themselves.

Is the difficulty internal or external to the learner?

EVALUATION AND REGULATION
OF COMPREHENSION OVERLAP

One consequence of the preceding analysis is that evaluation of comprehension cannot be separated from regulation of comprehension. Evaluation of comprehension (i.e. noticing a comprehension problem) involves having attempted to seek a solution (i.e., having attempted regulation) and deciding that one cannot find this solution. Consider the following sentences:

1. This milk was inside the refrigerator. The milk's temperature is 5°C.
2. This milk was inside the refrigerator. The milk's temperature is 60°C
3. This milk was inside the refrigerator. The milk's temperature is 200°C

Sentence 1 should not present any comprehension problem to a reader who is familiar with refrigerators. Inferences could be easily made that establish factual coherence by causally linking propositions corresponding to both sentences. That is, *Two bodies initially at different temperature that are put in contact eventually equate their temperatures, given enough time; Given enough time, the milk acquires the temperature of the refrigerator; The temperature of the refrigerator was 5°C or below.* Does Sentence 2 represent a comprehension problem? What would be the outcome of the evaluation phase of text comprehension in this case? Finding milk at 60°C inside a refrigerator is not what one would normally expect. The inconsistency is easily solved by some additional inferencing, for example, *Someone recently put the milk inside the refrigerator after having heated it.* Should we say that evaluation of comprehension is negative in this case, and that the comprehension problem is solved by regulation activity? If yes, something similar should be said for Sentence 1, because inferences also need to be made there to establish factual coherence between both propositions. This would imply that failures in evaluation would be ubiquitous in normal reading, and this is not a sensible situation. Finally, Sentence 3 constitutes a comprehension problem in normal situations. This does not mean that evaluation is negative without further attempt of regulation. A more parsimonious interpretation, supported by the observation of increased reading times in subjects faced with this class of difficulties (Baker & Anderson, 1982; O'Brien & Myers, 1985), would be that readers try to make deliberate inferences, as in Sentence 2, that would solve the problem. However, this attempt fails because creating a satisfactory situation model is difficult under such circumstances (an unusually high pressure on the milk would need to be supposed). The reader presumably reverts to explanations at the pragmatic level that could solve the inconsistency, as previously mentioned. For example, readers might assume that there is a typographical error.

According to the aforementioned reasoning, *noticing* a problem results from the existence of an initial negative assessment of coherence, that is G below MAL, *together with* an unsuccessful regulatory attempt, as shown in Fig. 12.1. This suggests that the apparently clear distinction between evaluation and regulation of comprehension, often shown in the comprehension-monitoring literature (Baker, 1985b; Otero, 1996; Zabrucky & Ratner, 1986, 1989, 1992), should be qualified. An evaluation of comprehension is *not* completely independent of the regulation of comprehension.

CONCLUSION

Collins et al. (1980) pointed out that "we do not typically teach children what to do when they cannot comprehend a text" (p. 404). This can be applied to science texts also. Adequate regulation is important when there is scientific information that cannot be comprehended because it is inconsistent with learners' knowledge. This is a frequent situation in science education. The model presented in this chapter suggests some ways that may improve regulation in this condition.

First, teaching readers to appropriately assess the coherence of text representations is expected to have a positive effect on the preliminary stage in the regulation process, that of detecting a difficulty. That involves being able to use all relevant comprehension-monitoring standards that relate both to local and global coherence of a text representation (Baker, 1985b).

Second, good regulation depends on maintaining an appropriate MAL. Suggesting ways to modify this parameter is not an easy task because some of the variables influencing MAL may be related to personality or permanent traits of the reader. However, one may speculate that a history of authoritarian teaching may have a negative effect on readers' acceptance levels. Science teaching has been frequently criticized as dogmatic (Brunkhorst, 1992;

Yager & Yager, 1985) leading students to take on faith, and by rote, scientific results that could have been learned meaningfully. This suggests a possible negative influence on acceptance levels: students may learn that not much coherence should be expected in representations of scientific texts. Thus, teaching scientific content that surpasses the understanding capabilities of students (because of lack of necessary prior knowledge or comprehension skills of students, e.g.) is not only useless, but it is actually detrimental to their metacognitive abilities. It may lower acceptance levels of students and affect all their subsequent regulation behavior. ✓

Third, adequate regulation depends on making every comprehension problem objective and not discounting it because of one's own limitations. It means that a difficulty has to be explicitly stated as a problem by the learner in the cases where he or she does not have available knowledge to generate repair inferences. For this, a social environment where showing ignorance is encouraged appears as a key supporting factor. Use of the so-called "choice procedure" (Acredolo & O'Connor, 1991), implying that all school questions have an answer, has probably taught students that showing uncertainty and ignorance is punishable. Improving students' regulation skills depends on raising their awareness of uncertainty as it has already been attempted in some science teacher education studies (Rowell & Pollard, 1995) or in approaches like *questioning the author* (Beck, McKeown, Hamilton, & Kucan, 1997). This last approach attempts to get readers to engage with texts by encouraging a change of attitude toward the status of these texts. An attempt is made to depose the authority of a text by letting students know that texts are just someone's ideas written down.

In summary, the complexity of the regulation process outlined in this chapter shows that reacting to comprehension difficulties is not a trivial task. Consequently, an educationally relevant recommendation for educational systems may be to teach students how *not to know* in addition to the traditional and accepted aim of teaching how to know. *Raise student awareness of uncertainty*

ACKNOWLEDGMENTS

This research was supported by Grant PB98-0711, of the Ministry of Education, Spain. Thanks are due to Juan Miguel Campanario for valuable help in gathering some of the data used in the chapter. I am also grateful to Jerry Keller, of the Universidad de Alcalá, for the linguistic revision of the manuscript.

Preparation of this chapter was also supported by a Travel Grant from the Spanish Ministry of Education to visit the Department of Psychology at the

University of Memphis from May 2000 to July 2000. I would like to thank Art and Nancy Graesser for their warm hospitality during this visit.

REFERENCES

Abelson, R. P. (1959). Modes of resolution of belief dilemmas. *Journal of Conflict Resolution, 3*, 343–352.

Abelson, R. P. (1968a). Psychological implication. In R. P. Abelson, E. Aronson, E. J. McGuire, T. M. Newcomb, M. J. Rosenberg, & P. H. Tannenbaum (Eds.), *Theories of cognitive consistency: A sourcebook* (pp. 112–139). Chicago: Rand McNally.

Abelson, R. P. (1968b). A summary of hypotheses on modes of resolution. In R. P. Abelson, E. Aronson, E. J. McGuire, T. M. Newcomb, M. J. Rosenberg, & P. H. Tannenbaum (Eds.), *Theories of cognitive consistency: A sourcebook* (pp. 716–720). Chicago: Rand McNally.

Acredolo, C., & O'Connor, J. (1991). On the difficulty of detecting cognitive uncertainty. *Human Development, 34*, 204–223.

Adams, J. S. (1968). A framework for the study of modes of resolving inconsistency. In R. P. Abelson, E. Aronson, E. J. McGuire, T. M. Newcomb, M. J. Rosenberg, & P. H. Tannenbaum (Eds.), *Theories of cognitive consistency: A sourcebook* (pp. 655–660). Chicago: Rand McNally.

Aronson, E. (1968). Dissonance theory: progress and problems. In R. P. Abelson, E. Aronson, E. J. McGuire, T. M. Newcomb, M. J. Rosenberg, & P. H. Tannenbaum (Eds.), *Theories of cognitive consistency: A sourcebook* (pp. 5–27). Chicago: Rand McNally.

Baker, L. (1979). Comprehension monitoring: Identifying and coping with text confusions. *Journal of Reading Behavior, 11*, 363–374.

Baker, L. (1984). Spontaneous versus instructed use of multiple standards for evaluating comprehension: Effects of age, reading proficiency, and type of standard. *Journal of Experimental Child Psychology, 38*, 289–311.

Baker, L. (1985a). Differences in the standards used by college students to evaluate their comprehension of expository prose. *Reading Research Quarterly, 22*, 297–313.

Baker, L. (1985b). How do we know when we don't understand? Standards for evaluating text comprehension. In D. L. Forrest-Pressley, G. E. Mackinnon, & T. G. Waller (Eds.), *Metacognition, cognition and human performance* (pp. 155–205). New York: Academic Press.

Baker, L., & Anderson, R. I. (1982). Effects of inconsistent information on text processing: Evidence for comprehension monitoring. *Reading Research Quarterly, 17*, 281–294.

Beck, I. L., McKeown, M. G., Hamilton, R. L., & Kucan, L. (1997). *Questioning the author: An approach for enhancing student engagement with text*. Newark, DE: International Reading Association.

Britton, B., & Eisenhart, F. J. (1993). Expertise, text coherence and constraint satisfaction: Effects on harmony and settling rate. In *Proceedings of the Fifteenth Annual Conference of the Cognitive Science Society* (pp. 266–271). Hillsdale, NJ: Lawrence Erlbaum Associates.

Brunkhorst, B. J. (1992). A study of student outcomes and teacher characteristics in exemplary middle and junior high science programs. *Journal of Research in Science Teaching*, 29, 571–583.

Burbules, N. C., & Linn, M. C. (1988). Response to contradiction: Scientific reasoning during adolescence. *Journal of Educational Psychology*, 80, 69–75.

Cacioppo, J. T., & Petty, R. E. (1982) The need for cognition. *Journal of Personality and Social Psychology*, 42, 116–131.

Campanario, J. M., & Otero, J. (1997). *Análisis del proceso de regulación de textos con inconsistencias* [Analysis of the regulation process of texts containing inconsistencies]. Unpublished manuscript. Universidad de Alcalá, Madrid, Spain.

Chan, C., Burtis, J., & Bereiter, C. (1997). Knowledge building as a mediator of conflict in conceptual change. *Cognition and Instruction*, 15, 1–40.

Chinn, C., & Brewer, W. (1993). The role of anomalous data in knowledge acquisition: A theoretical framework and implications for science instruction. *Review of Educational Research*, 63, 1–49.

Collins, A., Brown, J. S., & Larkin, K. M. (1980). Inference in text understanding. In R. J. Spiro, B. C. Bruce, & W. F. Brewer (Eds.), *Theoretical issues in reading comprehension* (pp. 385–407). Hillsdale, NJ: Lawrence Erlbaum Associates.

Coté, N., Goldman, S., & Saul, E. U. (1998). Students making sense of informational text: Relations between processing and representation. *Discourse Processes*, 25, 1–53.

Cuerva, J., & Otero, J. (1996, September). *Influence of epistemic authority and knowledge activation on the detection of inconsistencies in science texts*. Paper presented at the International Seminar "Using Complex Information Systems," UCIS'96, Poitiers, France.

Darden, L. (1992). Strategies for anomaly resolution. In R. N. Giere (Ed.), *Cognitive models of science* (pp. 251–273). Minneapolis: The University of Minnesota Press.

De Manuel, J. (1995). Por qué hay veranos e inviernos? Representaciones de estudiantes (12–18) y de futuros maestros sobre algunos aspectos del modelo sol-tierra [Why are there summer and winter? Students' (12–18) and prospective teachers' representations of some aspects of the model sun-earth] . *Enseñanza de las Ciencias*, 13, 227–236.

diSessa, A. (1982). Unlearning Aristotelian physics: A case study of knowledge-based learning. *Cognitive Science*, 6, 37–75.

Ericsson, K., & Kintsch, W. (1995). Long-term working memory. *Psychological Review*, 102, 211–245.

Festinger, L. (1957). *A theory of cognitive dissonance*. Evanston, IL: Row, Peterson.

García-Arista, E., Campanario, J. M., & Otero, J. (1997) Influence of subject matter setting on comprehension monitoring. *European Journal of Psychology of Education*, XXI, 427–441.

Glass, D. C. (1968). Individual differences and the resolution of cognitive inconsistencies. In R. P. Abelson, E. Aronson, E. J. McGuire, T. M. Newcomb, M. J. Rosenberg, & P. H. Tannenbaum (Eds.), *Theories of cognitive consistency: A sourcebook* (pp. 615–623). Chicago: Rand McNally.

Gorman, M. E. (1986). How the possibility of error affects falsification on a task that models scientific problem solving. *British Journal of Psychology*, 77, 85–96.

Graesser, A. C., Millis, K. K., & Zwaan, R. A. (1997). Discourse comprehension. *Annual Review of Psychology, 48,* 163–189.

Graesser, A. C., Person, N. K., & Huber, J. D. (1992). Mechanisms that generate questions. In T. Lauer, E. Peacock, & A. C. Graesser (Eds.), *Questions and information systems* (pp. 167–187). Hillsdale, NJ: Lawrence Erlbaum Associates.

Graeser, A. C., Singer, M., & Trabasso, T. (1994). Constructing inferences during narrative text comprehension. *Psychological Review, 3,* 371–395.

Grice, H. P. (1975). Logic and conversation. In P. Cole & J. Morgan (Eds.), *Syntax and semantics 3: Speech acts* (pp. 41–58). New York: Academic Press.

Hardyck, J. A., & Kardush, M. (1968). A modest modish model for dissonance reduction. In R. P. Abelson, E. Aronson, E. J. McGuire, T. M. Newcomb, M. J. Rosenberg, & P. H. Tannenbaum (Eds.), *Theories of cognitive consistency: A sourcebook* (pp. 684–692). Chicago: Rand McNally.

Hopfield, J. J. (1982). Neural networks and physical systems with emergent collective computational abilities. *Proceedings of the National Academy of Sciences, USA, 79,* 2554–2558. Reprinted in J. A. Anderson & E. Rosenfeld (Eds.), *Neurocomputing. Foundations of research* (pp. 460–464). Cambridge, MA: MIT Press.

Johnson, H. M., & Seifert, C. M. (1994). Sources of continued influence effect: When misinformation in memory affects later inferences. *Journal of Experimental Psychology: Learning, Memory, and Cognition, 20,* 1420–1436.

Johnson, H. M., & Seifert, C. M. (1999). Modifying mental representations: Comprehending corrections. In H. van Oostendorp & S. Goldman (Eds.), *The construction of mental representations during reading* (pp. 303–318). Mahwah, NJ: Lawrence Erlbaum Associates.

Just, M. A., & Carpenter, P. A. (1987). *The psychology of reading and language comprehension.* Boston: Allyn & Bacon.

Karabenick, S. A. (1996). Social influences on metacognition: Effects of colearner questioning on comprehension monitoring. *Journal of Educational Psychology, 88,* 689–703.

Kardash, C. M., & Scholes, R. J. (1996). Effects of preexisting beliefs, epistemological beliefs and need for cognition on interpretation of controversial issues. *Journal of Educational Psychology, 88,* 260–271.

Kelman, H. C., & Baron, R. M. (1968). Determinants of modes of resolving inconsistency dilemmas: A functional analysis. In R. P. Abelson, E. Aronson, E. J. McGuire, T. M. Newcomb, M. J. Rosenberg, & P. H. Tannenbaum (Eds.), *Theories of cognitive consistency: A sourcebook* (pp. 670–683). Chicago: Rand McNally.

Kintsch, W. (1988). The construction-integration model of text comprehension. *Psychological Review, 95,* 163–182.

Kintsch, W. (1998). *Comprehension: A paradigm for cognition.* Cambridge, England: Cambridge University Press.

Kuhn, D. (1989). Children and adults as intuitive scientists. *Psychological Review, 96,* 674–689.

Kuhn, D., Amsel, E., & O'Loughlin, M. (1988). *The development of scientific thinking skills.* Orlando, FL: Academic Press.

Lepper, M. (1996). Cognitive dissonance reduction as constraint satisfaction. *Psychological Review, 103,* 219–240.

Lightfoot, C., Bullock, M. (1990). Interpreting contradictory communications: Age and context effects. *Developmental Psychology, 26*, 830–836.

Luke, C., DeCastell, S., & Luke, A. (1983). Beyond criticism: The authority of the school text. *Curriculum Inquiry, 13*, 111–127.

Markman, E. M. (1977). Realizing that you don't understand: A preliminary investigation. *Child Development, 46*, 986–992.

Markman, E. M. (1979). Realizing that you don't understand: Elementary school children's awareness of inconsistencies. *Child Development, 50*, 643–655.

Markman, E. M., & Gorin, L. (1981). Children's ability to adjust their standards for evaluating comprehension. *Journal of Educational Psychology, 73*, 320–325.

McClelland, J. L., & Rumelhart, D. E. (1988). *Explorations in parallel distributed processing. A handbook of models, programs and exercises.* Cambridge, MA: MIT Press.

Miller, G. R., & Rokeach, M. (1968). Individual differences and tolerance for inconsistency. In R. P. Abelson, E. Aronson, E. J. McGuire, T. M. Newcomb, M. J. Rosenberg, & P. H. Tannenbaum (Eds.), *Theories of cognitive consistency: A sourcebook* (pp. 624–632). Chicago: Rand McNally.

Miyake, N., & Norman, D. A. (1979). To ask a question one must know enough to know what is not known. *Journal of Verbal Learning and Verbal Behavior, 18*, 357–364.

Mosenthal, P. (1979). Children's strategy preferences for resolving contradictory story information under two social conditions. *Journal of Experimental Child Psychology, 28*, 323–343.

O'Brien, E., & Myers, J. L. (1985). When comprehension difficulty improves memory for text. *Journal of Experimental Psychology: Learning Memory, and Cognition, 11*, 12–21.

Otero, J. (1987). Comprehension monitoring in learning from scientific text. In J. D. Novak (Ed.), *Proceedings of the Second International Seminar on Misconceptions and Educational Strategies in Science and Mathematics* (pp. 370–375). Ithaca, NY: Cornell University Press.

Otero, J. (1996). Components of comprehension monitoring in the acquisition of knowledge from science texts. In K. M. Fisher & M. R. Kibby (Eds.), *Knowledge acquisition organization and use in biology* (pp. 36–43). Berlin: NATO-Springer Verlag.

Otero, J. (1998). Influence of knowledge activation and context on comprehension monitoring of science texts. In D. Hacker, J. Dunlosky, & A. Graesser (Eds.), *Metacognition in educational theory and practice* (pp. 145–164). Mahwah, NJ: Lawrence Erlbaum Associates.

Otero, J., & Campanario, J. M. (1990). Comprehension evaluation and regulation in learning from science texts. *Journal of Research in Science Teaching, 27*, 447–460.

Otero, J., & Kintsch, W. (1992). Failures to detect contradictions in a text: What readers believe vs. what they read. *Psychological Science, 3*, 229–235.

Park, J., & Pak, S. (1997). Students' responses to experimental evidence based on perceptions of causality and availability of evidence. *Journal of Research in Science Teaching, 34*, 57–67.

Peng, K., & Nisbett, R. E. (1999). Culture, dialectics and reasoning about contradiction. *American Psychologist, 54,* 741–754.

Phillips, L., & Norris, S. P. (1999). Interpreting popular reports of science: What happens when the reader's world meets the world on paper? *International Journal of Science Education, 21,* 317–327.

Posner, G. J., Strike, K. A., Hewson, P. W., & Gertzog, W. A. (1982). Accommodation of a scientific conception: Toward a theory of conceptual change. *Science Education, 66,* 211–227.

Read, S. J., & Miller, L. C. (1994). Dissonance and balance in beliefs systems: The promise of parallel constraint satisfaction processes and connectionist modeling approaches. In R. C. Schank & E. Langer (Eds.), *Beliefs, reasoning, and decision making. Psycho-logic in honor of Bob Abelson* (pp. 209–235). Hillsdale, NJ: Lawrence Erlbaum Associates.

Reif, F., & Larkin, J. (1991). Cognition in scientific and everyday domains: Comparison and learning implications. *Journal of Research in Science Teaching, 28,* 733–760.

Roberts, R. M., Kreuz, R. J., Gilbert, D. K., & Bainbridge, E. A. (1994). Discourse expectation and perceived coherence. In H. van Oostendorp & R. Zwaan (Eds.), *Naturalistic text comprehension* (pp. 189–202). Norwood, NJ: Ablex.

Rowell, J. A., & Pollard, J. M. (1995). Raising awareness of uncertainty: A useful addendum to courses in the history and philosophy of science for science teachers? *Science & Education, 4,* 87–97.

Rukavina, I., & Daneman, M. (1996). Integration and its effect on acquiring knowledge about competing scientific theories from text. *Journal of Educational Psychology, 88,* 272–287.

Shultz, T. R., & Lepper, M. R. (1996). Cognitive dissonance reduction as constraint satisfaction. *Psychological Review, 103,* 219–240.

Tapiero, I., & Otero, J. (1999). Distinguishing between textbase and situation model in the processing of inconsistent information: Elaboration versus tagging. In H. van Oostendorp & S. Goldman (Eds.), *The construction of mental representations during reading* (pp. 341–365). Mahwah, NJ: Lawrence Erlbaum Associates.

van den Broek, P., Risden, K., & Husebye-Hartmann, E. (1994). The role of readers' standards for coherence in the generation of inferences during reading. In R. F. Lorch & E. J. O'Brien (Eds.), *Sources of coherence in text comprehension* (pp. 353–373). Hillsdale, NJ: Lawrence Erlbaum Associates.

van der Meij, H. (1988). Constraints on question asking in classrooms. *Journal of Educational Psychology, 80,* 401–405.

van Dijk, T., & Kintsch, W. (1983). *Strategies of discourse comprehension.* New York: Academic Press.

van Oostendorp, H. (1994). Text processing in terms of semantic cohesion monitoring. In H. van Oostendorp & R. Zwaan (Eds.), *Naturalistic text comprehension* (pp. 35–55). Norwood, NJ: Ablex.

van Oostendorp, H., Otero, J., & Campanario, J. M. (in press). Conditions of updating during reading. In M. Louwerse & W. Van Peer (Eds.), *Thematics: Interdisciplinary studies.* Amsterdam: John Benjamins.

Wilkes, A. L., & Leatherbarrow, M. (1988). Editing episodic memory following the identification of error. *The Quarterly Journal of Experimental Psychology, 40A(2),* 361–387.

Yager, S. O., & Yager, R. E. (1985). Changes in perceptions on science for third, seventh and eleventh grade students. *Journal of Research in Science Teaching, 22,* 347–358.

Zabrucky, K. (1986). The role of factual coherence in discourse comprehension. *Discourse Processes, 9,* 197–220.

Zabrucky, K., & Ratner, H. (1986). Children's comprehension monitoring and recall of inconsistent stories. *Child Development, 57,* 1401–1418.

Zabrucky, K., & Ratner, H. H. (1989). Effects of reading ability on children's comprehension evaluation and regulation. *Journal of Reading Behavior, 21,* 69–83.

Zabrucky, K., & Ratner, H. H. (1992). Effects of passage type on comprehension monitoring and recall in good and poor readers. *Journal of Reading Behavior, 24,* 373–391.

❧ 13 ❧

Updating Mental Representations During Reading Scientific Text

Herre van Oostendorp

Utrecht University, Utrecht, The Netherlands

Readers often do not adequately control their comprehension and consequently miss errors when reading texts. Studies in this area have mostly been carried out according to the "error detection paradigm" (Hacker, 1998; Winograd & Johnston, 1982). In this approach, subjects have to read texts containing some kind of error or correction, and the detection of these errors or corrections by subjects indicates that they have activated the corresponding standard of comprehension (Baker, 1985; Garner, 1987).

According to Baker (1985), the control of comprehension is carried out in two stages: *evaluation* and *regulation* of comprehension (see also Otero & Campanario, 1990; chap. 12, this volume). In the first step subjects detect problems of comprehension, such as encountering apparent contradictions between ideas in the text or detecting a contradiction between the text and prior knowledge. In the regulation phase, they try to solve the problem using some strategy, such as rereading the text, trying to find the meaning of an unknown word, making questions (see Graesser, McMahen, & G. S. Johnson, 1994), and so forth.

In this chapter I focus on the regulation phase, particularly on the sort of representation that comprehenders construct of information that has been corrected in the text. For example, one important question is whether the representation is completely reorganized according to the correction. This representational issue has not been adequately addressed by researchers in the mainstream error detection field, probably because they were primarily interested in the error detection task itself, and less in the representational consequences of the regulation strategies that follow after the evaluation phase.

The few studies on regulation of comprehension have demonstrated that the influence of incorrect or discredited information is hard to eradicate from memory by discrediting information (H. M. Johnson & Seifert, 1994, 1999; van Oostendorp & Bonebakker, 1999; Wilkes & Leatherbarrow, 1988; Wilkes & Reynolds, 1999). The memory record is not "updated" or edited effectively after reading discrediting information. Readers continue to make inferences based on the old information that has been corrected in the text and that also mentally should have been corrected. In these studies the texts were mainly narrative texts involving everyday events. An additional purpose of the studies presented here is to examine whether the same problems occur with reading expository text. Also readers of scientific text may frequently find information that does not fit the mental representation or situation model that they have built until that moment (see also van Oostendorp & Elshout-Mohr, 1999).

Van Oostendorp and Bonebakker, for example, presented college students with a story on a fire in a warehouse (see Table 13.1). Subjects in the experimental condition read that "inflammable materials were carelessly stored in a side room." Later in the story they read that "the side room happened to be empty." The control condition read a neutral, irrelevant sentence as "Both police and fire men are involved in the investigation"later they read "The side room happened to be empty. The conclusion was that the influence of old information in the experimental condition (like "inflammable, carelessly stored material in a room") could not be fully neutralized by new, discrediting information (such as "no inflammable, carelessly stored materials"), even though the new source even stated that the previous message had been incorrect. Answers to inference questions such as "What was the cause of the explosions?" or, "For what reason might an insurance claim be refused?" were frequently based on the old information, even by subjects who were aware of the fact that that information was discredited. Readers in the experimental condition more often gave answers such as "because of careless behavior of the owner" than did those in the control condition. Recall and direct questions showed that almost all readers had the corrections available but still did not use these during processing

TABLE 13.1

Example Story: Fire in a Warehouse

Message 1: Jan. 25, 9:00 P.M. Alarm call received from premises of a wholesale warehouse. Premises consist of offices, display room, and storage hall.

Message 2: A serious fire was reported in the storage hall, already out of control and requiring instant response. Fire appliance dispatched at 9:00 P.M.

Message 3: The alarm was raised by the night watchman, who referred to the presence of thick, oily smoke and sheets of flame.

Message 4: Jan. 26, 4:00 A.M. Attending fire officer suggests that the fire was started by a short circuit in the wiring of a side room off the main storage hall. Police now investigating.

Control Condition:
Message 5: 4:30 A.M. Police and firemen are involved in the investigation.

Experimental Condition:
Message 5: 4:30 A.M. Police says that they have reports that lightly inflammable materials including paint and gas cylinders had been carelessly stored in the side room before the fire.

Message 6: Firemen attending the scene report the fire developed an intense heat that made it particularly difficult to bring under control.

Message 7: It has been learned that a number of explosions occurred during the blaze, which endangered firemen in the vicinity, but no casualties resulted from this cause.

Message 8: Two firemen are reported to have been taken to the hospital as a result of breathing toxic fumes that built up in the area in which they were working.

Message 9: The works foreman has disclosed that the storage hall contained bales of paper and a large amount of photocopying equipment.

Experimental Condition:
Message 10: 10.40 A.M. A message received from the police about the progress of the investigation. It stated that the side room had been empty before the fire. The previous message had been incorrect.

Control Condition:
Message 10: 10.40 A.M. A message received from the police about the progress of the investigation. It stated that the side room had been empty before the fire.

Message 11: 10.00 A.M. The owner of the affected premises estimates that total damage will amount to many thousands of pounds, although the premises were insured.

continued on next page

TABLE 13.1   (*continued*)

Message 12: A small fire had been discovered on the same premises, 6 months previously. It had been successfully tackled by the workmen themselves.

Message 13: 11:30 A.M. Attending fire officer reports that the fire is now out and that the storage hall had been completely gutted.

Note. Originally written by the author in Dutch, adapted from Wilkes and Leatherbarrow (1988).

of the text. In these experiments, even the explicit instruction that information might be corrected did not lead to a better updating (see also Otero, 1998). Readers continued to use the misinformation represented in episodic memory, and kept making inferences based on the corrected information even afterwards.

There clearly is evidence that readers tend to use old, discredited information for making inferences. At the same time, however, there are limits within which old information may obstruct the updating of a previously formed mental representation (see also van Oostendorp, 1996, 2001; van Oostendorp, Otero, & Campanario, in press). The goal of four experiments presented in this chapter is to explore the limits within which readers hold on to old information, and fail to take into account the new, correcting information.[1] As mentioned earlier, one difference with previous studies is that in all four experiments expository text with scientific content is used.

EXPERIMENT 1: CLEAR-CUT CONTRADICTIONS

In the first experiment, a very strong manipulation was used in which there was a clear-cut contradiction between old and new information. It was expected that under this condition, in contrast with the conditions used in the studies cited previously, readers update their representation, and consequently use new information to a high degree.

Method

The experimental text we constructed explained a method for increasing the strength of ceramic materials. The text is presented in Table 13.2.

---

[1]These studies were conducted in Spain in cooperation with Dr. J. M. Campanario at the University of Alcala, Madrid. His contribution to these studies is greatly acknowledged.

The old scenario (in sentence 8) stated that the process takes *some days*, whereas the new scenario referred to the idea that the process can be carried out in a *few minutes* (in Sentences 15 and 16). Sentences placed between the two contradictory ones were compatible with both scenarios and provided opportunities to check the interpretation of the text by the readers. For instance, corresponding to Sentence 13 ("reaction speed can be measured by an external device"), an inference question after reading the text was presented: "The text mentions an external device to record reaction times. What time units should this device use to control the process of hardening ceramic materials?" Inference questions like this one can tap one or the other interpretation concerning the time needed for the process. If readers finally believe that the process takes some days, they will mention time units like hours or days, indicating that they base their answer on old information. However, when they generate answers as seconds or minutes, their answer is more probably based on new information. The research question is thus whether the final interpretation of the intervening events is influenced by the old information or rather by the new information.

Subjects were 93 first-year students, mostly from medical and chemical sciences. There were four conditions in our experiment: The first condition was the condition old & new, and the second condition was old & new+. These two conditions received the same text, but subjects in the old & new+ condition were warned beforehand that information in the text could be subsequently corrected. The text they read was the one described earlier. The third condition, only-new condition, was a control condition. In this condition, there was no old information, and instead an irrelevant sentence (8) was presented (see Table 13.2); only new information was provided at the end of the text (Sentences 15 and 16). This condition provided some base rate of old and an upper limit of new information. The fourth condition, only-old condition, was also a control condition; the OLD information was given in Sentence 8 but there was no new information correcting it; instead, irrelevant Sentences 15 and 16 were inserted. This condition is intended to check whether old information was available to students when answering inference questions as well as to have an upper limit of the use of old information by students when this information was not contradicted.

The text was presented as a booklet, each page containing two sentences. Students were told that they should not go back to reread previous pages of the booklet. They were also told that they would receive some questions to answer. After reading the text at their own pace, subjects returned the text and were given the inference questions.

TABLE 13.2

Text on Strengthening Ceramic Materials, used in Experiment 1

1. It is very difficult to increase the hardness of some new ceramic materials

2. For this reason, there are many problems using these materials to make special containers.

3. These containers are useful to store small amounts of radioactive substances because ceramic materials prevent radiation from escaping.

4. Thus, it could solve the problem of storing radioactive materials in hospitals and research centers that use such substances in their daily work.

5. So, it is important to obtain ceramic materials strong enough to be used as containers.

6. The reason for the lack of hardness of ceramic materials is that molecular bonds in such materials are very soft.

7. It is well known that the hardness of some substances increases if silicon atoms are put in a third of the molecular bonds in such substances.

OLD sentence

8. In order for Silicon to act on a third of the molecular bonds in ceramic materials, it is necessary for the treatment to take **some days**.

IRRELEVANT sentence

8. This is one of the methods that is being studied to increase the strength of the chemical bonds.

9. Silicon reacts chemically with the ceramic materials and it opens some chemical bonds in such materials.

10. Silicon atoms join to molecular bonds that are open, and they build new bonds.

11. These new silicon bonds increase the hardness of ceramic material.

12. In order for the method to work, reaction speed has to be constant.

13. Such speed can be measured by means of an external device that records reaction speed.

14. It is also necessary to record silicon concentration at the start, at the middle, and at the end of the reaction.

NEW sentences

15. In order for silicon to act on a third of the molecular bonds in ceramic materials, it is necessary for the treatment to take as little as **a few minutes**.

16. The above has been confirmed by numerous studies stating that the process is **fast and efficient**.

IRRELEVANT sentences

15. This is one of the methods that is being studied to increase the strength of chemical bonds.

16. There are many scientists working in this field and it is hoped that there will be advancements in the next years.

Note. Text originally in Spanish.

Six inference questions were included to check the understanding of the text. Each response to the questions was scored according to the use of old or new information. We scored the answers in three categories or *scenarios*:

Old: A response on the basis of information that in a later stage turned out to be incorrect (the corrected information).

New: A response on the basis of information that finally turned out to be correct (the correction). A response was also judged as new if it provided a plausible explanation that was not incompatible with the correction.

Other: All other responses that subjects gave, but that did not use old or new information. Thus, this category reflects the use of information not referring to the old or new topics, based on other information coming from the text or based on self-invented information. Questions that produced no responses, as well as responses like "don't know" and "don't remember," were also included in this category. There were only 12 instances of such "don't know" or "don't remember" answers.

Results and Discussion

Figure 13.1 shows the mean number of questions that subjects answered according to the old and new scenarios. In order to simplify presentation, the results concerning the other scenario are not presented. In principle, the scores on each scenario can range from 0 to 6 (because there were six inference questions, and the total score can, thus, be maximally 6).

In order to simplify the presentation of the outcomes of analyses of variance (ANOVAs), outcomes of these analyses are presented separately for each response category or scenario (old, new, and other information, respectively). First of all, there are significant differences in the use of old in-

Mean Number of Answers per Scenario

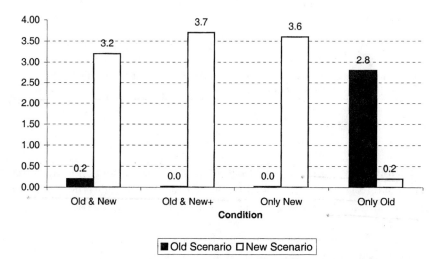

FIG. 13.1. Mean number of answers in the four conditions on the old and new scenarios (Experiment 1).

formation and new information across conditions, $F(1,92) = 105.99, p < .001$ and $F(1,92) = 66.31, p < .001$, respectively. The student–Newman–Keuls test showed that the only-old condition used significantly more old information, and less new information than the other three conditions. However, there are no significant differences between the only-new control group and the two experimental groups (the old & new and old & new+ conditions), nor among the experimental groups themselves. The experimental groups frequently used new information, so subjects in these groups changed their mental representation. In addition, subjects in control group only-old frequently recalled old information. This demonstrates that such information was available to experimental subjects when reading the correcting new information at the end of the text. There were no significant differences between conditions regarding other information.

The results of this experiment indicate that students reading scientific text tend to use new information when this new information clearly contradicts their previous mental representation of scientific content. Thus, in contrast with studies cited earlier that used a less stringent manipulation, when a clear-cut contradiction is used, subjects tend to update their mental model, or at least incorporate the new information in their representation.

EXPERIMENT 2: STRENGTHENING THE OLD AND WEAKENING THE NEW INFORMATION

To explore further the conditions that may lead subjects to use old or new information, a second experiment was designed in which the old information was strengthened and the new information was weakened. The main objective was to examine whether strengthening of old information would lead to less updating, that is, to less use of the new scenario. Similarly, does strengthening the new information result in more frequent use of new information? In this second experiment the strength of old information and the strength of new information were independently varied in order to examine the influence of both sources on the degree of updating.

In the strong version of the old scenario, an additional sentence reinforced the old scenario (see Table 13.3).

For instance, in Sentence 12 the content of Sentence 8 (that "the treatment or process takes some days") is *strongly* reinforced by stating that "a device plots a graphic each ten hours," while the *weak* old version is neutral to the duration, and does not reinforce it (Sentence 12: "a device plots a graphic at the end of the process"). Also the strength of the new information was varied. In the *strong* version of the new information, it is explicitly stated that the process takes a few minutes (by means of Sentences 15 and 16). In the *weak* version of the new scenario, the new scenario was stated in an indirect way, by mentioning in Sentence 15 that "only a few liters of water are needed."

Method

Strength of old vs. new info   Strength

Four versions of the text were constructed combining the strong and weak versions of the old and new scenarios as indicated previously. Therefore there was a 2 × 2 factorial design: *strength of old information* (with two values: strong vs. weak) and *strength of new information* (with two values: strong vs. weak). Subjects were 93 first-year students (not the same as in Experiment 1). The procedure, number of questions, scoring, and so on, were the same as in the previous experiment.

Results

Figure 13.2 presents the mean number of inference questions answered according to each the three scenarios. Analysis of the use of the new scenario showed only a main effect of the factor Strength of old Information ($F(1,89) = 6.81, p < .01$). No other main effect or interaction is statistically signifi-

TABLE 13.3
Text Used in Experiment 2

1. It is very difficult to increase the hardness of some new ceramic materials.

2. For this reason, there are many problems using these materials to make special containers.

3. These containers are useful to store small amounts of radioactive substances because ceramic materials prevent radiation from escaping.

4. Thus, it could solve the problem of storing radioactive materials in hospitals and research centers that use such substances in their daily work.

5. So, it is important to obtain ceramic materials strong enough to be used as containers.

6. The reason for the lack of hardness of the new ceramic materials is that molecular bonds in such materials are very soft.

7. It is well known that the hardness of some substances increases if silicon atoms are put in a third of the molecular bonds in such substances.

8. In order for silicon to act on a third of the molecular bonds in ceramic materials, it is necessary for the treatment to **take some days**.

9. Silicon reacts chemically with the ceramic materials and it opens some chemical bonds in such materials.

10. Silicon atoms join to molecular bonds that are open and they build new bonds.

11. These new silicon bonds increase the hardness of ceramic materials.

Strong old

12. An external device continuously records silicon concentration and **plots a graphic each 10 hours.**

Weak old

12. An external device continuously records Silicon concentration and plots a graphic **at the end of the process.**

13. The heat produced in the process is eliminated by means of a flow of water of 1 liter per minute.

14. The temperature of water rises notably and for this reason the water is not used again in the process and is eliminated by a pipe.

Strong new

15. In order for silicon to act on a third of the molecular bonds in ceramic materials it is necessary for the treatment to **take a few minutes.**

16. The above has been confirmed by numerous studies that show that the treatment is done in **a fast and efficient way.**

318

Weak new

15. The main advantage of the previous method is that **only a few liters of water** are needed from the start until the end of the treatment.

16. This is very important, because the authorities **check carefully** the ecological impact of the industrial process and the research methods.

Note. Text originally in Spanish.

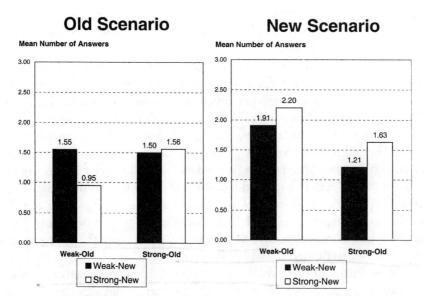

FIG. 13.2. Mean number of answers on the old and new scenarios (Experiment 2).

cant ($p > .05$). Subjects use more frequently the new scenario when they read the weak old version than when they read the strong old version, and the influence of the strength of the new information was weak and not significant. The results regarding the use of the old scenario are in the expected direction, that is, with strong old information yielding more frequently the old scenario, and strong new information leading less frequently to the old scenario. However, these effects were not statistically significant.

In summary, subjects who read the text in which the old information had been strengthened appeared to use less frequently the new information. Apparently, the extent of updating also depends upon the strength in the representation of the old information.

EXPERIMENT 3A: DIRECT VERSUS INDIRECT REFERENCE TO OLD INFORMATION

In the third experiment the old perspective was reinforced in a more subtle manner in two ways: by *indirectly referring* to the old perspective (or not), or by inserting information *implicitly fitting* to the old perspective. The purpose of this subtle manipulation was to examine whether activation and sustained activation of the old perspective can also be obtained by presenting schema- or model-related information. If this is the case, it supports the hypothesis that it is a scenario or situation model that exerts its influence on the difficulty in updating.

In the previous experiment the old information was strengthened almost at a surface (lexical) level. For instance, the old information that "the treatment takes some days" was rather directly reinforced (in Sentence 12, Table 13.3) by stating that "a device plots a graphic each 10 hours." In contrast, in the current experiment, an *indirect* mentioning of the old information was used. The old information was "Previous studies demonstrated that this method has to be carried out for some days," and the strong indirect reinforcement was "A drawback of this method is that it takes much time" (see Table 13.4). The weak control sentence was here "A drawback of this method is that it produces much heat" (weak indirect reinforcement). The research question is, thus, whether indirectly reinforcing the old perspective can also strengthen the old perspective.

The second question is whether activation of the old perspective can also be obtained by encountering contextual information that is *compatible* with old information, and thereby even more indirectly reinforcing the old perspective. By varying the distance between the old and new information, we were able to insert a different number of compatible information units. For instance, a sentence such as "To carry out the method computers have to monitor the process from the start until the end" was presented or "Special thermometers record the temperature at the start, at the middle, and at the end of the process" (see Table 13.4). The fragments "from the start until the end" as well as "at the start, at the middle, and at the end" are compatible to the old perspective "some days" without expressing it directly. In the long-distance condition, four of these compatible information units were presented between the old and new information, whereas in the short-distance condition only two compatible information units were inserted (and two *irrelevant* sentences). The old information (i.e., a treatment that takes some days) could in these cases be used and activated four versus two times before en-

TABLE 13.4

Text Used in Experiment 3A

1. The new ceramic materials used in research and in industry are originally very soft and they break easily.

2. There are some methods to increase the hardness of these ceramic materials in order to use them.

3. A widely used method is to make silicon act on intermolecular bonds of ceramic materials for **some days. (old)**

Strong Indirect Reinforcement

4. This method was developed in a leading research laboratory and its main drawback is that it takes **much time.**

Weak Indirect Reinforcement

4. This method was developed in a leading research laboratory and its main drawback is that it produces much heat.

Compatible Information Unit

5. To carry out the method computers have to monitor the process **from the start until the end.**

Irrelevant Information Unit

5. The basis of the method is the well-known fact that the hardness increases if silicon is put into a third of their molecular bonds.

(.............................

...............................).

Compatible Information Unit

14. Special thermometers record the temperature **at the start, at the middle and at the end of the process.**

Irrelevant Information Unit

14. This water cannot be reused because its temperature increases, and it is carried off through an external pipe.

15. However, recent advances in this method make it possible to reduce the amount of time necessary to carry out the method **to only a few minutes. (new)**

16. The above has been confirmed by recent studies that demonstrate that the process is now **very fast and efficient. (new)**

countering the new information that the method can be carried out in a few minutes (as in Sentence 15), and is fast and efficient (Sentence 16).

This experiment slightly changed the nature of the new information. In previous experiments there was a clear contradiction between the old and information source. That is, it was not easy to imagine how both could be true in the same world. In the present experiment we modified the new information into a correction of the old information; that is, recent advances make it possible now to carry out the method in a few minutes (Table 13.4, Sentence 15), and recent studies confirm that the process is now very fast (Sentence 16).

These two variables, indirect reinforcement (weak vs. strong) and distance (short vs. long), were combined in a 2 × 2 design. Therefore there were four text versions. The hypothesis was that a strong indirect reinforcement would lead to strengthening the old perspective, and thus to less updating. This prediction is based on the idea that reinforcing more strongly the old perspective leads to a higher degree of activation and stronger availability of the old perspective compared to a weak indirect reinforcement. Also using the old perspective more often during understanding, by encountering more compatible information units, should lead to less updating. Again, this is based on the idea that frequency correlates with activation degree and availability of the old perspective. Consequently, a long distance should lead here to less updating. Subjects were 65 first-year students, randomly assigned to conditions. The procedure, number of questions, scoring, and so on, were similar to those in the previous experiments.

Results

Figure 13.3 presents the mean number of inference questions answered as a function of the two scenarios (old and new).

A 2 × 2 ANOVA of the old scenario showed only a main effect of indirect reinforcement, $F(1,61) = 4.55$, $p < .05$. The stronger the old information was indirectly present in the text, the more the old scenario was used to answer the inference questions. The other main effect and the interaction were not significant. The results concerning the use of the new scenario also showed a significant effect of indirect reinforcement, $(F(1,61) = 3.71, p < .05)$, whereas the other effects were not significant. The stronger the old information is indirectly present, the less the new scenario was used. Taken together, indirect reinforcement of the old scenario leads to stronger holding on to the old scenario and less to the new scenario. Readers answer, then, inference questions more frequently on the basis of the old informa-

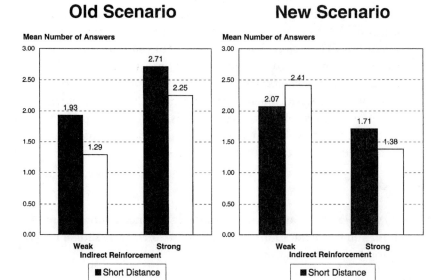

FIG. 13.3.   Mean number of answers on the old and new scenarios (Experiment 3A).

No distance factor

tion source, and less on the basis of the new information source (The distance factor did not have here a significant influence.)

EXPERIMENT 3B: FREQUENCY OF INDIRECT REFERENCE TO OLD INFORMATION

In Experiment 3A no significant effect of distance between old and new information was found. The number of intervening information units compatible with the old information did not have a reinforcing effect. Looking back to the construction of materials some confounding was present in the text, which might be responsible for the lack of an effect. In the short-distance condition, a few intervening compatible information units were included, but at the same time the old information was more recently mentioned. These two influences were both present in the experiment at the same time, causing some confounding. The net results could thus be "no difference" with the long-distance condition.

Because it seemed worthwhile to check this matter more closely, an experiment was conducted to examine more precisely the influence of varying the number of information units compatible to the old information source. Four conditions were included in this experiment (all with old and new information) consisting of *zero, one, two, or three* times respectively, indirectly mentioning the old information while keeping the exact location of old and new information constant. The research question is whether it can be demonstrated that the more often the old source is indirectly mentioned in the text, the more often the old source is used in answering the inference questions, compared to the new information source.

Method

Subjects were 93 first-year students, randomly assigned to conditions. The procedure, number of questions, scoring, and so forth, were similar to those the previous experiments.

Results

Figure 13.4 presents the mean number of inference questions answered as a function of scenario (old or new) in the four conditions.

Outcomes of ANOVAs showed significant differences between conditions in the use of the old scenario as well as that of the new scenario, $F(1,92) = 5.03, p < .05$ and $F(1,92) = 3.97, p < .05$, respectively. In the condition with no indirect repetition of the old information (the *none* condition), readers use less frequently the old scenario, and more frequently the new scenario compared to the other three conditions (see Fig. 13.4).

A useful index indicating the relative amount of old responses compared to new responses on the inference questions is the ratio of the frequency of old responses divided by the frequency of new responses. This analysis showed the following means (average proportions): zero repetitions: .25 (.62/2.50); one repetition: .57 (1.00/1.76); two repetitions: .42 (.90/2.15); three repetitions: .48 (.98/2.04). Statistical comparisons (Student–Newman–Keuls) revealed that only the zero repetition condition significantly differed from the other conditions. With *no* indirect repetition of old information, the ratio of using old information to new information on the inference questions is lower than *with* repetition of old information (irrespective of how often repeated). Thus, there is *no* linear effect of number of times that old information was indirectly mentioned on the frequency of mentioning old information. There was only a dichot-

Mean Number of Answers per Scenario

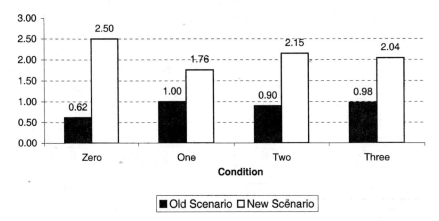

FIG. 13.4. Mean number of answers in the four conditions on the old and new scenarios (Experiment 3B).

omy between no repetition and repetition. Apparently with this kind of materials (rather short texts), it is sufficient to repeat information once to keep it active in the mental representation. Repeating it twice or three times does not add to the effect.

CONCLUSIONS

The results in Experiment 1 were different from results of previous studies mentioned in the introduction (H. M. Johnson & Seifert, 1994, 1999; van Oostendorp & Bonebakker, 1999; Wilkes & Leatherbarrow, 1988; Wilkes & Reynolds, 1999). Unlike their results, comprehenders in this study successfully edited their mental record and frequently used the new information to answer inference questions. In the first experiment, the texts placed subjects in an extreme situation of a rather strong contradiction between the old and new information. Confronted with such an explicit and strong contradiction, readers edited their memory record to accommodate their representation of the text to the new information. Given the fact that readers in the only-old condition in the first experiment, in which no new, contradictory information is presented, used the old information to answer inference questions, we can be rather sure that information derived from the first so-called contradictory sentence was also available to the subjects in the old & new and old & new+ conditions. Consequently, the frequent use of new information cannot be explained by assuming that the subjects in these conditions miss the old information. Thus, apparently the regulation of understanding of subjects in these conditions consisted of frequently leaning on new information to solve the contradiction. The conscious strategy of monitoring inconsistencies triggered by the warning instruction as in the second condition in the first experiment did not add much compared to the old & new condition (the condition without warning instruction).

Experiments 2, 3A, and 3B provided additional knowledge about the regulation strategies used by subjects when reading texts in which old, discredited information was challenged by new information. Results in these experiments indicate that readers tend to use more frequently the old and less the new scenario when new information is weakened and old information is reinforced, even when it is indirectly mentioned.

In summary, the results in these experiments point to a regulation mechanism that is based on weighting evidence in favor of the old and new sources of information. According to the outcomes of this evaluation process, readers choose one or the other point of view, and use that for making inferences, even backwards ones. Thus, in terms of the construction-integration model of Kintsch (1998), the exact balance between the strengths of sources may influence the degree of updating. In the construction-integration model, two stages of processing are distinguished. First, there is the construction phase in which propositions derived from the text are joined in a network together with propositions retrieved from memory. The old and new information sources are included in this network. The second stage consists of an integration process carried out in a connectionist manner. Activation spreads between propositions depending on existing links. Pieces of the network that hang together reinforce each other, whereas nodes that are isolated are deactivated. The integration process gives as a result the final activation of propositions. In the second phase strong support of one source may cause an increased activation of this source in the network, and inhibition of the other source. The balance of activation values of old and new information in the final representation after processing both sources determines what interpretation receives priority. Subtle reinforcements of old information and new information can, as we saw here, activate qualitatively different regulation (updating) strategies by subjects, such as holding on to the old information and rejecting the new information, or on the contrary, switching to a new perspective. This principle was not well controlled in previous studies, and differences in the exact balance might be responsible for differences in outcomes between previous experiments and the current ones. That is, in the van Oostendorp and Bonebakker (1999) experiments the old source was maybe strongly present. In contrast, the present experiments showed that the activation of information compared to new information can be manipulated, and consequently, depending on the balance, the degree of updating—switching to new information—varies.

However, we must also keep in mind that one important difference with the other studies mentioned in the introduction is the type of text. Our text was an expository text on a scientific mechanism whereas their stories were about everyday events. In addition, the nature of the old and new information differed across studies. In previous research, the old information identified a plausible cause of the central event of the story. In this study, it concerned a characteristic of a process "duration of some days" as old information) that was almost as plausible as the new characteristic ("duration of some minutes" as new information).

The studies presented here show that the regulation strategies of readers, more specifically taking into account new information, depend on *textual* conditions. At the least, the following characteristics may play a role:

1. How relevant or salient is the old and new information?
2. What is the exact character of the correction itself (the new information source)? Logical inconsistencies are probably easy to detect but difficult to repair, whereas a correction or reported change in the world may be more difficult to detect but easy to understand (and repair).
3. How explicit is the correction?
4. How credible is the old and new information source?

It is, of course, reasonable to assume that regulation strategies also depend on *contextual* constrictions and on *individual characteristics* of readers (see Otero, 1998, for a survey). The role of context on the regulation strategies of readers was shown in García-Arista, Campanario, and Otero (1996). In their study subjects were presented with the same text containing contradictions, either in a "science" or in a "newspaper" setting. Readers detected more contradictions and also better regulated their comprehension in the science setting than in the newspaper setting.

Individual characteristics constitute the third block of variables. Relevant here are prior knowledge (Otero, 1998). Also limitations in working memory capacity may influence a reader's representation of a text (see Mannes, 1994). Limitations of working memory may urge a reader to give priority to old or new information, respectively, for further processing. The suppressed information has then less chance to be used and to influence the final representation. Another individual characteristic that is relevant here are beliefs, such as the epistemological belief that integration of ideas implied by a text is important to understanding (Kardash & Scholes, 1996; Rukavina & Daneman, 1996; Schommer, 1990). Comprehenders with a low score on this epistemological belief are using a less deep reading strategy and they build only a compartmentalized representation. Opposed to this, comprehenders with a strong belief that ideas should be connected are more likely to reconcile inconsistencies in the text. So we may predict that these readers will try to integrate information derived from the old and new sources and use that for making inferences. At least they will try to keep both available.

REFERENCES

Baker, L. (1985). How do we know when we don't understand? Standards for evaluating text comprehension. In D. L. Forrest-Pressley, G. E. Mackinnon, & T. G. Waller (Eds.), *Metacognition, cognition and human performance* (pp. 155–205). New York: Academic Press.

García-Arista, E., Campanario, J. M., & Otero, J. (1996). Influence of subject matter setting on comprehension monitoring. *European Journal of Psychology of Education, 11*, 427–441.

Garner, R. (1987). *Metacognition and reading comprehension*. Norwood, NJ: Ablex.

Graesser, A. C., McMahen, C. L., & Johnson, G. S. (1994). Question asking and answering. In M. Gernsbacher (Ed.), *Handbook of psycholinguistics* (pp. 517–538). San Diego: Academic Press.

Hacker, D. J. (1998). Self-regulated comprehension during normal reading. In D. J. Hacker, J. Dunlosky, & A. C. Graesser (Eds.), *Metacognition in educational theory and practice* (pp. 165–192). Mahwah, NJ: Lawrence Erlbaum Associates.

Johnson, H. M., & Seifert, C. M. (1994). Sources of the continued effect: When misinformation in memory affects later inferences. *Journal of Experimental Psychology: Learning, Memory, and Cognition, 20*(6), 1420–1436.

Johnson, H. M., & Seifert, C. M. (1999). Modifying mental representations: Comprehending corrections. In H. van Oostendorp & S. R. Goldman (Eds.), *The construction of mental representations during reading* (pp. 303–318). Mahwah, NJ: Lawrence Erlbaum Associates.

Kardash, C. M., & Scholes, R. J. (1996). Effects of preexisting beliefs, epistemological beliefs, and need for cognition on interpretation of controversial issues. *Journal of Educational Psychology, 88*(2), 260–271.

Kintsch, W. (1998). *Comprehension. A paradigm for cognition*. Cambridge, England: Cambridge University Press.

Mannes, S. (1994). Strategic processing of text. *Journal of Educational Psychology, 86*(4), 377–388.

Otero, J. (1998). Influence of knowledge activation and context on comprehension monitoring of science texts. In D. J. Hacker, J. Dunlosky, & A. C. Graesser

(Eds.), *Metacognition in educational theory and practice* (pp. 145–164). Mahwah, NJ: Lawrence Erlbaum Associates.

Otero, J., & Campanario, J. M. (1990). Comprehension evaluation and regulation in learning from science texts. *Journal of Research in Science Teaching, 27*(5), 447–460.

Rukavina, I., & Daneman, M. (1996). Integration and its effect on acquiring knowledge about competing scientific theories from text. *Journal of Educational Psychology, 88,* 272–287.

Schommer, M. (1990). Effects of beliefs about the nature of knowledge on comprehension. *Journal of Educational Psychology, 82,* 498–504.

van Oostendorp, H. (1996). Updating situation models derived from newspaper articles. *Medienpsychologie. Zeitschrift für Individual- und Massenkommunikation, 8,* 21–33.

van Oostendorp, H. (2001). Holding on to established viewpoints during processing news reports. In W. van Peer & S. Chatman (Eds.), *New perspectives on narrative perspective* (pp. 173–188). Albany: State University of New York Press.

van Oostendorp, H., & Bonebakker, C. (1999). Difficulties in updating mental representations during reading news reports. In H. van Oostendorp & S. R. Goldman (Eds.), *The construction of mental representations during reading* (pp.319–340). Mahwah, NJ: Lawrence Erlbaum Associates.

van Oostendorp, H., & Elshout-Mohr, M. (1999). Thinking skills in reading and text studying. In J. H. M. Hamers, J. E. H. van Luit, & B. Csapó (Eds.), *Teaching and learning thinking skills* (pp. 283–312). Lisse, Netherlands: Swets & Zeitlinger.

van Oostendorp, H., Otero, J., & Campanario, J. (in press). Conditions of updating during reading. In M. Louwerse & W. van Peer (Eds.), *Thematics: Interdisciplinary studies.* Amsterdam/New York: John Benjamins.

Wilkes, A. L., & Leatherbarrow, M. (1988). Editing episodic memory following the identification of error. *The Quarterly Journal of Experimental Psychology, 40A*(2), 361–387.

Wilkes, A. L., & Reynolds, D. J. (1999). On certain limitations accompanying readers' interpretations of corrections in episodic text. *The Quarterly Journal of Experimental Psychology, 52A*(1), 165–183.

Winograd, P., & Johnston, P. (1982). Comprehension monitoring and the error detection paradigm. *Journal of Reading Behavior, 14,* 61–76.

IV

Coordinating Multiple Information Sources and Media

❧ 14 ❧

Using Illustrations to Promote Constructivist Learning From Science Text

Richard E. Mayer
University of California, Santa Barbara

Explaining how things work is at the heart of science so our research focuses on techniques for helping students understand scientific explanations. In particular, we begin with texts that explain how various physical, mechanical, and biological systems work such as how lightning storms develop, how a car's braking system works, or how a bicycle tire pump works. Verbal modes of instruction are dominant in education so the most common way of presenting scientific explanations is to use words—such as printed or spoken text. In our research, we explore the idea that adding visual modes of presentation—such as illustrations—can improve students' understanding of scientific explanations. In a series of studies we have found that adding illustrations to text in a book-based environment can greatly improve students' understanding of scientific explanations, as measured by performance on tests of problem-solving transfer. In addition, in our research we have pinpointed the conditions under which adding visual representations to text can help students to understand scientific explanations. Our work is guided by a cognitive theory of multimedia learning that assumes that there are separate verbal and visual information channels; that each channel is limited in processing capacity; and that constructivist learning occurs when students mentally select relevant verbal and visual material, mentally organize the selected material into verbal and visual mental models respectively, and mentally integrate the visual and verbal mental models with each other and with prior knowledge. It follows that an essential condition for effective multimedia instruction is that the learner be able to process corresponding visual and verbal material in working memory at the same time.

The Case of Active Learning From Passive Media

Is it possible to foster active learning from passive media? Active learning, which can also be called constructivist learning, occurs when learners actively seek to make sense of their experiences. Printed text has been characterized as a passive medium because the learner cannot interact with the text in a behavioral way.

Presenting a text-based message to a learner, such as a paragraph in a textbook, is often considered to be a form of teaching that leads to rote (nonconstructive) learning. In contrast, requiring the learner to actively participate in a learning episode, such as in a hands-on science lesson or an interactive computer game, is often considered to be a form of teaching that leads to meaningful (constructivist) learning. This view, which we call the *behavioral activity view*, is based on the premise that behavioral activity leads to cognitive activity. It is represented in the top panel of Fig. 14.1.

The behavioral activity view enjoys popularity in writings about teaching, including science teaching. For example, in a textbook for teachers, Lefrancois (1997) equated constructivist learning with active teaching methods: "The constructivist approach to teaching ... is ... based on the assumption that students should build (construct) knowledge for themselves. Hence constructivist approaches are basically discovery oriented" (p. 206). Similarly, the *National Science Education Standards* (National Research Council, 1996) appears to see active learning as incompatible with passive instructional methods in which a student reads or listens: "Emphasizing active science learning means shifting emphasis away from teachers presenting information ... " (p. 20). The implication that readers may draw from statements such as these is that passive media such as textbooks have no place in science programs aimed at promoting constructivist learning.

In contrast, Ausubel (1968) and others (Mayer, 1997, 1999b) have argued that teaching with text-based messages can lead to either meaningful

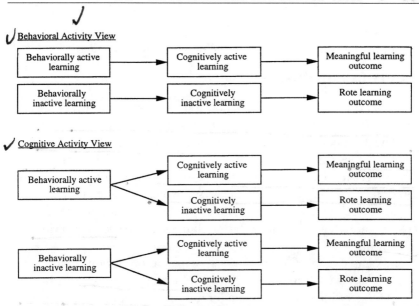

Fig. 14.1. Two views of the relation between behavioral activity and cognitive activity.

or rote learning, and teaching with learner behavioral activity can lead to either meaningful or rote learning. When a student reads a passage or listens to a lecture, the student is not behaviorally active but the student can be cognitively active, seeking to make sense of the presented material. When a student engages in a hands-on activity or plays an interactive game, the student is behaviorally active but may not be cognitively active; that is, the student may not reflect on what the experience means. This view, which we call the *cognitive activity view*, is based on the premise that behavioral activity is not the same as cognitive activity. It is represented in the bottom panel of Fig. 14.1.

We adopt the cognitive activity view, including the idea that meaningful learning can occur when students receive text-based messages such as in a textbook or lecture. This view is complemented by the view that text comprehension is a potentially active explanation-based constructive process (Graesser, Singer, & Trabasso, 1994). Our goal is to determine the conditions that promote constructivist learning from text-based messages. In particular, we focus on how to help learners understand scientific text that explains how something works, which we call *explanative text*. For the past 12 years, this issue has guided our research at the University of California, Santa Barbara. In order to address this issue, it is necessary to more clearly define the nature of the *text*, the nature of the *help*, and the nature of *understanding*.

What Is Explanative Text?

A cause-and-effect explanation of how some system works, which we refer to as explanative text, is an important rhetorical structure in science education. The distinguishing features of explanative text are that (a) it contains a series of steps (or changes in the states of parts of the system) in which each step is the cause or the result of an adjacent step, (b) it describes the operation of a system consisting of parts in which a change in the state of one part causes a change in the state of another part, and (c) the series of steps or state changes is not arbitrary but rather is based on principled mechanisms.

For example, Table 14.1 presents an explanation of how a bicycle tire pump works. As you can see, the cause-and-effect chain consists of several steps. The steps include the handle (or rod) moving up, causing the piston to move up, which causes the inlet valve to open and air to enter through the piston. The pump system consists of several parts, each of which can be in several different states: The handle can be up or down, the piston can be up or down, the inlet valve can be open or closed, the outlet valve can be open or closed, the air pressure in the cylinder can be high or low, the hose can have air moving out or not. A change in the state of one part is logically related to change in the state of another part. For example, when the handle is pulled up the piston moves up because the piston is attached to the handle by the rod, or when the piston moves up the inlet valve opens because air pressure is greater above than below the valve. We consider the pump passage to be an explanative text because it provides a cause-and-effect explanation of how a system works in which the causal steps are logically related to one another.

As another example, consider the explanation of how a car's braking system works as presented in Table 14.2. As you can see, the cause-and-effect chain includes the following steps: The driver steps in the brake pedal, a piston moves forward in the master cylinder, brake fluid is compressed, smaller

TABLE 14.1
Portion of an Explanative Text About How Pumps Work

As the rod is pulled out, air passes through the piston and fills the area between the piston and the outlet valve. As the rod is pushed in, the inlet valve closes and the piston forces air through the outlet valve.

TABLE 14.2
Portion of an Explanative Text About How Brakes Work

When the driver steps on the car's brake pedal, a piston moves forward inside the master cylinder. The piston forces brake fluid out of the master cylinder and through the tubes to the wheel cylinders. In the wheel cylinders, the increase in fluid pressure makes a smaller set of pistons move. These smaller pistons activate the brake shoes. When the brake shoes press against the drum, both the drum and the wheel stop or slow down.

---

pistons move forward in the wheel cylinders, smaller pistons push the brake shoes, brake shoes press against the brake drum, and the wheel slows down or stops. The brake system consists of several key parts, each of which can be in several possible states: The brake pedal can be up or down, the piston in the master cylinder can be forward or back, the brake fluid can be compressed on not compressed, the smaller pistons can be forward or back, the brake shoe can be pushing outward or not, the brake pad can be rubbing against the shoe or not, the wheel can be moving or coming to a stop. Each change in the state of one part of the system is logically related a change in the state of another part. For example, when the brake pedal is pushed, the master cylinder moves forward because they are connected by rods; and when the piston moves forward, brake fluid pressure is increased because the same·amount of fluid occupies less space. We classify the brake passage as an explanative text because it gives a cause-and-effect explanation of how a system works in which the causal links are based on mechanical or physical principles.

Finally, Table 14.3 presents a passage that explains how lightning storms develop. Some of the major steps in this cause-and-effect chain are: Warm moist air rises, warm moist air forms a cloud, the upper portion is composed of ice crystals, ice crystals drag air downward, negatively charged particles move to the bottom of the cloud, two leaders meet, negatively charged particles rush from cloud to ground, and positively charged particles rush upward along the same path. The lighting system consists of several components that can be in various states: The cloud can be below or at the freezing level, there can be ice or no ice in the top of the cloud, there can be negative charges or no negative charges in the bottom of the cloud, and so on. Each change in state in one part is related to a change in state in another part: When cool air moves over a warmer surface, for example, it becomes heated and rises. The lightning passage is classified as explanative text be-

TABLE 14.3

**Portion of an Explanative Text About How
Lightning Storms Develop**

Cool moist air moves over a warmer surface and becomes heated. Warmed moist air near the earth's surface rises rapidly. As the air in this updraft cools, water vapor condenses into water droplets and forms a cloud. The cloud's top extends above the freezing level, so the upper portion of the cloud is composed of tiny ice crystals. Within the cloud, the rising and falling air currents cause electrical charges to build. The charge results from the collision of the cloud's rising water droplets against the heavier, falling pieces of ice. The negatively charged particles fall to the bottom of the cloud, and most of the positively charged particles rise to the top. Eventually, the water droplets and ice crystals become too large to be suspended by the updrafts. As raindrops and ice crystals fall through the cloud, they drag some of the air in the cloud downward, producing downdrafts. When downdrafts strike the ground, they spread out in all directions, producing the gusts of cool wind people feel just before the start of the rain. A stepped leader of negative charges moves downward in a series of steps. It nears the ground. A positively charged leader travels up from such objects as trees and buildings. The two leaders generally meet about 165 feet above the ground. Negatively charged particles then rush from the cloud to the ground along the path created by the leaders. It is not very bright. As the leader stroke nears the ground, it induces an opposite charge, so positively charged particles from the ground rush upward along the same path. This upward motion of the current is the return stroke. It produces the bright light that people notice as a flash of lightning.

cause it provides a cause-and-effect explanation of how a lightning system works and is based on physical principles.

One of the primary goals of science is to explain how the world works, so it follows that an important goal of science education is to provide students with understandable explanations of how things work. Explanative text is an important tool for accomplishing this goal. In addition to explanation, there are many other important rhetorical structures used in communicating about science, including description, comparison, classification, and generalization (Brincones & Otero, 1992; Cook & Mayer, 1988; Meyer, 1975). Descriptive text provides a description of some object or event, such as telling what brake shoes are made out of and how they are shaped. In comparative text, a matrix is created in which two or more objects are compared across several dimensions, such as comparing the advantages and disadvantages of disk brakes and hydraulic brakes. In classification text, a hierarchy is created in which a category is broken into subcategories such as describing each kind of cloud. Generalization text consists of a main point followed by supporting evidence, such as stating that differences in air temperature are crucial to lighting formation and then supporting this claim through concrete examples. In this chapter we restrict our focus to one type of rhetorical structure, namely explanative text, because explanations are at the heart of scientific understanding.

What Is an Aid to Understanding Explanative Text?

Although the use of words is the most accepted medium for presenting an instructional message to a learner, sometimes learners have difficulty making sense of messages that are presented solely in words. In the case of scientific explanations, a potentially useful aid for promoting learner understanding is the use of illustrations. In our research we seek to use the power of words and pictures to help students understand how various scientific systems work.

For example, Fig. 14.2 shows a two-frame illustration depicting how a pump works. To help learners construct causal connections among state changes, the first frame depicts the state of each component in the system when the handle is up and the second frame depicts the state of each component in the system when the handle is down. To avoid overloading learners, only a few basic components and actions are presented, such as the

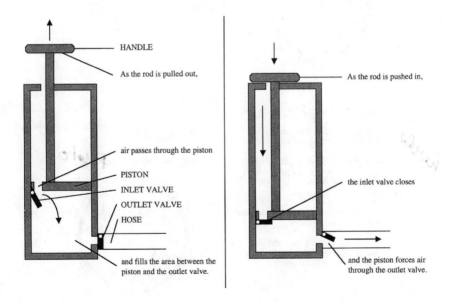

Fig. 14.2.   Illustration and text on how a pump works.

handle being up or down, the air going in or out, the inlet valve being open or closed, and the outlet valve being open or closed. To help learners build connections between corresponding words and pictures, each piece of text is placed next to the part of the illustration it describes.

Figure 14.3 shows a two-frame illustration depicting how a braking system works. To help learners construct causal connections among state changes, the first frame depicts the state of each component in the system before the driver steps on the car's brake pedal and the second frame depicts the state of each component after the driver steps on the brake pedal. To avoid overloading learners, only a few components and actions are presented, such as the pedal being up or down, the master cylinder being in or out, and so on. To help learners build connections between corresponding words and pictures, each portion of text is placed next to the part of the illustration it describes.

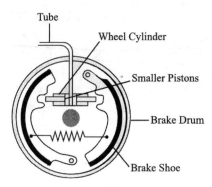

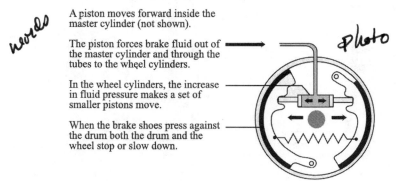

Fig. 14.3.   Illustration and text on how brakes work.

Finally, Fig. 14.4 shows a five-frame illustration depicting how lightning storms develop. The transition from one frame to the next allows the learner to focus on important state changes. By presenting only a few elements, the learner's information-processing system is not overloaded. The captions at the bottom of each frame help the learner connect relevant words with the illustration.

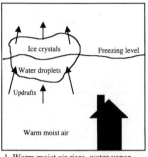

1. Warm moist air rises, water vapor condenses and forms a cloud.

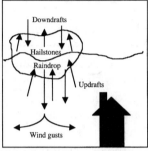

2. Raindrops and ice crystals drag air downward.

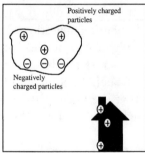

3. Negatively charged particles fall to the bottom of the cloud.

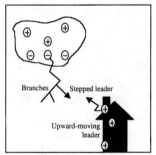

4. Two leaders meet, negatively charged particles rush from the cloud to the ground.

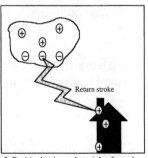

5. Positively charged particles from the ground rush upward along the same path.

Fig. 14.4. Illustration and text on how lightning storms develop. [From Mayer, Bove, Bryman, Mars, and Tapangco, Mayer, (1996)]. Copyright © 1996 by the American Psychological Association. Reprinted by permission.

How Can We Measure Understanding?

Constructivist learning occurs when learners make sense of their experiences, including the experience of receiving an instructional message. Our focus is on promoting the construction of meaningful learning outcomes, so our major measure of learning is a test of problem-solving transfer. Problem-solving transfer taps the ability to take what was learned and use it to solve new problems, and thus is the classic way of measuring understanding.

Table 14.4 lists some problem-solving transfer questions for the pump passage. As you can see, some questions involve troubleshooting (Question 3), some involve redesigning the system to meet a new functional requirement (Questions 1 and 2), and some ask for an underlying physical principle (Question 4). Students receive 1 point for each acceptable answer across all the questions. For example, some acceptable answers for the troubleshooting question (i.e., Question 3) include that the handle became disconnected from the piston, the inlet valve is stuck in the open position, the cylinder has a hole in it, the seal around the inlet valve leaks, and so on.

Table 14.5 lists some problem-solving transfer questions for the brakes passage. Questions 4 and 5 involve troubleshooting, Questions 2 and 3 involve redesign, and question 1 involves a physical principle. Students receive 1 point for each acceptable answer across all the questions. For example, some acceptable answers for the troubleshooting question about what went wrong (Question 4) include that the brake pedal is not connected to the rod, the master cylinder is stuck in one position, there is a hole in the brake line, and so on.

Table 14.6 lists some problem-solving transfer questions for the lightning passage. Question 2 is a troubleshooting question, Question 1 is a redesign question, and questions 3 and 4 are principle questions. Students receive

TABLE 14.4

Some Problem-Solving Transfer Questions Used to Evaluate Students' Understanding of the Pump Passage

1. What could be done to make a pump more reliable, that is, to make sure it would not fail?

2. What could be done to make a pump more effective, that is, to move air more rapidly?

3. Suppose you push down and pull up the handle of a pump several times but no air comes out. What could have gone wrong?

4. Why does air enter a pump? Why does air exit from a pump?

TABLE 14.5

Some Problem-Solving Transfer Questions Used to Evaluate Students' Understanding of the Brakes Passage

1. Why do brakes get hot?

2. What could be done to make brakes more reliable, that is, to make sure they would not fail?

3. What could be done to make brakes more effective, that is, to reduce the distance needed to bring a car to a stop?

4. Suppose you press on the brake pedal in your car but the brakes don't work. What could have gone wrong?

5. What happens when you pump the brakes (i.e., press the pedal and release the pedal repeatedly and rapidly)?

TABLE 14.6

Some Problem-Solving Transfer Questions Used to Evaluate Students' Understanding of the Lightning Passage

1. What could be done to decrease the intensity of lightning?

2. Suppose you see clouds in the sky, but no lightning. Why not?

3. What does air temperature have to do with lightning?

4. What causes lightning?

one point for each acceptable answer across all the questions. For example, some acceptable answers for the troubleshooting question include that the cloud did not reach the freezing level, the earth's surface was not warm, negative charges did not build in the bottom of the cloud, there are no positive charges on the earth's surface, and so on.

This chapter provides an overview of our research program on fostering learner understanding of scientific explanations. First, we examine the limitations of relying exclusively on verbal modes of presentation. Second, we examine ways of incorporating illustrations with text in book-based environments. Third, we examine the role of individual differences in learning from text and illustrations.

WHAT'S WRONG WITH USING TEXT ALONE?

Multimedia Principle: Use Text and Illustrations Rather Than Text Alone

Is there any evidence that adding pictures depicting the workings of a cause-and-effect system to words can improve people's understanding? For example, Tables 14.1, 14.2, and 14.3 contain text that explains the workings of a cause-and-effect system whereas Figs. 14.2, 14.3, and 14.4 contain text and pictures that depict the workings of the same systems, respectively. In a series of six comparisons involving explanations of pumps, brakes, and lightning, students who read a text explanation accompanied by corresponding illustrations generated a median of 79% more solutions on problem-solving transfer tests than students who read a text alone (Mayer, 1989, Experiments 1 and 2; Mayer, Bove, Bryman, Mars, & Tapangco, 1996, Experiment 2; Mayer & Gallini, 1990, Experiments 1, 2, and 3). The effect was present in each of the six comparisons, and yielded a median effect size of 1.37. Although both groups received the same explanation, students who received text supplemented with illustrations understood the explanation much better than did the students who received text alone. Based on these findings we propose the multimedia principle: Present a cause-and-effect explanation using text and illustrations rather than text alone.

WHAT'S THE BEST WAY TO INCORPORATE ILLUSTRATIONS WITH TEXT?

Spatial Contiguity Principle: Put Text Next to Corresponding Illustrations

The next issue concerns the arrangement of corresponding text and illustrations on the page. In Figs. 14.2, 14.3, and 14.4, the text is incorporated into the illustration so that each set of the words is placed next to the part of the picture it corresponds to. For example, in Fig. 14.2, the words, "the rod is pulled out," are printed next to the part of the illustrations showing the handle of the pump. In Fig. 14.3, the words, "a set of smaller pistons move" are placed next to the picture of the smaller pistons moving outward. In Fig. 14.4, the words, "negatively charged particles fall to the bottom of the cloud," are placed under the picture of a cloud with negative particles on the bottom. In each of these figures the corresponding words and pictures are contiguous, so the instructional message is high in spatial contiguity. We refer to this situation as *integrated presentation*.

Principles for incorporating illustrations

In contrast, the words in Figs. 14.2, 14.3, and 14.4 could be moved away from the illustrations so the text is presented on one page or one part of the page whereas the corresponding illustration (without any words) is presented far away on another page or another part of the page. In these revised figures the corresponding words and pictures are not contiguous, so the instructional message is low in spatial contiguity. We refer to this situation as *separated presentation.*

teaching talk text

In five separate comparisons of integrated and separated presentation involving passages about lightning and brakes, students receiving integrated presentation generated a median of 68% more solutions on problem-solving transfer tests than did students who received separated presentation *A study* (Mayer, 1989, Experiment 1; Mayer, Steinhoff, Bower, & Mars 1995, Experiments 1, 2, and 3; Moreno & Mayer, 1999, Experiment 1). The effect was present in each of the five tests and yielded a median effect size of 1.12. Although both groups received the same text and illustrations, the group that received the text and illustrations in an integrated arrangement understood the explanation much better than did the group that received the text and illustrations in a separated arrangement. These findings allows us to propose the spatial contiguity principle: Present corresponding text and illustrations near rather than far from one another on the page.

Coherence Principle: Eliminate Extraneous Text and Illustrations

The next issue concerns the role of interesting but extraneous text and illustrations in promoting learning. For example, the text used in Figs. 14.2, 14.3, and 14.4 is extremely concise. In Fig. 14.4, for example, only about 50 words are used to describe the process of lightning formation depicted in the five frames. In Figs. 14.2 and 14.3, even fewer words are needed to describe the two frames. In addition, Figs. 14.2, 14.3, and 14.4 contain only frames that are essential for depicting the states of the system. In Fig. 14.4, for example, only five frames are used to depict the steps in the lightning formation, whereas Figs. 14.2 and 14.3 require only two frames each. These figures contain only words and pictures that are essential to the cause-and-effect explanation, so they are high in coherence. We refer to this situation as *concise presentation.*

In contrast, the words or pictures in Figs. 14.2, 14.3, and 14.4, could be expanded to include interesting details. For example, the captions in Fig. 14.4 could be expanded to include all the words shown in Table 14.3, adding about 500 words to the message. Each caption would increase from about a dozen words to an average of over 100 words. Another way to expand this situation even further is to begin with the text shown on Table 14.3 and the captioned illustrations shown in Fig. 14.4, and then add more text and more captioned illustrations. For example, we could add a story about a boy who was struck by lightning: "Eyewitnesses in Burtonsville, Maryland, watched as a bolt of lighting tore a hole in the helmet of a high school football player during practice. The bolt burned his jersey, and blew his shoes off. More than a year later, the young man still won't talk about his near death experience." In addition, we could insert an illustration showing the boy looking at his lightning-burnt jersey and helmet. In these revised figures, words and/or illustrations have been added to describe many details extraneous to the basic cause-and-effect chain, so the instructional messages are low in coherence. We refer to this situation as *extraneous presentation*.

In eight separate comparisons of concise and extraneous presentation involving passages about lightning, students receiving concise presentation generated a median of 105% more solutions on problem-solving transfer tests than did students who received extraneous presentation (Harp & Mayer, 1997, Experiment 1; Harp & Mayer, 1998, Experiments 1, 2, 3, and 4; Mayer et al., 1996, Experiments 1, 2, and 3). The effect was present in each of the eight tests and yielded a median effect size of 1.66. Although both groups received the same core words and pictures explaining how lightning works, the group that did not receive extra words and/or pictures and illustrations understood the explanation much better than the group that received extra words and/or pictures. These findings allows us to propose the coherence principle: Exclude rather than include extraneous words and pictures.

WHO IS MOST LIKELY TO BENEFIT FROM WELL-DESIGNED MULTIMEDIA?

Prior knowledge Principle: Provide Well-Designed Multimedia to Low-Knowledge Learners Rather Than High-Knowledge Learners

The final issue concerns who benefits most from well-designed multimedia presentations. In particular, we examine the role of the learner's prior knowledge because this factor has been shown to be important in facilitating students' reading comprehension. Table 14.7 presents a knowledge questionnaire for the pumps passage, Table 14.8 presents a knowledge questionnaire for the brakes passage, and Table 14.9 presents a knowledge ques-

TABLE 14.7

A Knowledge Questionnaire for the Pumps Passage

Please place a check mark next to the items that apply to you:

_____ I own a screwdriver.

_____ I own a power saw.

_____ I have replaced the heads on a lawn sprinkler system.

_____ I have replaced the washer in a sink faucet.

_____ I have replaced the flush mechanism in a toilet.

_____ I have installed plumbing pipes or fixtures.

Please place a check mark indicating your knowledge of how to fix household appliances and machines:

_____ very much

_____

_____ average

_____

_____ very little

TABLE 14.8

A Knowledge Questionnaire for the Brakes Passage

Please place a check mark next to the items that apply to you:

_____ I have a driver's license.

_____ I have put air into a car's tire.

_____ I have changed a tire on a car.

_____ I have changed the oil in a car.

_____ I have installed spark plugs in a car.

_____ I have replaced the brake shoes in a car.

Please place a check mark indicating your knowledge of car mechanics and repair:

_____ very much

_____

_____ average

_____

_____ very little

TABLE 14.9

A Knowledge Questionnaire for the Lightning Passage

Please place a check mark next to the items that apply to you:

____   I regularly read the weather maps in a newspaper.

____   I know what a cold front is.

____   I can distinguish between cumulous and nimbus clouds.

____   I know what low pressure is.

____   I can explain what makes the wind blow.

____   I know what this symbol means. [Symbol for cold front.]

____   I know what this symbol means. [Symbol for warm front.]

Please place a check mark indicating your knowledge of meteorology (weather):

____   very much

____

____   average

____

____   very little

tionnaire for the lightning passage. In each case, we asked students to rate their knowledge of the subject on a 5-point scale from very little to very much, and we asked students to place a check mark next to the things that they had done. We scored the questionnaire by tallying 1 point for each level of the rating scale (e.g., 1 for very little to 5 for very much) and 1 point for each check mark (e.g., 1 point if one item was checked, 2 points if two items were checked, and so on). Based on a median split, approximately half of the students were classified as low-knowledge learners and approximately half can be classified as high-knowledge learners.

Our research examined whether the design effects just described occur differently for low-knowledge and high-knowledge learners. In four studies (Mayer et al., 1996, Experiment 2; Mayer & Gallini, 1990, Experiments 1, 2, and 3), we compared the transfer test performance of low-knowledge and high-knowledge learners who learned about pumps, brakes, or lightning from a well-designed multimedia presentation, such as concise, annotated illustrations, or from poorly designed multimedia, such as text alone or text separated from illustrations. In all four comparisons, the low-knowledge learners benefitted more from well-designed multimedia than did the high-knowledge learners. Low knowledge students who received well-designed multimedia presentations generated far more solutions in the problem-solving test than did low-knowledge who received poorly designed multimedia, but this pattern was not present for high-knowledge learners. Overall, the median gain in problem-solving transfer attributable to good design was 61 percentage points greater for low-knowledge students than for the high-knowledge students and the median effect size was .80 greater for the low-knowledge students as compared to high-knowledge students.

Our results show that implementing design principles is more likely to increase the understanding of low-knowledge learners than high-knowledge learners. In general, the high-knowledge learners perform well under all instructional treatments, whereas the low-knowledge learners only perform well when given well-designed multimedia presentations. Based on these findings we propose the prior-knowledge principle: Implement design principles particularly for low-knowledge rather than high-knowledge learners.

A THEORY OF MULTIMEDIA LEARNING

Our program of research is based on the premise that multimedia instructional design should be based on a theory of how students learn from text and pictures. Our research contributes to the development of a cognitive theory of multimedia learning that is summarized in Fig. 14.5. The theory is based on three basic assumptions concerning the nature of human learning: the dual channel assumption, the limited-capacity assumption, and the active processing assumption (Mayer, 2001).

Dual-Channel Assumption

The first assumption is that humans process incoming information through two separate channels, one channel for auditory/verbal processing and one channel for visual/pictorial processing. In Fig. 14.5, this assumption is reflected in having the top row of boxes for auditory/verbal processing and the bottom row for visual/pictorial processing. This assumption is adapted from Paivio's (1986; Clark & Paivio, 1991) dual coding theory. According to this view, text enters through the eyes but is transferred to the verbal channel for further processing whereas illustrations enter through the eyes and are processed in the pictorial channel.

Limited-Capacity Assumption

The second assumption is that humans are limited in the amount of processing that can occur in each channel. In Fig. 14.5, this assumption is re-

Model of Multimedia learning

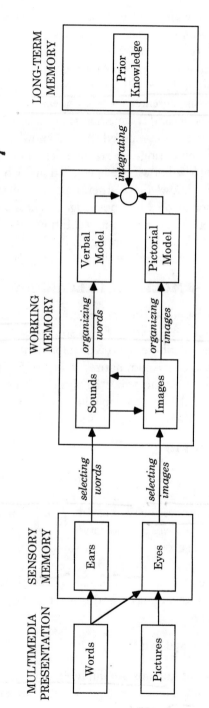

Fig. 14.5. A cognitive model of multimedia learning. From Mayer (2001). Copyright © 2001 by the Cambridge University Press. Reprinted by permission.

flected in center boxes labeled *working memory*. This assumption is adapted from Baddeley's (1992, 1998) working memory theory and Chandler and Sweller's (1991) cognitive load theory. According to this view, a learner can process only a limited amount of verbal material and a limited amount of pictorial material at one time.

Active Processing Assumption

[handwritten: org + create coherence!]

The third assumption is that meaningful learning depends on the learner's engaging in appropriate cognitive processing, including paying attention to relevant incoming material, mentally organizing the material into a coherent structure, and mentally connecting the structures they build with each other and with prior knowledge. In Fig. 14.5, this assumption is indicated by the arrows labeled *selecting words, selecting images, organizing words, organizing images*, and *integrating*. This assumption is adapted from Wittrock's (1989) theory of generative learning and Mayer's (1996b, 1999b) theory of meaningful learning. According to this view, a central condition for meaningful learning, integrating a verbal and pictorial representation of the material, is that learners be able to hold corresponding verbal and pictorial representations in working memory at the same time.

ARE THE DESIGN PRINCIPLES CONSISTENT WITH THE COGNITIVE THEORY OF MULTIMEDIA LEARNING?

Table 14.10 summarizes the four research-based principles of how to promote meaningful learning from science text. In addition to being consistent with empirical research, each of the four principles is consistent with the cognitive theory of multimedia learning. This theory assumes that the learner is actively trying to make sense of the presented explanation by mentally constructing a cause-and-effect chain. This construction process is enhanced when learners can process verbal and pictorial representations at the same time.

In contrast, a competing view of multimedia learning is what can be called the information delivery theory, the idea that media channels serve as delivery routes from the teacher to the student (see Mayer, 1996a). Words can be used to deliver information to a learner, or illustrations can be used to deliver information to a learner. As long the information is delivered, it does not matter whether it was delivered via words or pictures or both.

TABLE 14.10

**Four Principles for Promoting Understanding
of Scientific Text**

Name	Statement of Principle	Number of Tests	Median Gain	Median Effect Size
Multimedia	Use text and illustrations rather than text alone.	6 of 6	79%	1.37
Spatial contiguity	Put text next to corresponding illustrations.	5 of 5	68%	1.12
Coherence	Eliminate extraneous text and illustrations.	8 of 8	105%	1.66
Prior knowledge	Provide well-designed multimedia to low-knowledge rather than high-knowledge learners.	4 of 4	61%	0.80

Multimedia Principle

According to the cognitive theory of multimedia learning, meaningful learning occurs when the learner selects and organizes words into a coherent verbal representation, selects and organizes pictures into a coherent visual representation, and integrates the two representations. When material is presented only in verbal form, some of the processes are emphasized (such as selecting and organizing words) but the other processes may not be likely to occur. Although it is possible to form and organize mental images from words, this might not occur in a systematic way for all learners. Thus, for text-only presentations, one of the major conditions for meaningful learning is less likely to be met: having corresponding verbal and pictorial representations in working memory at the same time (Alternatively, when words and illustrations are presented in a coordinated way, all five cognitive processes are facilitated) Thus, the cognitive theory of multimedia learning predicts that students who learn from words and illustrations will understand an explanation better than students who learn from words alone. This prediction was overwhelming confirmed in our research.

In contrast, the information delivery theory predicts that students who learn from words alone should perform as well as students who learn from words and illustrations. According to the information delivery view, a well-written text explanation is all that is needed to deliver information to a learner; adding an illustration depicting the same information does not affect learning because the information is already being delivered by the words. The results summarized in the top line of Table 14.10 conflict sharply with this prediction, and offer no support for the information delivery theory.

Spatial Contiguity Principle

According to the cognitive theory of multimedia learning, meaningful learning is facilitated when a learner is able to hold corresponding pictorial and verbal representations in working memory at the same time. This cognitive condition is more likely to occur when corresponding words and pictures are presented near one another on the page than when they are separated from one another. Therefore, students who receive integrated presentation are expected to understand the explanation better than students who receive separated presentation.

In contrast, the information delivery theory holds that words and pictures are two ways of delivering information to the learner. When both deliveries come at the same time (as in integrated presentation), the learner essentially receives the information once. However, when words and pictures are presented separately (as in separated presentation), the learner is exposed to the same information twice—once when processing the words and once when processing the pictures. Therefore, students who receive separated presentation are expected to understand the explanation better than students who receive integrated presentation.

The results summarized in the second row of Table 14.10 are consistent with the cognitive theory of multimedia learning and inconsistent with the information delivery theory.

Coherence Principle

According to the cognitive theory of multimedia learning, learners are working hard to make sense of the presented explanation by mentally constructing a cause-and-effect chain. This process of knowledge construction is enhanced when the adjacent links in the chain are presented near one another, and this process is obstructed when irrelevant material is presented between successive links. The tactic of interspersing details that are interesting but irrelevant may signal learners to use inappropriate organizing schemata instead of a cause-and-effect chain. Therefore, students who receive concise presentation are expected to understand the explanation better than students who receive extraneous presentation—a prediction that coincides with the results summarized on the third line of Table 14.10.

In contrast, the information delivery theory posits that the teacher's job is to transmit information and the learner's job is to receive it. In both the concise presentation and extraneous presentation, the same information is presented concerning the cause-and-effect chain. Therefore, students who receive the extraneous presentation are expected to understand the explanation as well as students who receive the concise presentation. The results summarized in the third row of Table 14.10 are consistent with the cognitive theory of multimedia learning and inconsistent with the informational delivery theory.

Prior-Knowledge Principle

According to the cognitive theory of multimedia learning, a major step in meaningful learning is to connect corresponding visual and verbal representations. When text is presented alone or separated from the illustrations, this process is hindered. However, students who possess high prior knowledge may be able to form appropriate mental images from words alone, whereas students who lack prior knowledge may be less able to accomplish this feat. Therefore, good multimedia design is expected to benefit low-knowledge learners more than it benefits high-knowledge learners. This pattern was obtained in our research, as summarized in final row of Table 14.10.

In contrast, the information delivery theory assumes that students who have more knowledge may be more effective in receiving information whereas students who possess low knowledge may be less effective in receiving information. Similarly, good multimedia design serves to deliver the information more effectively to all learners. Therefore, good multimedia design is expected to have the same effects on improving the knowledge acquisition of both high- and low-knowledge learners. The results summarized in the final row of Table 14.10 are consistent with the cognitive theory of multimedia learning and inconsistent with the information delivery theory.

CONCLUSION

Our research demonstrates that it is possible to foster active learning from passive media. Active learning occurs when learners actively make sense of the presented material by constructing a coherent cognitive structure. Printed text is generally considered to be a passive medium because the learner cannot interact with it in a behavioral way. The focus of our re-

generate active learning

search is on how to design text-based instructional messages so that they
foster active learning. Based on a series of research studies we offer four
principles of text design that warrant further study: (a) the multimedia principle, the idea that students understand an explanation better when it is
presented in words and pictures rather than in words alone, (b) the spatial
contiguity principle, the idea that students understand an explanation
better when corresponding words and pictures are presented near rather
than far from each other on the page, (c) the coherence principle, the idea
that students understand an explanation better when extraneous material
is excluded rather than included, and (d) the prior-knowledge principle, the
idea that these design principles benefit low-knowledge students more than
high-knowledge students.

Other reviews include parallel principles for the design of computer-based multimedia messages involving animation and narration
(Mayer, 1999a, 1999c, 2001). For example, students learn more deeply from
animation and narration rather than narration alone (multimedia principle), students learn more deeply when on-screen text is placed near rather
than far from the corresponding action in the animation (spatial contiguity
principle), students learn more deeply when corresponding portions of animation and narration are presented simultaneously rather than successively (temporal contiguity principle), and students learn more deeply
when extraneous music, sounds, and videoclips are excluded rather than
included from a narrated animation (coherence principle). Overall, our research shows that passive media can promote active learning when the materials are designed on the basis of how people learn.

REFERENCES

Ausubel, D. P. (1968). *Educational psychology: A cognitive view.* New York: Holt,
    Rinehart & Winston.
Baddeley, A. (1992). Working memory. *Science, 255,* 556–559.
Baddeley, A. (1998). *Human memory* (Rev. ed.). Boston: Allyn & Bacon.
Brincones, I., & Otero, J. (1992). Students' conceptions of the top-level structure
    of physics texts. *Science Education, 78,* 171–183.
Chandler, P., & Sweller, J. (1991). Cognitive load theory and the format of instruc-
    tion. *Cognition and Instruction, 8,* 293–332.
Clark, J. M., & Paivio, A. (1991). Dual coding theory and education. *Educational
    Psychology Review, 3,* 149–210.
Cook, L. K., & Mayer, R. E. (1988). Teaching readers about the structure of scien-
    tific text. *Journal of Educational Psychology, 80,* 448–456.
Graesser, A. C., Singer, M., & Trabasso, T. (1994). Constructing inferences during
    narrative text comprehension. *Psychological Review, 101,* 371–395.

Harp, S., & Mayer, R. E. (1997). Role of interest in learning from scientific text and illustrations: On the distinction between emotional interest and cognitive interest. *Journal of Educational Psychology, 89,* 92–102.

Harp, S., & Mayer, R. E. (1998). How seductive details do their damage: A theory of cognitive interest in science learning. *Journal of Educational Psychology, 90,* 414–434.

Lefrancois, G. R. (1997). *Psychology for teachers* (9th ed.). Belmont, CA: Wadsworth.

Mayer, R. E. (1989). Systematic thinking fostered by illustrations in scientific text. *Journal of Educational Psychology, 81,* 240–246.

Mayer, R. E. (1996a). Learners as information processors: Legacies and limitations of educational psychology's second metaphor. *Educational Psychologist, 31,* 151–161.

Mayer, R. E. (1996b). Learning strategies for making sense out of expository text: The SOI model for guiding three cognitive processes in knowledge construction. *Educational Psychology Review, 8,* 357–371.

Mayer, R. E. (1997). Multimedia learning: Are we asking the right questions? *Educational Psychologist, 32,* 1–19.

Mayer, R. E. (1999a). Multimedia aids to problem-solving transfer. *International Journal of Educational Research, 31,* 611–623.

Mayer, R. E. (1999b). *The promise of educational psychology.* Upper Saddle River, NJ: Prentice–Hall.

Mayer, R. E. (1999c). Research-based principles for the design of multimedia instructional messages: The case of multimedia instructional messages. *Document Design, 1,* 7–20.

Mayer, R. E. (2001). *Multimedia learning.* New York: Cambridge University Press.

Mayer, R. E., Bove, W., Bryman, A., Mars, R., & Tapangco, L. (1996). When less is more: Meaningful learning from visual and verbal summaries of science textbook lessons. *Journal of Educational Psychology, 88,* 64–73.

Mayer, R. E., & Gallini, J. K. (1990). When is an illustration worth ten thousand words? *Journal of Educational Psychology, 82,* 715–726.

Mayer, R. E., Steinhoff, K., Bower, G., & Mars, R. (1995). A generative theory of textbook design: Using annotated illustrations to foster meaningful learning of science text. *Educational Technology Research and Development, 43,* 31–44.

Meyer, B. J. F. (1975). *The organization of prose and its effects on memory.* Amsterdam: North-Holland.

Moreno, R., & Mayer, R. E. (1999). Cognitive principles of multimedia learning: The role of modality and contiguity. *Journal of Educational Psychology, 91,* 358–368.

National Research Council. (1996). *National science education standards.* Washington, DC: National Academy Press.

Paivio, A. (1986). *Mental representations: A dual coding approach.* Oxford, England: Oxford University Press.

Wittrock, M. C. (1989). Generative processes of comprehension. *Educational Psychologist, 24,* 345–376.

❧ 15 ❧

Understanding Machines From Multimedia and Hypermedia Presentations

---

Mary Hegarty
University of California, Santa Barbara

N. Hari Narayanan
Auburn University

Pam Freitas
University of California, Santa Barbara

What is the best way to communicate to someone how a complex system, such as a mechanical or biological system, works? The traditional way is to produce a printed book that combines textual descriptions with different kinds of illustrations, presented on sequential pages. With the advent of multimedia computers and hypermedia authoring tools, however, we no longer need to be confined to this traditional medium. For example, we can now choose to present verbal information as written text or as an audio commentary. Similarly, we can present diagrams as static or animated, and images as still photographs or video clips. *Multimedia* presentations, combining some or all of the aforementioned media, are becoming increasingly available as educational CD-ROMs and on the World Wide Web. Furthermore, with the availability of new authoring tools, we do not have to be constrained by the linear format of the printed book, in which information is presented and typically read in a sequential order. In *hypermedia* systems, information is presented in a collection of hyperlinked documents, so that information can be browsed in any order.

These technological advances present a tantalizing spectrum of choices to authors of instructional materials. However, there are few empirically validated guidelines for how to choose among the various capabilities for optimal design of hypermedia presentations. There are some widely held beliefs about the effectiveness of these new developments. These include the beliefs that diagrammatic representations are better than sentential representations, three-dimensional representations are better than two-dimensional ones, animated diagrams, are more effective than static diagrams and interactive graphics are better than noninteractive graphics (Scaife & Rogers, 1996). However, most of these beliefs have not been tested systematically.

This chapter describes a research program in which we designed, prototyped and evaluated several versions of a hypermedia presentation explaining how a mechanical system works. Our prototypes describe a specific mechanical system, the flushing cistern. However, our approach to the design of hypermedia presentations can be applied to explaining any complex system, for example, a biological system such as the human circulatory system. In a parallel research project, we have applied our guidelines to the development of interactive animations of computer algorithms (e.g., Hansen, Narayanan, Schrimpsher, & Hegarty, 1998; Hansen, Schrimpsher, & Narayanan, 1998) and we are currently extending our research to the domain of meteorology.

Our design process (illustrated in Fig. 15.1) begins with a review of research on multimodal comprehension, leading to a preliminary model of this process. An initial design for a hypermedia presentation is derived from this model. Then basic research is conducted to refine and elaborate this model. At the same time, the design principles are used to create an initial presentation, which is evaluated by assessing how people interact with the presentation and how well they understand the mechanical systems it explains. The experimental research and evaluation therefore proceed in parallel. The results of the evaluation can be used to redesign the presentation and to suggest further experimental studies (e.g., to examine the causes of particular comprehension failures). The results of the experiments can refine the model that forms the basis of the next design cycle. This process can be repeated to iteratively improve both the design of the hypermedia manual and the model of comprehension on which it is based.

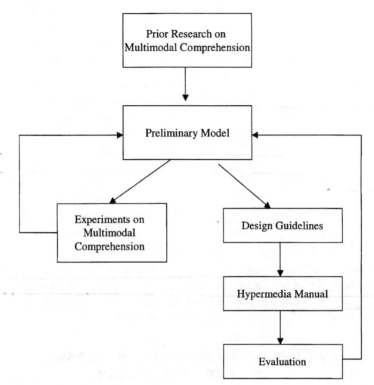

Fig. 15.1.   Overview of our research design.

This design process makes two types of prescriptions about instruction. First, it specifies the *content* of instruction, that is, what information should be communicated in the hypermedia presentation and in what order. Second, it makes prescriptions about the *format* of instruction, that is, the media and modalities in which different types of information should be presented. Many studies of the effects of new media and visualizations in education investigate situations in which a new medium is used in the context of a novel method of instruction, such as discovery or collaborative learning (e.g., Edelson, 1999; White, 1993). Effects of instruction are compared to learning from traditional lecture and textbook formats. In these situations it is difficult to evaluate whether differences in learning outcomes are due to the new media used, the instructional method, or instructional goals embodied in different pedagogies. In our research, we attempt to design instructional treatments that systematically vary the content and the format of instruction, so that we can evaluate the separate effects of each.

Our research builds on recent research examining the conditions under which multimedia instruction is most effective (e.g., Faraday & Sutcliffe, 1997a, 1997b; Mayer, 1997; Mayer & Moreno, 1998; Mousavi, Low, & Sweller, 1995; see also chap. 14, this volume). For example, Mayer and his colleagues have shown that students learn better from text and diagrams if related visual and verbal information is presented as close as possible in space (Mayer & Gallini, 1990), that people learn more effectively from animations if they are accompanied by simultaneous commentaries (Mayer & Sims, 1994), and that people learn more effectively from multimedia information if visual information and verbal information are presented in different modalities (Mayer & Moreno, 1998). Similarly, Faraday and Sutcliffe (1997a, 1997b) showed that students learn more effectively from movies accompanied by commentaries, if visual cues such as arrows and highlighting draw their attention to the relevant parts of the display as they are described in the commentary. Our research addresses a different question. We ask whether multimedia presentations, including animations, commentaries, and hyperlinks, lead to different learning outcomes, compared to traditional printed media when both contain the same information and when both are designed according to available empirically validated guidelines.

A MODEL OF MACHINE COMPREHENSION FROM TEXT AND DIAGRAMS

Explaining how machines work using the printed book is a well-established craft since the 15th century (Ferguson, 1977). This medium consists of written text interspersed with various kinds of illustrations, such as schematic diagrams, cross-sectional views, exploded views, and realistic depictions of machines. Popular books like How Things Work (1967) and The Way Things Work (Macaulay, 1988) are excellent examples of this medium. Readers of such books typically have some specific comprehension goal in mind. For example, a reader might want to understand how the machine operates so that he or she can predict its behavior, operate it, or troubleshoot it.

Our approach to developing a hypermedia manual was to first construct a model (essentially a task analysis) of the process of understanding a machine from text and diagrams (Hegarty, Quilici, Narayanan, Holmquist & Moreno, 1999; Narayanan & Hegarty, 1998). This model can be seen as an extension of constructivist theories of text processing (e.g., Chi, de Leeuw, Chiu, & LaVancher, 1994; Goldman, Graesser, & van den Broek, 1999; Graesser, Singer, & Trabasso, 1994). These theories view comprehension as a process in which the comprehender uses his or her prior knowledge of the domain and integrates it with the presented information to construct a mental model of the object or situation described. In addition to text comprehension skills, our model proposes that comprehension is dependent on spatial skills for integrating information in text and graphics, and encoding and inferring information from graphic displays (Hegarty & Kozhevnikov, 1999; Hegarty & Sims 1994).

According to this model, people construct a mental model of a dynamic system by first decomposing it into simpler components, retrieving relevant background knowledge about these components, and mentally encoding the relations (spatial and semantic) between components to construct a static mental model of the situation. They then mentally animate this static mental model to construct a kinematic/dynamic mental model of the system. We postulate that mental model construction under these circumstances requires the stages described next. Although we list them in order, we acknowledge that they are not always accomplished in this order:

1. *Machine Decomposition by Diagram Parsing*. Diagrams of mechanical systems are made up of elementary shapes, such as rectangles, circles, and cylinders, that represent objects such as pistons, gears, and tubes. The first step in comprehension is to parse the connected diagram into these elementary shapes, that is, units in the diagram that correspond to subcomponents of the mechanical system.

2. *Constructing a Static Mental Model by Making Representational Connections*. The second stage in multimodal comprehension involves making appropriate connections in memory among the components identified in Stage 1. This stage involves making two types of connections: (a) connections to prior knowledge and (b) connections to the representations of other machine components.

First, the user must identify the components, that is, make connections between the diagrammatic elements identified at Stage 1 and their real-world referents. For example, the user might represent that a rectangle represents a piston or a circle represents a gear. Prior knowledge can also provide additional information about components, such as what they are typically made of and whether they are rigid or flexible. This information is valuable in making inferences about how components move and constrain each other's behaviors.

Second, the user must represent the spatial relations between different machine components by building connections between the representations of these components (Mayer & Sims, 1994). In understanding how a machine works, information about the spatial relations between mechanical components forms the basis for inferences about the motions of components, because these spatial relations determine how components affect and constrain each other's motions.

3. *Making Referential Connections.* When diagrams are accompanied by text, an additional stage in comprehension is that of resolving coreference between the two media, that is, making referential links between a noun phrase in the text (e.g., "the piston") and the diagrammatic unit that depicts its referent (e.g., a rectangle) (Novak, 1995). This step is crucial to constructing an integrated representation of the common referent of the text and diagram in memory as opposed to separate surface-level representations of the text and diagram.

4. *Determining the Causal Chain of Events.* When asked to predict the behavior of machines from static diagrams, people tend to reason about machine operation along the direction of causal propagation in the machine (Hegarty, 1992; Narayanan, Suwa, & Motoda, 1994, 1995). Therefore, we hypothesize a fourth stage of comprehension that involves identifying the potential causal chains of events in the operation of the machine, or "lines of action" in the machine.

5. *Constructing a Dynamic Mental Model by Mental Simulation and Rule-Based Inference.* The final stage of comprehension is that of constructing a dynamic mental model of the machine, that is, a representation of how the components move and constrain each other's motion when the machine is in operation. Our previous research (Hegarty, 1992; Narayanan et al., 1994, 1995) suggests that people can often infer this information from a static diagram by a process that we call *mental animation.* Computational models and empirical evidence suggest that this is an incremental process in which the reasoner considers the components or subsystems individually, assesses the influences acting on each, infers the resulting behavior of each, and then proceeds to consider how this behavior affects the next component or subsystem in the causal chain. It depends on both prior knowledge (e.g., rules that govern the behavior of the system in question) and spatial visualization processes.

INITIAL DESIGN OF A HYPERMEDIA MANUAL

In a recent article (Narayanan & Hegarty, 1998), we identified potential sources of comprehension error that users might encounter in each stage of comprehension, and developed hypermedia design guidelines intended to ameliorate these difficulties. These were applied to develop a prototype hypermedia manual that explains how a toilet tank (a flushing cistern) works. Although this is a familiar device, its inner workings are not intuitively obvious. It is relatively complex, having two main subsystems: a water output system that flushes water into the toilet tank, and a water inlet system that refills the tank for the next use. Explaining a flushing cistern presents interesting challenges for our theory because its operation involves two causal chains of events that occur in tandem but are also temporarily dependent on each other. The particular toilet tank explained in our manual also contains a siphon (see Fig. 15.2). A siphon works by the principle that fluids move from areas of higher pressure to areas of lower pressure. This raises the interesting question of how to explain a basic physics principle in the context of explaining how a specific machine works.

The initial design for our hypermedia manual contained seven sections designed to guide users through the stages of comprehension in our model. Figure 15.2 contains an image of a screen from the first section of this manual. The seven sections are as follows:

1. *Section 1, "Parts":* The primary objectives of this section are to help the user in decomposing the machine into its components and building referential connections between elements of text and diagrams. Previous research has pointed out that diagrams are often underspecified in that they do not contain enough information for a user to identify whether two or more connected units in a diagram represent separate objects or parts of a single object (Novak, 1995). For example, a diagram element, such as a line, might represent the edge of an object, or an object itself (a rope). Furthermore, resolving coreference between text and graphics can be a source of comprehension difficulty (Mayer & Sims, 1994). To facilitate users in these processes, the first section of the manual presents a cross-sectional diagram of the toilet tank, in which decomposition is facilitated by labeling the different functional components, by presenting them in different colors, and by allowing users to click on the label of any component and have the component highlighted in the diagram (see Fig. 15.2).

2. *Section 2, "Subsystems":* The decomposition of a mechanical system is often hierarchical, such that the system breaks down into functional subsystems, which can themselves be broken down into more elementary components. The objective of Section 2 is to facilitate identifying the functional subsystems to which the components belong, that is, the water output system and the water input system. The first presentation in this section is a schematic diagram with accompanying text that outlines

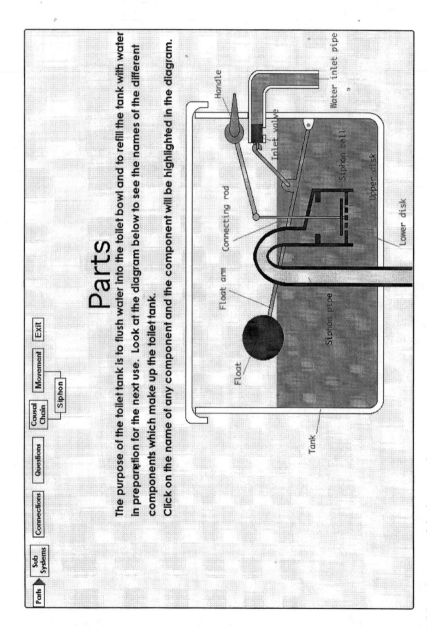

Fig. 15.2. A screen of the hypermedia manual.

the various subsystems of the machine. This presentation also allows the user to animate an exploded view of the machine in which the input and output systems are separated in space. In two further presentations, the user views diagrams highlighting the components of first the output system and then the input system, each accompanied by text describing the function of the relevant subsystem.

3. *Section 3, "Connections"*: The objective of Section 3 is to facilitate construction of a static mental model of the machine. This includes identifying the real-world components to which diagram units refer, and retrieving prior knowledge about these components (what they are made of, their principles of operation, etc.). This information is not included in highly schematized depictions, but is necessary for correct inferences about how the machine works (Schwartz & Black, 1996). In this section, the user is shown a cross-sectional view of the toilet tank and taken on a guided tour of the components. Text describes each of the components in turn, pointing out its linkages to other system components, and other information that is not visible in the diagram, such as its material composition and function. Only the text about one component is visible at a time, and to aid the construction of referential connections, the component in question is highlighted in the diagram concurrently with the presentation of the textual description.

4. *Section 4, "Questions"*: This section is designed to encourage the user to reason about the causality and dynamics of the machine. Previous research has shown that the generation of ideas or self-explanations improves learning (Chi et al., 1994). Therefore one of our guidelines is that users should be encouraged to mentally animate the machine (i.e., attempt to predict its behavior) before they are shown animations of the causal chain and movement of the machine. Section 4 does this by presenting users with the static diagram, and a set of multiple-choice questions in which users are asked to imagine that a component of the system is moving in a given way and have to predict how another component of the system will be moving. Users are given feedback on their answers.

5. *Section 5, "Causal Chain"*: The purpose of this section is to help the user in understanding the propagation of causality in the entire machine. It contains an audio commentary describing the operation of the toilet tank, explaining causal propagation within and across the water output and water inlet subsystems. Synchronized with the commentary, the corresponding components and paths of causal propagation are highlighted in the static schematic diagram. An "explain siphon principle" button

gives users the option to access a description of the fundamental physics principle underlying the operation of the water output system—the siphon (see Section 7).

6. *Section 6, "Movement"*: The objective of this section is to convey how the machine actually operates by describing and showing the movements of its components. It includes the same auditory commentary as Section 5. An animation in which all component behaviors are concurrently shown continuously cycles through the operation of the device during this commentary. At the end of this narrated animation, users have the option of replaying it, or viewing a silent animation. An "explain siphon principle" button again gives users the option to access a description of how a siphon works.

7. *Section 7, "The Siphon"*: The purpose of this section is to explain a fundamental physics principle underlying the behavior of the toilet tank—the siphon. It contains a schematic diagram of the machine with the siphon bell and pipe highlighted. The text describes how a siphon works and how it applies to the operation of the water output system of the toilet tank. Users can also view a silent animation of the siphon effect. This section is not part of the sequential path through sections of the manual. Instead, it is reached from Sections 5 or 6, in response to a user clicking the "explain siphon principle" button.

Navigation and Guidance. The model of machine comprehension outlined previously suggests a sequence of comprehension stages, such that the later stages are at least somewhat dependent on successful completion of the earlier ones. In particular, representation of the spatial relations between device components (Stage 2b) is dependent on first decomposing the system into individual components (Stage 1), and the stages of finding lines of action and constructing a kinematic mental model (Stages 4 and 5) are dependent on successful construction of a static model of the machine (Stages 2 and 3). Therefore, in the initial version of the hypermedia presentation, we constrained navigation. Users studied the sections of the manual in order, starting with Section 1 ("Parts"). An exception to this forward traversal was Section 7 ("The Siphon"), which could be accessed optionally from Section 5 or 6. Once the user had seen a section, he or she was allowed to return to it at any time. Users proceeded from section to section using an overall "map" of the hypermedia manual, which showed icons for all the sections of the manual and was color coded to show users their current place in the system, the sections that they had already studied, and the sections that they were allowed to move to at any given time (see the upper left corner of Fig. 15.2). Sections of the map were highlighted and became mouse sensitive based on the user's history, so that clicking on a section was successful only if it was consistent with these navigation constraints.

EMPIRICAL STUDIES OF MULTIMEDIA AND HYPERMEDIA COMPREHENSION

We now summarize the results of several experiments designed to evaluate different aspects of the hypermedia presentation. First, we examine whether people learn differently from hypermedia presentations, including hyperlinks and animations, compared to printed manuals containing the same visual and verbal information. Second, we ask whether people learn differently from hypermedia presentations that direct the learner to view the information in a specific order as opposed to those that allow free navigation. Third, we ask whether people learn more from an animation of a mechanical system if they first try to mentally animate the system.

Do People Learn Differently From Hypermedia Presentations, Compared to Printed Materials Containing the Same Information?

The initial hypermedia manual design embodied guidelines about both the format and the content of instruction. Therefore it was important to evaluate the separate effects of format differences and content differences between our manual and typical instructional materials. First, the hypermedia manual differed from standard printed manuals in the format of instruction. It included dynamic elements, that is, constrained navigation, hyperlinks, and animations that are not available in the print medium. In the first experiment that we describe here, we compare the learning outcomes of interacting with the hypermedia manuals to those of studying printed text and diagrams containing the same content.

Experiment 1a

Hegarty et al. (1999) compared three groups. The first learned from the hypermedia presentation (described earlier). A second learned from a paper printout of the text and diagrams used in the manual (which we refer to as the *full-text* condition). The third learned from a paper printout of the labeled diagram of the toilet tank accompanied by printed text describing the movement of the components in order of the causal chain (the *causal-text* condition). The main differences between the hypermedia manual and full-text conditions were the absence of hyperlinks and animations in the full-text condition and the presentation of the verbal description of the causal chain and movement of components, which was presented visually as text rather than auditorally. The main difference between the full-text and causal-text conditions was that the causal text did not include the sections explicitly pointing out the subsystems of the toilet tank, the connections between components, and the material composition of the components.

Twenty undergraduate students studied how a toilet tank works from the manual, 20 more students studied the full text, and 20 more students studied the causal text. All students were timed as they studied the materials. Afterwards, their comprehension was tested with the following types of questions:

Mental animation questions, which required them to predict how a component of the system would be moving, given that another component was moving in a specified way. For example, one question asked "Imagine the connecting rod is moving up. What is happening to the float arm?"

Function Questions, which are questions about the function of a component in the system, for example, "What is the function of the float and float arm?

"Fault-behavior" questions, which described a particular fault in a component of the system and asked participants to predict how the system would behave, for example, "How would the tank function be affected if the inlet valve was stuck in the water inlet pipe? (list all possible answers)."

"Troubleshooting" questions, which described faulty behavior of the system and asked what components might be faulty, for example, "Suppose that after flushing the toilet, you notice that water is continuously running into the tank. What could be wrong? (list all possible answers)."

A background questionnaire asked participants to list any courses they had taken in physics, mechanics, or mechanical engineering, to list any mechanical or electrical items that they had attempted to repair, and specifically whether they had ever tried to fix a toilet, change the oil in a car, or unblock a drain. Finally, they were asked to rate on a scale of 1 to 7 how interesting they thought the material was (with 1 meaning not interesting at all and 7 meaning very interesting).

Results. The main difference between the three groups was in their study times. The causal group spent the least time studying the materials

(4.62 minutes, $SD = 1.89$) Although the full-text and hypermedia manual groups received the same content, the latter group spent longer (14.57 minutes, $SD = 4.09$) than the full-text group (10.43 minutes, $SD = 3.39$). This may reflect time learning and interacting with the computer interface and the fact that participants had to view the whole animations in Sections 5 and 6 of the manual. These animations were played at a constant rate that was probably slower than the time taken to read the relevant text and integrate it with the diagram in the full-text condition. It might also reflect higher motivation induced by the hypermedia presentation. However, the type of instruction did not influence participants' ratings of interest in the materials. The mean rating was 4.05 for the hypermedia group, 4.10 for the full-text group, and 4.30 for the causal-text group.

These differences in study times did not lead to differences in comprehension. There were no significant differences between the three groups on any of the comprehension measures. The only effect of prior knowledge was on the mental animation questions. Participants with more practical experience with machines (i.e., those who had attempted to repair more machines) had higher mental animation scores (12.12, $SD = 4.26$) compared to those with less practical experience (9.73, $SD = 2.52$), $F(1, 54) = 6.24$, $p < .05$. None of the measures of training or experience had significant interactions with the type of instruction suggesting that the various instructional conditions were not differentially effective for individuals with different amounts of prior knowledge or experience.

Discussion. In summary, Experiment 1a showed no differences in learning outcomes between the three groups, despite differences in study times. The similarity in performance between the full-text and hypermedia groups indicates that whether people view information on a computer screen or on paper, interact with a hypermedia interface including hyperlinked text and diagrams rather than reading printed material, and view animations with commentaries rather than static text and diagrams does not have significant effects on learning this material. This result suggests that the media and modalities through which information is presented do not affect comprehension, when the instruction is designed according to our comprehension model.

A comparison of the full-text and hypermedia groups with the causal-text groups also reveals no differences in learning outcomes. This suggests that explicitly describing the functions of the toilet tank subsystems, the connections between components, and the material composition of the components does not affect people's ability to understand the causal chain or kinematics of the device. On first glance this appears to contradict the principles of our theoretical model. However, it is possible that the labeled diagram of the device provided to participants in the causal-text condition provided sufficient information about the decomposition of the diagram and the spatial relations between components so that the additional text describing these aspects of the system was superfluous. Furthermore, because a toilet tank is a household item, participants might have already been familiar with the functions and material composition of its parts, so that the additional information on these topics in the full-text and multimedia conditions (Section 3 of the manual) might have been superfluous. Hegarty et al. (1999) replicated this result in two further experiments, in which students learned about car brakes and a bicycle pump, in addition to the toilet tank, indicating that it generalizes to other relatively familiar devices.

Experiment 1b

Experiment 1a indicated that the media and modalities through which information is presented does not affect comprehension, when the instruction is designed according to our comprehension model. In a recent experiment, we compared hypermedia and printed versions of our manual to hypermedia and printed instruction on the same type of flushing cistern from commercially available hypermedia and multimedia presentations (*The Way Things Work* book and CD-ROM by David Macaulay, 1988, 1998). This experiment also allowed us to compare learning from our materials to learning from materials that were designed according to the intuitions of an award-winning designer, but that were not informed by our comprehension model.

In this experiment, some participants learned from a version of our hypermedia manual, which was revised according to the results found by Hegarty et al. (1999). Because we found that students learned as much from the causal text as from the full text in Experiment 1a, we omitted Section 3 of the original presentation in the revised manual. The revised manual combined Sections 1 and 2 of the original model, so that students first saw the cross-sectional diagram of the whole system (as in Section 1 of the original manual), then saw it decomposed into the water output and water inlet systems (with all the functionality described in Section 2 of the original manual), and then were allowed to click on individual components and have them highlighted in the diagram (as in Section 1 of the original manual). The revised manual also combined Sections 5 and 6 of the original manual, so that students saw an animation of the system in which successive components in the causal chain were pointed out, using a red arrow, as they were described in the accompanying commentary (the arrow thus performed the same function as the successive highlighting in Section 5 of the original manual). This embodies a design principle suggested by Faraday and Sutcliffe (1997a, 1997b) to direct students' attention to the part of the visual presentation that is being described in the auditory commentary. The manual therefore had four sections: an initial section that showed the hierarchical decomposition of the systems, a questions section (identical to Section 4 of the original manual), a movement section, in which successive components in the causal chain were indicated with an arrow, and the siphon section (identical to Section 7 of the original manual).

Other students learned from the description of the toilet tank in *The Way Things Work* book or CD-ROM (Macaulay, 1988, 1998). The description in the book shows a large labeled diagram of the toilet tank, which differed from the diagram in Fig. 15.2 in that it showed the third dimension and is a rather whimsical depiction, showing fish swimming in the tank, and fishermen sitting on the float arm. Several small diagrams are shown as insets to the main diagram. One shows a side view of a toilet indicating the location of the tank, two more show the operation of a siphon and are accompanied by text explaining how a siphon works, and three more show different stages in the flushing of the cistern and are accompanied by a description of the flushing process. The CD-ROM version shows the same large labeled diagram on a single screen of text. From this, the user has the option of clicking on two "movie" icons, one of which brings them to another screen showing a schematic diagram of the toilet tank that is animated in response to a mouse click. This animation is very fast (takes no more than a couple of seconds) and is not accompanied by a commentary. Clicking on the other "movie" icon brings the user to a screen describing how a siphon works, which is also accompanied by a diagram that the user can animate.

Method. Fifteen undergraduate students studied our hypermedia manual, 16 studied a paper printout of the text and diagrams used in the manual, 14 students studied the hypermedia presentation on the toilet tank from *The New Way Things Work* CD-ROM (Macaulay, 1998), and 16 students studied the corresponding materials from *The Way Things Work* book (Macalulay, 1988).

Afterwards, all students wrote a description of how the device worked. They were instructed to imagine that they push down on the handle of the toilet tank and describe, step-by-step, what happens to each of the other parts of the tank as it flushes. Then they answered function questions and troubleshooting questions as described earlier in Experiment 1a. Finally they were administered a test of spatial visualization ability—the Paper Folding Test (Ekstrom, French, Harman, & Derman, 1976).

Results. Students spent on average 9.06 minutes studying the hypermedia manual, 6.18 minutes studying the printed version of the manual, 5.32 minutes studying the *New Way Things Work* (Macaluay, 1998), CD-ROM and 4.79 minutes studying *The* way *Things Work* book (Macaulay, 1988). There was a large effect of instruction on ability to describe how the toilet tank worked. Students who learned from the materials developed according to our comprehension model described more steps in the causal chain (12.20 steps for the hypermedia group, 12.25 steps for those who received the printed materials) than students who learned from the Macaulay materials (7.36 steps for the CD-ROM group, 7.81 steps for those who received the printed materials). However, there were no significant differences in this measure between the printed and multimedia versions of either presentation.

Students who learned from the materials developed according to our comprehension model also had better performance on the function questions. For the troubleshooting questions, those who learned from our materials were better than those who learned from the Macaulay book, but not the Macaulay CD Rom. Spatial ability was marginally related to the ability to describe how the toilet tank worked and had a significant effect on troubleshooting performance. However there were no interactions of the format of instruction with either spatial ability, prior knowledge, or practical experience with machines, indicating that the instruction was equally effective for students with different backgrounds and abilities.

Discussion. In summary, the results of this experiment are consistent with those of Experiment 1a in showing no difference between printed versions of instructional materials and hypermedia versions, including animations and hyperlinks, when the content of the materials is the same. It also showed that the materials that were designed according to our comprehension model were superior to award-winning commercially available materials, suggesting that our theoretically derived and empirically supported guidelines are a significant improvement over the conventional wisdom in multimedia design. These studies clearly indicate that it is the content and structure of instructional materials, and not the media and modalities in which they are presented that is important for comprehension of complex devices.

Do People Learn Differently From Hypermedia Presentations That Direct the Learner to View the Information in a Specific Order Compared to Those That Allow Free Navigation?

Our model of machine comprehension suggests that a presentation should provide information about the decomposition of the device, the spatial relations between components, the causal chains of events in the operation of the machine, and the behaviors of the components. In our initial hypermedia design, we constrained navigation in the manual to ensure that users worked through each section. In a sense, this made our hypermedia manual more like a digitized book, in which information is presented on sequential pages, rather than a true hypermedia system that allows information to be viewed in any order.

Our decision to constrain navigation in the initial version of the hypermedia presentation was based on evidence that people, especially novices in the domain of interest, do not search these media optimally. For example, users can search haphazardly, get lost and fail to get an overview of how the information in the different displays is integrated (Hammond & Allinson, 1989; Spoehr, 1994). On the other hand, Shapiro (1998) found that students indicated a deeper level of learning from a less structured hypermedia document, compared to one in which the hierarchical structure was made obvious, and one in which the presentation was linear. She interpreted this result in relation to research on text comprehension showing that more knowledgeable readers learn more from less elaborate and less coherent texts compared to texts that are easier to comprehend (McNamara, E. Kintsch, Songer, & W. Kintsch, 1996), because the less structured texts promote more active processing. In general, there is no clear consensus in the literature regarding the relative effectiveness of hypermedia systems compared to more linear forms of presentation. In a meta-analysis of 13 studies comparing hypertext to linear text, Chen and Rada (1996) reported that hypertext was more effective in 8 cases and the opposite was true in the other 5 cases.

In Experiment 2, we compared learning outcomes from our initial hypermedia manual that constrained the order of navigation, and a version that contained the same information, but allowed students to view the sections in any order.

Experiment 2

N=36

Method.   Thirty-six students took part in this experiment. Eighteen learned from the hypermedia presentation described previously in which they were restricted to view the sections of the presentation in the order prescribed by our comprehension model. The other 18 students learned from a presentation that contained the same sections and information within the sections, but they were free to view the sections in any order. Afterwards, all students answered the mental animation questions, function questions, fault-behavior questions and troubleshooting questions, used in Experiment 1a described earlier.

Results. Participants who learned from the restricted-navigation version of the manual spent more time studying ($M = 15.21$ minutes, $SD = 03.23$) than participants who viewed the free-navigation manual ($M = 11.39$ minutes, $SD = 02.37$). In general, participants viewing the restricted version revisited a section ($M = 1.82, SD = 1.6$) more often than did participants viewing the free version ($M = 1.38, SD = 1.2$).

The type of presentation studied (free vs. restricted navigation) did not affect performance on any of the four categories of comprehension questions. Furthermore, there were no significant effects of the interactions between previous experience or mechanical training with type of manual presented for any of the categories of questions.

Although participants in the free-navigation condition were allowed to view the sections in any order, in fact, most of them viewed them in the order prescribed in the restricted navigation version of the manual. Twelve of the 18 participants in the free-navigation condition viewed the sections in the order prescribed in the constrained-navigation version of the manual and most of the others did not depart much from this order. This may be because the icons that people clicked to gain access to the sections of the manual were aligned from left to right on the screen (see upper left corner of Fig. 15.2). Therefore most participants did not use the freedom that they were afforded to view sections in any order, a result that has been reported elsewhere (White, 1993).

This study therefore showed no differences in effectiveness of hypermedia presentations with free and restricted navigation. It was a limited test of the differences between free and restricted navigation, given that the number of sections in the presentation seven was relatively small. Differences may emerge in more complex hypermedia systems, or in systems where the interface used for navigation does not suggest an order in which to view the information. However, as reviewed earlier, the issue of whether hypermedia are more effective than linear presentations is clearly an open question, and probably depends on many aspects of the design of specific presentations (Chen & Rada, 1996; Shapiro, 1998).

Do People Learn More From an Animation of a Mechanical System If They First Try to Mentally Animate the System?

Experiments 1a and 1b, described earlier, showed no advantage of learning from animations accompanied by commentaries, compared to learning from text and static diagrams presenting the same information. This result is contrary to many people's intuitions about the effectiveness of computer animations (Scaife & Rogers, 1996). We might expect animations to be more effective than static diagrams. For example, animations portray the temporal changes in the operation of a machine *explicitly*, rather than relying on the user to visualize these changes, and they might be closer to a mental model of a mechanical system than would a static depiction (Lowe, 1999).

However, there are also several reasons why animations accompanied by commentaries might be less effective than static text and diagrams. First, animations accompanied by commentaries take a specified amount of time to display. In contrast, reading of static diagrams and text is self-paced. There is a question, therefore, of whether comprehension processes can keep up with the pace at which an animation is presented (see also Lowe, 1999).

Second, a realistic animation of a mechanical system shows all components moving simultaneously. In contrast, when people attempt to understand how a machine works, or answer questions about how a device works, they mentally animate the components one by one, in order of a causal chain of events (Baggett & Graesser, 1995; Hegarty, 1992; Hegarty & Sims, 1994, Narayanan et al., 1994, 1995). Furthermore, in a complex machine such as the flushing cistern, there are two causal chains that operate simultaneously. Therefore, to understand an animation, people need to attend to and relate changes that occur simultaneously in different regions of space (Lowe, 1999). However our visual attention is typically focused on only one location at a time.

Third, viewing an animation is a passive process. Phenomena such as the self-generation effect (Slamencka & Graf, 1978) and the self-explanation effect (Chi et al., 1994) suggest that people learn more effectively if they are more active in the learning process, and actually generate ideas or explanations. Similarly, people learn more from information presentations if they first participate in activities that activate their knowledge relevant to the topic of the presentation (Britton & Graesser, 1996; W. Kintsch, Britton, Fletcher, Mannes, & Nathan 1993; McNamara et al., 1996) or generate the important distinctions relevant to understanding the topic (Schwartz & Bransford, 1998).

In contrast to passively viewing an animation, previous research has shown that people can be quite successful in mentally animating mechanical systems (Hegarty, 1992; Narayanan et al., 1994, 1995). Furthermore, people with high spatial ability are more successful at mental animation than people with low spatial ability (Hegarty & Kozhevnikov, 1999; Hegarty & Sims, 1994; Hegarty & Steinhoff, 1997). Even if people are not successful in mentally animating a machine, if they first attempt to do so before viewing a computer animation, they might discover which mechanical linkages they can easily visualize and which linkages they cannot visualize. The mental animation process might also induce them to articulate their intuitions about how the machine works, so that when they view the animation they can compare these intuitions to the actual physical process shown in the animation. They might then use the animated display to check the accuracy of their mental animations and to encode information about the motions of components that they could not infer from the diagram. We recently tested the effects of learning from computer animations versus learning by mentally animating static diagrams in three experiments.

Experiment 3a

Method. Eighty-eight undergraduate students participated in four different conditions of this experiment. Twenty-three studied a static diagram of the flushing cistern, shown in Fig. 15.2 (diagram group). Twenty students studied the static diagram and then attempted to explain to the experimenter orally how the system worked (mental animation group). Twenty-five students studied the static diagram and then viewed an animation, accompanied by a commentary explaining how the flushing cistern worked (computer animation group). Twenty students viewed the static diagram, then attempted to explain to the experimenter how the system worked and finally viewed the computer animation (combination group). Afterwards all students answered mental animation questions, function questions, and troubleshooting questions similar to those used in Experiment 1a, described previously. Finally, students were given the Paper Folding Test (Ekstrom et al., 1976) as a test of spatial visualization ability.

Results. Viewing the animation and commentary significantly improved performance on all three types of questions. First, students in the computer animation and the combination groups (combined) answered more mental animation questions correctly ($M = 19.11$, $SD = 4.21$) than students in the other two groups ($M = 17.02$, $SD = 3.62$). They were also better able to state the function of components ($M = 3.22$, $SD = 1.00$) than were students who did not view the animation ($M = 2.74$, $SD = 1.00$). Finally, they were better able to predict and diagnose faults in the system ($M = 5.39$, $SD = 1.84$) than were students in the other groups ($M = 4.47$, $SD = 1.90$). Students with high spatial ability also answered more function and troubleshooting questions correctly. For the mental animation questions, there was a trend for students in the mental animation groups to have better performance than those in the other groups, but this trend did not reach statistical significance.

Experiment 3b

Experiment 3a indicated that students could learn how a mechanical system works from an animation accompanied by a commentary. No significant effects of first attempting to mentally animate the system were observed. However the participants in Experiment 3a might not have been given enough information to generate an explanation of how the system worked. They were shown a static diagram of the system, and this diagram was not present when they attempted to explain how the system worked, so they had to mentally animate the system from memory. In Experiment 3b, students in the mental animation and combination groups were shown three static diagrams showing different stages in the operation of the device, and these three diagrams were visible while they attempted to explain how the system worked.

We were also concerned that the mental animation questions were not diagnostic of the differences between the groups, because they were multiple-choice questions, and therefore students had a good chance of answering them correctly if they could eliminate one or two of the answer choices. Therefore in this experiment, the multiple-choice questions were replaced by a task in which the students were asked to describe, step-by-step, how the flushing cistern works (as in Experiment 1b described earlier).

Method.   Eighty students participated in this experiment, 20 in each of the conditions (diagram only, mental animation, computer animation, and combination mental + computer animation). The procedure was similar to that of Experiment 3a with the changes noted earlier.

Results.   Students who viewed the animation and commentary wrote more complete descriptions of how the flushing cistern worked; that is, they included more steps in the causal chain in their description ($M = 14.53$, $SD = 4.33$) compared to students who did not view the animation ($M = 10.12$, $SD = 10.12$). Furthermore, students who mentally animated the mechanical system also wrote more complete descriptions ($M = 13.50$, $SD = 4.39$)

than those who did not mentally animate the system ($M = 11.15$, $SD = 4.26$). The effects of these two manipulations were additive, such that students in the combination condition (who first mentally animated the system and then viewed the computer animation) had the best performance of all four groups on this measure ($M = 15.64$, $SD = 4.30$). This indicates that students learn more from viewing an animation of a mechanical device if they first attempt to mentally animate the device. Students with higher spatial ability also had better performance on this measure.

Students who viewed the animation and commentary also had better performance on the troubleshooting questions. Although there were trends for mental animation and spatial ability to improve performance on this measure, the trends did not reach statistical significance. None of the experimental manipulations had significant effects on the function questions.

Experiment 3c

Experiments 3a and 3b showed that people are better able to describe how a mechanical system works after viewing an animation accompanied by a commentary than after viewing a static diagram. Experiment 3b also showed that they are better able to describe how a machine works if they attempt to mentally animate the machine before viewing an animation. However, Experiments 1a and 1b, described previously, indicate that students learn as well from static diagrams accompanied by text as from animations. In this experiment we examined the effects of two factors on students' ability to describe how the flushing cistern works. The first factor was whether they learned how the system worked from an animation accompanied by a commentary or from a static diagram accompanied by text. The second factor was whether they first attempted to mentally animate the mechanical system before receiving an explanation of how it worked.

Method. One hundred students participated in this experiment. Twenty-six students first studied a diagram of the flushing cistern and then read a text, accompanied by a diagram describing how it worked (text-and-diagram group). Twenty-five students viewed a static diagram of the device, then attempted to explain to the experimenter how it worked, and then read a text-and-diagram description of how it worked (mental animation + text-and-diagram group). Twenty-four students studied the diagram and then viewed an animation accompanied by a commentary explaining how the device worked (computer animation group). Twenty-five studied a static diagram of the device, then attempted to explain to an experimenter how it worked, and then viewed an animation accompanied by a commentary explaining how the device worked (mental animation + computer animation group). Afterwards, all participants were asked to describe in writing, step-by-step, how the flushing cistern works (as in Experiment 1b earlier) and answered the troubleshooting and function questions.

Results.   As in Experiment 3b, students who mentally animated the mechanical system (i.e., attempted to explain how it works) before viewing an animation of the mechanical system wrote more complete descriptions of how the device works ($M = 17.44$ causal steps, $SD = 3.02$) compared to those who viewed the animation without first mentally animating ($M = 14.75$, $SD = 4.49$). This replicates the result (see Experiment 3b) that students learn more from viewing an animation of a mechanical device if they first attempt to mentally animate the device. However, for the text-and-diagram conditions, there were no differences on the outcome measures between those who mentally animated before reading the text and diagram ($M = 17.76$, $SD = 4.15$) and those who did not ($M = 16.68$, $SD = 4.26$). Furthermore, there were no differences on the outcome measures between those who viewed animations accompanied by commentaries and those who viewed text and diagrams.

How might we explain these results? First, it is possible that the process of understanding a text accompanied by a static diagram involves mental animation (Hegarty & Just, 1993). That is, when one views a static diagram of a mechanical device and reads a text describing how it operates, the comprehension process involves visualizing how the different parts of the diagram will move to accomplish the function of the machine. In this view, first mentally animating a diagram before reading a text and diagram does not affect comprehension because the comprehension process itself involves mental animation. In contrast, viewing a computer animation does not involve mental animation, and therefore learning from an animation is enhanced if one first mentally animates the device. Second, consistent with Experiments 1a and 1b described earlier, this experiment indicates that it is the content and structure of instructional materials, and not the media and modalities in which they are presented that is important for comprehension of mechanical systems.

SUMMARY AND CONCLUSIONS

In summary, we developed a theoretical model of comprehension of mechanical systems from text and diagrams. From this we derived design guidelines and implemented several versions of a hypermedia presentation that explains how a mechanical device, the flushing cistern, works. We described six different experiments, some of which evaluated different versions of our hypermedia presentation and some of which were focused on specific aspects of our model.

We obtained support for our theoretical model in that people learned more from materials designed according to this model than from commercially available books and CD-ROMs that explained the same materials. One specific design guideline (that people should be induced to mentally animate a mechanical system before seeing a computer animation of the device) was also empirically validated. These advantages were most evident in participants' ability to describe, step-by-step, how the machine works. In contrast, differences between conditions were not always observed for troubleshooting tasks that require the user to reason with the information given in the multimedia presentation.

Our experiments provide no evidence that the *format* of instruction, that is, the media and modalities in which different types of information are presented, has any effect on comprehension and learning. The comprehension measures were not affected by whether information was presented in static text and diagrams or as animations accompanied by commentaries. Furthermore, there were no effects on comprehension of hyperlinking information or allowing participants free rather than restricted navigation of the hypermedia presentations. We have observed similar results in a parallel project on teaching computer algorithms.

A particularly notable result of our experiments was the fact that the provision of an animation did not lead to better understanding of the system than viewing a static diagram. The ineffectiveness of the animation might be specific to the type of machine explained here, for example, because people already have some familiarity with the system or because it is relatively simple. It is important to examine whether these results generalize to explanations of other mechanical systems. However, our results are not isolated findings. For example, Mayer (1997) reported only a 3% difference in comprehension outcomes from animations compared to static text and diagrams in a reanalysis of several studies in which people learned about a variety of different mechanical systems. Noneffects of animations have also been reported in teaching physics (Rieber, 1989) and computer interaction (Palmiter & Elkerton, 1993). Our results are consistent with a growing body of research showing no significant effects of animations over static media when they present the same information (Morrison, Tversky, & Betrancourt, 2000; Pane, Corbett, & John, 1996).

What can we conclude about the effectiveness of animations and hypermedia in science instruction? Our research shows no advantages of these new media over traditional print formats. However there have been several excellent demonstrations of the effectiveness of animations in science teaching. Notable examples are White and Frederiksen's studies of teaching mechanics and electrical circuits using interactive microworlds that allow students to run animations of the phenomena being explained (Frederiksen, White, & Gutwill, 1999; White, 1993). However, in this case, the animations are embedded in a wider curriculum in which students articulate their intuitions about the phenomena being studied, and are taught basic scientific inquiry skills. Similarly, in Edelson's (1999) work on teaching students about climate using an interactive visualization system, successive iterations of the instructional program included more structured activities for students, because it was observed that students did not use much of the functionality of the system if they were not given specific learning goals and supporting conceptual information.

We expect that new media have the potential to be powerful instructional tools in scientific communication and teaching. However, our research has shown that merely translating information from a traditional print medium to a hypermedia system including animations, commentaries, and hyperlinks does not affect comprehension and learning when the content of the information is held constant. Basic research is needed to study the conditions under which these powerful new media can be used in the instructional process.

ACKNOWLEDGMENTS

We thank Selma Holmquist, who assisted with data collection and analysis for Experiment 2, Jill Quilici, Christina Cate and Narisa Hoevatanaku, who assisted with data collection for the other experiments, and Roxana Moreno, who assisted in development of the hypermedia presentations. This research is supported by the Office of Naval Research under contracts N00014-96-10525 to the University of California, Santa Barbara, and N00014-96-11187 to Auburn University

REFERENCES

Baggett, W. B., & Graesser, A. C. (1995). Question answering in the context of illustrated expository text. In *Proceedings of the 17th Annual Conference of the Cognitive Science Society* (pp. 334–339). Hillsdale, NJ: Lawrence Erlbaum Associates.

Britton, B. K., & Graesser, A. C. (Eds.). (1996). *Models of understanding text.* Mahwah, NJ: Lawrence Erlbaum Associates.

Chen, C., & Rada, R. (1996). Interacting with hypertext: A meta-analysis of experimental studies. *Human–Computer Interaction, 11,* 125–156.

Chi, M. T. H., de Leeuw, N., Chiu, M., & LaVancher, C. (1994). Eliciting self-explanations improves learning. *Cognitive Science, 18,* 439–478.

Edelson, D. C. (1999). Addressing the challenges of inquiry-based learning through technology and curriculum design. *Journal of the Learning Sciences, 8,* 391–450.

Ekstrom, R. B., French, J. W., Harman, H. H., & Derman, D. (1976). *Kit of factor-referenced cognitive tests.* Princeton, NJ: Educational Testing Service.

Faraday, P., & Sutcliffe, A. (1997a). Designing effective multimedia presentations. In *Proceedings of the ACM Conference on Human Factors in Computing Systems (CHI '97)* (pp. 272–278). New York: ACM Press.

Faraday, P., & Sutcliffe, A. (1997b). An empirical study of attending and comprehending multimedia presentations. *Proceedings of the ACM Multimedia '96 Conference* (pp. 265–275). New York: ACM Press.

Ferguson, E. S. (1977). The mind's eye: Non-verbal thought in technology. *Science, 197,* 827–836.

Frederiksen, J. R., White, B. Y., & Gutwill, J. (1999). Dynamic mental models in learning science: The importance of constructing derivational linkages among models. *Journal of Research in Science Teaching, 36,* 806–836.

Goldman, S. R., Graesser, A. C., & van den Broek, P. (Eds.). (1999). *Narrative comprehension, causality, and coherence: Essays in honor of Tom Trabasso.* Mahwah, NJ: Lawrence Erlbaum Associates.

Graesser, A. C., Singer, M., & Trabasso, T. (1994). Constructing inferences during narrative text comprehension. *Psychological Review, 101,* 371–395.

Hammond, N., & Allinson, L. (1989). Extending hypertext for learning: An investigation of access and guidance tools. In A. Sutcliffe & L. Macaulay (Eds.), *People and computers V: Proceedings of HCI '89* (pp. 293–304). Cambridge, England: Cambridge University Press.

Hansen, S. R., Narayanan, N. H., Schrimpsher, D., & Hegarty, M. (1998). *Empirical studies of animation-embedded hypermedia algorithm visualizations* (Tech. Rep. No. CSE98–06). Auburn, AL: Auburn University, Department of Computer Science and Software Engineering.

Hansen, S. R., Schrimpsher, D., & Narayanan, N. H. (1998). Learning algorithms by visualization: A novel approach using animation-embedded hypermedia. In *Proceedings of the Third International Conference on the Learning Sciences* (pp. 125–130). Charlottsville, VA: Association for the Advancement of Computing in Education.

Hegarty, M. (1992). Mental animation: Inferring motion from static diagrams of mechanical systems. *Journal of Experimental Psychology: Learning, Memory, and Cognition, 18,* 1084–1102.

Hegarty, M., & Just, M. A. (1993). Constructing mental models of machines from text and diagrams. *Journal of Memory and Language, 32,* 717–742.

Hegarty, M., & Kozhevnikov, M. (1999). Spatial abilities, working memory and mechanical reasoning. In J. Gero & B. Tversky (Eds.) *Visual and spatial reasoning in design*. Sydney, Australia: Key Centre of Design and Cognition.

Hegarty, M., Quilici, J., Narayanan, N. H., Holmquist, S., & Moreno, R. (1999). Multimedia instruction: Lessons from evaluation of a theory-based design. *Journal of Educational Multimedia and Hypermedia, 8*, 119–150.

Hegarty, M., & Sims, V. K. (1994). Individual differences in mental animation during mechanical reasoning. *Memory & Cognition, 22*, 411–430.

Hegarty, M., & Steinhoff, K. (1997). Use of diagrams as external memory in a mechanical reasoning task. *Learning and Individual Differences, 9*, 19–42.

George Allen & Unwin Ltd. (1967). *How things work: The universal encyclopedia of machines*. (1967). London: Allen & Unwin. Great Britain.

Kintsch, W., Britton, B. K., Fletcher, C. R., Mannes, S. M., & Nathan, M. J. (1993). A comprehension-based approach to learning and understanding. In D. L. Medin (Ed.), *The psychology of learning and motivation* (Vol. 30, pp. 165–214). New York: Academic Press.

Lowe, R. K. (1999). Extracting information from an animation during complex visual learning. *European Journal of Psychology of Education, 14*, 225–244.

Macaulay, D. (1988). *The way things work*. Boston: Houghton Mifflin.

Macaulay, D. (1998). *The new way things work* [CD-ROM]. New York: DK Interactive Learning.

Mayer, R. E. (1997). Multimedia instruction: Are we asking the right questions? *Educational Psychologist, 32*, 1–19.

Mayer, R. E., & Gallini, J. (1990). When is an illustration worth ten thousand words? *Journal of Educational Psychology, 83*, 715–726.

Mayer, R. E., & Moreno, R. (1998). A split-attention effect in multimedia learning: Evidence for dual processing systems in working memory. *Journal of Educational Psychology, 90*, 312–320.

Mayer, R. E., & Sims, V. K. (1994). For whom is a picture worth a thousand words? Extensions of a dual-coding theory of multimedia learning. *Journal of Educational Psychology, 86*, 389–401.

McNamara, D. S., Kintsch, E., Songer, N. B., & Kintsch, W. (1996). Are good texts always better? Interactions of text coherence, background knowledge and levels of understanding in learning from text. *Cognition and Instruction, 14*, 1–43.

Morrison, J. B., Tversky, B., & Betrancourt, M. (2000). Animation: Does it facilitate learning? In A. Butz, A. Kruger, & P. Olivier (Eds.), *Smart graphics: Papers from the 2000 AAAI Spring Symposium* (pp. 53–60). Menlo Park, CA: AAAI Press.

Mousavi, S. Y., Low, R., & Sweller, J. (1995). Reducing cognitive load by mixing auditory and visual presentation modes. *Journal of Experimental Psychology, 87*, 319–334.

Narayanan, N. H., & Hegarty, M. (1998). On designing comprehensible hypermedia manuals. *International Journal of Human–Computer Studies, 48*, 267–301.

Narayanan, N. H., Suwa, M., & Motoda, H. (1994). A study of diagrammatic reasoning from verbal and gestural data. In *Proceedings of the 16th Annual Conference of the Cognitive Science Society* (pp. 652–657). Hillsdale, NJ: Lawrence Erlbaum Associates.

Narayanan, N. H., Suwa, M., & Motoda, H. (1995). Diagram-based problem solving: The case of an impossible problem. In *Proceedings of the 17th Annual Conference of the Cognitive Science Society* (pp. 206–211). Hillsdale, NJ: Lawrence Erlbaum Associates.

Novak, G. (1995). Diagrams for solving physics problems. In J. I. Glasgow, N. H. Narayanan, & B. Chandrasekaran (Eds.), *Diagrammatic reasoning: Computational and cognitive perspectives* (pp. 753–774). Boston: MIT Press.

Palmiter, S., & Elkerton, J. (1993). Animated demonstrations for learning procedural computer-based tasks. *Human–Computer Interaction, 8,* 193–216.

Pane, J. F., Corbett, A. T., & John, B. E. (1996). Assessing dynamics in computer–based instruction. In *Proceedings of the ACM Conference on Human Factors in Computing Systems (CHI '96),* (pp. 797–804). New York: ACM Press.

Rieber, L. P. (1989). The effects of computer animated elaboration strategies and practice on factual and application learning in an elementary science lesson. *Journal of Educational Computing Research, 5,* 431–444.

Scaife, M., & Rogers, Y. (1996). External cognition: How do graphical representations work? *International Journal of Human–Computer Studies, 45,* 185–213.

Schwartz, D. L., & Black, J. B. (1996). Analog imagery in mental model reasoning: Depictive models. *Cognitive Psychology, 30,* 154–219.

Schwartz, D. L., & Bransford, J. D. (1998). A time for telling. *Cognition and Instruction, 16,* 475–522.

Shapiro, A. M. (1998). Promoting active learning: The role of system structure in learning from hypertext. *Human–Computer Interaction, 13,* 1–35.

Slamencka, N. J., & Graf, P. (1978). The generation effect: Delineation of a phenomenon. *Journal of Experimental Psychology: Human Learning and Memory, 4,* 592–604.

Spoehr, K. T. (1994). Enhancing the acquisition of conceptual structures through hypermedia. In K. McGilly (Ed.) *Classroom lessons: Integrating cognitive theory and practice* (pp. 75–101). Cambridge, MA: MIT Press.

White, B. Y. (1993). Intermediate causal models: A missing link for successful science education? In R. Glaser (Ed.), *Advances in instructional psychology* (pp. 177–252). Hillsdale, NJ: Lawrence Erlbaum Associates.

⊰ 16 ⊱

Toward an Integrative View of Text and Picture Comprehension: Visualization Effects on the Construction of Mental Models

---

Wolfgang Schnotz
Maria Bannert
Tina Seufert
University of Koblenz-Landau, Germany

Human communication is based on signs, which are used by individuals in order to exchange information (Bühler, 1934). These signs can be verbal signs, as in the case of words that are combined into sentences that hopefully form coherent texts. They can also be pictorial signs as in the case of realistic pictures or graphs, often referred to as logical pictures. Comprehension of texts and pictures is fundamental to the functioning of the human cognitive system in contemporary civilization. Current psychological approaches emphasize the active, constructive nature of human cognition. Accordingly, when an individual learns from text and pictures, the person actively searches for information, selects particular information,

385

evaluates the relevance of the information for specific purposes, and builds a knowledge structure that accommodates present or anticipated demands (Shuell, 1988; Wittrock, 1989). Usually, text and picture comprehension do not occur in isolation. Instead, text comprehension occurs in the context of pictures and picture comprehension occurs in the context of text. A comprehensive theory of text and picture comprehension is needed that is embedded in a broader framework of human cognition and that considers the active, constructive nature of the human mind.

The aim of this chapter is to contribute to such a theory. In the first part, we develop an integrated model of text and picture comprehension that is based on a semiotic and cognitive analysis of verbal and pictorial information processing. In the second part, we report an empirical study that was motivated by the assumptions of this model. The study had several objectives. We analyzed how learners use text and pictures under the conditions of self-directed learning, when pictures vary in terms of difficulty. We investigated whether the *form* of visualization used in a picture affects the structure of mental representations constructed by the learner. We analyzed the conditions in which pictures have positive versus negative effects on learning.

THEORY

Whereas text comprehension has been investigated rather intensively during the last 25 years (Graesser, Millis, & Zwaan, 1997), research on picture comprehension has always been a secondary field of research. Studies on text and picture comprehension focused primarily on the mnemonic function of pictures illustrating a text. The main assumption of these studies was that text information is remembered better when it is illustrated by pictures than when there is no illustration. The majority of studies confirmed this hypothesis (Levie & Lentz, 1982; Levin, Anglin, & Carney, 1987).

The facilitation of pictures on learning from text was usually explained by Paivio's dual coding theory (Clark & Paivio, 1991; Paivio, 1986). According to this theory, verbal information and pictorial information are processed in different cognitive subsystems: a verbal system and an imagery system. Words and sentences are usually processed and encoded only in the verbal system, whereas pictures are processed and encoded both in the imagery system and in the verbal system. Thus, the high memory for pictorial information and the memory-enhancing effect of pictures in texts is ascribed to the advantage of a dual coding as compared to single coding in memory. As an amendment to the dual coding theory, Kulhavy, Stock, and Kealy (1993) explained the mnemonic function of pictures by the simultaneous availability of text information and pictorial information in working memory, which is assumed to facilitate retrieval and processing of information.

Relatively few investigations were concerned with the use of pictures to foster comprehension and to support the answering of question in the context of illustrated expository text (Baggett & Graesser, 1995; Larkin & Simon, 1987). Mayer and his coworkers, for example, conducted a series of experiments that identified the conditions under which pictures support understanding of technical or physical phenomena (Mayer, 1997). They found that pictures support comprehension when both texts and pictures are explanatory, when verbal and pictorial content are related to each other, when verbal and pictorial information are presented closely together in space or time (i.e., in contiguity), and when individuals have low prior knowledge about the subject domain but high spatial cognitive abilities. In order to explain these results, Mayer developed a model of multimedia learning, which combines the assumptions of dual coding theory with the notion of comprehension as a construction of multilevel mental representations.

Although these approaches can explain findings of various empirical studies, they do not seem to be an adequate basis for an integrated theory of text and picture comprehension. They do not sufficiently take into account the different sign systems that underlie texts and pictures and do not recognize the fundamentally different principles of representation. In the following sections we try to clarify these differences with the help of some concepts of semiotics and representation theory.

FORMS OF REPRESENTATION

A representation is an object or an event that stands for something else (Peterson, 1996). Texts and pictures are external representations. These external representations are understood when a reader or observer constructs internal mental representations of the content described in the text or shown in the picture. Comprehension is usually task-oriented. That is, the mental construction is performed by the individual in a way that allows him or her to deal effectively with current or anticipated requirements. In other words comprehension of text and pictures is a task-oriented construction of mental representations (Kolers & Brison, 1984).

Representations can differ from one another with respect to their informational content and their usability. The informational content of a representation is the set of information that can be extracted from the representation with the help of available procedures (Palmer, 1978). Thus, the informational content of a representation depends both on its structure and on the procedures that operate on the structure. Two representations are informationally equivalent if every information item that can be taken from one representation can also be taken from the other representation (Larkin & Simon, 1987). A piece of information can be relevant for some tasks and irrelevant for other tasks, so it is possible to define the informational content of a representation with respect to a specific set of tasks. Accordingly, two representations are (in a task-specific sense) informationally equivalent, if both allow the extraction of the same information that is required to solve the specific tasks.

An example of two representations that are informationally equivalent in a task-specific sense is given in Figs. 16.1 and 16.2. Both figures illustrate the fact that different daytimes and dates exist on earth at the same point in time. The two figures show the division of the earth surface into time zones, the Greenwich Meridian, the Date Line, and the position of various cities in the world. The kind of visualization used in the two figures, however, is quite different. Figure 16.1 shows the earth as a rectangle moving across a time axis like a flying carpet. We hereafter call this kind of visualization *carpet diagram*. Figure 16.2 depicts the earth as a circle (or sphere) seen from the North Pole, which rotates in a swirl of different daytimes and dates. This kind of visualization is hereafter called *circle diagram*.

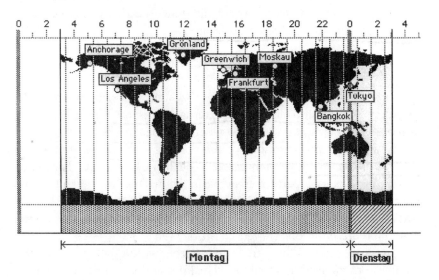

FIG. 16.1. Visualization of geographic time differences by a carpet diagram.

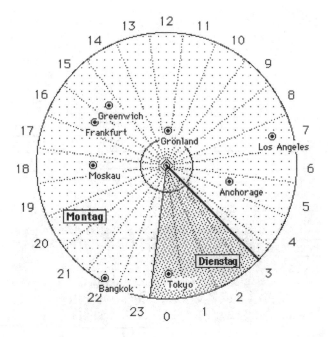

FIG. 16.2. Visualization of geographic time differences by a circle diagram.

The two figures differ from each other in various respects. Figure 16.1 shows the northern and the southern hemispheres, whereas Fig. 16.2 shows only the northern hemisphere. In Fig. 16.1, the distances between east and west become more and more distorted (i.e., enlarged) the closer one comes to the poles, whereas such a distortion does not exist in Fig. 16.2. Figure 16.1 depicts the earth with its continents, whereas no continents are shown in Fig. 16.2. If one is interested in time differences between the depicted cities, however, then both figures furnish the information despite their differences. In other words, both figures are informationally equivalent from the perspective of this kind of task.

When two representations are informationally equivalent they can nevertheless differ in their usefulness. Representations are used to retrieve information about what they represent. Depending on the structure of the representation and the processes operating on it, information retrieval (which often means the computation of new information) can be easy or difficult. For example, it might be easier to read off information about time differences between cities in the world from a carpet diagram, because big spatial (left–right) differences in the diagram correspond to big differences in time. This is not the case in a circle diagram, where there exists a very small spatial distance between the east and west of the Date Line, whereas the corresponding time difference is very high. On the other hand, a circle diagram might be better to imagine circumnavigations around the earth, because circumnavigations can be envisioned here as continuous movements. This is not the case in carpet diagrams, where a jump is required from the left edge to the right edge of the carpet or vice versa. Representations, which are not only informationally equivalent, but also equivalent in terms of retrieving information, are referred to as computationally equivalent. Two representations are (in a task-specific sense) computationally equivalent if each task-relevant information can be retrieved from one representation as easily as from the other representation (Larkin & Simon, 1987).

Texts and pictures are based on different sign systems that capture descriptive and depictive representations. Texts (or mathematical equations, e.g.) are descriptive representations. A descriptive representation consists of symbols that have an arbitrary structure and that are associated with the content they represent simply by means of a convention (Peirce, 1906). If we describe something in a text, we use nouns to refer to its parts and we use verbs and prepositions to relate these parts to each other (e.g., *Seen from the North Pole, the earth rotates counterclockwise around its axis*). Pictures (or sculptures or physical models, e.g.) are depictive representations. A depictive representation consists of iconic signs. These signs are associated with the content they represent through common structural features. Depictions do not contain signs for relations; instead the relations are inferred. In Fig. 16.1, for example, the left–right dimension in the carpet diagram is used to represent earlier–later dimension in time.

Descriptive representations and depictive representations have different uses for different purposes. Descriptive representations have a higher representational power than depictive representations. For example, there is no problem in a descriptive representation to express a general negation (*No pets allowed!*) or a general disjunction (*Seat reserved for infirm people and for mothers with babies*). In a depictive representation, however, one can express only specific negations (e.g., a picture showing a dog combined with a prohibitive sign). Disjunctions are depicted through a series of pictures (e.g., a picture showing an old man plus a picture showing a mother with her baby). On the other hand, depictive representations encompass a specific class of information in its entirety. For example, it is possible to read off from a geometric figure (like a triangle) all its geometric properties. Similarly, a picture of an object is not limited to information about its form, but also has information about its size and its orientation in space. In contrast, in a description it is possible to mention only a few geometric characteristics of a figure or to specify only the form of the object, without providing information about its size or orientation. Accordingly, depictive representations are especially useful to gain new information from already known information. A depiction constructed on the basis of already known information contains necessarily further information that has not been made explicit so far (Kosslyn, 1994). If one draws a triangle based on information about two sides and one angle, one can read off the size of the third side, the size of the other two angles, the area of the triangle, and many more geometric characteristics. The new information is not generated in the sense of a logical conclusion, but rather can be read off directly from the representation (Johnson-Laird, 1983). These have sometimes been called pseudoinferences (Garrod, 1985).

EXTERNAL AND INTERNAL REPRESENTATIONS

The distinction between descriptions and depictions can be applied not only to external representations like texts and pictures, but also to internal mental representations, which are constructed during text and picture comprehension. Current approaches in text comprehension research assume that in understanding a text a reader constructs multiple mental representations. The representations include a surface representation of the text, a propositional textbase, a mental model of what the text is about, a communication level, and a genre level (Graesser et al., 1997). The text surface representation includes the detailed linguistic information, such as the specific words, phrases, and syntactic structures. The textbase represents the semantic content of the text in the form of propositions. The mental model represents the referential content of the text. In narrative texts this is frequently referred to as a situation model (van Dijk & Kintsch, 1983). The mental model is constrained both by the textbase and by domain-specific world knowledge. The communication level represents the pragmatic context of the communication between reader and writer. The genre level captures knowledge about the class of text and its corresponding text function. Evidence for a differentiation between the surface code, the textbase, and the mental model level has been found in several investigations (Kintsch, Welsch, Schmalhofer, & Zimny, 1990; Schmalhofer & Glavanov, 1986).

In picture comprehension, the individual also constructs multiple mental representations. This set also includes a surface structure representation, a mental model, a propositional representation, as well as a communication-level and a genre-level representation (Kosslyn, 1994). The surface structure representation corresponds to the perceptual (visual) image of the picture in the individual's mind. The mental model represents the subject matter shown in the picture on the basis of common structural features (i.e., based on an analogy) between the picture and its referential content. The propositional representation contains information, which is read off from the model and which is encoded in a propositional format. The communication level represents the pragmatic context of the pictorial communication, whereas the genre level represents knowledge about the class of pictures and their corresponding functions.

Propositional representations, whether constructed during text comprehension or during picture comprehension, are descriptive representations. They consist of internal symbols, which can be decomposed, similar to sentences of natural language, into simple symbols. The proposition "SHIFTS (agent: CARPET, from: LEFT SIDE, to: RIGHT SIDE)," for example, has symbols of entities, arguments (CARPET, LEFT SIDE, RIGHT SIDE), and a symbol of a relation (the predicate SHIFTS), which relates the arguments into a complex meaningful unit. Accordingly, propositional representations are symbolic representations and contain signs for relations, which are main characteristics of descriptive representations. Propositional representations can be viewed as internal descriptions in the language of the mind (Chafe, 1994).

The perceptual images created as surface structure representations during picture comprehension are internal depictive representations. They retain structural characteristics of the picture and use these inherent structural characteristics as a means of representation. Perceptual images created in picture comprehension are sensory specific because they are linked to the visual modality. The proximity of these images to perception can be attributed to the fact that visual images and visual perceptions are based on the same cognitive mechanisms (Kosslyn, 1994). Mental models, whether constructed during picture comprehension or during text comprehension, are also internal depictive representations, as they have inherent structural features in common with the depicted object. That is, they represent the object based on a structural or functional analogy (Johnson-Laird, 1983; Johnson-Laird & Byrne, 1991). Such an analogy does not imply that mental models represent only spatial information. A mental model can represent, for example, also the increase or decrease of birth rates or incomes during a specific period of time (as it can be described in a text or displayed in a line graph), although birth rates and incomes are certainly not spatial information.

Contrary to visual images, mental models are not sensory specific. For example, a mental model of a spatial configuration (say, of a room) can be constructed not only by visual perception, but also by auditory , kinesthetic, or haptic perception. Because mental models are not bound to specific sensory modalities, they can be considered as more abstract than perceptual images. On the one hand, a mental model constructed from a picture contains less information than the corresponding visual image, because of its abstraction. That is, irrelevant pictorial details that are included in the visual image are omitted from the mental model. On the other hand, the mental model contains more information than the corresponding visual image, because it also includes prior knowledge that is not present in the visual perception. For example, a mental model of a brake can contain information about causal relationships that are not explicitly included in the corresponding picture of the brake (Mayer & Anderson, 1992).

AN INTEGRATED MODEL
OF TEXT AND PICTURE COMPREHENSION

Mayer and his coworkers have adopted Paivio's dual coding theory to develop a model of text and picture comprehension that has been tested in various studies on multimedia learning (Mayer, 1997). A main assumption of the model is that verbal and pictorial information are processed in different cognitive subsystems and that processing results in the parallel construction of two kinds of mental models that are finally mapped onto each other. Accordingly, an individual understanding a text with pictures selects relevant words, constructs a propositional representation or textbase, and then organizes the selected verbal information into a verbal mental model of the situation described in the text. Similarly, the individual selects relevant images, creates what is called a pictorial representation or image base, and organizes the selected pictorial information into a visual mental model of the situation shown in the picture. The final step is to build connections through a one-to-one-mapping between the text-based model and the picture-based model. This requires that the corresponding entities in the two models are in working memory at the same time (Baddeley, 1992; Chandler & Sweller, 1991).

The parallelism of text processing and picture processing assumed in this model is problematic, however, because texts and pictures are based on different sign systems and use quite different principles of representation. Thus, we propose another model of text and picture comprehension, which gives more emphasis to these representational principles. An outline of this model is shown in Fig. 16.3. It consists of a descriptive (left side) and a depictive (right side) branch of representations. The descriptive branch comprises the (external) text, the (internal) mental representation of the text surface structure, and the propositional representation of the text's semantic content. The interaction between these descriptive representations is based on symbol processing. The depictive branch comprises the (external) picture, the (internal) visual perception or image of the picture, and the (also internal) mental model of the subject matter presented in the pic-

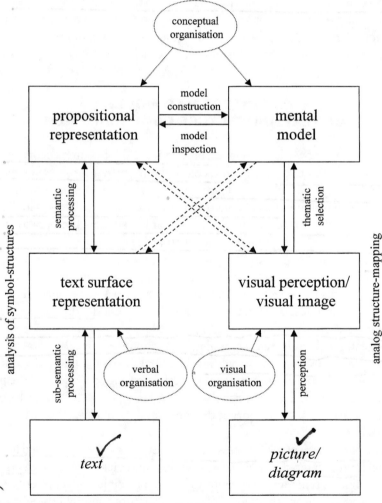

FIG. 16.3. Schematic illustration of an integrated model of text and picture comprehension.

ture. The interaction between these depictive representations is based on processes of structure mapping due to the structural correspondences (i.e., analogy relations) between the representations (Gentner, 1989).

According to this model, the reader of a text constructs a mental representation of the text surface structure, generates a propositional representation of the semantic content (i.e., a textbase), and finally constructs from the textbase a mental model of the subject matter described in the text (Schnotz, 1994; van Dijk & Kintsch, 1983; Weaver, Mannes, & Fletcher, 1995). These construction processes are based on an interaction of bottom-up and top-down activation of cognitive schemata, which have both a selective and an organizing function. Task-relevant information is selected through top-down activation, and the selected information is then organized into a coherent mental representation of the text surface structure. Processes of conceptual organization, starting from the text surface representation, result in a coherent propositional representation, which in turn triggers the construction of a mental model.

In picture comprehension, the individual first creates through perceptual processing a visual mental representation of the picture's graphic display. Then the individual constructs through semantic processing a mental model and a propositional representation of the subject matter shown in the picture. In perceptual processing, task-relevant information is selected through top-down activation of cognitive schemata and then visually organized through automated visual routines (Ullman, 1984). Perceptual processing includes identification and discrimination of graphic entities, as well as the visual organization of these entities according to the Gestalt laws (Wertheimer, 1938; Winn, 1994). The resulting mental representation is the visual perception of the picture in the imagery part of working memory, the so-called visual sketchpad (Baddeley, 1992; Kruley, Sciama, & Glenberg, 1994; Sims & Hegarty, 1997). Perception and imagery are based on the same cognitive mechanisms, so the same kind of representation can also be referred to as a perceptual image if the representation is created on the basis of internal world knowledge rather than external sensory data (Kosslyn, 1994; Shepard, 1984).

Semantic processing is required to understand a picture, as opposed to merely perceiving it. During this process the individual constructs a mental model of the depicted subject matter through a schema-driven mapping process, in which graphic entities are mapped onto mental model entities and in which spatial relations are mapped onto semantic relations. In other words, picture comprehension is considered to be a process of analogical structure mapping between a system of visuo-spatial relations and a system of semantic relations (Falkenhainer, Forbus, & Gentner, 1989/1990;

Schnotz, 1993). This mapping can take place in both directions; it is possible to construct a mental model bottom-up from a picture, and it is also possible to evaluate an existing mental model top-down with a picture. While understanding realistic pictures, the individual can use cognitive schemata of everyday perception. While understanding logical pictures, however, the individual requires specific cognitive schemata (so-called graphic schemata) in order to be able to read off information from the visuo-spatial configuration (Pinker, 1990).

Although the construction of mental models in picture comprehension is triggered by visuo-spatial information in the visual sketchpad, mental models are not simply visual images. First, they are more abstract than visual images, because they are not bound to a specific sensory modality. Second, mental models differ from visual images with respect to their information content. On the one hand, a task-oriented selection takes place in mental model construction. Those parts of the graphic configuration that are relevant to current or anticipated tasks are included in the process of structure mapping. On the other hand, the mental model is also elaborated through information from world knowledge and thereby adds information to the representation.

When a mental model has been constructed, new information can be read off from the model through a process of model inspection. The new information gained in this way has to be made explicit, which is performed by encoding it in a propositional format. The new propositional information is used to elaborate the propositional representation. In other words, there is a continuous interaction between the propositional representation and the mental model (Baddeley, 1992). In text comprehension, the starting point of this interaction is a propositional representation, which is used to construct a mental model. When understanding pictures, the starting point of the interaction is a mental model, which is used to read off new information that is added to the propositional representation. Besides the interaction between the propositional representation and the mental model, there may also exist an interaction between the text surface representation and the mental model, as well as an interaction between the perceptual representation of the picture and the propositional representation. This is shown in Fig. 16.3 by the dotted diagonal arrows.

In summary, one can say that there is no one-to-one relationship between external and internal representations. A text as an external descriptive representation leads to both an internal descriptive and an internal depictive mental representation. A picture, on the other hand, as an external depictive representation leads to both an internal depictive and an internal descriptive mental representation.

Formally, one can consider the construction of a propositional representation and of a mental model as a kind of dual coding. Nevertheless, our view is fundamentally different from the traditional dual coding theory. First, dual coding presumably applies not only to the processing of pictures, but also to the processing of words and texts. Second, the construction of a mental model is regarded as more than simply adding a further code that elaborates the mental representation and provides a quantitative advantage compared to a single code. Rather, the essential point is that propositional representations and mental models are based on different sign systems and different principles of representation that complement one another.

RESEARCH QUESTIONS AND HYPOTHESES

According to the theoretical model presented earlier, text comprehension and picture comprehension are to be considered as complementary ways of creating mental representations. Comprehension and knowledge acquisition are active constructive processes, in which the individual decides by him or herself when each kind of information is to be processed. Accordingly, if a learner is given a text with pictures, a number of questions become relevant. To what extent does the person use the text or the pictures? Which factors influence the use of verbal and pictorial information? Does the form of visualization used in a picture affect the structural characteristics of the mental representation? Does it affect solutions for different tasks? Is adding a picture to a text always beneficial for learning, or is there also a possibility of interference between text and picture comprehension?

Use of Verbal and Pictorial Information

Texts and pictures can be seen as complementary sources of information so learners can focus on one source more than the other. One important question is whether the use of verbal and pictorial information follows the principle of cognitive economy. According to this principle, learners try to construct a mental representation that is sufficient to handle tasks with a minimum of cognitive effort. Constructing a mental model from a picture might be generally easier than constructing a mental model from a text, because understanding a picture requires only a process of structure mapping from one analog representation onto another analog representation. Text comprehension, on the contrary, requires a shift from a symbolic propositional representation to an analog representation. However, there can be differences with regard to the ease or difficulty of pictures. A series of carpet diagrams, for example, showing the earth at different times and dates (see Fig.

16.1) might require less cognitive effort than an equivalent series of circle diagrams (Fig. 16.2). There are two reasons for this assumption. First, in the carpet diagrams, the earth is always shown from the same perspective so the east–west relations on the earth are always represented by right–left relations in the diagram. In the circle diagrams, the fact that the earth rotates makes different points on the earth appear at different places at different points in time, so east–west relations on the earth can be represented by right–left, top–bottom, left–right, or bottom–top relations (Franklin & Tversky, 1990). Second, as mental translations require less cognitive effort than do mental rotations, simulating the time course should be easier with carpet diagrams than with circle diagrams (Hegarty & Sims, 1994; Logie & Baddeley, 1990; Reed, Hock, & Lockhead, 1983; Shepard & Hurwitz, 1984).

Based on our theoretical model and the previous assumptions, three hypotheses can be derived on the use of verbal and pictorial information. A first, very simple hypothesis is that the use of verbal information is independent from the use of pictorial information, and vice versa. A second hypothesis is that text processing and picture processing can *substitute* for each other. A third hypothesis is that text processing and picture processing can *stimulate* each other. These three hypotheses lead to different predictions about the use of verbal and pictorial information.

Independence Hypothesis. This first hypothesis simply assumes that text and picture do not affect each other with respect to the extent they are used. Thus, when a learner is given a text with a picture (a carpet or circle diagram), the text would be used as intensively as when no picture would be offered (text only). The picture is simply used in addition to the text.

Use of text:

(1) carpet = text only.

(2) circle = text only.

Furthermore, if the form of visualization would have no effect, then there would be also no difference in the extent of using text and picture information when we compare the groups who receive different visualizations (carpet vs. circle):

Use of text:

(3) carpet = circle.

Use of pictures:

(4) carpet = circle.

Substitution Hypothesis.   If knowledge acquisition from text and pictures is an active, constructive process, in which the learners decide when to access a particular source of information, it is also possible that text comprehension and picture comprehension substitute for one another. We call this second possibility the substitution hypothesis. It is supported by research of van Dam, Brinkerik-Carlier, and Kok (1986), who found that the retention of text content is poorer when the text is accompanied by an illustrative picture than when the text is given alone. In our case one would expect that a text combined with carpet diagrams or circle diagrams is used to a lesser extent than the same text without diagrams:

Use of text:

(5) carpet < text only.

(6) circle < text only.

The next question is whether the preference for the pictorial representation compared to the preference for the text is the same for both forms of visualization. According to the principle of cognitive economy, one can assume that easy pictures will be used more extensively than demanding pictures. That is, the carpet pictures are more often used than the more demanding circle pictures. Based on the substitution hypothesis, one can also predict that a learner will pay less attention to the text if the text is combined with easy carpet pictures than when it is combined with difficult circle pictures:

Use of text:

(7) carpet < circle.

Use of pictures:

(8) carpet > circle.

Stimulation Hypothesis.   A third possibility is that text comprehension and picture comprehension do not substitute for, but rather stimulate each other. For example, questions can arise while reading a text, which the reader attempts to answer by inspecting the pictures. Conversely, questions can arise while inspecting a picture, which the reader seeks to clarify by consulting the text. Findings supporting this hypothesis are reported by Rusted (1984; Rusted & Hodgson, 1985). In these studies, both illustrated and nonillustrated text information was remembered better than in comparable nonillustrated text. According to the stimulation hypothesis, one would expect that a text combined with carpet diagrams or with circle diagrams is used more intensively than the corresponding nonillustrated text:

Use of text:

(9) carpet > text only.

(10) circle > text only.

According to the stimulation hypothesis, difficult pictures elicit more questions than easy pictures. Thus, difficult pictures should lead to more intensive picture processing, and should also stimulate text processing more than easy pictures. Consequently, the use of circle diagrams should be higher than the use of carpet diagrams, but also that a text combined with circle diagrams would be used more extensively than would a text combined with carpet diagrams:

Use of text:

(11) carpet < circle.

Use of pictures:

(12) carpet < circle.

The Impact of the Form of Visualization on the Structure of Mental Models

Designers of instructional material do not only have to ask whether a picture should be used or not. They also have to ask which kind of picture should be used. There is often more than one way to illustrate a subject matter, so one has to decide which visualization seems to be best suited under the given circumstances. This question cannot be asked independently from the given task, because one picture may be more effective to solve a certain task whereas another picture is better suited to solve another task, even if the pictures contain the same information.

In our example presented earlier, the carpet and circle diagrams are informationally equivalent with respect to *time difference tasks* and *circumnavigation tasks*. In the time difference tasks, the learner is asked to find the time difference between specific cities, for example, *What time and which day is it in Los Angeles when it is Tuesday 2 o'clock P.M. in Tokyo?* In the circumnavigation tasks, the learner has to travel mentally around the world, for example, *Why did Magellan's sailors believe that they arrived on a Wednesday after sailing around the world, although it was already Thursday?* Both kinds of question can be answered with both forms of visualizations. Nevertheless, the two kinds of pictures can differ in their computational efficiency with respect to the two different kinds of tasks. If one assumes that in picture comprehension the structural characteristics of the picture are mapped on the mental model, then the corresponding mental models should also differ in their computational efficiency. This leads to the structure-mapping hypothesis.

Structure-Mapping Hypothesis. The basic assumption of this hypothesis is that structural features of the external graphic representation are mapped onto a mental model. Accordingly, different forms of visualization should result in mental models with different structures, even if the visualizations are informationally equivalent.

The efficiency of a mental model constructed from carpet diagrams for answering time difference questions should be higher than the efficiency of a mental model generated on the basis of circle diagrams. Conversely, the efficiency of a mental model constructed from circle diagrams should be higher for solving circumnavigation tasks than the efficiency of a mental model constructed from carpet diagrams. Consequently, one should expect that performance in solving time difference tasks with a mental model based on carpet diagrams is higher than performance with a mental model constructed from circle diagrams. On the other hand, performance in solving circumnavigation tasks should be higher with a mental model based on circle diagrams than with a model based on carpet diagrams:

Time difference task performance:

(13) carpet > circle.

Circumnavigation task performance:

(14) carpet < circle.

An alternative view would be that the structural characteristics of a picture do not affect the structure of the mental model created by picture comprehension. In this case, one would expect no differences between different kinds of pictures with regard to task performance.

Supportive Versus Interference Effects of Pictures

Previous research on learning from verbal and pictorial information in line with the dual coding theory has suggested that adding pictures to a text leads generally to better learning outcomes. If the form of visualization affects the structure of mental models, however, this view could be too simplistic. Two further possibilities should be considered. One possibility is that pictures with task-appropriate visualization support the mental model construction. We call this the structure support hypothesis. Another possibility is that pictures with task-inappropriate visualization interfere with mental model construction. We call this the structure interference hypothesis.

Circle diag vs carpet diag

Dual Coding Hypothesis.   According to the dual coding theory, texts combined with pictures lead to more elaborated cognitive structures than texts without pictures. As a consequence, learning from text with pictures leads to better memory for the learned information and to better performance in knowledge acquisition. The dual coding theory makes no assumptions about whether one kind of picture is better than another one, so it predicts that learners who received a text with carpet diagrams or with circle diagrams will perform better in solving time difference tasks than learners who received the text without pictures.

Elab — Memory

Time difference task performance:

(15) carpet > text only.

(16) circle > text only.

Similarly, one can assume that learners who received a text with carpet diagrams or with circle diagrams will perform better in solving circumnavigation tasks than learners who received a nonillustrated text.

Circumnavigation task performance:

(17) carpet > text only.

(18) circle > text only.

However, if the form of visualization has an effect on the structure of mental models in picture comprehension, then adding pictures to a text can have differential effects depending on the interplay between the form of visualization and the kind of task.

Structure Support Hypothesis.   Previous research has suggested that pictures support mental model construction if learners have low prior knowledge (Levie & Lentz, 1982; Mayer, 1993). If picture comprehension includes a process of structure mapping between the picture and the mental model, then one can assume that adding task-appropriate pictures facilitates the construction of a task-appropriate mental model. This facilitation should be especially obvious for learners with low prior knowledge, who would not be able to construct a mental model only from a text. According to the structure support hypothesis, adding carpet diagrams to the text should help such learners to construct a mental model appropriate for solving time difference tasks. Similarly, the addition of circle diagrams to a text should help such learners to construct a mental model appropriate for solving circumnavigation tasks. Thus, one can predict that performance would in both cases be better than after learning from nonillustrated text.

Low Know learner

Time difference task performance:

(19) carpet > text only.

Circumnavigation task performance:

(20) circle > text only.

If pictures are not task-appropriate, on the contrary, one can assume that these pictures would neither support nor hinder the construction of a task-appropriate mental model. Accordingly, one can predict that individuals learning from text with task-inappropriate pictures show about the same performance as individuals learning from nonillustrated text.
Time difference task performance:

(21) circle = text only.

Circumnavigation task performance:

(22) carpet = text only.

Structure Interference Hypothesis. Learners with high prior knowledge and cognitive abilities are often in the position to construct a task-appropriate mental model only from a text. In this case one can expect that adding task-appropriate pictures would be a support that is not required by the learner. Thus, the pictures would not help to increase performance. Accordingly, after learning from a text with carpet diagrams, one would not expect better performance with time difference tasks than after learning from a text without pictures. Correspondingly, one would not expect better performance with circumnavigation tasks after learning from a text with circle diagrams than after learning from a text without pictures:
Time difference task performance:

(23) carpet = text only.

Circumnavigation task performance:

(24) circle = text only.

If a picture with a task-inappropriate form of visualization is added to the text, however, then these learners could be hindered in their comprehension process. The structure of the picture interferes with the required mental model construction. For example, circle diagrams interfere with the construction of a carpetlike model, and carpet diagrams interfere with the construction of a circlelike model. Accordingly, one can predict that individuals, after learning from a text with circle diagrams, would perform poorer in solving time difference tasks than after learning from a text without diagrams. Similarly, one would expect that individuals after learning from a text with carpet diagrams would show lower performance in solving circumnavigation tasks than after learning from nonillustrated text.

Time difference task performance:

(25) circle < text only.

Circumnavigation task performance:

(26) carpet < text only.

EXPERIMENTAL TESTS OF PREDICTIONS

Method

Participants.   Sixty university students majoring in different fields participated in the experiment. They were randomly assigned to three groups of 20 persons corresponding to three experimental conditions: text only, text with carpet diagrams, and text with circle diagrams.

Instructional Material.   The learning material consisted of a hypertext about the topic "time differences on earth," which had 32 text cards. Learners had access to these cards via a hierarchical menu. The complete text consisted of 2,750 words. The text-only group received only this hypertext. The carpet group received the text with carpet diagrams (see Fig. 16.1), whereas the circle group was given the text with circle diagrams (see Fig. 16.2). Learners were able to retrieve carpet diagrams or circle diagrams by clicking on a button. Texts in the three experimental treatments were informationally equivalent except for some differences in wording that were necessary in order to refer to the different figures.

Procedure.   Verbal and spatial intelligence of the subjects was assessed in a pretest session using subtests of the Intelligenzstrukturtest IST 70 (Amthauer, 1973). Moreover, the subjects' prior knowledge was assessed by an essay-type test concerning time differences on earth.

The main experimental session consisted of three phases: practice, learning, and test. In the *practice phase*, the subjects were given hypermedia software on a different topic in order to learn how to handle the medium. The practice phase was followed by the *learning phase* in which the subjects acquired knowledge about the reasons for time differences on earth. As an orientation about what kind of tasks they had to expect later on, subjects were given 10 questions that addressed time differences between specific cities (i.e., time difference tasks) and changes in time related to circumnavigations around the world (i.e., circumnavigation task). The subjects could freely access text information as they liked. Subjects in the carpet group and in the circle group could also freely access the picture information. In the following *test phase*, the subjects were given a computer-supported comprehension test consisting of time difference tasks (16 items) and circumnavigation tasks (16 items). The items had to be answered without consulting the instructional material. The experiment was conducted in individual sessions and lasted approximately 2 hours.

Scoring. The verbal and spatial abilities of each subject were determined by standardized scores of the corresponding IST-70 subtests. In the prior knowledge test, points were given for correctly answered questions. The differences between the groups with regard to verbal ability, spatial ability, and prior knowledge were negligible.

During the learning phase, the frequency of access to the text information and the picture information was registered automatically. The frequency of text retrievals was used as an indicator of the incidence of using text information. Similarly, the frequency of picture retrievals was used as an indicator of the incidence of using picture information. Learning time was registered automatically by computer. There were no significant group differences with respect to learning time. Comprehension test performance was measured with two subscores: Time difference performance was determined by adding the number of correctly solved time difference tasks. Circumnavigation performance was determined by adding the number of correctly solved circumnavigation tasks.

Results

Use of Text and Picture Information. In the introduction of this chapter, we considered three alternative hypotheses about the use of verbal and pictorial information: the independence hypothesis, the substitution hypothesis, and the stimulation hypothesis. The independence hypothesis simply assumes that the incidence of using text information is independent of the incidence of using picture information, and vice versa (see Predictions 1–4). The substitution hypothesis assumes that text and picture can substitute for each other (see Predictions 5–8). The stimulation hypothesis assumes that text processing stimulates picture processing and vice versa (see Predictions 9–12).

Means and standard deviations of the frequency of text information re-trieval are shown in Table 16.1. The carpet group retrieved about one third less text information than the circle group and the text-only group, which had both retrieved about the same amount of text information. Although an analysis of variance did not show a significant main effect for the factor *form of presentation (text-only, text + carpet, text + circle)*, $F(2,57) = 2.17$, $p = .12$, a priori contrasts revealed that the form of presentation neverthe-less affected the retrieval of text information. Text information with carpet diagrams was used much less than text information with circle diagrams, $t(38) = 2.15, p = .04$. Text information with carpet diagrams was also used less than text information without pictures, although this difference was only marginally significant, $t(38) = 1.82, p=.08$. In contrast, no significant differences were found between the carpet group and the text-only group with regard to the use of text information, $t(38) = 0.06, p = .96$.

Means and standard deviations of the frequency of picture information retrieval in the carpet group and the circle group are also shown in Table 16.1. Accordingly, the carpet group retrieved about one third less picture information than the circle group. An analysis of variance with the factor *form of visualization* (carpet, circle) revealed a marginally significant differ-ence, $F(1,38) = 3.61, p = .07$.

In Table 16.2 the predictions of the independence hypothesis, the substi-tution hypothesis, and the stimulation hypothesis are compared with the experimental findings. The predictions supported by the empirical data are highlighted with asterisks. As can be seen from this table, the results clearly

TABLE 16.1
Use of Text and Picture Information and Comprehension Performance

		Text-only group n = 20	Carpet group n = 20	Circle group n = 20
Text retrieval	M	34.30	21.80	34.75
	SD	27.75	13.24	23.40
Picture retrieval	M		13.15	19.10
	SD		6.01	12.64
Time difference	M	10.30	9.05	7.20
performance	SD	3.34	2.86	2.17
Circumnavigation	M	10.15	8.50	10.85
performance	SD	3.12	2.57	3.23

TABLE 16.2

Predictions and Empirical Findings regarding Retrieval of Text and Picture Information

		Text Retrieval		Picture Retrieval
Theoretical predictions				
Independence hypothesis:				
–With / without pictures	Ca = To	Ci = To	–	–
–Picture difficulty	–	–	Ca = Ci	Ca =Ci
Substitution hypothesis:				
–With / without pictures	Ca < To*	Ci < To	–	–
–Picture difficulty	–	–	Ca < Ci**	Ca > Ci
Stimulation hypothesis:				
–With / without pictures	Ca > To	Ci > To	–	–
–Picture difficulty	–	–	Ca < Ci**	Ca < Ci*
Empirical findings				
	Ca < To	Ci > To	Ca < Ci	Ca < Ci
Significance	$p < .10$	n.s.	$p < .05$	$p <.10$

Note. To = Text only. Ca = Text with carpet diagrams. Ci = Text with circle diagrams.

**$p < .05$, *$p < .10$.

contradict the independence hypothesis: Predictions 1, 3, and 4 are falsified by the data, whereas the only supported prediction (Prediction 2) fits an alternative explanation.

It is more difficult to assess the status of the remaining two hypotheses, the substitution hypothesis and the stimulation hypothesis. The comparison between the carpet group and the text-only group with regard to the use of text information appears to support the substitution hypothesis rather than the stimulation hypothesis: Prediction 5 is confirmed, whereas Prediction 9 is falsified. The circle group did not differ from the text-only group, so this comparison provides no indication for or against one of the other hypothesis (Predictions 6 and 10). If one compares the carpet group and the circle group, however, the results support the stimulation hypothesis rather than the substitution hypothesis: Prediction 12 about the use of picture information is confirmed, whereas Prediction 8 is falsified. The two equivalent predictions about the use of text information (Predictions 7 and 11) were both supported by the data. In other words, the difficult circle pictures were retrieved more frequently and also had triggered more frequent retrieval of text information than the easy carpet pictures.

To sum up, one can conclude from these results that easy pictures (like the carpet diagrams) lead to rather superficial text processing. Accordingly, less text information is used compared to a text without pictures, which is in line with the substitution hypothesis. On the contrary, demanding pictures (like the circle pictures) trigger more intensive picture processing as well as more intensive text processing, which corresponds to the stimulation hypothesis. In other words, the substitution hypothesis and stimulation hypothesis are valid under different conditions.

Influences of the Form of Visualization on the Structure of Mental Models. We earlier discussed the structure-mapping hypothesis of picture comprehension. According to this hypothesis, the structure of a picture influences the structure of the mental model created during picture comprehension and thus its computational efficiency for specific tasks. This resulted in predictions 13 and 14. Accordingly, the structure-mapping hypothesis can be tested by analyzing the pattern of comprehension test performance.

Means and standard deviations of the time difference performance and the circumnavigation performance for the three groups are shown in Table 16.1. When considering the time difference tasks, the best performance was shown by the text-only group, closely followed by the carpet group, with the poorest performance being exhibited by the circle group. An analysis of variance with the factor *form of presentation* showed a significant main effect, $F(2,57) = 6.07, p = .004$. An a priori contrast revealed that the carpet group performed significantly better with the time difference tasks than did the circle group, $t(38) = 2.31, p = .03$. This result confirms prediction 13 of the structure-mapping hypothesis.

With regard to the circumnavigation tasks, on the contrary, the circle group showed the highest performance. An analysis of variance with the factor *form of presentation* resulted in a significant main effect, $F(2,57) = 3.27, p = .05$. An a priori contrast revealed that the circle group performed significantly better on the circumnavigation tasks than did the carpet group, $t(38) = 2.55, p = .02$. This result confirms Prediction 14 of the structure-mapping hypothesis.

In summary, the predictions of the structure-mapping hypothesis were clearly confirmed. Obviously, the form of visualization used in a picture influences the structure of the mental model constructed by picture comprehension. The mental models based on carpet diagrams seem to be more appropriate to solve time difference tasks than mental models based on circle diagrams. On the other hand, mental models based on circle diagrams seem to be more appropriate to solve circumnavigation tasks than mental models based on carpet diagrams. One can conclude from these results that the surface structure of the picture is mapped (at least partially) onto the structure of the mental model and thereby affects the computational efficiency of the model for specific tasks.

Supportive Versus Interference Effects of Pictures. We earlier considered different hypotheses about how learning is affected by adding pictures, when these pictures use different forms of visualization: the dual coding hypothesis, the structure support hypothesis, and the structure interference hypothesis. The dual coding hypothesis assumes that adding pictures to a text is always beneficial for learning (which results in predictions 15–18). The structure support hypothesis assumes that, if learners are unable to construct a mental model only from the text, then the addition of task-appropriate pictures supports the construction of a task-appropriate mental model (which results in Predictions 19 and 20); the addition of task-inappropriate pictures does not affect their mental model construction (Predictions 21 and 22). On the contrary, the structure interference hypothesis assumes that, if learners are able to construct a task-appropriate mental model only from the text, then they do not benefit from adding task-appropriate pictures (resulting in Predictions 23 and 24), whereas the addition of task-inappropriate pictures interferes with the construction of a task-appropriate mental model (Predictions 25 and 26). Thus, the three hypotheses can be tested by comparing both the carpet group and the circle group with the text-only group with regard to their comprehension test performance shown in Table 16.1.

When we analyzed the time difference tasks, the circle group performed significantly poorer than the text-only group, $t(38) = 3.48, p = .001$, whereas the difference between the carpet and the text-only group was not significant, $t(38) = 1.27, p = .21$. When we analyzed the circumnavigation tasks, the carpet group performed marginally poorer than the text-only group, $t(38) = 1.83, p = .08$, whereas the difference between the circle group and the text-only group was not significant, $t(38) = 0.70, p = .49$.

Table 16.3 summarizes the results and the predictions of the dual coding hypothesis, the structure support hypothesis, and the structure interference

TABLE 16.3

Predictions and Empirical Findings That Test the Dual Coding, the Structure Support, and the Structure Interference Hypothesis

	Time Difference performance		Circumnavigation performance	
Theoretical predictions				
Dual coding	Ca > To	Ci > To	Ca > To	Ci > To
Structure support	Ca > To	Ci = To	Ca = To	Ci > To
Structure interference	Ca = To	Ci < To***	Ca < To *	Ci = To
Empirical findings				
	Ca < To	Ci < To	Ca < To	Ci > To
Significance	n.s.	$p < .01$	$p < .10$	n.s.

Note. To = Text only. Ca = Text with carpet diagrams. Ci = Text with circle diagrams.

***$p < .01$, **$p < .05$, *$p < .10$.

hypothesis with respect to time difference performance and circumnavigation performance. Predictions, which are supported by the empirical data, are highlighted through asterisks. As can be seen from the Table 16.3, no empirical support is found for the dual coding hypothesis. Predictions 15, 16, and 17 were falsified by differences in the opposite direction. Prediction 18 was also not confirmed by a significant result. To sum up, the dual coding hypothesis seems not to be a good candidate to explain the empirical findings.

There is also no support for the structure support hypothesis because none of its predictions were confirmed by significant results. Predictions 19, 21, and 22 were falsified by differences in the opposite direction. The empirical data fit relatively well, however, to the structure interference hypothesis. Prediction 25 was robustly confirmed and Prediction 26 had a marginally significant difference in the predicted direction. When no differences had been expected (Predictions 23 and 24), the results were far from significant.

In summary, contrary to a commonly held belief, adding pictures to a text is not always helpful for the learner. It is also possible that task-inappropriate pictures hinder the learner's construction of a task-appropriate mental model. The presentation of a circle diagram, for example, can interfere with the construction of a carpetlike mental model, when the learner would able to construct such a model also from the text alone. Similarly, the presentation of a carpet diagram can interfere with the construction of a circlelike mental model when the learner has the required prior knowledge and cognitive abilities. The present study was conducted with university students, so presumably the subjects' prior knowledge and cognitive abilities were relatively high. Mental model construction was not facilitated through pictures. Instead, the pictures interfered with the learners' mental model construction.

DISCUSSION

Text comprehension and picture comprehension are goal-driven processes in which the individual actively selects and processes verbal and pictorial information in a fashion that allows them to construct mental representations that are suited to the current or anticipated demands. Thus, a comprehensive theory of text and picture comprehension should take this active and constructive nature of information processing into account and should be embedded into a broader framework of human cognition. Such a theory should be able to predict the conditions in which individuals select verbal versus pictorial information in order to construct mental representations for specific tasks. The theory should also take into account that pictures can visualize one and the same subject matter in different ways. It should be able to predict the particular effects that different forms of visualization will have on the structure of the mental representation created in the comprehension process as well as on the computational efficiency of this representation for specific tasks. Finally, the theory should be able to predict under which conditions the addition of a picture to a text is beneficial for comprehension or knowledge acquisition and under which conditions it has a detrimental effect.

The findings of the present study indicate that the dual coding theory is not a satisfactory basis for the development of such a theory. First, the dual coding theory is not able to make predictions about the use of verbal and pictorial information under the conditions of self-directed knowledge acquisition. Second, it does not take into account that subject matter can be visualized in different ways and that the form of visualization affects the structure of the mental representation. Third, it assumes that adding pictures to a text is generally beneficial for learning. It cannot account for the conditions in which pictures interfere with the process of mental model construction.

The combined model of text and picture comprehension presented earlier seems to be better suited for an explanation of the empirical findings of our study. In this model, text and pictures are considered as alternative sources of information for the construction of knowledge structures. They can substitute for each other under specific conditions, but can also stimulate each other under other conditions. The results of our study suggest that adding easy pictures to a text can make text processing more superficial. In this case, the pictorial information seems to distract the individual's attention from the verbal information; that is, the pictures are used instead of the text. Adding more demanding pictures, on the contrary, seems to result in deeper text processing. In this case, the picture processing seems to stimulate text processing, and vice versa. Further studies are required to study the conditions of substitution and the conditions of stimulation more closely.

The model considers picture comprehension as a process of analogical structure mapping. Accordingly, the model allows us to explain why the form of visualization used in a picture affects the structure of the mental model created during picture comprehension. Obviously, the surface structure of the picture is mapped (at least partially) onto the structure of the mental model and, thus, affects the computational efficiency of this model for specific tasks.

Finally, the model allows us to explain why adding pictures to a text is not always beneficial, but can have detrimental effects on the construction of task-appropriate mental representations. Previous research on children's processing of narrative texts has shown that it is the poor readers who benefit most from text illustrations with respect to comprehension and learning (Cooney & Swanson, 1987; Levie & Lentz, 1982; Mastropieri & Scruggs, 1989; Rusted & Coltheart, 1979). This suggests that poor readers are able to construct a mental model from a text with pictures, whereas they would fail on the basis of a text alone. Similar results have been found for adult learners' processing of expository texts. Learners with low prior knowledge benefit from pictures in a text, whereas learners with higher prior knowledge are able to construct a mental model of the described content also from the text alone (Mayer, 1997). These results and our own findings suggest that pictures facilitate learning only if individuals have low prior knowledge and if the subject matter is visualized in a task-appropriate way. However, if good readers with high prior knowledge receive a text with pictures in which the subject matter is visualized in a task-inappropriate way, then these pictures may interfere with the construction of a task-appropriate mental model.

From the perspective of practice, the findings of our study emphasize that in the design of instructional material that include texts and pictures, the form of visualization used in the pictures should be considered very carefully. The question is not only which information is to be conveyed. One must also ask how demanding the processing of a specific picture is and whether the form of visualization used in the picture supports the construction of a task-appropriate mental model. Good graphic design is not only important for individuals with low prior knowledge who need pictorial support in constructing mental models. Well-designed pictures are also important for individuals with high prior knowledge because these individuals can be hindered in their mental model construction through inappropriate forms of visualization.

The model of text and picture comprehension presented herein provides a theoretical framework for research on the construction of mental representations through the combined processing of verbal and pictorial information. The empirical results of our study can be explained within this framework and, at the same time, they help to specify the relationships hypothesized in this framework. In order to make the model fruitful both under theoretical and practical aspects, however, further research is needed. The studies should focus especially on the interplay between external and internal forms of representation during the acquisition of knowledge under different conditions, learning domains, groups of subjects, learning requirements, text characteristics, and forms of visualization. The findings of these studies should help to further elaborate an integrative view of text and picture comprehension.

ACKNOWLEDGMENTS

The authors thank Beatriz Barquero, Susan Goldman, Art Graesser, Mary Hegarty, Richard Mayer, Ric Lowe, Phil Moore and José Otero for helpful discussions about theoretical issues of this chapter.

REFERENCES

Amthauer, R. (1973). Intelligenz-Struktur-Test 70 (IST 70). Göttingen, Germany: Hogrefe.

Baddeley, A. (1992). Working memory. *Science, 255*, 556–559.

Baggett, W. B., & Graesser, A. C. (1995). Questions answering in the context of illustrated expository text. In *Proceedings of Seventh Annual Conference of the cognitive Science Society* (pp. 334–339). Hillsdale, NJ: Lawrence Erlbaum Associates.

Bühler, K. (1934). *Sprachtheorie* [Theory of Language]. Jena, Germany: Fischer.

Chafe, W. L. (1994). *Discourse, consciousness, and time*. Chicago: University of Chicago Press.

Chandler, P., & Sweller, J. (1991). Cognitive load theory and the format of instruction. *Cognition and Instruction, 8,* 293–332.

Clark, J. M., & Paivio, A. (1991). Dual coding theory and education. *Educational Psychology Review, 3,* 149–210.

Cooney, J. B., & Swanson, H. L. (1987). Memory and learning disabilities: An overview. In H. L. Swanson (Ed.), *Memory and learning disabilities: Advances in learning and behavioral disabilities* (pp. 1–40). Greenwich, CT: JAI.

Falkenhainer, B., Forbus, K. D., & Gentner, D. (1989/1990). The structure-mapping engine: Algorithm and examples. *Artificial Intelligence, 41,* 1–63.

Franklin, N., & Tversky, B. (1990). Searching imagined environments. *Journal of Experimental Psychology: General, 119,* 63–76.

Garrod, S. C. (1985). Incremental pragmatic interpretation versus occasional inferencing during fluent reading. In G. Rickheit & H. Strohner (Eds.), *Inferences in text processing* (pp. 161–181). Amsterdam: North-Holland.

Gentner, D. (1989). The mechanisms of analogical learning. In S. Vosniadou & A. Ortony (Eds.), *Similarity and analogical reasoning* (pp. 197–241). Cambridge, England: Cambridge University Press.

Graesser, A. C., Millis, K. K., & Zwaan, R. A. (1997). Discourse comprehension. *Annual Review of Psychology, 48,* 163–189.

Hegarty, M., & Sims, V. K. (1994). Individual differences in mental animation during mechanical reasoning. *Memory & Cognition, 22,* 411–430.

Johnson-Laird, P. N. (1983). *Mental models. Towards a cognitive science of language, interference, and consciousness.* Cambridge, England: Cambridge University Press.

Johnson-Laird, P. N., & Byrne, R. M. J. (1991). *Deduction.* Hillsdale, NJ: Lawrence Erlbaum Associates.

Kintsch, W., Welsch, D., Schmalhofer, F., & Zimny, S. (1990). Sentence memory: A theoretical analysis. *Journal of Memory and Language, 29,* 133–159.

Kolers, P. A., & Brison, S. J. (1984). Commentary: On pictures, words, and their mental representation. *Journal of Verbal Learning and Verbal Behavior, 23,* 105–113.

Kosslyn, S. M. (1994). *Image and brain.* Cambridge, MA: MIT Press.

Kruley, P., Sciama, S. C., & Glenberg, A. M. (1994). On-line processing of textual illustrations in the visuospatial sketchpad: Evidence from dual-task studies. *Memory & Cognition, 22,* 261–272.

Kulhavy, R. W., Stock, W. A., & Kealy, W. A. (1993). How geographic maps increase recall of instructional text. *Educational Technology Research and Development, 41,* 47–62.

Larkin, J. H., & Simon, H. A. (1987). Why a diagram is (sometimes) worth ten thousand words. *Cognitive Science, 11,* 65–99.

Levie, H. W., & Lentz, R. (1982). Effects of text illustrations: A review of research. *Educational Communication and Technology Journal, 30,* 195–232.

Levin, J. R., Anglin, G. J., & Carney, R. N. (1987). On empirically validating functions of pictures in prose. In D. M. Willows & H. A. Houghton (Eds.), *The psychology of illustration,* (Vol. 1, pp. 51–86). New York: Springer.

Logie, R. H., & Baddeley, A. D. (1990). Imagery and working memory. In P. J. Hampson, D. F. Marks, & J. T. E. Richardson (Eds.), *Imagery: Current developments* (pp. 103–128). London: Routledge.

Mastropieri, M. A., & Scruggs, T. E. (1989). Constructing more meaningful relationships: Mnemonic instruction for special populations. *Educational Psychology Review, 1*, 83–111.

Mayer, R. E. (1993). Illustration that instruct. In R. Glaser (Ed.), *Advances in instructional psychology* (Vol. 5, pp. 253–284). Hillsdale, NJ: Lawrence Erlbaum Associates.

Mayer, R. E. (1997). Multimedia learning: Are we asking the right questions? *Educational Psychologist, 32*, 1–19.

Mayer, R. E., & Anderson, R. B. (1992). The instructive animation: Helping students build connections between words and pictures in multimedia learning. *Journal of Educational Psychology, 84*, 444–452.

Paivio, A. (1986). *Mental representations: A dual coding approach.* Oxford, England: Oxford University Press.

Palmer, S. E. (1978). Fundamental aspects of cognitive representation. In E. Rosch & B. B. Lloyd (Eds.), *Cognition and categorization* (pp. 259–303). Hillsdale, NJ: Lawrence Erlbaum Associates.

Peirce, C. S. (1906). Prolegomena to an apology for pragmaticism. *The Monist*, pp. 492–546.

Peterson, D. (1996). *Forms of representation.* Exeter, England: Intellect.

Pinker, S. (1990). A theory of graph comprehension. In R. Freedle (Ed.), *Artificial intelligence and the future of testing* (pp. 73–126), Hillsdale, NJ: Lawrence Erlbaum Associates.

Reed, S. K., Hock, H. S., & Lockhead, G. R. (1983). Tacit knowledge and the effect of pattern configuration on mental scanning. *Memory & Cognition, 11*, 137–143.

Rusted, J. M. (1984). Differential facilitation by pictures of children's retention of written texts: A review. *Current Psychological Research and Reviews, 3*, 61–71.

Rusted, J. M., & Coltheart, M. (1979). Facilitation of children's prose recall by the presence of pictures. *Memory & Cognition, 7*, 354–359.

Rusted, J. M., & Hodgson, S. (1985). Evaluating the picture facilitation effect in children's recall of written texts. *British Journal of Educational Psychology, 25*, 288–294.

Schmalhofer, F., & Glavanov, D. (1986). Three components of understanding a programmer's manual: Verbatim, propositional, and situational representations. *Journal of Memory and Language, 25*, 279–294.

Schnotz, W. (1993). On the relation between dual coding and mental models in graphics comprehension. *Learning and Instruction, 3*, 247–249.

Schnotz, W. (1994). *Aufbau von Wissensstrukturen* [Construction of Knowledge Structures]. Weinheim, Germany: Beltz.

Shepard, R. N. (1984). Ecological constraints on internal representations: Resonant kinematics of perceiving, thinking, and dreaming. *Psychological Review, 91*, 417–447.

Shephard, R. N., & Hurwitz, S. (1984). Upward direction, mental rotation and discrimination of left and right terms in maps. *Cognition, 18*, 161–193.

Shuell, T. J. (1988). The role of the student in the learning from instruction. *Contemporary Educational Psychology, 13*, 276–295.

Sims, V. K., & Hegarty, M. (1997). Mental animation in the visuospatial sketchpad: Evidence from dual-tasks studies. *Memory & Cognition, 25*, 321–332.

Ullman, S. (1984). Visual routines. *Cognition, 18,* 97–159.

van Dam, G., Brinkerik-Carlier, M., & Kok, I. (1986). The influence of visual and verbal embellishment on free recall of the paragraphs of a text. *American Journal of Psychology, 94,* 103–110.

van Dijk, T. A., & Kintsch, W. (1983). *Strategies of discourse comprehension.* New York: Academic Press.

Weaver, C. A., III, Mannes, S., & Fletcher, C. R. (Eds.). (1995). *Discourse comprehension.* Hillsdale, NJ: Lawrence Erlbaum Associates.

Wertheimer, M. (1938). *Laws of organization in perceptual forms in a source book for Gestalt psychology.* London: Routledge & Kegan Paul.

Winn, W. D. (1994). Contributions of perceptual and cognitive processes to the comprehension of graphics. In W. Schnotz & R. Kulhavy (Eds.), *Comprehension of graphics* (pp. 3–27). Amsterdam: Elsevier.

Wittrock, M. C. (1989). Generative processes of comprehension. *Educational Psychologist, 24,* 345–376.

"Mining for Meaning": Cognitive Effects of Inserted Questions in Learning From Scientific Text

Jean-François Rouet
Université de Poitiers

Eduardo Vidal-Abarca
Universidad de Valencia

Most current theories of text learning assume that comprehension results from the interaction between the propositional content of a text and the reader's previous knowledge (Kintsch, 1998; van Dijk & Kintsch, 1983). However a full theory of comprehension must also take into account a number of contextual factors that influence the nature of the text–reader interaction. Among these factors is the way the study situation is designed, and especially the type of instructional objective or question that motivates the study of a particular text. In this chapter we examine the cognitive processes of answering questions from text, and their effects on comprehension. First, we review a number of assumptions concerning the cognitive processes of text comprehension. We emphasize the crucial role of study objectives, especially when reading lengthy scientific texts. Next, we examine

417

the processes of question answering from memory and from text. In the third section we discuss three factors that influence the role of inserted questions in text comprehension: type of questions, metatextual cues, and individual variables (such as previous knowledge and study skills). Finally, we draw some instructional implications concerning the design of instructional study tasks that promote effective learning from text.

WHY SCIENTIFIC TEXTS ARE DIFFICULT TO UNDERSTAND: THE ROLE OF BACKGROUND KNOWLEDGE AND STRATEGIC READING

The comprehension of complex instructional texts requires elaborate study strategies. According to van Dijk and Kintsch (1983), comprehension can be defined as the construction of a mental representation of the situation described in the text, or what they called the *situation model*. The construction of a situation model involves several subprocesses, such as parsing the literal linguistic content, constructing micro- and macro-semantic propositions, generating various kinds of inferences, and integrating text information with one's previous knowledge (Kintsch, 1998; Kintsch & van Dijk, 1978). The precise nature of comprehension processes (e.g., the extent to which readers generate specific types of inferences) depends on the reader's comprehension strategy (van Dijk & Kintsch, 1983). When reading simple narratives, readers normally use a strategy that consists in establishing and maintaining referential and causal coherence (Kintsch & van Dijk, 1978; Trabasso & van den Broek, 1985; Van den Broek, Young, Tzeng, & Linderholm, 1999). When reading lengthy expository texts for specific learning purposes, however, more elaborate strategies may be warranted. For instance, when studying a physics text describing the evolution of atomic models, the reader needs to construct a representation of each model, then to understand the problems of the model and the features of a better model that replaced it. Such elaborate strategies are often a problem for students, because of the knowledge required to process information at multiple levels within a limited-capacity working memory. To illustrate this point, consider the excerpt of an introductory physics text presented in the central column of Table 17.1.

The theory proposed by Kintsch and van Dijk (Kintsch, 1998; Kintsch & van Dijk, 1978; van Dijk & Kintsch, 1983) provides an account of the psychological processes that occur when a student tries to read and understand a passage like this. According to Kintsch and van Dijk (1978), the passage is comprehended through a series of processing cycles. During each cycle, the reader acquires a small amount of information, roughly corresponding to

TABLE 17.1.

Excerpt From an Introductory Physics Text on Atomic Models With Various Types of Questions and Related Information

Inserted Question	Passage Excerpt	Related Information
What did Rutherford find out about atoms?	"In 1911, Rutherford conducted an experiment that was critical in challenging Thomson's atomic model. The experiment consisted in bombarding a leaf of gold foil with packets of alpha particles positively loaded, of much larger mass than that of electrons and launched at high velocities. Rutherford observed that most of the particles traversed the leaf, while some were deviated and a few others bounced back. Rutherford concluded that atoms had to be made essentially of empty space since most of the particles traversed the leaf without being deviated."	Thomson defined atoms as compact but penetrable spheres
What type of particles did Rutherford use in his experiment?		in a solid body atoms are squeezed together
How did Rutherford's atomic model differ from Thomson's?		the particles could not go through the gold leaf except through the atoms themselves

Note. The data in this table are drawn from the materials used in the study by Vidal-Abarca, Gilabert, and Rouet (2001).

one sentence. This involves constructing semantic propositions that underlie the meaning of the sentence, connecting the propositions through various types of links (e.g., coreference, causal and temporal relationships), and maintaining a small subset of propositions in working memory, in order to connect them to the next processing cycle. In the example presented in Table 17.1, upon reading the first sentence the reader must understand that Rutherford conducted an experiment, that the experiment was critical, that the experiment challenged Thomson's model, and so forth. Then, the reader retains a subset of information, for example, "Rutherford conducted a critical experiment". This process goes on during each subsequent cycle, allowing the reader to construct progressively an interconnected network of semantic propositions, or a "textbase" in Kintsch and van Dijk's (1978) terminology.

Comprehension of the passage in Table 17.1 also involves the retrieval of knowledge from the reader's long-term memory (LTM). Retrieval from LTM is cued by the concepts and propositions encountered in the cycle being processed. For instance, upon encountering the phrase "Thomson's model" in the first sentence, a knowledgeable reader may retrieve some characteristics of Thomson's model that he or she may have learned previously, for example, that "Thomson defined atoms as compact but penetrable spheres." Knowledge retrieved from LTM is integrated with text information and becomes part of the reader's representation in LTM, or "situation model" (van Dijk & Kintsch, 1983). The amount of knowledge available prior to reading a text determines the elaborateness of a reader's situation model. For instance, a reader may simply memorize the assertion that "Rutherford concluded that atoms must be essentially empty" and relate it with the fact that "most of the particles traverse the gold leaf." Another, more knowledgeable reader may elaborate upon this conclusion by activating the previous idea that "in a solid body atoms are squeezed together" and conclude that "the particles could not go through the gold leaf except through the atoms themselves." In the terms of van Dijk and Kintsch, the first reader has formed a good textbase, but a poor situation model, whereas the second one has constructed a good representation at both levels.

Comprehension of the passage is further constrained by working memory capacity. In order for two pieces of information to be integrated in LTM, both must be activated simultaneously at some point. For instance, if the passage in Table 17.1 were preceded by a presentation of Thomson's atomic model, the reader should be able to (re)activate some of its features while reading about Rutherford's model, strengthening the connection between the two models (van den Broek et al., 1999). If synchronous activation does not occur to a satisfactory extent, however, the reader will not be able to relate information concerning atomic models presented in distinct paragraphs. Ericsson and Kintsch (1995) established a relationship between domain expertise and the processing capacity in working memory. A reader who possesses a densely interconnected network of relevant concepts prior to reading a text will be able to use it as a cueing system or *long-term working memory*. The cueing system will ensure the spread of activation through a larger set of concepts in LTM, thus maximizing integration of text information with the reader's previous knowledge. Conversely, for readers with a low-level of prior knowledge, the probability that activation of previous information occurs to a sufficient extent is low. For this reason, low-knowledge students typically do not perform inferences that would allow them to repair the numerous gaps in coherence typically found in expository texts (McNamara & Kintsch, 1996).

The assumptions just summarized, which have received ample support from research conducted during the past 20 years, provide a partial explanation of why many students experience serious difficulties when asked to acquire new knowledge from text. Because they do not possess much prior knowledge of the topic, they cannot integrate incoming textual information into a richly interconnected conceptual network. As a result, their representation of the text is piecemeal, and they cannot establish connections between distant pieces of information. Later on, such students may have trouble remembering the information they have read. Consequently, they might not be able to use this information in order to answer questions, to solve problems, or to transfer and generalize it to new situations. In other words, part of the difficulties of understanding scientific text is attributable to the very process of text comprehension, a process that relies heavily on the subject's ability to activate prior knowledge, which, in the case of science texts, is precisely what students are missing.

Psychologists and instructional scientists have proposed several means to alleviate students' comprehension difficulties. One of them consists in guiding the student's activity toward appropriate information and/or levels of processing. Guidance is usually provided by inserting questions in the text or asking the student to perform specific tasks while reading. However there have been few attempts to interpret the effect of adjunct questions in terms of a cognitive theory of text comprehension. In the next section we review the main findings concerning the effects of inserted questions, and we examine current theoretical approaches to question answering from memory and/or from text.

THE ROLE OF QUESTION ANSWERING
IN THE COMPREHENSION OF SCIENTIFIC TEXT

The role of Inserted Questions in Text Comprehension

Rothkopf (1982) studied extensively the role of questions in comprehension and learning. For Rothkopf, questions are a means to stimulate and guide what he called mathemagenic activities, or activities that promote learning. Questions focus the reader's attention to specific aspects of the materials to be learned, or to specific forms of reasoning or inference generation. They play a role similar to other adjuncts, for example, study directions or instructional objectives. Indeed, there is ample evidence that adjunct information deeply influences the processing of instructional materials (for reviews, see Andre, 1979; Hamilton, 1985; Hartley & Davies, 1976; Rickards, 1979). Moreover, the effect of instructional adjuncts varies qualitatively as a function of a number of parameters. For instance, Rickards elicited two main dimensions of inserted questions: the *direction* of their effect (forward or backward) and the *kind of processing* they induced (specific or general). *Backward questions* encourage the mental review of the previously read text, whereas *forward questions* focus students' attention on specific information in the upcoming portion of the text (Rothkopf & Bisbicos, 1967). *Specific questions* focus on a single piece of information whereas *general questions* may involve whole text passages.

General, or "higher level" questions facilitate deep comprehension, that is, the integration of text elements and the production of inferences (Andre, 1979). Andre argued that higher level questions encourage readers to pay attention to broader portions of the text and thus help them structure the mental representation of the text. Wixson (1983) found that textually explicit, textually implicit, or schema-based questions each promoted the corresponding type of inferences in 10th graders, as evidenced in a delayed recall task. Vidal-Abarca, Mengual, Sanjose, and Rouet (1996) asked high school students to study a physics text, then to review it in order to solve either text-explicit or inference questions. The students who received inference questions scored better on recall and inferential comprehension tests. However, these results were only partially replicated in another study (Vidal-Abarca, Gilabert, & Rouet, 1998), possibly because the latter study involved students with much more prior knowledge of the topic.

In summary, many studies have provided convergent evidence that inserted questions facilitate comprehension, especially if they promote the production of inferences and/or the integration of text elements. One issue of theoretical interest is how the processes of question answering relate to the general model of text comprehension outlined earlier. In order to address this complex issue, a close examination of the cognitive processes involved in answering questions from memory and from text is needed.

Cognitive Processes of Question Answering From Memory

Suppose that a student is asked to read the passage on atomic models presented in Table 17.1. Now suppose that after reading the passage the student is asked a question, for example, "What did Rutherford find out about atoms?" Exactly what kind of processes will the student bring to bear in order to provide an answer to this question? The processes depend in part on the organization of the task. If the student is required to answer from memory only, the process will consist of inspecting the mental representation of the text, retrieving relevant information, and constructing an answer. If, however, the student is allowed to review the text in order to locate information relevant to the question, the process will consist in both memory search and text search.

Let us start with the first option. Psychological research suggests that answering questions from memory is in itself a fairly complex process. According to Graesser and Franklin's (1990) QUEST model, question answering involves a categorization mechanism that identifies the *type* of question (e.g., *what-*, *why-*, *how-* type of question), its *focus* (e.g., "Rutherford found something about atoms" in the example aforementioned), and the relevant information *sources*. In the case of questions about concepts newly learned, the identification of the question focus may be affected by low-level processes, for example, correct recognition of key words. Concerning young students with limited reading skills, this aspect of question answering is far from trivial. For instance, Rouet (1991) reported that after reading the question "What kind of customs did the Man of Neanderthal have?" a sixth grader (11-year-old) answered "None. They only wore some kinds of shorts." This type of complete misinterpretation may be quite exceptional, but students' comprehension of questions about scientific texts is nevertheless considerably hindered by their lack of familiarity with the vocabulary employed in the question.

In the case of memory search, *information sources* are the episodic or general-knowledge structures that may be tapped for answers to the question. If the search occurs after reading a scientific text that introduced unfamiliar or complex information, the subject may have to decide whether to search from his or her text representation only, from other episodic structures if any are available, or from a broader knowledge base. Again, the selection of a relevant source in memory may be a problem for novice readers. For instance, Rouet (1991) asked sixth and eighth graders to read a biology text on sharks and to answer a series of comprehension questions. Quite unexpectedly, some answers reported dramatic (and irrelevant) details, for example, sharks' huge size, intelligence, and vindictive temper. A tentative explanation was found when the researcher discovered that the movie *Jaws* had been watched on TV by most subjects the evening before the experiment. Only one eighth-grade participant asked whether it was "compulsory to answer from the text or whether they could use their own knowledge as well."

The latter observation suggests that the selection of an appropriate source may rely on students' metatextual skills, for example, their awareness that several sources exist and that they are not equally useful or relevant (see Rouet, Britt, Mason, & Perfetti, 1996; Rouet & Eme, in press). Indeed, Raphael and Pearson (1985) reported a relationship between sixth graders' awareness of information sources (i.e., students' awareness that a question may be better answered from text or from one's own knowledge base) and their actual performance on comprehension questions. Furthermore, they demonstrated that explicit training in question–answer relationships increased students' recognition of various types of questions as well as the quality of their answers.

According to the QUEST model, questions differ in the size of the conceptual structure needed to build up an answer. Simple questions focus on a single concept or semantic proposition. For instance, "What year did Rutherford conduct his famous experiment?" calls for just a number to be found. More complex questions focus on broader conceptual structures. For instance, "How did Rutherford's atomic model differ from Thomson's?" calls for two knowledge structures to be activated and compared.

In the QUEST model, the actual process of answering a question starts with the activation of a knowledge node, either directly if the node matches a term in the question, or indirectly through the contextual activation of relevant knowledge structures (see also Whilite, 1985). Search continues through a radiation mechanism called *arc-search procedure*. Arc-search allows the propagation of activation through a knowledge network, based on constraints specific to each type of question. For instance, how-questions call for the search of causal antecedents or subordinate goals. Arc-search reduces the search space by identifying those knowledge nodes that may be chosen for an answer. The search space is further reduced by constraint propagation and pragmatic rules. For instance, comparing Rutherford's and Thomson's models may take a line, a paragraph or several pages of text, depending on practical conditions and the type of knowledge one is expected to exhibit. Notice that, for complex questions, note taking while thinking about the question can play a crucial role, as a means to relieve working memory from maintaining intermediate information. However the interactions of note taking and memory search have been seldom studied so far.

A model like QUEST accounts in part for the "mathemagenic effect" of inserted questions. Because of the limitations in students' knowledge and processing resources outlined in the previous section, one single reading of a scientific text may not be enough for the student to establish connections between information distant in the text. Answering questions from memory allow the students to reactivate selectively part of the information (the question acts as a retrieval cue), and to reinforce connections between the information pieces needed to answer (through arc-search and coactivation in working memory). These processes also explain the differential effects of high- and low-level questions. Strictly speaking, only questions that require the reactivation of at least two pieces of knowledge have a chance to improve the integration of representational constituents in LTM. Questions that require the retrieval of a single piece of information may only strengthen the memory trace of this information. However, the effectiveness of high-level questions is conditional upon the student's ability to retrieve the various pieces of relevant information from memory, a process that requires a minimal level of comprehension to be achieved.

The Cognitive Processes of Text-Based Question Answering

Let us now turn to a situation where the student is allowed to search the answer in a text. Do the assumptions of the QUEST model still hold in that case?

There is no obvious reason to believe that the subprocesses of parsing the question and identifying the question category and question focus are fundamentally different in the case of text-based question answering, because these subprocesses require only a question to be read. One distinction occurs at the level of *source selection*. The student has to decide whether he or she can answer based on prior knowledge, or whether searching the text is necessary. The cognitive processes that underlie the decision to conduct an external or internal search are still unclear. As mentioned previously, the students must at least be aware of the options. The decision-making process may then be affected by their general level of comprehension skill (Raphael, 1984; Raphael & Pearson, 1985), their feeling of knowing (Koriat & Levy-Sadot, 1999) or their selection of a retrieval strategy (Singer, 1990).

Let us assume that the student acknowledges the text as a relevant source of information. The next steps will be locating relevant information, and using it to construct an answer. Searching a text in order to locate information relevant to a question is a complex process. Mosenthal (1996) identified four variables that influence text inspection:

1. *Document complexity* is a function of the structural organization of the document (e.g., simple list vs. nested list) and the amount of raw information included in the document.
2. *Type of information requested* varies form the most concrete (e.g., identifying a person or a place) to the most abstract (e.g., identifying equivalence or difference between trends).

3. *Type of match* is a complex aggregated variable that encompasses both the type of search strategy (e.g., locate a single piece vs. integrate several pieces of information) and the amount and type of inferencing required to match document information with requested information (no inference, low text inference, high text inference).
4. *Plausibility of distractors* depends on the presence and location of information that shares some features with the requested information.

Based on the analysis of 217 document search tasks taken from five national surveys on adult document literacy, Mosenthal showed that the four variables accounted for 80% of the variance in task difficulty. Thus, when searching an external source, the subject's strategy is strongly influenced by the amount of information to be searched, its internal organization, and the relationship between the search question and the nature of the information found in the external source.

Mosenthal's (1996) typology suggests that, depending on the type of question, text search may involve superficial or deeper comprehension processes. For instance, imagine that a student is asked to search the text on atomic models in order to locate "the type of particles used in Rutherford's experiment." Based on the analysis of the question focus, the student may expect the target to be a name or a code that will most likely appear next to the word *particles*. This defines a rather precise criterion that can be met without engaging in deep reading comprehension processes (at least when the answer is explicit). On the other hand, using text information to "compare Rutherford's and Thomson's models" will require the student to reconstruct coherent representations of the respective properties of the two models by carefully rereading the relevant text passages. Moreover, as pointed out earlier, the student will have to establish connections between the two macrocomponents of the mental representation, which he or she may have failed to do while reading the text for the first time (Einstein, McDaniel, Owen, & Coté, 1990; see also Newell & Winograd, 1989).

There is evidence that searching a text in order to answer questions is a learning-effective activity. Andre and Thieman (1988) found that students who reviewed the text in order to check the correctness of their answers obtained better scores on the same questions repeated later, compared to students who received external feedback or no feedback on their answers. There is also some evidence that simple, well-structured search tasks may be of some help to less efficient learners in the elementary grades. Cataldo and Cornoldi (1998) observed that when sixth- and seventh-grade poor comprehenders were asked to locate and underline relevant information in the text before actually answering a set of comprehension questions, they later obtained better scores on a comprehension posttest.

An important condition for text search to be effective is that an explicit answer has to be constructed. Newell and Winograd (1989) compared the effects of note taking, question answering, and analytic essay writing on eight 11th-grade students' recall of 400- to 650-word expository passages on various topics. Compared to note taking and question answering, analytic essay writing fostered the recall of gist and relational information. They concluded that analytic essay writing "seemed to provide an occasion for the students to represent to themselves relationships that occurred in the connected discourse" (p. 211). This process may also underlie the difference between different types of inserted questions.

FACTORS THAT INFLUENCE THE EFFECT
OF TEXT-BASED QUESTION ANSWERING

The research studies presented in the preceding sections suggest that (a) answering questions as part of a text study task is an efficient means to improve students' comprehension and (b) searching a text to find relevant information can be a fairly complex activity depending on the type of questions, length, complexity of the text to be searched, and other factors. Thus, there is an apparent contradiction between the facilitative effect of inserted questions and the fact that they can cause specific difficulties for students. The contradiction can be partially explained by examining a number of factors that influence the *processes* and *products* of searching a text to answer questions.

Differential Effects of High- Versus Low-Level Questions

The distinction between high-level and low-level questions has been used extensively in the literature (see Andre, 1979; Halpain, Glover, & Harvey, 1985; Whilite, 1985), but their precise definition varies from one author to another. In the context of text-based question answering, a distinction between high-level and low-level questions corresponds to at least three distinct criteria: the raw amount of information relevant to a question (see "type of match" in Mosenthal's, 1996, typology); the fact that questions refer to the *microstructure* or *macrostructure* of the text, and the fact that they refer to the *textbase* or to the *situation model*. High-level questions are often implicitly defined as questions that focus on a broad set of concepts, for example, a paragraph or a section of a text, whereas low-level questions focus on a single proposition or sentence. The distinction between high-level and low-level questions is also partly related to Kintsch and van Dijk's (1978) concept of a text's microstructure and macrostructure. The microstructure is a hierarchically structured list of semantic propositions that are found in a text. The macrostructure is made of a network of macropropositions, or propositions that condense and subsume detailed information. Part of the macrostructure is usually explicit in the text (e.g., through introductions or summaries) whereas the other part must be constructed by the reader through the application of macrorules (van Dijk & Kintsch, 1983). The third way to look at the distinction between high- and low-level questions has to do with the amount of reasoning or inferences on the part of the reader. Some questions may be answered by using information found explicitly in the text, whereas others require the reader to draw in both textual information, and his or her own previous knowledge. In practice high- and low-level questions often differ according to the amount of information, type of information and type of processing required, with no attempt to isolate these distinctions. An exception is the study by Hofman and van Oostendorp (1999) who manipulated the level (micro vs. macrostructure) and the nature (textbase vs. situation model) of postpassage comprehension questions.

The processing differences between high- and low-level questions are further assessed by measures of their respective attentional demands. Halpain et al. (1985) conducted five experiments in order to study the influence of question type on the allocation of cognitive resources during reading. They presented university students a 1,200-word expository text, in which high- and low-level questions dealing with the contents of each paragraph were inserted. Using a secondary task method, Halpain et al. found that reading paragraphs preceded by high-level questions required more cognitive resources than did reading paragraphs preceded by low-level questions. The authors also found that when the questions were presented after the corresponding paragraphs, reading high-level questions took more resources than did reading low-level questions. The difference disappeared when questions were presented before the relevant paragraphs. Thus, when the students did not have the opportunity to read the text prior to the questions, the amount of resources devoted to high- and low-questions did not differ. These findings confirm the view that high-level postquestions require the reader to review and integrate several text elements, creating more connections in LTM. According to this view, the process of answering text-based high-level questions is more resource consuming, but promotes deep comprehension.

Differences in answering high- versus low-level questions are also apparent in the pattern of information search that they trigger. Vidal-Abarca et al. (1998) conducted two experiments in which high school (Experiment 1) and university students (Experiment 2) read a 2,500-word physics text presented paragraph-by-paragraph on a computer screen. Then half of the students in each experiment answered text-based explicit questions whereas the other half answered global and inference questions. In both conditions, the students were allowed to search information in the text to answer the questions. Answering both types of questions required that students focus on the same textual information. Students who answered explicit questions searched fewer paragraphs per question than those answering global and inference questions. Moreover, students who answered global and inference questions spent significantly less time searching information than students who answered text-based explicit questions. Using a similar procedure, Rouet, Vidal-Abarca, Bert-Erboul, and Millogo (2001) asked undergraduate students to search a 35-paragraph text in order to answer high-level or low-level questions. They observed that each type of question promoted specific review patterns. Figure 17.1 shows examples of search patterns for one high-level question and one low-level question.

The high-level question required the students to compare Thomson's and Rutherford's atomic models. Figure 17.1 shows that two subsections of the text were the most reviewed: the passage comprised of Paragraphs 17 through 20, which presented the features of Thomson's atomic model, and the passage comprised of Paragraphs 30 through 33, which presented those

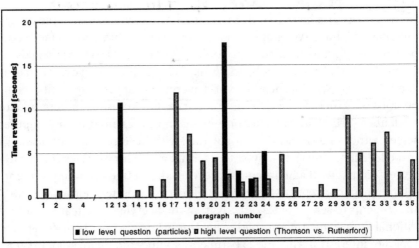

FIG. 17.1.   Patterns of text review for one high-level and one low-level question. This figure is based on the raw data collected in the study by Rouet, Vidal-Abarca, Bert-Erboul, and Millogo (2001).

of Rutherford's model. Some paragraphs of the introduction (1–3) and the sections surrounding the critical ones were also reviewed. In contrast the low-level question required the students to identify the type of particles used in Rutherford's experiment. This information was found in Paragraph 21, which was the most reviewed by students in the low-level questions group, as shown in Figure 17.1. Some students also reviewed the paragraphs following the target paragraph. The unexpectedly high review time on Paragraph 13 was due to one student who mistakenly thought that the question had to do with radioactivity, the topic dealt with in Paragraph 13, which also dealt with particles. In this particular case reviewing the wrong paragraph still allowed the student to provide the correct answer ("alpha particles").

The analysis of review patterns further confirms that answering high-level questions is more demanding because the target information is less precisely located and must be integrated across different text paragraphs. But the higher demand probably contributes to making high-level questions more learning effective than lower level questions.

The Role of Metatextual Cues

In order to locate relevant information, students must be able to read in a selective way, that is, to select only those sections that appear to be of interest while ignoring the others. Metatextual cues, that is, cues that signal the thematic organization of the text, play an important role in guiding students' search processes. *Use of theme cues*

Several studies have found that textual organizers, for example, headings, paragraphing, typography and connectives, facilitate main-idea comprehension (Goldman, Saul, & Coté, 1995; Mayer, 1984; Spyridakis & Standal, 1987). Lorch, Lorch, and Inman (1993) presented evidence that combination of spacing, headings, and overviews improved students' memory for text structure. Dee Lucas and Larkin (1995) asked undergraduate students to study an introductory physics text presented on a computer screen either in a traditional format (i.e., with headings and subheadings embedded in the text), in a hypertext format with a list overview, or in a hypertext format with a hierarchical overview (i.e., a tree diagram representing the main concepts to be learned). The two hypertext formats allowed the students to select topics directly from the overview, whereas in the traditional format the students had to flip through pages in order to locate the topics of interest. In the first experiment, 45 undergraduate students read one of the three versions in order to prepare for a test on its contents, that is, for general-comprehension purposes. Compared to the traditional and the list formats, the hierarchical overview increased students' reviewing of important text units. Even though the students in the traditional condition also spent a long time reviewing, part of this time was spent seeking irrelevant information. Furthermore there was no correlation between the importance of text units and the time spent reviewing them. The hierarchical overview also improved students' memory for main ideas and the quality of their summaries.

In Experiment 2 students were explicitly instructed that they would be asked to write a summary after reading. The rate of reviewing increased, and no difference was found between the three presentation formats. The authors concluded that "With the specific goal of summarizing, readers with the list overview are able to overcome the difficulty through additional processing of the text (i.e., repeated review) so that this is not an insurmountable problem" (Dee Lucas & Larkin, 1995, p. 465). In other words, specific study directions may override the effects of presentation formats. Without such specific study directions, students' willingness to review a science text may depend on the user-friendliness and/or the instructional effectiveness of the top-level content representation.

The effects of top-level content representations may also vary as a function of the reader's level of prior knowledge. Hofman and van Oostendorp (1999) compared the effects of a graphical overview and a topic list on first-year university students' comprehension of a 1,800-word scientific text about the effects of sun rays on health. Based on a pretest, the students were characterized as either high knowledge or low knowledge. After reading the text, students were asked textbase and situation model questions, at the micro- and macrostructure levels. For textbase questions, there was no effect of prior knowledge or presentation format. For situation model questions, the authors found an interaction between prior knowledge level, type of overview, and question level. Low-knowledge students in the graphical overview condition performed less well on microquestions than did students in the topic list version. The authors suggested that the graphical overview hindered low-knowledge students' comprehension of detailed aspects of the situation model because the overview drew their attention to the textual macrostructure at the expense of the microstructure. It is worth noticing that contrary to the simple hierarchical diagram used by Dee Lucas and Larkin (1995), Hofman and van Oostendorp's graphical organizer was a rather complex network diagram, with no clear orientation and several types of links whose meaning was only suggested. It remains to be found whether a more explicit diagram would be more profitable to less knowledgeable readers.

Metatextual cues are essential when performing search tasks in lengthy texts. Evidence comes in part from the literature on electronic text search. For instance, Foss (1989) reported that users of a hypertext system experienced difficulties locating information because of the lack of usual rhetorical cues. Simpson and McKnight (1990) found that subjects searching a hypertext with a hierarchical content list opened fewer irrelevant cards and recalled the document structure more accurately.

Rouet et al. (2001) compared undergraduate science students' search strategies in an electronic text with an implicit or an explicit overview (table of contents). The explicit overview had a major impact on students' reading strategies. During the initial study phase, the explicit overview increased study time by promoting students' spontaneous reviewing of a larger proportion of paragraphs (55% vs. 15% reviewed in the explicit and implicit conditions, respectively). After the initial study phase, the students were asked to search the text in order to answer a series of questions. Subjects in the explicit overview condition opened fewer paragraphs per question than did subjects in the implicit overview condition. The explicit overview also improved their memory for the text's expository structure.

Again, however, there is evidence that the benefits of structured overview depend on students' search skills. In a study by Dreher and Guthrie (1990), 31 10th-grade students searched a textbook chapter presented on a computer screen in order to answer simple and complex questions. Efficient versus less efficient searchers were identified based on their total search time. For complex questions, efficient searchers spent a larger proportion of time selecting information categories from the index or table of contents. Less efficient searchers spent more time extracting information from selected categories. The strategy employed while studying the text affected students' performance in further tests. In the study by Vidal-Abarca et al. (1998), the students who were able to answer more search questions performed better on a recall task 2 days later.

CONCLUSIONS

When considering the theoretical and empirical work reviewed in this chapter, several conclusions can be drawn about the effects of inserted questions on the comprehension of scientific text. First, answering questions based on text information requires both the reprocessing of the text and the reactivation of knowledge from memory. Both components are needed in order to improve students' integration of information and, consequently, their ability to recall and use it later on. Each component involves specific cognitive constraints. Retrieving information from memory requires the student to have achieved at least a minimal level of comprehension, in order for the appropriate arc-search procedures to be executed (Graesser & Franklin, 1990). Locating information in a text requires the student to locate relevant text sections and to match text information with the focus of the question (Mosenthal, 1996; Rouet et al., 2001). *matching*

There has been ample evidence of the positive influence of high-level, inserted questions on students' comprehension. A detailed analysis of the cognitive processes involved in answering high-level questions sheds some additional light on the nature of this effect. High-level questions encourage students to review broader portions of the text, as evidenced in the studies by Vidal-Abarca et al. (1996; 1998) and Rouet et al. (2001). High-level questions promote an integrative type of processing; that is, the student must summarize and compare information across text sections. Integration of information is especially likely to occur when students are asked to produce explicit answers (Newell & Winograd, 1989). This aspect of high-level, inserted questions is especially valuable in instructional settings because the integration of information is often poorly achieved when students read expository texts under general-comprehension objectives, due to their lack of relevant background knowledge and limited processing resources. As a result, their mental representation lacks the relational features necessary to remember in the long run, and to achieve transfer, problem-solving, generalization, and other instructional objectives. In that sense, high-level questions promote the type of processes that are complementary to those that are naturally brought to bear by the students (Einstein et al., 1990).

The benefits of high-level questions depend on students' ability to locate the relevant portions of the text. For this reason, a clearly signaled text structure may add to the benefits of high-level questions. However, there is currently only indirect evidence of the interaction between the presence of metatextual cues and the benefits of integrative search tasks. Moreover, the picture is complicated by the fact that students' search skills also seem to play a specific role in their ability to consider text cues while searching. Although the studies reviewed in this chapter have uncovered parts of the complex interaction between reader, text, and task characteristics, further research is clearly needed before researchers and educators can enjoy an explicit theory of the role of questions in science text comprehension.

ACKNOWLEDGMENTS

Parts of this chapter are adapted from Vidal-Abarca, Gilabert, and Rouet (in press). We thank Alain Bert-Erboul and Victor Millogo for their participation in the experiments.

REFERENCES

Andre, T. (1979). Does answering higher level questions while reading facilitate productive reading? *Review of Educational Research, 49,* 280–318.

Andre, T., & Thieman, A. (1988). Level of adjunct question, type of feedback, and learning concepts by reading. *Contemporary Educational Psychology, 13,* 296–307.

Cataldo, M. G., & Cornoldi, C. (1998). Self-monitoring in poor and good reading comprehenders and their use of strategy. *British Journal of Developmental Psychology, 16,* 155–165.

Dee-Lucas, D., & Larkin, J. H. (1995). Learning from electronic texts: Effects of interactive overviews for information access. *Cognition and Instruction, 13,* 431–468.

Dreher, M. J., & Guthrie, J. T. (1990). Cognitive processes in textbook chapter search tasks. *Reading Research Quarterly, 25,* 323–339.

Einstein, G. O., McDaniel, M. A., Owen, P. D., & Coté, N. C. (1990). Encoding and recall of texts: The importance of material-appropriate processing. *Journal of Memory and Language, 29,* 566–581.

Ericsson, K. A., & Kintsch, W. A. (1995). Long term working memory. *Psychological Review, 102,* 211–245.

Foss, C. L. (1989). *Detecting lost users: Empirical studies on browsing hypertext.* (Tech. Rep. No. 972). Sophia-Antipolis, France: INRIA.

Goldman, S. R., Saul, E. U., & Coté, N. (1995). Paragraphing, reader, and task effects on discourse comprehension. *Discourse Processes, 20,* 273–305.

Graesser, A. C., & Franklin, S. P. (1990). QUEST: A model of question answering. *Discourse Processes, 13,* 279–303.

Halpain, D. R., Glover, J. A,. & Harvey, A. L. (1985). Differential effects of higher and lower order questions: Attention hypotheses. *Journal of Educational Psychology, 77,* 703–715

Hamilton, R. J. (1985). A framework for the evaluation of the effectiveness of adjunct questions and objectives. *Review of Educational Research, 55,* 47–85.

Hartley, J., & Davies, I. K. (1976). Preinstructional strategies: the role of pretests, behavioral objectives, overviews and advance organizers. *Review of Educational Research, 46,* 239–265.

Hofman, R., & van Oostendorp, H. (1999). Cognitive effects of a structural overview in a hypertext. *British Journal of Educational Technology, 30,* 129–140.

Kintsch, W. (1998). *Comprehension: a paradigm for cognition.* Cambridge, MA: Cambridge University Press.

Kintsch, W., & van Dijk, T. A. (1978). Toward a model of text comprehension and production. *Psychological Review, 85,* 363–394.

Koriat, A., & Levy-Sadot, R. (1999). Processes underlying metacognitive judgments: Information-based and experience-based monitoring of one's own knowledge. In S. Chaiken & Y. Trope (Eds.), *Dual process theories in social psychology* (pp. 483–502). New York: Guilford.

Lorch, R. F., Jr., Lorch, E. P., & Inman, W. E. (1993). Effects of signaling topic structure on text recall. *Journal of Educational Psychology, 85,* 281–290.

Mayer, R. E. (1984). Aids to text comprehension. *Educational Psychologist, 19,* 30–42.

McNamara, D. S., & Kintsch, W. (1996). Learning from texts: Effects of prior knowledge and text coherence. *Discourse Processes, 22,* 247–288.

Mosenthal, P. (1996). Understanding the strategies of document literacy and their conditions of use. *Journal of Educational Psychology, 88,* 314–332.

Newell, G. E., & Winograd, P. (1989). The effects of writing on learning from expository text. *Written Communication, 6,* 196–217.

Raphael, T. E. (1984). Teaching learners about sources of information for answering comprehension questions. *Journal of Reading, 27,* 303–311.

Raphael, T. E., & Pearson, P. D. (1985). Increasing students' awareness of sources of information for answering questions. *American Educational Research Journal, 22,* 217–235.

Rickards, J. P. (1979). Adjunct postquestions in text: A critical review of methods and processes. *Review of Educational Research, 49,* 181–196.

Rothkopf, E. (1982). Adjunct aids and the control of mathemagenic activities during purposeful reading. In W. Otto & S. White (Eds.), *Reading expository material* (pp. 109–138). New York: Academic Press.

Rothkopf, E. Z., & Bisbicos, E. (1967). Selective facilitative effects of interspersed questions on learning from written materials. *Journal of Educational Psychology, 58,* 56–61.

Rouet, J.-F. (1991). Compréhension de textes didactiques par des lecteurs inexpérimentés dans des situations d'interaction sujet-ordinateur [Comprehension of expository text by inexperienced readers in subject-computer interaction situations]. Unpublished doctoral thesis, University of Poitiers, Poitiers, France.

Rouet, J.-F., Britt, M. A., Mason, R. A., & Perfetti, C. A. (1996). Using multiple sources of evidence to reason about history. *Journal of Educational Psychology, 88,* 478–493.

Rouet, J.-F., & Eme, P. E. (in press). The role of metatextual knowledge in text comprehension: Issues in development and individual differences. In P. Chambres, M. Izaute, & P. J. Marescaux (Eds.), *Metacognition: Process, function and use.* Amsterdam: Kluwer Academic Publishers.

Rouet, J.-F., Vidal-Abarca, E., Bert-Erboul, A., & Millogo, V. (2001). Effects of information search tasks on the comprehension of instructional text. *Discourse Processes, 31*(2), 163–186.

Singer, M. (1990). Answering questions about discourse. *Discourse Processes, 13,* 261–278.

Simpson, A., & McKnight, C. (1990). Navigation in hypertext: Structural cues and mental maps. In R. McAleese & C. Green (Eds.), *Hypertext: The State of the Art* (pp. 74–83). Oxford, UK: Intellect Books Ltd.

Spyridakis, J. H., & Standal, T. C. (1987). Signals in expository prose: effects on reading. *Reading Research Quarterly, 22,* 285–298.

Trabasso, T., & van den Broek, P. (1985). Causal thinking and the representation of narrative events. *Journal of Memory and Language, 24,* 612–630.

van den Broek, P., Young, M., Tzeng, Y., & Linderholm, T. (1999). The landscape model of reading: Inferences and the online construction of a memory representation. In H. van Oostendorp & S. R. Goldman (Eds.), *The construction of mental representations during reading* (pp. 71–98). Mahwah, NJ: Lawrence Erlbaum Associates.

van Dijk, T. A., & Kintsch, W. (1983). *Strategies of discourse comprehension.* Hillsdale, NJ: Lawrence Erlbaum Associates.

Vidal-Abarca, E., Gilabert, R., & Rouet, J.-F. (1998, July). *El papel del tipo de preguntas en el aprendizaje de textos cientificos* [the role of question type on learning from scientific text]. Paper presented at the *seminar "Comprension y produccion de textos cientificos"* [Comprehension and production of scientific texts]), Aveiro, Portugal.

Vidal-Abarca, E., Gilabert, R., & Rouet, J.-F. (2001). El papel de las preguntas y cuestiones en el aprendizaje de las ciencias [The role of questions and objectives in science learning]. In J. Otero & H. Caldeira (Eds.), *La comprensión y utilización de los libros de textos de ciencias.* Manuscript submitted for publication.

Vidal-Abarca, E., Mengual, V., Sanjose, V., & Rouet, J.-F. (1996, September). Levels of comprehension of scientific prose: The role of text and task variables. *Paper presented at the International Seminar on Using Complex Information Systems,* Poitiers, France.

Whilite, S. C. (1985). Differential effects of high-level and low-level postpassage questions. *American Journal of Psychology, 98,* 41–58.

Wixson, K. K. (1983). Postreading question-answer interactions and children's learning from text. *Journal of Educational Psychology, 75,* 413–423.

Author Index

A

Abelson, R. P., 92, 98, 160, 163, 282, 291, 292
Acredolo, C., 301
Adams, J. S., 282, 287
Adelson, B., 164
Afflerbach, P., 236
Ajewole, G. A., 40
Albrecht, J. E., 180, 181, 182, 183
Alexander, P., 57
Alexander, P. A., 20, 23, 37, 41, 223
Allinson, L., 373
Alonso, M. A., 205
Alverman, D. E., 55
American Psychological Association, 24, 26
Amsel, E., 293
Amthauer, R., 404

Anderson, C., 110
Anderson, C. A., 92, 105, 121
Anderson, J. R., 117, 122
Anderson, R. B., 393
Anderson, R. C., 56, 224, 230
Anderson, R. D., 39
Anderson, R. I., 300
Anderson, T. H., 68
Andre, T., 422, 426, 427
Andrusiak, P., 166
Anglin, G. J., 78, 386
Aquires, A., 75
Armbruster, B. B., 60, 68
Aronson, E., 281, 287
Asoko, H., 20
Ausubel, D. P., 224, 334
Avgerinou, M., 79
Ayers, M. S., 230

B

Baddeley, A., 351, 393, 395, 396
Baddeley, A. D., 398
Baggett, W. B., 156, 161, 166, 202, 204, 213, 375, 387
Bainbridge, E. A., 289
Baird, W., 57
Baker, L, 224, 225, 227, 228, 282, 283, 289, 300, 309
Ballstaedt, S.-P., 224
Banks, G., 92
Barlex, D., 75
Barman, C., 59
Barnard, Y., 224, 247
Barnett, J. E., 272
Baron, R. M., 282
Barrett, T., 68
Bartlett, F. C., 160
Bauer, H. H., 39
Baumann, J. F., 57
Bazerman, C., 21, 22, 26, 28, 29, 231, 248
Beck, I. L., 4, 56, 57, 161, 224, 233, 301
Begley, S., 68
Benjamin, A. S., 259
Bereiter, C., 41, 283
Berkenkotter, C., 21, 22, 26, 28, 29, 58
Berry, S. L., 258
Bert-Erboul, A., 429, 432, 433
Bertus, E. L., 10, 159, 161, 166, 167
Bertus, L. B., 200, 201, 204, 216
Betrancourt, M., 380
Bevridge, M., 79
Bisanz, G. L., 31, 34, 36, 37, 38
Bisanz, J., 31, 34, 36, 37, 38
Bisbicos, E., 422
Bishop, B., 110
Bjork, R. A., 259
Black, J. B., 160, 161, 166, 365
Blackwood, P. E., 59, 61, 62
Blanquer, E., 209

Bloom, B. S., 9
Bloom, C. P., 139
Bluth, G. J., 57
Bock, J. K., 204
Boeschen, J. A., 59, 61, 62
Bonebakker, C., 310, 325, 327
Bonnotte, I., 206
Borkowski, J. G., 272
Bovair, S., 204
Bove, W., 40, 341, 344, 346, 348
Bower, G., 54, 56, 345
Bower, G. H., 166
Bowers, C. A., 261
Bramuci, R. S., 230
Brainerd, L. E., 8
Brandt, D. H., 57
Bransford, J. D., 13, 188, 375
Brasil, 77
Breuker, J. A., 236
Brewer, W., 283, 293
Brewer, W. F., 92, 95, 97, 122, 158, 204, 224
Brincones, I., 338
Brinkerik-Carlier, M., 399
Brison, S. J., 387
Britt, M. A., 20, 29, 424
Britton, B., 286
Britton, B. K., 160, 161, 204, 375
Brooks, C., 6
Brouwer, W., 30, 32
Brown, A. L., 41, 224, 236
Brown, D., 55, 67
Brown, J. S., 180, 290, 295, 297, 300
Brown, R., 57
Brumby, M., 110
Bruner, J., 158, 159, 160, 165
Bruner, J. S., 4
Brunkhorst, B. J., 300
Brunning, R. H., 268
Bryant, D. S., 257, 259, 261, 272
Bryman, A., 40, 341, 344, 346, 348
Buchanan, B., 92

Budd, D., 230
Bühler, K., 385
Bullock, M., 292, 295
Bunge, M., 157
Burbules, N. C., 283, 286
Burnett, R., 57
Burns, K. D., 257, 259
Burtis, J., 283
Burtis, P. J., 41
Butler-Songer, N., 264
Buxton, W. M., 57
Bybee, R. W., 39
Byrne, R. M. J., 392

C

Cacioppo, J. T., 289
Caldwell, A., 39
Calfee, R. C., 39, 51, 52, 53, 56, 58, 60,
    65, 68
Calvo, M. G., 202
Camp, C., 55, 67
Campanario, J. M., 162, 163, 225, 282,
    284, 288, 289, 294, 295, 296,
    297, 298, 309, 312, 327
Caplan, D., 133
Caramazza, A., 38
Carenni, G., 92
Carey, S., 156
Carin, A. A., 59, 61, 62
Carney, R. N., 78, 386
Carpenter, P. A., 133, 141, 282
Carré, C., 75
Carreiras, M., 205
Carretero, M., 144, 163
Carriedo, N., 205
Casteel, M. A., 132, 139
Castillo, M. D., 202
Cataldo, M. G., 426
Chafe, W. L., 392
Chall, J. S., 60

Chambliss, M. C., 58, 60
Chambliss, M. J., 39, 51, 52, 53, 56, 58,
    60, 65, 68
Champagne, A. B., 54
Chan, C., 283
Chan, C. K. K., 41
Chandler, P., 351, 393
Chapman, M. L., 58
Chen, C., 373, 374
Cheng, P. W., 163
Chi, M. T. H., 7, 13, 41, 92, 110, 164,
    227, 360, 365, 375
Chiapetta, E. L., 4
Chincaro, A., 76
Chinn, C., 283, 293
Chinn, C. A., 92, 95, 97, 122, 224
Chiu, M. H., 7, 13, 41, 92, 227, 360,
    365, 375
Clancey, W. J., 92
Clark, H. H., 200
Clark, J. M., 349, 386
Clark, L. F., 132, 161, 166, 180, 189,
    190, 202
Clark, M. B., 133
Clement, J., 55, 67
Cobb, R. E., 158
Cochran, C., 57
Cohen, M. R., 63
Coleman, E., 41
Collins, A., 290, 295, 297, 300
Collins, A. M., 180
Coltheart, M., 412
Connors, R. J. 58, 59
Conrad, P., 32, 33, 34
Cook, L. K., 338
Cooney, J. B., 412
Cooney, T. M., 63
Cooper, E. K., 59, 61, 62
Corbett, A. T., 380
Corkill, A. J., 268, 269
Cornoldi, C., 426

Coté, N., 7, 10, 30, 38, 41, 149, 158, 166, 224, 227, 232, 239, 286, 426, 433, 430
Craig, M. T., 21
Crane, R. C., 239
Crane, R. S., 202
Crittenden, A., 151
Cuerva, J., 289
Cunay, P. K., 158

D

Dale, E., 60
Dall'Alba, G., 232
Daneman, M., 133, 282, 328
Darden, L., 283
Davies, I. K., 422
Davis, J. N., 30
Davison, A. L., 60
Day, J. D., 236
DeBoar, G. E., 39
DeCastell, S., 298
Dee-Lucas, D., 30, 40, 204, 430, 431
De Glopper, K., 236, 247
de Leeuw, N., 7, 13, 41, 92, 227, 360, 365, 375
De Manuel, J., 288
Demastes, S., 110
Denhière, G., 205
de Posada, J. M., 40
Derman, D., 372, 376
Dewey, J., 160
Dickinson, P., 114
diSessa, A., 53, 283
Dispezio, M., 59
Dopkins, S., 181, 182
Dorfman, D., 185
Doster, E. C., 41
Dreher, M. J., 432
Dretske, F., 98
Driver, R., 20, 75
Duchastel, P., 79

Duffy, S. A., 156
Duffy, T. M., 57
Duit, R., 54, 55
Dunbar, K., 20
Dunlosky, J., 258, 263, 265, 268, 273
Durán, R. P., 40
Duschl, R. A., 20

E

Eddy, D. M., 164, 165, 170
Edelson, D. C., 359, 381
Einhorn, H., 155, 158, 163, 165
Einhorn, H. J., 99
Einsiedel, E. G., 21, 31, 34
Einstein, G. O., 158, 261, 426, 433
Eisenhart, F. J., 286
Ekstrom, R. B., 372, 376
Elkerton, J., 380
Ellenbogen, K., 20
Elshout, J. J., 236
Elshout-Mohr, M., 226, 227, 233, 234, 236, 247, 310
Eme, P. E., 424
Englert, C. S., 56, 57
Entwistle, N., 224, 237
Epstein, W., 258, 260
Ericson, J., 79
Ericsson, K., 181, 184, 185, 186, 288
Ericsson, K. A., 9, 257, 420
Escudero, I., 162, 163, 166, 171, 204
Escudero, J., 168, 172
Everson, M. G., 151

F

Falkenhainer, B., 398
Faraday, P., 360, 371
Faust, M. E., 261
Ferguson, E. S., 360
Fernández, A., 205
Ferrari, M., 110
Ferreira, F., 166, 202

Festinger, L., 281
Filippatou, D., 79
Fillman, D. A., 4
Fincher-Kiefer, R., 166, 200, 202, 204
Fischer, B., 185
Fitzpatrick, S. M., 33
Fleming, M., 79
Fletcher, C. R., 133, 137, 139, 147,
        202, 262, 375, 395
Fodor, J. A., 100
Foley, J. M., 259
Fonte Boa, M., 78
Forbus, K., 115
Forbus, K. D., 395
Forgy, C. L., 115
Forsythe, D., 92
Foss, C. L., 432
François, J., 205
Franklin, N., 398
Franklin, S. P., 423, 433
Frederiksen, J. R., 381
Freebody, P., 56
Freedle, R. O., 56
Freedman, A., 58
Freeburn, G., 225
Freitas, C., 76
French, J. W., 372, 376
Fritz, J. B., 57
Fuchs, C., 205

G

Gaddy, M., 133, 135, 140, 144, 145
Gagnon, N., 166
Gallini, J. K., 344, 348, 360
Gamas, W. S., 41, 54, 55
García-Arista, E., 225, 289, 327
Garner, R., 57, 225, 272, 309
Garnett, P. J., 40
Garrod, S. C., 391
Gee, J. P., 21, 22
Gelman, R., 156

Gentner, D., 67, 115, 395
George Allen, 360
Gernsbacher, M. A., 132, 139, 261
Gertzog, W. A., 283
Giddings, M. G., 59, 61, 62
Gilabert, R., 419, 422, 428, 432, 433
Gilbert, D. K., 289
Gillingham, M., 57
Glanzer, M., 185
Glaser, H., 164
Glass, D. C., 287
Glass, G. V., 41, 54, 55
Glavanov, D., 391
Glenberg, A. M., 188, 258, 260, 395
Glenn, C. G., 159, 160
Glover, D., 59
Glover, J. A., 268, 427, 428
Glynn, S. M., 39, 41, 204
Goetz, E. T., 57
Golding, J., 166, 200
Golding, J. M., 200, 202
Goldman, S., 125, 286
Goldman, S. R., 7, 10, 13, 20, 23, 30, 38,
        39, 40, 41, 133, 149, 166, 224,
        227, 232, 239, 360, 430
Goldsmith, E., 79
Good, R., 40, 110
Gopnik, A., 92, 123
Gordon, D. H., 37
Gordon, S. E., 8
Gorin, L., 225, 288
Gorman, M. E., 289
Gottfried, S. S., 4
Gould, S. J., 116
Gowin, D. B., 247
Graesser, A. C., 4, 7, 8, 10, 13, 37, 92,
        98, 122, 132, 137, 138, 144,
        156, 159, 160, 161, 166, 167,
        180, 181, 182, 186, 189, 190,
        199, 200, 201, 202, 204, 205,
        206, 213, 216, 217, 224, 225,
        227, 228, 258, 260, 263, 264,

282, 283, 290, 309, 335, 360, 375, 386, 387, 391, 423, 433
Graf, P., 375
Graham, S., 223
Green, B., 38
Greenbowe, T. J., 40
Greene, E., 141
Greene, S., 200
Greene, S. B., 205
Grice, H. P., 298
Groen, G. J., 164, 170
Gromoll, E. W., 233
Guimarães, L. A., 78
Gunstone, R. G., 54
Gustafson, M., 137
Guthrie, J. T., 432
Guthrie, V., 59
Gutwill, J., 381
Guzetti, B. J., 41
Guzman, A. E., 203
Guzzetti, B. J., 40, 41, 54, 55

H

Haberlandt, K., 166, 200
Hacker, D. J., 232, 255, 309
Haenggi, D., 272
Hager, M., 68
Hall, V. C., 258
Hallden, O., 228, 232
Halldorson, M., 166
Halliday, M. A., 79, 80
Halliday, M. A. K., 181
Halpain, D. R., 427, 428
Hamilton, R. J., 20, 422
Hamilton, R. L., 301
Hammond, N., 373
Hanesian, H., 224
Hansen, S. R., 358
Hardyck, J. A., 282
Hare, V. C., 56, 57
Harkness, D., 159, 166, 167

Harman, H. H., 372, 376
Harmon, J. M., 224
Harp, S., 346
Harp, S. F., 57
Harris, J. L., 158
Harris, K. R., 223
Hart, H. L. A., 159
Harter, D., 7
Hartley, J., 422
Hartman, N., 158
Harvey, A. L., 427, 428
Hasan, R., 181
Haugen, D., 57
Haviland, S. E., 200
Hawthorne, C. M., 63
Hegarty, M., 358, 360, 361, 362, 367, 370, 375, 376, 379, 395, 398
Heider, F., 156
Hemmerich, J., 92
Hempel, C. G., 91, 94
Hemphill, D., 92, 122, 161, 204, 205, 206, 217
Henderson, J., 36, 37
Hertzog, C., 258
Hesse, F. W., 172
Hesslow, G., 163
Hewson, P. W., 283
Hewstone, M., 156
Hidi, S., 57, 224
Hiebert, E. H., 56, 57
Higginbotham, M. W., 37
Higgins, L., 57
Hill, C., 57
Hilton, D., 94, 122
Hilton, D. J., 163
Hock, H. S., 398
Hodgson, S., 399
Hofman, R., 428, 431
Hogarth, R. M., 99, 155, 158, 163, 165
Holmquist, S., 360, 367, 370
Holyoak, K., 114, 115
Holyoak, K. J., 55, 67, 163, 164, 170

Honoré, T., 159
Hopfield, J. J., 285
Huber, J. D., 283
Huckin, T. N., 21, 22, 26, 28, 29, 58
Huitema, J. S., 181, 182
Hummel, J. E., 137
Hurd, P. D., 39, 68
Hurwitz, S., 398
Husebye-Hartmann, E., 137, 146, 287
Hynd, C. R., 40, 41, 55, 58, 59

I

Inman, W. E., 430
Intrator, S., 39

J

Jaquette, D., 91
Jennings, T. M., 200
Jimenez Aleixandre, M. P., 78
John, B. E., 380
Johnson, B. K., 156, 166, 202, 204, 213
Johnson, C., 92
Johnson, G. S., 309
Johnson, H. M., 282, 294, 310, 325
Johnson, M. K., 188
Johnson, N. S., 159, 160
Johnson-Laird, P. N., 180, 186, 187,
     188, 189, 391, 392
Johnston, P., 309
Joly, M., 78
Jonas, D., 261
Jones, R., 92
Jordan, P., 7
Joseph, N., 68
Just, M. A., 133, 141, 282, 379

K

Kahneman, D., 165
Kajer, W. K., 259
Kallod, M., 261

Kamas, E. N., 230
Kamil, M. L., 39
Kantor, R. N., 68
Kaplan, B., 185
Karabenick, S. A., 262, 283, 299
Karau, S. J., 225
Kardash, C. M., 289, 328
Kardush, M., 282
Kassler, M. A., 4
Kealy, W. A., 386
Kearsey, J., 79
Keefe, D. E., 202, 203
Keenan, J. M., 166, 200, 202
Keil, F. C., 92, 95, 99, 120, 122
Kelly, M., 57
Kelman, H. C., 282
Kemper, S., 200
Kempff, H. J., 167, 201
Kesidou, S., 39
Kieffer, R., 39
Kieras, D. E., 204
Kim, H., 39
King, A., 41, 228
Kintsch, E., 10, 40, 225, 227, 231, 246,
     264, 373, 375
Kintsch, W., 7, 9, 10, 13, 20, 26, 40, 54,
     56, 57, 60, 125, 132, 133, 137,
     140, 141, 159, 179, 180, 181,
     182, 184, 185, 186, 187, 189,
     204, 223, 224, 225, 227, 231,
     232, 239, 241, 246, 247, 260,
     261, 263, 264, 282, 286, 288,
     294, 295, 326, 373, 375, 391,
     395, 417, 418, 419, 420, 421,
     428
Kitcher, P., 92, 93, 105
Klaczynski, P. A., 37
Klein, J., 31, 34, 37
Klein, P., 31, 34, 37
Klin, C. M., 181, 182, 202, 203
Klopfer, L. E., 54
Klusewitz, M. A., 144

Kluttz, C., 202
Koh, K., 163
Koizumi, C., 166
Kok, I., 399
Kolers, P. A., 387
Koriat, A., 259, 262, 263, 425
Korpan, C., A., 36, 37
Kosslyn, S. M., 391, 392, 395
Kozhevnikov, M., 361, 376
Krapp, A., 224
Kremer, K., 151
Kress, G., 75, 79, 80, 81, 84, 85, 86
Kruez, R. J., 4, 289
Krug, D., 268
Kruley, P., 395
Krull, D., 92, 105, 121
Krull, D. S., 92
Krupa, M., 91
Kucan, L., 56, 301
Kudukey, J., 55, 67
Kuhn, D., 283, 293
Kulhavy, R. W., 386
Kulikowich, J. M., 20, 23, 37, 41, 57
Kunda, Z., 37
Kyle, W. C., 4

L

Labbo, L. D., 39
Lalljee, M. G., 163
Lange, D. L., 30
Langer, J. A., 224
Langston, M., 92, 99, 156, 158, 161, 166
Langston, M. C., 133, 144, 186
Larkin, J., 288
Larkin, J. H., 30, 40, 204, 387, 388, 390, 430, 431
Larkin, K. M., 180, 290, 295, 297, 300
LaVancher, C., 41, 92, 227, 360, 365, 375
La Vancher, M., 7, 13
Lave, G., 22

Law, K., 115
Law, M., 41
Lawson, A., 110
Leach, J., 20
Leake, D. B., 92, 99, 120
Lear, J. C., 166
Leatherbarrow, M., 282, 293, 310, 312, 325
Lebiere, C., 117, 122, 230
Leddo, J., 92, 98
Lefrancois, G. R., 334
Lehrer, R., 40
Lehtinen, E., 115, 123
Lemke, J., 81
Lemke, J. L., 4, 203
Lentz, R., 78, 386, 402, 412
Lenzen, V. F., 157
León, J. A., 144, 162, 163, 164, 166, 168, 171, 172, 201, 203, 204
Lepper, M., 286
Lepper, M. R., 286
Levie, H. W., 386, 402, 412
Levine, W. H., 78, 203
Levin, J. R., 78, 386
Levy, D. H., 66
Levy-Sadot, R., 425
Leyden, M. B., 59
Lightfoot, C., 292, 295
Lin, L. M., 259
Lindem, K., 188
Linderholm, T., 133, 137, 143, 147, 151, 161, 418, 420
Linn, M. C., 283, 286
Little, L. D., 258
Locke, E. Q., 224
Lockhead, G. R., 398
Logie, R. H., 398
Long, D. L., 166, 167, 200
Lorch, E. P., 144, 430
Lorch, R. F., 4, 179
Lorch, R. F., Jr., 133, 137, 144, 430
Low, R., 360

Lowe, R. K., 375
Loxterman, J. A., 4, 161
Luke, A., 298
Luke, C., 298
Lynch, P. P., 40

M

Macaulay, D., 360, 370, 371, 372
Mackie, J. L., 144, 155, 158, 163
MacNamara, D., 10
Mac Whinney, B., 205
Magliano, J. P., 156, 166, 202, 204, 205,
    210, 213, 225, 258
Maki, R. H., 231, 257, 258, 259, 260,
    261, 262, 263, 267
Mallow, J. V., 34
Mandler, J. M., 4, 159, 160
Manes Gallo, M. C., 206
Mann, W. C., 182
Mannes, S., 327, 395
Mannes, S. M., 375
Manzo, A., 40
Manzo, U. C., 40
Markman, E. M., 225, 284, 285, 288
Mars, R., 40, 54, 56, 341, 344, 345,
    346, 348
Marsolek, C. J., 137
Martin, B. E., 30, 32
Martins, I., 75, 76, 78, 84, 86
Marton, F., 224, 237
Marx, R. W., 225
Mason, R. A., 424
Mastropieri, M. A., 412
Maury, P., 205, 209
Mayer, R. E., 40, 54, 56, 57, 58, 60, 65,
    78, 204, 265, 268, 269, 334,
    338, 341, 344, 345, 346, 348,
    349, 350, 351, 355, 360, 361,
    363, 380, 387, 393, 402, 412,
    430

Mayr, E., 107
McCaffrey, M., 57
McCauley, R. N., 123
McClelland, J. L., 285
McCloskey, M., 38
McConnell, M. C., 30, 68
McCormack, A. J., 63
McCormack, B. B., 21
McCormick, C. B., 271
McDaniel, M. A., 78, 158, 202, 203,
    261, 426, 433
McDonald, J. L., 205
McDonald, S., 263, 265
McDonald, S. L., 263
McGill, A. L., 163
McGillicuddy, K., 86
McKenna, M., 39
McKeown, M. G., 4, 57, 161, 224, 233,
    301
McKnight, C., 432
McKoon, G., 132, 179, 180, 181, 199,
    200, 202, 203, 204, 205
Mclain-Allen, B., 4
McMahen, C. L., 309
McMahon, M. M., 21
McNamara, D. S., 40, 225, 231, 246,
    264, 373, 375, 421
McWhorter, J. Y., 55, 58, 59
Means, M. L., 4
Mehlenbacher, B., 57
Meltzoff, A. N., 123
Mengual, V., 422, 433
Mercier, S., 59
Metcalfe, J., 257, 273
Meyer, B. J. F., 57, 60, 225, 338
Meyer, M., 188
Michotte, A., 156
Miller, G. A., 133
Miller, G. R., 287, 289
Miller, L. C., 282, 286, 288
Millis, K., 7

Millis, K. K., 166, 167, 200, 203, 204, 213, 217, 227, 263, 264, 265, 273, 282, 386, 391
Millogo, V., 429, 432, 433
Minstrell, J., 55, 67
Mischinski, M., 151
Miyake, N., 298
Moore, J., 92
Moore, J. D., 92
Moreno, R., 345, 360, 367, 370
Morgan, D., 166, 167, 202
Morris, C., 260
Morris, C. C., 259
Morrison, J. B., 380
Mortimer, E., 20, 78
Moschman, D., 13
Mosenthal, P., 292, 425, 426, 427, 433
Motoda, H., 362, 375, 376
Mousavi, S. Y., 360
Murachver, T., 161
Murray, J. D., 202
Muth, K. D., 39
Myers, J., 181, 182
Myers, J. L., 13, 132, 133, 139, 141, 156, 180, 181, 182, 183, 201, 202, 300

N

Narayanan, N. H., 358, 360, 362, 367, 370, 375, 376
Narvaez, D., 132, 137
Nathan, M. J., 7, 375
National Research Council, 334
National Science Resources Center, 68
Neisser, U., 232
Nelson, T. O., 226, 266
Newell, G. E., 426, 427, 433
Newton, D. P., 165
Nisbett, R. E., 163, 287
Noordman, L. G. M., 155, 164, 165, 167, 168, 201
Norman, D. A., 298

Norris, S. P., 20, 21, 30, 36, 37, 38, 298
Novak, G., 362, 363
Novak, J. D., 224, 247
Nwogu, K. N., 21, 31, 33, 34, 36

O

Oatley, K., 58
O'Brien, E., 300
O'Brien, E. J., 13, 132, 133, 139, 141, 180, 181, 182, 201
O'Connor, J., 301
Oestermeier, U., 172
Ogborn, J., 75, 84, 86
Ohlsson, S., 92, 98, 104, 105, 106, 115, 117, 123, 124
O'Loughlin, M., 293
Olson, T. L., 74
Oppenheimer, P., 91, 94
Oppy, B. J., 167
Osborn, J. H., 60
Osborne, J., 78
Ostlund, K., 59
O'Sullivan, J., 272
Otero, J., 41, 162, 163, 189, 224, 225, 282, 283, 284, 288, 289, 294, 295, 296, 297, 298, 300, 309, 312, 327, 338
Owen, P. D., 158, 426, 433

P

Paivio, A., 78, 349, 386
Paivio, A. V., 13
Pak, S., 283
Palincsar, A. M., 224
Palmer, D., 55, 67
Palmer, S. E., 388
Palmiter, S., 380
Pane, J. F., 380
Paris, C. L., 92
Park, J., 283
Parker, S. B., 5
Partridge, T., 85, 86

Pasachoff, J. M., 63
Pasachoff, N., 63
Patel, V. L., 164, 170
Pazzani, M. J., 99
Pearson, P. D., 224, 424, 425
Peirce, C. S., 390
Peñalba, G., 168, 172
Peng, K., 287
Pérez, O., 162, 163, 164, 168, 172, 201
Perfetti, C. A., 20, 29, 200, 201, 224,
        272, 424
Person, N. K., 224, 227, 228, 283
Peterson, D., 387
Petrosino, A. J., 40
Petty, R. E., 289
Pfundt, H., 54
Phares, V. L., 55, 58, 59
Phillips, L., 298
Phillips, L. A., 36, 37, 38
Phillips, L. M., 20, 21, 30, 36, 37
Piaget, J., 156, 160
Pinker, S., 396
Pitt, J. C., 95, 122
Plewes, S., 182
Ploetzner, R., 40
Pollard, J. M., 301
Pollatsek, A., 201
Posner, G. J., 283
Potts, G. R., 166, 200, 202
Premack, A., 99, 155
Premack, D., 99, 155
Pressley, M., 78, 225, 236, 271, 272
Pumfrey, P., 79

Q

Qualls, C. D., 158
Quilici, J., 360, 367, 370

R

Rabinowitz, M., 56, 57
Rada, R., 373, 374

Radvansky, G. A., 186, 187
Rakestraw, J. A., Jr., 20, 23, 39
Raphael, T. E., 424, 425
Ratcliff, R., 132, 179, 180, 181, 199,
        200, 202, 203, 204, 205
Ratner, H. H., 282, 300
Rawson, K. A., 263, 265, 268, 273
Rayner, K., 201
Read, S. J., 163, 282, 286, 288
Reder, L. M., 202, 230
Reed, S. K., 398
Rees, E., 164
Regan, S., 115, 124
Reid, D., 79
Reif, F., 288
Reinking, D., 39
Reitz, L., 139
Resnick, L. B., 247
Reynolds, D. J., 310, 325
Rhines, K. L., 63
Rice, G. E., 225
Rickards, J. P., 422
Rieber, L. P., 380
Risden, K., 133, 137, 146, 147, 202, 262,
        287
Ritchie, B. G., 133, 202
Ritchot, K. F. M., 133
Rivkin, I. D., 41
Rizella, M. L., 181, 182
Roberts, R. M., 289
Robertson, S. P., 37
Robinson, J. T., 39, 68
Rodriguez, M., 57
Rogers, K., 21, 36, 37
Rogers, W. A., 158
Rogers, Y., 358, 375
Rohleder, L., 132
Rokeach, M., 287, 289
Rose, C., 7
Roseman, J. E., 39
Ross, N. M., Jr., 39, 68
Rothkopf, E. Z., 421, 422

Rouet, J.-F., 20, 29, 419, 422, 423, 424,
  428, 429, 432, 433
Rowell, J. A., 301
Rowen, K. E., 58, 59
Ruiz, A. B., 137
Rukavina, I., 282, 328
Rumelhart, D. E., 160, 285
Rushworth, P., 75
Russell, B., 158
Rusted, J. M., 399, 412

S

Sadoski, M., 57
Salmon, W. C., 91, 95, 97, 122, 155,
  157, 161
Samarapungavan, A., 92, 95, 97, 110,
  122
Samuels, S. J., 30, 151
Sandberg, J., 224, 244, 247
Sanger, M. J., 40
Sanjose, V., 422, 433
Sanocki, T., 260
Saul, E. U., 7, 10, 30, 38, 41, 149, 166,
  224, 227, 232, 239, 286, 430
Scaife, M., 358, 375
Scardamalia, M., 41
Schallert, D. L., 78
Schank, R. C., 4, 57, 92, 94, 105, 117,
  121, 123, 160
Schauble, I., 40
Schellings, G. L. M., 225
Schieble, K. M., 56, 57
Schiefele, U., 24
Schleich, M. C., 205, 210
Schmalhofer, F., 391
Schnotz, W., 224, 395, 396
Scholes, R. J., 289, 328
Schommer, M., 231, 241, 246, 328
Schrimpsher, D., 358
Schultz, K., 55, 67
Schultz, T. R., 286

Schulze, S. K., 23, 37
Schustack, M. W., 156
Schwab, J. J., 53, 59
Schwartz, B. L., 259
Schwartz, D. L., 365, 375
Sciama, S. C., 395
Scott, P., 20
Scruggs, T. E., 412
Secco, T., 132, 144, 156, 161, 166
Seefeldt, R. W., 272
Seely, M. R., 167
Seifert, C. M., 282, 294, 310, 325
Selman, R., 91
Sell, M., 161
Serra, M., 263
Sethna, G. H., 4
Settlage, J., 110
Shapiro, A. M., 373, 374
Shapiro, B. P., 139
Shepard, R. N., 395, 398
Shimabukuro, J., 55, 67
Shinjo, M., 156
Shortliffe, E. H., 92
Shuell, T. J., 386
Shymansky, J. A., 40
Simpson, A., 432
Simpson, G. B., 132
Simon, H. A., 95, 102, 257, 387, 388,
  390
Simon, S., 265, 273
Sims, V. K., 204, 360, 361, 363, 375,
  376, 395, 398
Sinatra, G. M., 4, 161
Singer, M., 4, 10, 13, 92, 98, 133, 137,
  138, 159, 166, 167, 180, 181,
  182, 199, 200, 202, 204, 217,
  290, 335, 360, 425
Skeels, S. A., 40, 41, 54
Slamencka, N. J., 375
Slesnick, I. L., 63
Slisko, J., 203
Sloane, S., 57

Slugoski, B. R., 163
Smith, D., 21, 36, 37
Smith, S., 57
Smith, W. R., 37
Snyder, T. E., 41, 54, 55
Son, L. K., 257, 273
Songer, N. B., 10, 40, 225, 231, 246, 373, 375
Sosa, E., 91, 99
Sperber, D., 99, 155
Sperry, L. L., 156, 160, 161
Spoehr, K. T., 373
Sprangers, M., 234
Springen, K., 68
Spyridakis, J. H., 430
Standal, T. C., 430
Stein, N. L., 159, 160
Steinberg, M., 55, 67
Steinhoff, K., 54, 56, 345, 376
Stern, L., 39
Stevens, D. T., 261
Stewart, S. T., 159, 166, 167
Strike, K. A., 283
Stock, W. A., 386
Strube, P., 40
Suh, S. Y., 139, 140, 144, 160
Sung, Y., 133, 135, 140, 144, 145
Suppe, F., 91
Surber, J. R., 231, 241, 246
Sutcliffe, A., 360, 371
Suttles, C. W., 55, 58, 59
Suwa, M., 362, 375, 376
Swales, J. M., 21, 22, 24, 26, 30, 34, 57
Swarner, S. S., 161
Swanson, H. L., 412
Sweller, J., 351, 360, 393

T

Tamir, P., 110
Tapangco, L., 40
Tapiero, I., 189

Taylor, C., 98
Teisserenc, A., 205
tenBroek, N. S., 265, 273
Thagard, P., 55, 67, 114, 115
Thiede, K. W., 256, 265, 268, 273
Thiele, R. B., 41
Thieman, A., 426
Thompson, L., 110
Thompson, P., 91
Thompson, R. C., 259
Thompson, S. A., 182
Thorndyke, P. W., 159, 160
Thurlow, R., 133, 147, 262
Tooley, M., 91
Trabasso, T., 4, 10, 13, 92, 98, 99, 132, 133, 137, 138, 139, 140, 144, 156, 158, 160, 161, 166, 180, 181, 182, 199, 200, 202, 204, 217, 290, 335, 360, 418
Treagust, D. F., 40, 41
Truitt, T. P., 205
Tsatsareis, C., 78
Tufte, E. R., 60
Turner, A., 141
Turner, S., 79
Tversky, A., 165
Tversky, B., 380, 398
Tyler, R. W., 52, 53, 59
Tzeng, Y., 133, 137, 143, 147, 161, 418, 420
Tzou, C. T., 20

U

Uleman, J. S., 163
Ullman, S., 395
Unwin Ltd., 360

V

van Daalen-Kapteijns, M. M., 233, 234, 236, 247
van Dam, G., 399

Van den Akker, J., 39
van den Broek, P., 4, 92, 99, 132, 133,
        135, 137, 138, 139, 140, 143,
        144, 145, 146, 147, 151, 156,
        158, 160, 161, 166, 167, 171,
        179, 202, 204, 262, 287, 360,
        418, 420
van der Meij, H., 283
van Dijk, T. A., 20, 26, 31, 33, 36, 132,
        137, 141, 181, 182, 187, 260,
        282, 294, 391, 395, 417, 418,
        419, 420, 428
van Dusen, L., 204
van Etten, S., 225
van Hout-Wolters, 224
van Leeuwen, T., 79, 80, 81, 85
VanLehn, K., 7, 40, 92
van Meter, P., 225
van Oostendorp, H., 125, 137, 225, 226,
        229, 230, 282, 287, 310, 312,
        325, 327, 428, 431
van Someren, M. W., 236
Varma, S., 133
Varner, K. R., 261
Veneman, V., 55, 67
Vézin, J. F., 79
Vézin, L., 79
Vidal-Abarca, E., 419, 422, 428, 429,
        432, 433
Virtue, S., 147
Vonk, W., 155, 164, 165, 166, 167, 168,
        201
Voss, J., 4
Voss, J. F., 228, 232
Vye, N. J., 13

W

Wade, S. E., 57
Waldmann, M. R., 163, 164, 170
Wallace, D., 57
Walczyk, J. J., 224, 258

Waring, D. A., 202
Warren, R. P., 6
Waters, S., 133
Weaver, C., 259
Weaver, C. A., III, 257, 259, 261, 272,
        395
Webb, N. M., 7
Weiner, B., 92, 163
Welsch, D., 391
Wenger, E., 22
Wertheimer, M., 395
Whilite, S. C., 424, 427
White, B. Y., 359, 374, 381
White, J., 57
White, P. A., 159
Whitehead, A. N., 52, 53, 54, 59, 66
Whitney, P., 133, 202, 230
Whittaker, A., 56
Wielinga, B. J., 236
Wiers, R., 110
Wilkes, A. L., 282, 293, 310, 312, 325
Willert, M. G., 259
Williams, K. D., 225
Williams, S., 20
Williams, W. O., 40, 41, 54
Wilson, R. A., 92, 95, 99, 120, 122
Winn, W. D., 395
Winne, P. H., 225
Winograd, P., 309, 426, 427, 433
Winter, L., 163
Wittrock, M. C., 351, 386
Wixson, K. K., 422
Wong, I., 58
Wood-Robinson, V., 75
Worthy, J., 57
Wright, K., 33
Wu, S. M., 54

Y

Yager, R. E., 4, 301
Yager, S. O., 301

Yarbrough, J. C., 56
Yeaton, W. H., 21, 36, 37
Yokoi, L., 236
Yore, L. D., 4, 21, 39, 40
Young, E., 7
Young, M., 133, 137, 143, 147, 161,
        418, 420

Z

Zabrucky, K. M., 259, 282, 292, 300
Zimmerman, C., 31, 34, 36, 37, 38
Zimny, S., 391
Zohar, A., 110
Zwaan, R. A., 7, 13, 144, 186, 187, 204,
        205, 217, 225, 227, 263, 264,
        282, 386, 391

Subject Index

A

Accuracy assumption, 263, 265
Active learning, *see* Constructivist
    learning
Active processing assumption, 350-351
Ad hoc knowledge, 53
Adjunct tasks, 248
Advance organizers, 268–272
    metacomprehension judgments, 270
    prior knowledge, 268–270
    test performance, 270
Alternative explanation schema, 120
Analogy, 55, 57
Analytical structure, 83
Animation, 375–381
    commentary accompaniment,
        377–379
    explicit changes, 375
    mentally, 376–379

Arc-search procedure, 424, 433
Argument transformation, 295

B

Basic processing, 226, 231, 238
Behavioral activity view, 334–335
Bolstering, 291

C

Carpet diagram, 388–390, 398, 400–412
Causal cognition, 156
Causal explanation, 156, 162–164
Causal inference, 166–167
    antecedents, 166–167
    consequences, 166–167
Causal-text condition, 367
Causality, 155–172

analytic versus chronological, 171
 definition, 157
 prior knowledge, 163–64
Circle diagram, 388–390, 398, 400–412
Circumnavigation task, 400
Circumstance transformation, 295
Classification of representational struc-
  tures, 81–83
Clear-cut contradiction, 312–316
 results, 316
 scenarios, 315–316
Cognitive activity view, 335
Cognitive conflict, 283
Cognitive dissonance, 286
Cognitive economy, 397, 399
Cognitive processes, 9–10
Cognitive theory of multimedia learning,
  333–334, 349–354
Coherence gaps, 225–226
Coherence index, 285, 287–291,
  295–297, 300
Coherence principle, 345–346, 353–355
 concise presentation, 345
 extraneous presentation, 346
Cohort activation, 139
Conceptual structure, 81–82
Comprehension, 3–13, 56–57, 367–369,
  418–419
 definition, 418
 familiarity, 56
 individual differences, 4
 interestingness, 57
 monitoring, 11
 strategies, 418
 text structure, 56
Comprehension evaluation, 299, 309
Comprehension monitoring, 232–244,
  255–274, 282, 289, 300–301
 introductory text, 233, 235
 self-regulated, 255–259
 rereading, 257, 268, 271–272
 standards, 289, 300
 think aloud method, 236
Comprehension process, 228–230
Comprehension questions, 368

Comprehension regulation model,
  281–301, 309–312
 elements, 284
 fire in a warehouse example,
  310–312
 limitations, 283
 representation, 310
Conceptual change, 282–283
Conflict resolve, 117–120
 ACT-R theory, 117
Construction-integration model,
  326–327
 construction-phase, 326
 integration process, 326
Constructionist theory, 180, 360
Constructivist learning, 334, 342,
  354–355
Content of instruction, 359, 372
Content transformations, 292
Context and change verbs, 209–215
Context of reading, 225
Contextual constrictions, 327
Contradiction paradigm, 282, 284, 296,
  298
Conventional expository schemata, 227
Cueing system, *see* Long-term working
  memory
Curriculum, 51–54, 57–60
 epistemic purposes, 58–60
 explanation, 58–60
Cyclic processing, 232

D

Deep knowledge, 6–7
Deep representation, 247
Deference epistemic stance, 298
Delete the textbook approach, 3
Denial, 291
Depictive representation, 390–391
Descriptive representation, 390–391
Differentiation, 291
Directional causal schema, 165
 chronological order, 165

Discourse communities, 21–22
Dissonance, 281, 286–287
Document model representation,
    29–30
Dual-channel assumption, 349–350
Dual coding theory, 386–387, 393, 397,
    401–402, 409, 411
    hypothesis, 402
    mnemonic function of pictures,
        386–387

E

Effort after meaning, 290
Elimination strategy, 292
Empirical research report, 26–30
Enumeration, 238
Error detection paradigm, 309
Exigency threshold, 297
Explanandum, 95–96
    recurring events, 96
    unique events, 96
Explanation, 91–125
    ambiguity, 94
    cognitive processes, 121
    deep structure, 94
    definition, 93, 95, 98
Explanation schematas, 103–110
    bad weather elsewhere, 104–105
    evaporation-transportation, 105
    natural selection, 107
    standard scientific
Explanative text, 335–341
    definition, 336
    illustrations, 339–341
    rhetorical structures, 338–339
Explicit proposition, see Textbase
Expository schemata, 239–245, 248
Expository text, 140–141
    intratextual relations, 140
External representation, 387, 394, 396

F

Factor analysis, 278
Feedback, 260–261

Form of presentation, 406, 408
Form of visualization, 406
Formal education, 38–42
    internet, 39
    textbooks, 39–42
Formal explanation, 98
Format of instruction, 359, 369–370,
    372, 380
Frequency of indirect reference to old
        information, 323–325
    repetition, 324
    results, 324–325
Full-text condition, 367

G

Generative relations, 99–103, 110–114
    activation, 111–112
    assembly, 112
    building blocks, 103
    cause and effect, 99
    primitive, 102
Genre, 22–42
    formative, 24
    function, 22–23, 31–32
    incidental audience, 23, 30, 42
    integrative, 24
Global coherence model, 180–182, 192,
    195
    referential model, 192
Graphic schemata, 396
Gravity, 97

H

Higher level questions, 422, 425,
    427–430, 433
    benefits, 433
Higher order processing, 226, 238
Hyperlinking, 380
Hypermedia design guidelines, 362–366
Hypermedia manual, 363–367, 370–371
    map, 366–367
    screen, 364
    sections, 371
Hypermedia presentation, 358–373

comprehension, 367–369
research design, 358–359
structure, 373

I

Illusion of knowing, 231, 246
Illustrations, 333, 339–355
scientific explanations, 333, 339
with text, 339–341
Images in science text, 73–79, 88–89
function, 75–79
implications of use, 88–89
relationship with text, 76
results, 78–79
rhetorical devices, 77
Implication relations, 190, 192
Inappropriate inferences, 296
Inconsistency, 283, 286–287, 291, 293, 298
external, 283
internal, 283
readers' reactions, 286–287, 295
Independence hypothesis, 398, 405, 407–408
Inference, 199–217, 229
bridging, 200
elaborative, 200, 204
Inference assumption, 262, 264
Inference encoding score, 213–215
Information delivery theory, 351–354
Information sources, 423
Instruction, 54–56
Integrated text and picture comprehension, 386–413
construction processes, 395
schematic illustration, 394
Intelligence, 278–279
Intentional explanation, 98
Internal representation, 391–396
depictive, 392
Intraindividual correlation, 258

J

Journalistic reported versions, 32–38

challenges, 33–34
example, 36–36
processing, 36–38

L

Lag, 256
Landscape model, 133–136, 147, 150–151
Learner characteristics, 224
Learning how to learn, 247
Learning phase, 404
Levels of disruption hypothesis, 262–265, 267, 271–274
Lexical decision study, 206–210
Limited-capacity assumption, 349–351
working memory, 351
Local coherence model, 179–180, 182–183
cohesion, 182
minimalist hypothesis, 180
Long-term memory, 420, 428
Long-term working memory, 180, 184–186, 420
coherence, 185–186
situation model, 186
Low level questions, 427–430

M

Machine comprehension model, 360–367, 379
navigation and guidance, 366
text and diagrams, 360–362
Macroproposition processing, 261
Macrostructure, 427–433
definition, 428
Memory representation of text, 132
connections, 132
Mental model, *see also* Situation model
model inspection, 396
Mental model construction, 361–362
stages, 361–362
Mental representation, 19–20
prior knowledge, 20

Metacomprehension accuracy, 259–274
    test question type, 260
Metacomprehension judgments,
        256–259, 272
    rereading, 266, 272
    test performance, 270
Metatextual cues, 423, 430, 432–433
Microproposition processing, 261
Microstructure, 427–433
    definition, 428
Minimum acceptance level, 287–291,
        295–297, 300
    factors, 288
Modes of cognitive functioning,
        158–160
Monitoring process, 229–230, 245
Moses illusion, 230–231
Multimedia learning model, 387
Multimedia presentation, 357, 360,
        367, 372
    constructivist theory of text process-
        ing, 360
Multimedia principle, 344, 352, 355
    cause and effect explanation, 344
    computer based, 355

N

Narrative text, 81, 149, 160–161
    comprehension, 160–161
    structure, 81
Nonscientific images, 87
Novice schemas, 107–110
    evolutionary biology, 107–110
    frequency, 109

O

Objective comprehension problem,
        285, 298
Off-line measures, 3
Old information reinforcing, 320–323
    implicit fitting, 320
    indirect referring, 320
    results, 322–323
Old information strengthening, 317–31

results, 317–319
Online measures, 3

P

Passive media, 334
Physics first approach, 2–3
Popularized science, 31–38
    general public, 31
    public awareness, 31–32
    public understanding, 32
Practice phase, 404
Pragmatic communication, 8
Predicate transformation, 294
Predictive accuracy, 260
Predictive inferences, 202–203, 206–217
    stimulus on set asynchrony, 202, 208
Pretest, 264
Prior knowledge, 223, 226–228,
        230–248, 421, 431
    matching textual information, 230,
        244–245
Prior knowledge principle, 346–349,
        354–355
Problem model, 7–8
Problem-solving transfer, 342–343
Process analysis, 278
Processing cycles, 418–421
Proposition, 188–189
Propositional representation, 392,
        395–397
Peudoinferences, 391

Q

QUEST, 161–163, 423–425
Question answering from memory,
        422–425
Question answering from text, 425–427
Questioning the author, 301
Questions, 421–433
    direction of effect, 422
    kind of processing, 422

role, 421

R

Rationalization, 291
Readers' individual characteristics,
    327–328
  beliefs, 328
  prior knowledge, 327
  working memory limitations, 327
Reference transformations, 292–293
Refutational text, 54–55, 58
Regulation processes, 226
Regulatory actions, 291–292
Relational transformations, 292–293
Relevant schemata, 227–239
Representation, 387–390
  computationally equivalent, 390
  informationally equivalent, 388
Representation assumption, 263
Rereading, 265–268 271–274
Research report, 24–31
  example, 27–28
  scientist as reader, 28–30
Resonance model, 182–195
  contextual cue, 183–184
  target sentences, 183
Restructuring strategy, 292
Retrieval structures, 186
Roles for communication of scientific
    information, 21

S

Schema articulation, 114–117
  Darwinian explanation, 116
  natural selection, 116
Science, 5–6
  definition, 5
Science text, 2–13, 44–45, 161–163
  background knowledge, 2
  comprehension, 161–163
  content, 4, 6
  definition, 6
  implications, 44–45
  inference, 10–12

  knowledge representation, 8
  visual images, 12
Self-correction, 261
Self-explanation, 227, 232, 375
Self-generation effect, 375
Semantic features, 205–217
Semantic processing, 395
Semantic relations identification, 133
Shallow knowledge, 6
Short-term memory, 179–182
Signs, 385
Situated regulation strategy, 223
Situation model, 7, 10, 20, 186–189,
    196, 199–201, 203, 210, 216,
    239, 241–242, 264–274, 282,
    293–294, 300, 391–393,
    396–397, 400–401, 411,
    418–433
  alteration, 242
  causal inferences, 201
  coherence, 187
  global coherence, 189
  links, 187–188
Songbird passage, 141–150
  episodic memory representation,
    141, 143
  mental representation, 147
  mixed results, 149
  typographical cues, 144, 151
Source selection, 425
Sources of activation, 137
Spatial contiguity principle, 344–345,
    353, 355
  integrated presentation, 344
  separated presentation, 345
Spatial relations, 188–189
Split focus, 224, 245
Standards of coherence, 137–139
Stimulation hypothesis, 399–400, 405,
    407–408
Strategic processing, 226, 238
Structure inference hypothesis, 401,
    403–404, 409–411
Structure-mapping hypothesis, 401,
    408–409

Structure support hypothesis, 401–403,
    409–411
Study objectives, 417
Subject matter knowledge, 53
Subjective comprehension problem,
    285, 298
Substitution hypothesis, 399, 405,
    407–408
Surface code, 7
Symbolic processes, 82

T

Talk-aloud protocols, 209
Task characteristics, 225
Telelogical relation, 205
Test phase, 405
Text characteristics, 224, 241, 244
    coherence, 224
Text comprehension, 397
Text inspection, 425–426, 429, 433
    learning-effective activity, 426, 433
    type of question, 426
Text orientation, 37–38
    critical stance, 37–38
    deferential stance, 38
    dominant stance, 38
Text type, 205–217, 327
Textbase, 7, 187–189, 294, 419–421,
    427, 431
    links, 187
Textbook, 39–42, 168–170
    analogies, 41

difficulties, 40
    explanations, 41
    order of information, 168–170
Textbook evaluation, 60–69
    algorithms, 60
    example, 62–65
    graphic organization, 60
    subexplanations, 61–68
    trade book, 65–66
Textbook image research, 83–86
    dimension of operation, 86
    engagement, 84
    image functions, 85
    learning resources, 84
Textual conditions, 327
Textual organizers, 418, 430
Time difference task, 400
Tolerance level, 287–288
    factors, 288
Trascendence, 291

U

Uncommitted browsing, 84

V

Verb tense, 205–216
Verification judgment task, 211–215
    verification subject, 211, 213
Visual design, 79–81
    grammar, 79–81
Visual presentation, 333–355